Enterprise-Wide Computing: How to Implement and Manage LANs

Enterprise-Wide Computing: How to Implement and Manage LANs

Thomas W. Madron

John Wiley & Sons, Inc.

New York ▪ Chichester ▪ Brisbane ▪ Toronto ▪ Singapore

Library of Congress Cataloging-in-Publication Data:

Madron, Thomas William, 1937–
Enterprise-wide computing : how to implement and manage LANs / Thomas Wm. Madron.
p. cm.
Includes bibliographical references.
ISBN 0-471-53297-5 (paper)
1. Business—Data processing. 2. Local area networks (Computer networks) 3. Strategic planning. I. Title.
HF5548.2.M238 1991
658'.05468—dc20 91-13590

Printed in the United States of America

10 9 8 7 6 5 4 3 2 1

Preface

This book is my effort to provide an overview of the issues and technologies involved in thinking about, designing, and implementing an enterprise-wide computing environment. "Enterprise-wide" computing (EWC) is a new name for a set of integration objectives many people have had for years. Unlike the computing and communications environments of only a few years ago, today it is actually possible to design and implement EWC with off-the-shelf products.

The EWC concept is not only for large organizations but also for any organization of any size that wishes to use computer and networking technologies to help its employees work better. There are several strategies for implementing EWC: centering on a central minicomputer, centering on a mainframe computing environment, or centering on a local area network (LAN) or some other network philosophy. For reasons that will become apparent, my focus in on LANs as the centerpiece for EWC. Yet this is *not* a book on LANs. Notwithstanding some thinking in the industry, mainframes and minicomputers are not drying up and blowing away, but their use for integrating computing environments is being superceded. Consequently, all computing devices are becoming peripherals of networks rather than the reverse. Even though I have emphasized LANs for integrating computing environments, thus making this book relevant to even small organizations, the problems facing those environments with minicomputers and mainframes have not been ignored or forgotten.

Some of the figures, illustrations, and other materials used in this book have previously appeared in some of my related books published by John

Wiley & Sons. Specifically, some materials have been used from *Local Area Networks: The Next Generation*, 2nd Edition (Wiley, 1990) and from *LANs: Applications of IEEE/ANSI 802 Standards* (Wiley, 1989). Thanks are extended to Wiley for permission to use these materials. If more detail on relevant issues is needed, these books can provide further insights, especially into the use and technology of LANs.

Although I am solely responsible for any errors of commission and omission, I wish to thank Dr. Gregory Stone for his thoughtful review of the manuscript of this book. My wife, Beverly, deserves thanks not only for her support but also because she is periodically drafted into reading sections of this and other manuscripts.

Thomas W. Madron

Somerset, New Jersey
June 1991

Contents

Introduction

The growth of networking—originally conceived to support access to mainframe computer systems—has generated an increasing demand for the integration of computing resources in many organizations in modern society. The idea of integrated, organization-wide computing resources has been talked about for a number of years. Some institutions, Carnegie Mellon being among the most ambitious experiments, sought to implement such systems as long ago as the early 1980s. This book is directed toward the concepts, the issues, and, to an extent, the products available for constructing an integrated computer and communications environment that will contribute to the strategic and tactical success of the organization of which you are a part.

Today, the concept of integrated, organization-wide computing is often referred to as *enterprise computing*. Yet the concept of "enterprise-wide computing" is still not widely understood even though there have been many attempts to provide integrated networks for corporations, universities, governmental agencies, and other organizations. A major part of the reason why organizations do not have true enterprise-wide computing is due more to failures in management than to a lack of technology, for today much of the technology to implement widespread integration is available "off-the-shelf."

At least one caveat is needed at the outset. This is *not* a book about IBM's Enterprise Systems Connection (ESCON) Architecture, although that is briefly discussed as one possible approach. Neither is it a treatise on the way in which Digital Equipment Corporation (DEC) is approaching the issue of enterprise computing, although this too is discussed. The core of the approach by both IBM and DEC is peer computing (and communications) similar to or the same as that outlined in the Open System Interconnection (OSI) model. It is not true as some assume that these topics can be discussed only in IBM or DEC terms. A great deal of what this book is about has to do with peer computing, however.

Management's failure to use information technology well is not a recent phenomenon but rather stems from the fact that information systems are not often part of an institution's strategic planning. The lack of strategic thinking about information systems has meant that in many organizations mainframe systems are controlled and planned by one group, networks by another, minis by a third, and micros by a fourth. In many organizations it often seems that getting one's own ideas accepted, or obtaining enhancements for one's own department, always takes precedence over the strategic needs of the institution or the public policies of the body politic. In fact, it often seems that networks are implemented more as a function of political patronage than of rational planning.

When local networks (LANs) became feasible, yet a fifth group may have been formed. Moreover, most organizations were slow to adopt organization-wide standards for hardware and software, which has led to the inability to communicate adequately. Many organizations still resist adopting such standards, but support organizations cannot realistically maintain a random selection of hardware and software in today's market. Sometimes, when organizations have been willing to plan for information systems, the technology has not been quite ready; however, the lack of strategic planning and its implementation has probably been a more frequent problem than the lack of technology. These historical factors have provided impediments to the development of true enterprise-wide computing. Yet, in many institutions, planning for enterprise-wide computing is taking place, sometimes by default rather than by design. It is important, therefore, to understand the importance of enterprise-wide computing generally, and the role of networking in particular, in this endeavor.

Does a comprehensive definition of enterprise-wide computing exist? Perhaps not one that will last forever, but issues that contribute to such a definition can be identified. Enterprise-wide computing means at least the following:

- a strategic concern for the total computing needs of the organization;

- the ability to do distributed computing using distributed databases;
- the capacity for each computing entity on the network to communicate with any other entity as required by the organization;
- provisions to protect the integrity of information throughout the organization (security);
- adoption of internal and international standards;
- an integrated network management system capable of managing components from multiple vendors;
- enhancements that improve the capacity to use the system by the people in the organization, possibly including:
    - a common user interface (CUI);
    - sufficient bandwidth to move multimedia information (including not only voice, video, and images but also text) in a timely fashion;
    - "seamless" and "transparent" interactions among users of diverse computing hardware; and
    - access to information internal to the organization and the acquisition of relevant information available on networks external to the organization.

In the characterization just given, I have not tried to specify approaches to enterprise networking suggested by mainframe/mini vendors such as IBM and DEC, on the one hand, or LAN vendors such as Novell and Banyan, on the other hand. Moreover, much of the essence of enterprise networking is tied up in network management, and the availability of management resources is still sparse in the early 1990s. According to James Herman, the "industry has set its sights on open, multivendor networks and distributed computing, but missing in action so far are the enterprise management architectures that can integrate diverse and far-flung network devices into a cohesive, controllable whole."[1] IBM's catchall for enterprise computing is the new ESCON Architecture, while DEC's contribution is called Enterprise Management Architecture. Both Novell and Banyan are explicitly aimed at the enterprise networking market, as well.[2] Chapter 11 discusses this definition in light of other material in this book.

There are a variety of reasons why organizations should think strategically about computing and networking. First, in an era of scarce funding, it is necessary to improve the economic efficiency of business, government, and education. Second, there seems to be a dearth of successful planning. Consequently, I suspect that very little of what is planned is ever implemented. Third, without planning and consequently, without a vision of what networking can achieve, the organization will never be pointed in an appropriate direction.

Highly connective networks can be found on a number of corporate and university campuses, and their installation started at least in the early 1980s. An example of such an institution with a campus-wide, fully connective network is the University of North Texas (UNT) in Denton, Texas. When I was manager of computer services at UNT, we planned the network–based on cable television technology—in 1982, and implementation was started in 1983. By 1984 all campus buildings were connected, and all academic and administrative computing took place over that single network. Since that time, of course, modifications have been made, including the addition of some fiber-optic links, but the central theme of a consolidated network is still in place. In today's computing and networking environment, the economies of scale tend to be more with networking and less with computing than was true in earlier periods. There are, however, still many organizations that do not view their networks as strategic components of their competitive posture and are not, therefore, maximizing the use of their people and other resources.

But what does enterprise computing mean to you? In the characterization of enterprise computing given earlier, several points were mentioned that have direct bearing on the answer to this question. Other points bear on the technical nature of the network itself, and some of those points will be taken up in various chapters of this book. Some points, of course, will have to be discussed from both points of view. Recasting those points that are of importance now, however, provides the following list:

- A strategic concern for the total computing needs of the organization.

  The fundamental question to be asked here is, "how can we maximize resources for the institution and the institution's goals? rather than, "what's in it for me?" The point is that planning needs to be done from a relatively universal perspective rather than from any provincial point of view.

- The capacity for each computing entity on the network to communicate with any other entity as required by the organization.

  Networks are designed to facilitate communication. To the extent that those communications support the professional and social processes among people, then information networking is possibly more a sociological than a technical process. The technical need, however, is to have widespread connectivity and interoperability so that resources can be distributed to the people and places where they will be used most appropriately.

- Provisions to protect the integrity of information across the organization (security).

  The most frustrating problems for users are the apparent roadblocks often placed in the way of "user-friendly" computing. These roadblocks are often part of the security process. One of the disadvantages of the decentralization that has come with the widespread use of microcomputers is that information security has suffered. Information security is the state of certainty that computers, programs, data, and program files cannot be accessed, obtained, or modified by unauthorized personnel. Security is implemented by restricting the physical area around the computer system to authorized personnel, using special software, and the security built into the computer's operating procedure. This definition is true of any computer, although with micros not many, if any, of these are implemented. Likewise, the network that supports the computers must also be secured.

  Who needs security in a university? Probably everyone. Security can be breached by accident as well as by design. The object is to protect all information. The administration may perceive problems with financial or student information. With researchers the data collected under the auspices of a research grant may be equally important and difficult to recover if something happens. Everyone needs security, but it must be implemented to the level of need rather than to some level of paranoia.

- Adoption of internal and national/international standards.

  Internal standards are those that allow people within an organization to make use of a consistent set of software and hardware technologies. The purpose of internal standards is to provide a manageable set of hardware and software products so that the organization can benefit from quantity purchases and provide maintenance in a cost-effective manner. Such standards do not, in fact, need to be excessively restrictive, but they do need to limit supported hardware and software to what can be appropriately and economically managed.

The use of devices that conform to national or international standards is important to ensure that those devices will be supported both now and in the future. An example is the selection of LAN protocols. Some protocols, such as ARCnet, have been around for a number of years but have not won official national or international support. IEEE 802.3 (Ethernet) and IEEE 802.5 (Token Ring) are the most common of the standard LAN protocols supported not only in the United States but also by the International Organization for Standardization (ISO). As it happens, ARCnet hardware is often less expensive than either 802.3 or 802.5 hardware. To adopt ARCnet solely because of cost, however, would be a very short-term strategy, since support for the ARCnet protocols is based entirely on the whims of current manufacturing and marketing trends.

There can also be confusion within a system that apparently conforms to a standard. Ethernet, which is a proprietary name given by Xerox, its original developer, to the technology that was a precursor of the current 802.3 standards, is often used popularly as a synonym for 802.3. I do so myself, although I try to be clear when I am so using it. One of the primary supporters of Ethernet has been DEC. Digital Equipment Corporation has used for several years, an Ethernet frame structure (Ethernet V2.0) that is slightly different from the 802.3 standard.[3] While DEC is today away from proprietary protocols toward standard protocols the older Ethernet frame format is still used by some installations. This means that while 802.3 standard network interface cards (NICs) can reside on the same physical network as Ethernet V2.0 NICs, they cannot communicate with one another without some form of protocol conversion. The clear implication is that for long-term, continued network support, officially accepted national and international standards should be employed when available.

- A CUI.

A CUI is one where, when a user sits down at a randomly selected workstation, access to network resources will occur in about the same fashion as with any other randomly selected node. In other words, the screens will look about the same, the commands and command structures will be about the same, and the end user will not have to go through a new learning curve just because a move has taken place. It is also easier to diagnose problems when there is a single set of error messages and when the screens are similar. If Microsoft has its way, a product like Windows 3.x will become the standard user interface for all activities, including the use of networks. It is quite possible that some form of Graphical User Interface (GUI) will, indeed, become the user interface of choice. If the choices are something like Apple's MacIntosh interface, Windows 3.x, and XWindows on Unix, then the appearance of these products is likely to converge over time, or versions of these interfaces will become available for all systems over time. The state of the art is not yet to the point where a true CUI can be established in a multivendor environment, but that should certainly be a goal and has been an objective of several development efforts over the years.

- The ability (bandwidth) to deal with multimedia information in a timely fashion.

  One of the newest buzz phrases in the computer community is "multimedia information," by which is meant not only the usual character data, but also voice, video, and images. The problem with digitized voice, video, and image data is that in order for it to be delivered in a timely and *appropriate* fashion the network needs to operate at rather high speeds. When LANs were first developed they carried only character data and were used primarily as replacements for slow, voice-grade, analog communications. Thus, LANs operating at 1, 2.5, 10, or 16 Mb/s all seem wonderfully speedy compared to .3, 1.2, 2.4, 4.8, 9.6 or even 19.2 Kb/s. Yet, when the amount of data traversing a network is expanded by many orders of magnitude, then even LAN speeds may seem slow. The increase in amounts of data come from two sources: greater numbers of users and larger amounts of data per user. The latter is or will be largely a function of larger file sizes generated by digital voice, video, or image technologies. Consequently, in the very near future networks will have to be very much faster or the actual throughput will slow down considerably. If your network supports a FAX Server, for example, providing you with means of generating and receiving facsimiles, each page of returning FAXed information requires about 25,000 bytes of file storage. If that page had been simple ASCII character data, the file size would be substantially smaller. FAX is based on one form of image data.

- Seamless interactions among users of diverse computing hardware.

  In one sense this point is an expansion of the earlier discussion regarding a CUI. Yet this discussion must go beyond the CUI to the point where the transfer of information takes place. A person with a MAC, for example, should be able to transfer a file to a user with an MS-DOS or Unix machine. Any of these three should be able to do work in a straightforward manner with an IBM mainframe or a VAX supermini. With a GUI, the ideal situation would be one in which a mouse could be used to drag an icon representing data from a mainframe window to a MAC window to a DOS window. In fact, an even more ideal situation would be one in which the data icon could be dragged from a VAX application window to a DOS or MAC application window, and the conversions would be made without the direct intervention of the user other than to drag the data icon from one window to another. There are, however, a number of complexities that must be overcome in order to make these things happen, and off-the-shelf support software is not yet available for a multivendor environment, although more and more is becoming accessible.

- Access to information internal to the organization and acquisition of relevant information available on networks external to the organization.

  Most end users want to share information, manipulate information, analyze information, look up information, or something similar. Transactional database systems usually allow many users to look at information and a few to update information. Examples might be university registration files and library catalogues. Many people might need to look up selected information when trying to assist a student, a few would need to update that information. Similarly, virtually everyone in a college or university should need to use the library from time to time, but only a few should be allowed to add information to the database. The information obtained from each inquiry is limited, and access often means the ability to see one or a related set of records. On the other hand, if one were writing an article jointly with a colleague, each coauthor might need to access the word processing document regardless of whether they were across the hall from one another or on opposite sides of the Earth. Sometimes one might need to acquire documents that are available locally, with a bibliographic service, or somewhere on Internet. The other side of all this is that individuals may need to add to the information rather than to extract from it.

The common characteristic of all these activities is that they require a solid, high-speed network to be accomplished in a timely fashion. That network needs to be secure and reliable. It needs to be capable of being accessed by a wide variety of hardware and software. In short, it needs to be able to assist users to communicate with colleagues regardless of location.

Notes

1. James Herman, "Enterprise Management Vendors Shoot It Out," *Data Communications*, Vol. 19, No. 14, Nov. 1990, p. 92.
2. See, for example, Cheryl Snapp, "Cerberus on the Enterprise," *LAN Times*, Vol. 6, No. 8, Aug. 1989, p. 85(2)
3. See the appropriate discussions in Thomas W. Madron, *LANs: Applications of IEEE/ANSI 802 Standards* (New York: John Wiley & Sons, 1989), and/or *Local Area Networks: The Next Generation*, 2nd Edition (New York: John Wiley & Sons, 1990), for further details.

CHAPTER 1

Enterprise-Wide Computing

Anyone seriously engaged in business today needs a network! Moreover, organizations both large and small need to give some consideration to enterprise-wide computing (EWC) in order to make networking and computer technologies work effectively. These are premises I and others have been working toward for the past decade or so. It has taken some time, but there is a developing consensus in favor of networking, and this is exhibited in that fact that even popular periodicals are now running cover stories on the changes being wrought by networking technology. In a recent issue of *BusinessWeek*, for example, it was observed that "Networks are altering the way businesses work. So software companies need new products, new ways to sell them, and a new service mentality."[1]

Although some of the popular coverage of the impact of networking technology sometimes sounds like the authors have just had some sort of revelation, those of us closely affiliated with the industry have been pointing out these changes for years.[2] A second premise can also be stipulated, one that has been somewhat less obvious until recently: anyone seriously engaged in a business of virtually *any size* needs a network! This is as true of a two-person office (or maybe even a one-person office) as for a corporation or government agency with tens of thousands of employees.

This book covers and updates some of the issues in a previous work entitled, *Micro–Mainframe Connection*[3] (now out of print). The original intent of that book was to provide an account of the manner in which microcomputers could be used in the context of mainframe computing. Even in the relatively short time since *Micro–Mainframe Connection* was published, however, the technology and the marketplace have changed in very significant ways. In particular, while the concerns evidenced in the original still hold true, there is now a better understanding in the industry of the need for using networks generally, and local area networks (LANs) in particular, as the integrating tool of choice in the computing world. Moreover, for the past few years we have also witnessed a growth in the use of a variety of computing resources in addition to the micro and mainframe with the resultant need for broader integration.

The impact of micros on the way in which people think about computing in organizations has been enormous. The potential for distributing computing people once thought must be centralized have been touched in only superficial ways. The question from users (not necessarily from data processing personnel) is not only simply "how can we transfer information to our micro workstation so that we can use it more effectively?" but also "how can we work more effectively using the network's resources?" This book is an effort to answer those questions in terms of the problems, opportunities, and technologies involved in using LANs, and by inference other networks, for EWC.

In 1986, as I was writing *Micro–Mainframe Connection*, I suggested that "Easy, user transparent, communications between or among systems is a major computing problem to be resolved in the 1980s."[4] It is, unfortunately, necessary to report that while there have been improvements, two of the most important factors that prevent people from taking advantage of new communication technologies are lack of technological skills and lack of access to navigational tools.[5] One problem is that appropriate software development has not kept apace of the ability to build networks. A second problem is that there has been no consensus on what the navigational tools should look like. This problem is no doubt due, at least in part, to a focus on "electrical connectivity whereas our constituents have been concentrating on information connectivity."[6] And a third problem is the continuing turf wars between centralized management information systems (MIS) departments and microcomputer/LAN users in larger organizations.[7]

About a year after *Micro–Mainframe Connection* was published in 1987, some vendors started pushing the concept of EWC, although as Bill Dooley commented at the time, "Enterprise-Wide Computing (EWC) is a phrase that conjures up visions of the 21st century, but like the 21st century, it isn't here yet."[8] Several things have happened during the intervening period that will contribute to the growth in EWC, especially the growth in the acceptance of networking protocols associated with the Open System Interconnection (OSI) model. In the context of OSI the key word that connotes EWC is "interoperability." This concept of interoperability is somewhat more complicated than "simply getting everyone 'talking' to anyone else," as Dooley put it, but that imperative is at the heart of the matter.

There are several important reasons why doing EWC proves to be more difficult than one would first suppose. Some of the reasons are technical, some sociological, some political, and some economic. While most of this book will dwell on the technical issues it is necessary at the outset to understand that EWC and interoperability implies the real deployment of what used to be called distributed data processing (DDP). Distributed data processing is the organization of information processing so that both the processing and the data may be distributed over several machines at one or more sites. Data communication is fundamental to making DDP work, and increasingly LANs constitute the basic building block for such a data communication system. As soon as people start talking about distributing information processing, however, they realize that the usual social, political, and economic relationships within an organization (and within society as whole, for that matter) will be changed. Change has a tendency to threaten people, and many, perhaps most, will resist it. Furthermore, it requires both imagination and money to implement EWC, although it is also true, as Dooley noted, that any "industry that states 'Time is money' is in need of EWC."

While IBM has attempted to provide large-scale integration, even that giant of the information age has found it impossible to impose its will on buyers of products. Thus even IBM in 1990 was a distant second to Novell in its sales of network operating systems (NOSs) for LANs. In a purely mainframe world IBM was able to specify its System Network Architecture (SNA) and make its customers generally (though not completely) adhere to its proprietary standards. Similarly, Digital Equipment Corporation (DEC) was, for a time, able to convince many DEC minicomputer environments to use its Digital Network Architecture (DNA) components. Once many—perhaps most—large-scale installations became multicomputer users (as happened with the onslaught of micros) it became difficult for IBM and

DEC to maintain customer purity. Part and parcel of this trend has been the movement away from mainframe and high-end minis to LANs, particularly at the departmental level. This trend can clearly be seen in the data illustrated by Figure 1.1.[9]

In the last decade of the twentieth century computer technology cannot be divorced from information communications (networking) technology. In the earlier days of the information revolution, networks started out as peripherals to computers—today, however, computers have become the peripherals of the networks. How this description of the relationship between computers and communications looks may be seen in Figure 1.2. The growth of communication technology and the deployment of networks have the potential for making, of this collective technology, tools for the enablement and empowerment of human beings. Ethical tools, so to speak. This point of view was recently illustrated by James Marston, senior vice

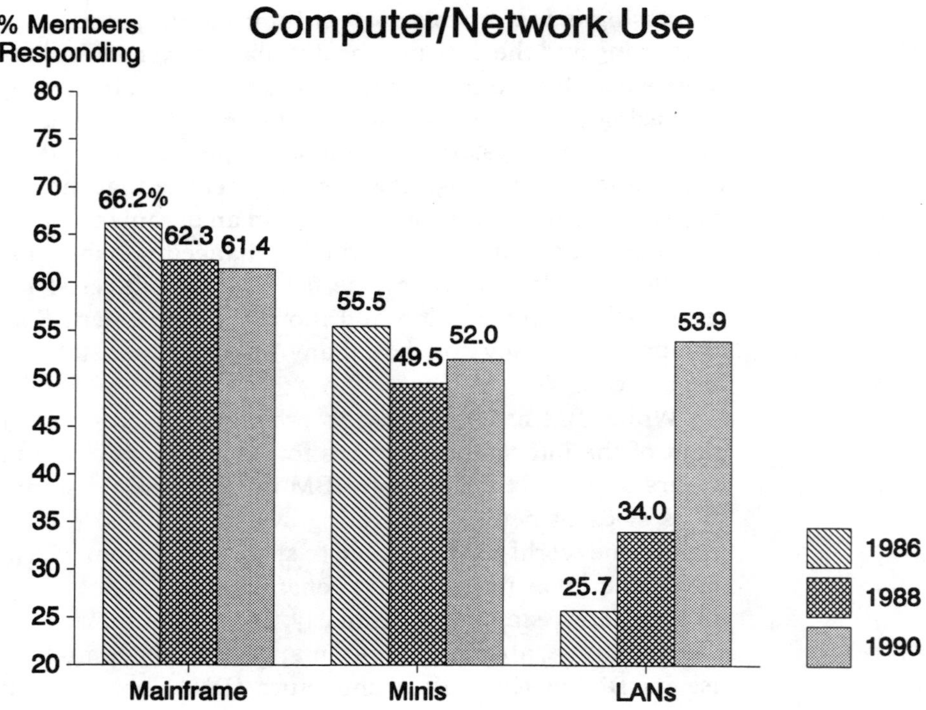

Figure 1.1. Trends in the Use of Mainframes, Minis, and LANs.
Source: Data Processing Management Association, used by permission.

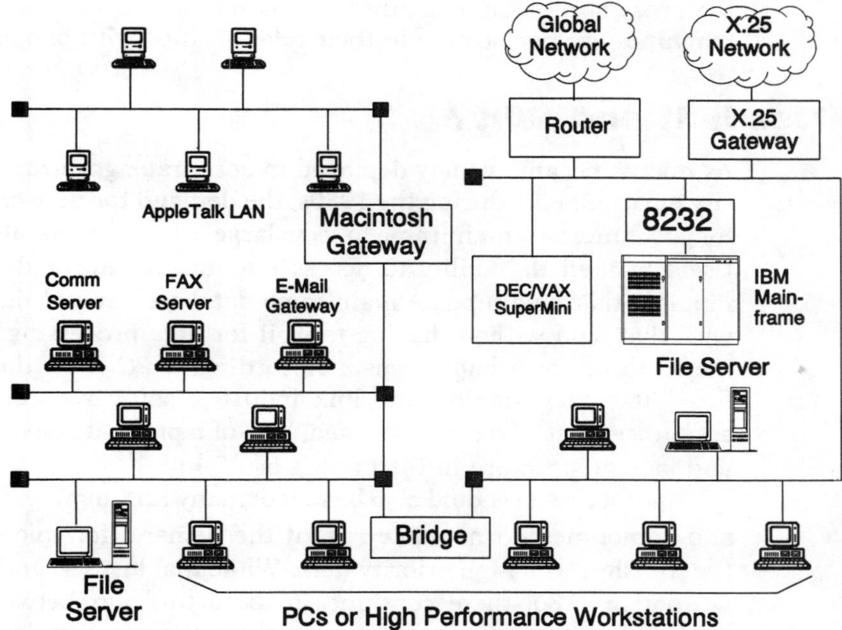

Figure 1.2. Computers as Peripherals to Networks.

president and CIO, American Companies Ltd., Oakland, CA, when he noted that networking "has empowered our people in some remote areas to participate more in the day-to-day activities of the company."[10]

One additional point should be noted: a conceptual change away from the idea of the "micro-to-mainframe" link, and classifying computers as micros, minis, and mainframes, to a growing understanding of the wider complexity of computer-to-computer relationships. Original micro-to-mainframe or terminal-to-host associations were structured as *master–slave* connections. A better basis for thinking about the relationship among computers will probably revolve around notions such as *peer* or *client–server* relations, and *host* functions. These are, in turn, based on a recognition that many of the functions once thought of as mini or mainframe characteristics are actually based on multitasking, multiuser functionality. Thus, both the micro–mini–mainframe and micro-to-mainframe terminology has become suspect and is of declining value in understanding the way in which computers communicate with one another. In other words, it is no longer the gross size of the machines that is important, but the functions those machines are performing in their relationships with one another.

Who Needs It and Why?

As micros became widely deployed in corporate, government, and university environments during the 1980s, the demand for networking, especially for *good* micro-to-mainframe links in large organizations, also grew rapidly. Users wanted the ability to access mainframe data with their PCs, manipulate that data, update mainframe databases in real time, and interact with that data without having to wait for data processing or MIS departments to perform batch runs.[11] According to *PC Week* three factors confused the micro–mainframe link industry: software products that were announced but never materialized, lack of a product standard for PC links, and lack of structure in the pricing of PC links.[12]

Another issue should also be noted: many MIS managers simply did not and sometimes do not now regard the demand for micro-to-mainframe file transfers as a high priority item. While that last sentence was originally written in 1986, there continues to be a turf war between central MIS organizations and micro users. By the late 1980s and early 1990s, however, it became clear that organizations needed an *integrated* approach to dealing with automation in order to make effective use of the technology. It is this latter realization that has an impact on all organizations, not just large ones. Virtually all organizations need some concept of EWC and how to achieve it.

Various commentators on the micro-to-mainframe link have pointed out the importance of the link to computer users in large organizations for a number of years. G. Briggs, for example, writing in *MIS Week*, stressed that micro-to-mainframe link software is a user-driven demand that companies will have to provide or fail. Writing in 1984 Briggs noted that the link software probably required electronic mail, word processing, and spreadsheet analysis.[13] In 1990 one needed only to talk to a few users in a large organization to realize that there is significant dissatisfaction with the way in which mainframe data are made available to micro users, although some organizations have been more successful than others in providing the service.[14] Two of the most common requests from users revolve around transactions with the corporate database and transferring data from that database.[15] But how does this affect people in smaller organizations with no mainframe? Or for that matter, how might these concepts affect home computers in the not too distant future?

It has become increasingly clear that concerns once confined to the use of computers in large organizations now affect people in the smallest offices. An example of this phenomenon is a recent client of mine, an attorney with a very small two-person office: the attorney and her secretary. In such an environment it is frequently necessary for the attorney and the secretary to work on the same document (not different versions of the document). Moreover, there is a need for a message system, a time-keeping system, and other software that must also be accessed by both the attorney and secretary. This was a classic situation in which a local network of some form was required and desired. In addition, there was a broader data communications function since the attorney needs to access legal databases such as Lexus.

That attorney clearly needs to be concerned about integrated EWC, albeit on a small scale. In the context of larger organizations the problem is compounded by many more people with a wider variety of needs. Both kinds of organizations need reliable and intuitively obvious methods for navigating around their respective systems. Everyone knows how to use the telephone system's navigational tools: telephone directories and operator assistance. Everyone also knows how to "address" a phone call by pressing the telephone number into the telephone's keypad. Organizations large and small need navigational tools for their computer and networking environments that will allow them to access services as easily as making a telephone call. Other aspects of the electronic communications process, such as FAX and voice mail, also need integration in an EWC environment.

Navigational Tools and the User Interface

An effective user interface is one that presents the human being using the system with a minimum number of problems in accessing all the electronic services available. Organizational decisions can encourage or inhibit this effort, as can decisions made by software and hardware manufacturers. For many years it has been recognized that such tools must be more user-friendly, better integrated, and provide compatibility between various manufacturers' products.[16] Unfortunately, the problem has become more, not less, complicated. As late as the mid-1980s writers were still talking in futures about the micro-to-mainframe link and suggesting that terminal emulation would continue to be the most important micro-to-mainframe link.[17] By 1990 it was still possible to complain about the lack of integration and the difficulty of navigating in an electronic computer/communication environment in most organizations. (Note that the industry has gone beyond the terms micro-to-mainframe link, or computer access, or even electronic mail, to an *electronic environment*.) That environment, as was previously illustrated, is already with us—the problem is to make it usable by everyone.

Micro software manufacturers must confront the fact that, although the condition is changing, there are few data communications or data transfer standards in universal use. Many of the available integrated packages—packages that attempt to provide a user-friendly method for transferring data—can do so only over asynchronous communications lines (see Chapter 3), even though most IBM mainframe communications are synchronous. Getting a "flat" or rectangular file from a mainframe system can often be accomplished well, but if the data required is part of a database system, then a separate extraction program will be needed or specialized programs suited for that particular manufacturer's products. It is easy to imagine a downloading procedure requiring anywhere from two to four or five steps—hardly transparent. Solutions are in the wings, however. As the industry moves to OSI standards it will become increasingly easy for software manufacturers to access network resources. Of particular importance is the File Transfer, Access, and Management (FTAM) applications layer standard (ISO 8571).

The ideal user interface would be one in which the human user is not aware of two different computer systems. One in which he or she always operates in an apparent mainframe environment or an apparent micro environment without having to consciously shift back and forth. *Integration* in this sense would mean not only the integration of microcomputer functions, but also the integration of micro–mini–mainframe functions. Some manufacturers of mainframe and micro software have moved in this direction for, at least, their applications. An example is FOCUS (Information Builders, Inc.), a database retrieval and reporting system available on both micros and mainframes with the ability of the two software systems to (more-or-less) transparently communicate with one another. FOCUS supports some variety in communications techniques, and will interact with several common database systems, as well. But the complete FOCUS system is expensive and is limited to the few mainframe Teleprocessing Monitors (see below) it supports. A further problem with the approach used in FOCUS is that it is an application-specific solution rather than a system level or universal solution to user-transparent file transfers.

There is software and hardware available in the marketplace that can reduce the navigational problems significantly. The difficulty with their use is more organizational and financial than technical. Many, if not most organizations take the view that the benefits to be derived from an easily used information navigation system are more than offset by the cost involved in deploying the technology. Navigational tools designed to stimulate computer use have been debated almost since the dawn of the computer age and certainly since the late 1950s. The early arguments revolved around how easy it was to use a program when the basic input device was a punched card. When microcomputers first started appearing, their operating systems all provided command-driven access based on a character user interface (CUI)—a holdover from minicomputer and mainframe operating system concepts. The first major deviation was the development of what has come to be the graphical user interface (GUI), which was first pioneered by Xerox with its Xerox Star in the early 1980s. The Xerox approach was adopted in the mid-1980s by Apple in its MacIntosh series of computers. By 1990 it was possible to obtain several windowing/graphical interface environments for IBM PC/clones. One should note that windowing and GUI environments are not the same. A windowing environment helps to provide differing views of one or more tasks but may itself have either a CUI or a GUI.

With products such as Quarterdeck's Desqview (a CUI) or Microsoft's Windows* (a GUI) working in conjunction with communication software such as Datability Software System's Remote Access Facility (RAF) (see Chapter 6), it would be possible to provide an end user with the ability to access a mini or mainframe application as though it were running on a local micro. Both Desqview and Windows provide multitasking windowing environments as enhancements to MS/DOS, and the production of OS/2 by IBM/Microsoft was a recognition of the need for a true multitasking operating system in a networking environment. The increasing popularity of Unix has resulted in the development of GUI products in that environment, as well. DOS products such as Desqview provide essentially a CUI while Windows offers a GUI. Combine these items with the ability of some LAN Network Operating Systems (NOSs) to run on a large system used as a very large file server, and one has the basis for impressive integration and easily

*With the advent of Microsoft Windows 3.0 in 1990 some people have been led to believe that products such as Desqview are dead. As of this writing Desqview is still alive and well and had some advantages over Windows, particularly in the way in which standard DOS programs are handled and in the overhead required by the two systems.

accessed software and tools. In order to set up such a system, however, there would be overhead in the acquisition and maintenance of the software, acquisition and maintenance of possibly some new hardware, and a considerable amount of personnel time expended in getting the system set up and running smoothly. With other priorities at hand, most organizations have not elevated the "ease of use" issue very high. Yet in the long run it will be desirable to make these investments because an easily used environment can help people work better and more efficiently so that finally the benefits will outweigh the costs.[18]

Transferring Data from Here to There

One approach that many organizations have used is to simply create their own micro-to-mainframe links. This is costly, of course, since a team of programmers will have to be dedicated to the project, probably on an ongoing basis. On the other hand, such an approach is guaranteed to provide the user interface the organization wants, not one micro or mainframe software/hardware manufacturers think is appropriate. Frequently, however, it is organizationally easier to buy off-the-shelf software and hardware that does not exactly meet anyone's needs than it is to hire the talent to solve the problem. Either solution may be expensive and both require corporate commitment.

Moving Quantities of Data

There are several reasons for moving large quantities of data among micros, minis, mainframes, and other computing devices, and every year the number of reasons expands. New microcomputer users frequently want to download data from the corporate database on the mainframe (or host) to the micro for further analysis or inclusion in reports. Less apparent, but nevertheless real, is the need to upload data captured or massaged on the micro to the host for additional analysis with host tools. The host can also be used as a storage medium for the micro, although this approach is underused in most organizations. Output from the micro can be moved to the host so that specialized host peripherals, such as high speed laser printers, may be used by the micro user. Each of these problems can be solved in somewhat different ways. Nor should these services be regarded as existing only for large organizations. Service bureaus and "information utilities" such as CompuServe often offer similar capacity and services. The acquisition of services for the purposes just cited is often quite competitive with other, less secure approaches. With the advent of relatively fast (9.6 kb/s and 19.2 kb/s) dialup modems, remote services may prove appropriate for providing some services that people in large organizations take for granted. The coming of Integrated Services Digital Networks (ISDN) through the telephone system will push these data transfer speeds even higher. In most areas it is still difficult to acquire ISDN services. The result of this difficulty is that if better ISDN distribution is not achieved by the mid-1990s, it may end up as a failed technology.

One common need for each of the problems just listed is the requirement that some host software interact with software on the micro. That interaction may not be sophisticated, but it must take place. Downloading from the host to the micro is at once easy to implement and difficult to implement effectively. In an asynchronous communications environment it is particularly easy to implement a simple system of data transfer. If the data to be transferred has only printable characters in a sequential file, the only thing necessary on the host end is some listing utility that allows the listing of the data to the terminal. On the micro end the terminal emulator must only be smart enough to capture the data in a file or memory. The speed at which data transfer takes place will depend on a number of elements: the implementation of some form of flow control, the speed of the microcomputer hardware and software, the ability to do interrupt programming on the micro, and the communications interfaces and modems (when necessary) on both the micro and host ends of the connection. If the communications lines are not clean, then some error-checking protocol is desirable. Many asynchronous terminal emulators allow such file transfer. If the emulator is smart enough, a simple host program may be written that prompts the user for a filename, then controls the micro to do the transfer, making the downloading more automatic. This requires a terminal emulator that can be remotely controlled.

In the micro-to-mini environment, a simple approach is often used. In an IBM 3270–oriented or other database environment, however, the problem becomes more complex. The first problem is that the software at the host end will be more complicated because files are rarely in simple sequential format. Furthermore, data are often accessed via a data dictionary, which requires intervention of a more sophisticated data-retrieval program to obtain information. The block-oriented nature of synchronous communications (used by the 3270 Display System) can also complicate the software. If all these problems have been overcome, then the micro software must also be smart enough to respond in an appropriate manner. Many of the manufacturers of 3270 hardware/software emulators are attempting to confront this problem but it is complicated by a variety of teleprocessing monitors and database systems. The same technique cannot be used for IBM's CICS and IMS, much less for systems like Software AG's COMPLETE and ADABAS.

A different approach to this problem is the use of a software system on the micro that turns the micro into an IBM 3780 or HASP Workstation Remote Job Entry (RJE) terminal. An advantage of this approach is that IBM systems have the appropriate mainframe software as a more or less standard feature. Another advantage is that if appropriate IBM mainframe software is implemented, routing can take place to many other mainframe peripherals. A major disadvantage is that an RJE line must be specified in the system generation on the IBM mainframe, and the RJE line may not be accessible by more than one remote device. The micro acting as an RJE terminal will also take up a synchronous port on the mainframe's communications processor. Where it is appropriate, however, this can be a useful file transfer for both uploading and downloading.

Mainframes as Micro Peripherals

A more interesting and exciting class of software are systems that allow the micro to use the mainframe as a peripheral. In a large organization this could prove to be extremely useful for archiving documents and data originating on micros since the mainframe disk drives are always backed up, usually on a daily basis, and security is normally much better. One early product of this type was Tempus-Link from Micro Tempus Inc., of Montreal, Canada. Another for IBM mainframes is RDISK from Tangram Systems, Inc., of North Carolina. Other products are available for use on DEC's VAXs, and one, in particular, will be discussed in some detail.

These systems consist of both micro and host software providing a communications link that allows the micro user to think simply of the host as another (although large) disk or diskette on the micro accessed in apparently the same way the micro's operating system accesses a local disk. The speed of these products is dependent on the communications line speed and the method used by the designer to access communications on the host.

Tempus-Link uses standard teleprocessing systems on the IBM/PCM (plug compatible mainframe/machine) end, such as CICS or TSO, to facilitate communications (a limited technique); RDISK uses direct access to IBM's Virtual Telecommunications Access Method (VTAM), which results in a more flexible and possibly faster system. These products may optionally provide access to database systems such as IMS or ADABAS as well as have the capacity to transfer files off the virtual micro disk for access by other host software. Although such products will probably operate best in a synchronous communications environment, they will typically allow either synchronous or asynchronous communications.

This review of the micro to host issues is summarized in Table 1.1. The two broad needs are generally for transaction processing and sizable data transfers. The fundamental purposes for which all this may be needed vary. One common need is for data to be downloaded so that it can be acted upon by microcomputer spreadsheet programs, word processing systems, or both. Another need may be for economical data storage for the micro user or data storage as a matter of organizational policy. The user interface is also of some concern. If organizational policy demands that even when the user is accessing microcomputer applications it should appear to be in the context of host software, then one set of solutions is appropriate. If, by way of contrast, the objective is to make the system appear to be an extension of the micros' operating environment, then another set of solutions is necessary. There are clearly a variety of products on the market that will provide various resources and facilities, and more are on the way.

Organizational Problems and Opportunities

Although there are significant technical difficulties associated with the micro-to-host link—and these are the primary focus of this book—it must be recognized that organizational problems can inhibit the free flow of information between central and distributed computers. On the other hand, significant opportunities can also accrue to the organization that manages the link well. As early as 1984 somewhere between 38 percent[19] and 48 percent[20] of larger companies and organizations had some form of micro-to-host link. An additional 38 percent[21] had plans to install a micro–host link within 18 months of the survey.

From the inception of micro–host links most organizations allowed read-only access with one-way downloading of data from the host to the

TABLE 1.1. The Micro-to-Host Issues

	Hardware	*Software*	*Communications*
Micro	• Communication Interfaces Synchronous Asynchronous LAN (802.x) X.25 • Protocol Conversion	• Terminal Emulations Asynchronous 3270 Synchronous • LAN Software • File Transfer • Appls. with Communications • Format/Character Conversion • Protocol Conversion • Protocol Suites Open System Interconnection (OSI) TCP/IP IBM SNA Other	• Access Technology • Bridges/Gateways/Routers • Servers • Physical Medium • Attachment Hardware Modems LAN Interface Cards • Data Link Technologies HDLC, SDLC (or bisync) (IBM) IEEE 802, Asynchronous, Others
Mainframe	• Communication Interfaces Front-End Processor (FEP) Terminal Controllers LAN Controllers X.25 • Protocol Conversion	• IBM VTAM or equivalent • Protocol Suites OSI TCP/IP IBM SNA Other • Data Extraction • Format/Character Conversion • Protocol Conversion	• Access Technology • Routing Systems Bridges/Gateways/Routers RSCS (IBM) Other • Servers • Physical Medium • Attachment Hardware Modems LAN Controllers/Cards FEP • Data Link Technologies HDLC, SDLC (and/or bisync) (IBM) IEEE 802, Asynchronous, Others

micro. The reasons for such limited use of the link have been seen as a by-product of the issues of data integrity, data administration, and data security,[22] although there are good reasons to allow uploading to the host, as well. One common reason users may wish to upload data is to prepare documents off-line on the micro, then transfer them to others through electronic mail systems. The ability to upload does not necessarily imply the ability to modify the corporate database.

One objective of the micro-to-host link should be to provide true information exchange: the ability to freely exchange documents among those who need access. In addition to the issues of data integrity, data administration, and data security, noted previously, there are a variety of other organizational problems:

- By 1990, standards (particularly those based on OSI) for the link were just emerging and products using those standards were not yet widely deployed. Because of this, and because most organizations finally resolve the issue through some committee structure composed of data processing (DP) management and end users or end users only,[23] organizational politics can play an important role in decisions made, overriding rational analysis and planning. It should be noted, however, that decisions to implement a link should include information from more than just technical people.
- The installation of a micro-to-host link may be expensive if done correctly and well,[24] although the challenge has always been to implement a cost-effective interconnection methodology. Many organizations that do "quick and dirty" fixes,[25] apparently cheap, may find they spend more in the long run.
- Because of the newness of the demand for micro-to-host links, technical decisions made earlier do not always fit well with changing demands. Any analysis of the micro–host link must include an evaluation of the host system with its protocols, teleprocessing monitors, operating systems, and communications access methods.[26]
- Few if any products exist that will properly integrate a multivendor hardware and software environment. This is, of course, related to the lack of standards for the link throughout the industry. More will be said of this in later chapters.
- The unwillingness of many organizations to recognize that in the contemporary computing environment central DP organizations

will have to employ microcomputer programmers and related support personnel.

Notwithstanding the problems that must be confronted in providing an effective micro-to-host connection, the organizational benefits of the link can be significant. One basic premise implicit in any discussion of distributed computing is the (almost always untested) assumption that some things can be done less expensively on small computers than on large central systems. Off-line data preparation can reduce the load on the host. Any transactional system that consists primarily of data entry could be written or rewritten to be accomplished off-line with batch transfer to the database. Text preparation for electronic documents can often be accomplished more conveniently on a micro, then uploaded to the appropriate system. Many micro-based software packages provide good-to-superior presentation graphics and spreadsheet functions that allow report writing that are either expensive or not available on large systems.

Composition of documents that ultimately end up as books or magazines is gravitating toward micro-based desktop publishing systems. In fact, the compositors of this book used Ventura Publisher from Xerox. A recently distributed communications program from CompuServe is another example of the situation. The *CompuServe Information Manager* is a very inexpensive package designed specifically to make it easy to deal with CompuServe. Much, if not most, editing is done on the micro end of the connection, and the document (or electronic mail) is then automatically uploaded to the CompuServe computer system. Other elements of the user interface that were once thought to be a necessary part of large-scale host computing have been transferred to the micro end of the connection. In such an environment the whole issue of file transfer becomes much more central to the process than ever before.

The underlying reason micros made such an impact on organizations during the 1980s is that end users see micros as an aid to productivity. Such an aid should help the organization reduce costs—not increase them. In many, if not most, organizations, neither the end user nor the DP department has total control over the situation. The result is often a chaotic situation. Chaos usually costs money. To avoid a chaotic, and inappropriate, micro-to-host link, it is desirable in most organizations to have central planning and control over shared micro–host applications.[27] Even more important, it is necessary to have a comprehensive understanding and perspective concerning the way in which computing and communications are to be incorporated into the organizational milieu.

Centralized, Decentralized, and Distributed Processing

Traditional DP environments in most organizations of any size are centralized systems. Centralized systems are the historical product of the economy-of-scale philosophy, which says that many people using expensive equipment is more cost-effective than each person or group having their own computing facilities. In addition, for a large organization, there is a considerable amount of data that must be centrally controlled and maintained. These two issues led to the establishment of central DP facilities in most large organizations and many small ones. The growth in the use of inexpensive microcomputers and the falling costs of minicomputers has called this entire approach to computing into question.

Two alternatives to centralized computing exist: decentralized and distributed. Decentralized computing implies that an organization has no need for a centralized database, that it is cost-effective to provide multiple small computer systems, and that centralized planning for computing is either unnecessary or undesirable. Distributed processing, by way of contrast, recognizes the need for centralized planning, but also recognizes that economy-of-scale arguments are no longer as compelling as they were in earlier times.

Distributed processing (and/or cooperative computing) assumes that work will be accomplished on whatever level of computer system is most appropriate to the function. A further assumption is that all computers in a distributed system will be linked with a data communications system transparent to the user. While a decentralized system does not preclude the use of data communications among systems, neither is communications required. In a distributed system communications is required. Although the DP community has been talking about distributed systems for a long time, there are still few good examples. It has turned out that distributed systems are easier to talk about than to design and build.

The microcomputer, during the 1980s, was thrust into the controversy over centralized/decentralized/distributed computing. Rather than simplifying the discussion and resolution of the issue, micros have vastly expanded the scope of the problem in many organizations. One way in which the scope has expanded is that many of the computing problems that once were done on a remote host, can now be accomplished on micros, providing the data are available. This will ultimately mean that the role of the central DP operation will change. The most likely direction is that the central operation will become primarily a data communications/information utility, providing data communications and centralized data availability and maintenance with most actual manipulation of the data being accomplished on a worker's desk. This may create a new computing environment that lies somewhere between distributed and decentralized systems.

Especially in large organizations, the mainframe will continue to play a major role simply because it supports the corporate database—that central repository of the "soul" of the institution. The deployment of micros across an organization, however, changes the way in which the corporate database can be used. With the coming of micros there is the immediate demand for the ability to move data from the host to the micro and from the micro to the host. The ability to transport data is further complicated because there will be the need to move data from one micro to another. Another reason for moving data from micro to host may not involve the corporate database at all—it may be a function of using the most cost-effective storage technology.

In today's marketplace this discussion centers primarily around IBM/PCMs as distinguished from minis or superminis. What can be said of IBM/PCM mainframes is also applicable, however, to multiuser systems from many manufacturers. This book makes only limited use of the traditional distinctions among micro, mini, and mainframe. This is partly because such distinctions have only limited value with today's technology, and partly because the logical distinction is between single-user workstations and multiuser systems. Although I will mention IBM, DEC, and other (host) systems, this is mostly to clarify the issues under discussion or to emphasize technological implications of a problem or process.

In most organizations there will not be a single solution to the micro-to-host problem. The solution will be partly determined by the intended use of the micro-to-host link, the communications standard(s) used, the composite use of the micros, and the sophistication of end users. Clearly, with these different objectives in mind, *the* solution will probably be a compromise among contending interests within the organization.

Organizational Objectives

Another way of confronting the micro-to-host link is to address the corporate problems involved in deploying microcomputers. I, for one, applaud that deployment but recognize that just as micros can contribute to the solution of many bottlenecks, they can also be the cause of others. The appropriate use of microcomputers in an organization can improve white-collar productivity, limit the growth in the demand for clerical employees, and provide the tools for producing better information for better decisions. The demand for a reasonable micro-to-host link can also lead to decreased security for corporate data, require more sophisticated communications between micro and host, and require the establishment of an extensive support structure for education, maintenance, and systems development for micros.

In organizations there are several objectives for using micro-to-host links.[28] In the list and associated diagrams that follow, several points should be noted in that they give clues about the underlying technology necessary for successful implementation. Note first that almost all the applications, and this is only an illustrative list, require some form of batch transfer. Second, the micro in the illustrations is not always the client.

1. The most frequent use—terminal emulation of one kind or another.

Micro-Mainframe Terminal Emulation Flow:

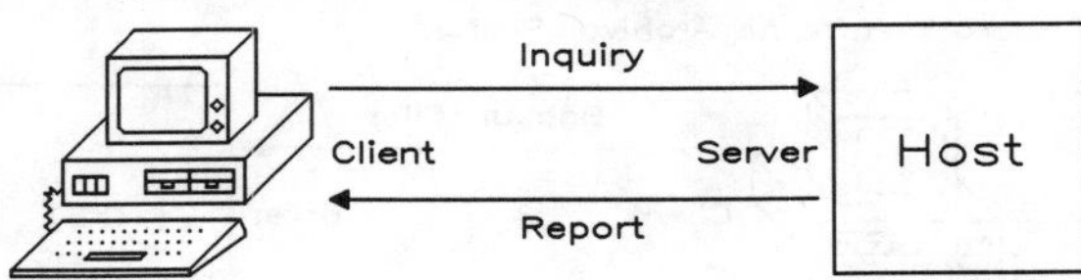

MODE: Interactive Transfer

2. The ability to extract data from the corporate database, download it, massage it, and produce reports locally.

Micro-Mainframe Data Extraction Flow:

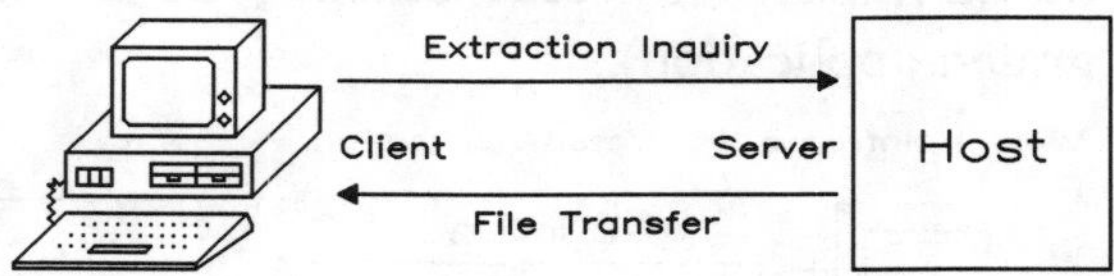

MODE: Interactive/Batch Transfer

3. Electronic report distribution, instead of the physical distribution of printed reports, is technologically feasible, and economically desirable.

Mainframe-Micro Document Transfer:

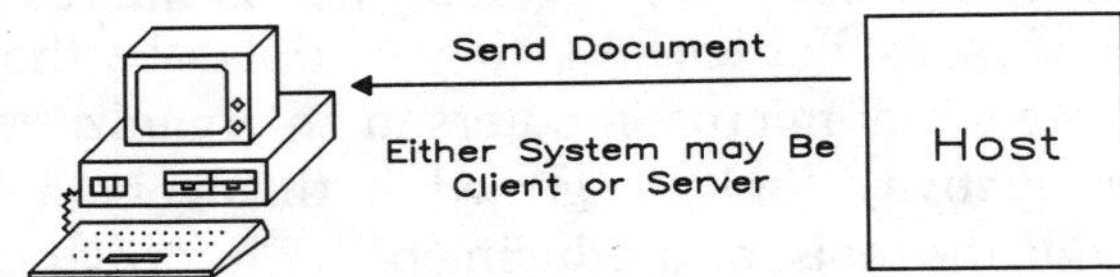

MODE: Batch Transfer

4. Composing documents locally, then transmit them to some other target system, which might be an electronic mail system, an automated composition machine in the print shop, or some other expensive (or esoteric) device.

Micro-Mainframe Document Transfer:

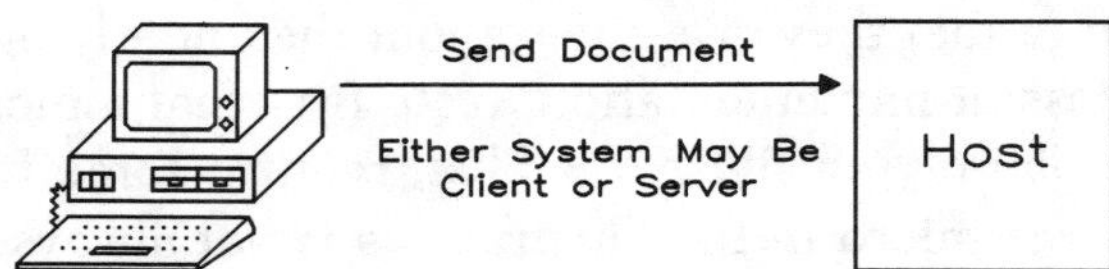

MODE: Batch Transfer

5. Using the host as an archival peripheral for the micro.

Micro-Mainframe Archival System:

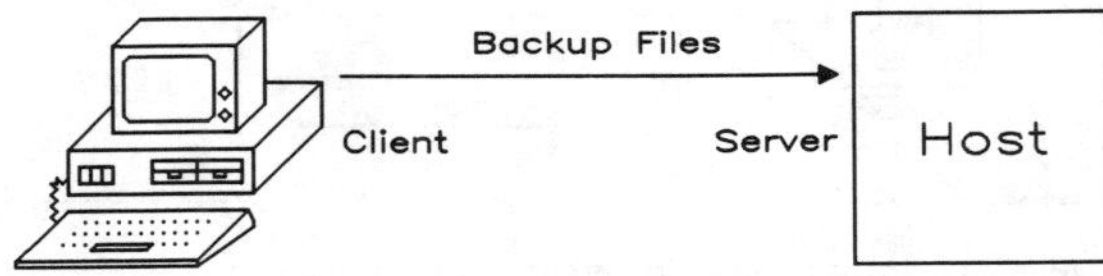

MODE: Batch Transfer

6. The effort to make the host more user-friendly with an off-line transaction set-up system, which presumably would lead to a reduced impact on host resources (this is sometimes called an integrated application).

Micro-Mainframe Integrated Application:

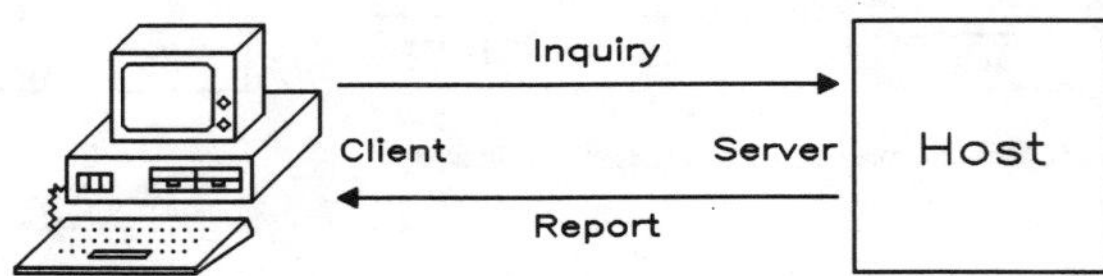

MODE: Integrated Application with Batch Transfer

7. The ability to act as an intelligent node in a distributed processing environment (transparent service).

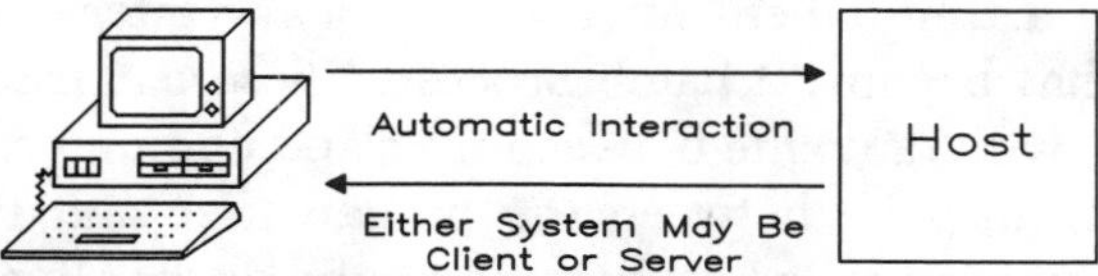

Many observers of the micro-to-host link have reduced their objectives to three: terminal emulation, file transfer, and intelligent links.[29] The first objective, terminal emulation, is the simplest approach to the link. Emulation can be slow and allows the host to dictate the role of the micro, usually as a passive or dumb terminal. Terminal emulation requires an appropriate micro-based software (or software/hardware) package, which turns the micro into a terminal. In large systems that terminal is often in the DEC VT100* family or the International Business Machines (IBM) 3270 family. More will be said of these emulations in later chapters. When terminal emulation is the objective, transactional processing is the usual objective of the user.

The second objective, file transfer, represents a somewhat more complicated and varied form of the micro-to-host link. The flow of such transfers may be from the host to the micro, from the micro to the host, or both. Either system may serve as client or server. If the transfer is from the host to the micro, then the purpose of the transfer may be to provide data to a micro application program, such as a spreadsheet, or to simply distribute information to selected employees. Local printing of an extended report is a special form of file transfer. While transferring data, reformatting the data may be required for further processing on either the micro or the host. File transfer is essentially a batch (instead of an interactive) process. Although batch processes may be seen by some as a problem, it has

*The DEC VT100 has now been superceded by the VT200 and VT300 series. Moreover, the screen handling system adopted by DEC for the VT100 was the basis for American National Standards Institute (ANSI) standard X3.64. "VT100" is still the more-or-less popular (and now generic) designation for the escape code definitions and associated protocol implementing those escape code definitions.

come almost full circle from the time when all processing was batch oriented because the input medium was normally punched cards, to a time when user–host interactions were almost on a character-by-character basis, back to a time when much of the heavy interaction between client and server has become a batch process. These batch processes are now interspersed with dialogue between user and computer, but today some of that dialogue may be between the human user and the local computer, the human user and the host computer, and/or the client and server computers. Part of this development has been the result of a recognition that much of what happens in a computer/communications environment consists of file transfers, and this in turn has been made ever more evident by the expanded use of the packetizing of data for use by the networks over which the information moves. It is no longer very efficient to move data one character at a time.

The third objective, intelligent links, typically implies a tighter integration of micro and host applications than either terminal emulation or simple file transfers. The objective of such links is to minimize user intervention in the micro-to-host relationship with messaging, commands, controls, and actions being performed more or less automatically and under the control of either the micro or the host. As a result, the relationship becomes automatic, transparent, and anticipatory. In other words, this approach is user-friendly. There may be claims that intelligent links involve the use of artificial intelligence (AI) or "fourth generation" (4GL) languages. In the context of the micro-to-host link, however, it appears that the terms AI and 4GL are more often marketing artifacts than technological realities. As with simple file transfers, the intelligent link may involve reformatting data from the file structure at one end to the file structure at the other.

System-Dependent Issues

Although there were by the mid-1980s many acceptable ways to solve the micro-to-host link, it turns out to be an almost insolvable problem in many organizations. Certainly—given the current state of technology—there is no *one* way of solving the problem. This situation arises because of decisions that may have predated the advent of micros or decisions that continue to be made without considering the effect of micros on the organization. The problems are both hardware and software related at both the micro and host ends of the connection. An illustration will serve to make the point.

One organization, using IBM-compatible mainframes, decided in the early 1980s to adopt ADABAS—a database system from Software AG. To access the database with IBM's 3270 Display System (more of this in a later chapter) it was necessary to have an item of mainframe software called a teleprocessing monitor (TP monitor), which along with software implementing an access method, allows communications to take place. The organization adopted Software AG's COM-PLETE, not one of IBM's "standard" TP monitors or systems (such as CICS, TSO, CMS, or IMS), and its associated access method, CTAM (COM-PLETE Telecommunications Access Method) instead of IBM's more standard VTAM (Virtual Telecommunications Access Method). At that time (before the arrival of the IBM PC) Software AG did not have a plan in effect to provide micro-to-mainframe connections at all.

Shortly thereafter, but before the impact of the IBM PC (or PCs in general) had become apparent, a decision was also made to employ the Texas Instrument Professional Computer (TIPC) as the organization's standard micro. Both decisions were appropriate, providing good software and hardware. With the growth in demand for micro-to-host communications, especially the extraction of data from the ADABAS database, Software AG produced a product call the "Natural Connection." Unfortunately the Natural Connection supported *only* the IBM PC family of micros, not the TIPC. At the same time, third-party vendors of micro and mainframe software provided appropriate software that would work with the TIPC and with ADABAS, but would not work with Software AG's COM-PLETE TP monitor or with CTAM.

It turned out that at that time only about 20 percent of the installations using ADABAS also used TIPCs, and only about 20 percent of Software AG's installed base used COM-PLETE. Consequently there was no incentive for Software AG to produce Natural Connection to support the TIPC and no incentive for third-party software manufacturers to support Software AG's COM-PLETE and CTAM. In the long run, to support appropriate micro-to-mainframe connections, the organization in question had to maintain multiple TP monitors, switch from CTAM to VTAM, and move from the TIPC standard to an IBM PC or IBM PC Compatible microcomputer. These were expensive alternatives but are problems common in many organizations. While the illustration just given is several years old, essentially the same problems continue to occur in many organizations today.

The issues just noted, along with others, make the host-to-micro connection a complicated problem in most real organizations. In a distributed processing environment there should be two primary objectives: connectivity and end user transparency. In a truly distributed environment ultimate connectivity is the ability to establish an "any-to-any" session between or among any of the devices attached to the network. The ability to establish and use a connection should be transparent to the user to the extent that the major complexities of the connection are established by micro-and-mainframe (or micro-and-micro or micro-and-mini) software with a minimum of user intervention. This section is designed to introduce you to some of the issues that must be solved to effect a satisfactory relationship between micros and hosts. Most of these problems will become the focus of subsequent chapters.

Networks and Enterprise Computing

Networks make EWC possible. Chapters 3 and 4 will explore some of the networking issues in detail. This section, however, attempts to identify some of the major issues with which designers of enterprise-wide integration must deal. What started out as a project to solve the micro-to-host link has now become a quest for organization-wide integration of computing resources. The first issue is, of course, "what kind of network do we have?" The second issue is, "is software available to support a sophisticated micro–host link over the network available to us?" It has long been understood that when sophisticated software is developed it will allow the microcomputer/workstation to look like a true computer to its host peer.[30] The third issue concerns objectives in constructing an integrated computing environment. Even at the level of the micro-to-host link the successful implementation of stated objectives may well determine what hardware and software communications technology to use. Certainly for broader integration efforts that would hold true. If, for example, one were doing "real time" process control a network protocol that is deterministic and predictable would be necessary, while an office automation environment may allow protocols that are more probabilistic in their behavior during data transfers. Even more fundamental is the selection of a network architecture. Will the network be structured by what is essentially a wide area network architecture such as IBM's SNA, or will it be built around LAN concepts and technologies?

Although the network might be a serial, asynchronous, RS-232-C based communications system, an IBM synchronous link, a LAN, an X.25 Wide Area Network (WAN), or something else, the way in which the micro-to-host connection works will depend on what network environment it's working in. In many organizations, systems may have to confront all these, and other, networks. Even within the general types noted, there are variations. Not all asynchronous networks use the same methods for preventing data overflow (called "flow control" or "speed matching"). Many installations still use IBM's older bisynchronous communications rather than the currently promoted SDLC/SNA. Gateways (interfaces between two different kinds of networks) and bridges (interfaces between two networks of the same kind) allow data to flow between and among networks. Although there are still some difficulties in their use, there are a significant number of gateways and bridges commercially available that can provide good, if not universal, connectivity among networks.[31] The manufacturers of micro-to-host software have problems in structuring a truly universal interface in part because of the difficulty in dealing with the various network products available.

Micro Communications and Host Extraction

Most of the terminal emulator programs for micros provide uploading and downloading to and from standard software on the host. Typically this means some character-by-character or record-by-record transfer system. Database systems on either the host or micro end of the connection, however, typically do not transfer simple flat or rectangular files. Alternately, a database inquiry is necessary to retrieve appropriate data elements for a specified unit (in a rectangular file, a "record"), compose a record, and send it out the communications line.

Some systems, like FOCUS, can handle the chore for some database management systems in a simple manner. As R. Roth has noted, the grand solution involves the use of a 4GL database system, often at great expense.[32] If such a system is unavailable, however, the only alternative is to write a transaction to do the job. That transaction might be generalized (so that different people with different needs can use it) or specific to a particular task. In either case it is hardly transparent.

In any event, a complete micro-to-host link must provide the following data conversion services:

- Extract the data from the host database system, whatever that may be.
- Reformat the data for transfer to the micro.

- Reformat the data after reception at the micro for use with the appropriate software on the micro end.

A complete end-to-end system would provide these services, and for some applications are currently available if the software fits into the rest of the system available, if the host can support the system and, if the micro can support the system, and if appropriate communications facilities are available. "Support" and "appropriate" means that the software designer has understood and implemented the necessary interfaces to both software and hardware at both ends of the connection.

Protocols

A protocol is a formal set of conventions governing the format and relative timing of message exchange in a communications network. Many protocols deal with maintaining the integrity of data when on the network. Different kinds of networks provide different challenges when transferring data. Networks based on unshielded twisted pairs of copper wires—such as telephone systems—are subject to considerable electrical interference. Everyone has heard static on the telephone line. That static, or "noise," can garble the data coming down the line. At some point a protocol must be used that will allow reliable data transfer between or among computers.

I hasten to note that the integrity of transmitted data is not solely dependent on protocol robustness, although data-transfer protocols have been constructed to ensure that integrity. Telephone lines, for example, can be conditioned to compensate for such things as phase and amplitude perturbations. Cable television systems are specifically designed to take care of such problems. Nevertheless, since many transmission media can be affected by external electrical noise, file-transfer protocols are usually necessary to protect the data-transfer process. All modern networks, except for the most primitive, low-speed systems, use some form of error-correcting data-transfer protocol.

Sometimes the network itself will take care of the data-transfer protocol. Local Area Networks and other networks have the capacity for checking the integrity of the data passed around the system. This is a function of the need to ensure that the network itself does not corrupt the data. If all the data to be transferred consist of printable characters in the same character set (ASCII or EBCDIC, usually), then such networks will likely have sufficient services to handle the problem. On the other hand, to transfer binary data (programs, for example), additional software will be necessary at both the transmitting and receiving end as an additional protocol to ensure correct transfer and to ensure that the data being transferred will not interfere with the network. But data integrity exists at several different layers in a network (see Chapter 3).

A file transfer controlled by an end user is an *application* on any computer system and related network. At the lowest network levels (physical and data link) data are also passed in frames or packets and participate in much of the same behavior as more widely understood forms of file transfer. In both situations error checking takes place and can result in a request for retransmission. High-speed dial-access modems typically access each other over a synchronous link using an appropriate transfer technique (often Microcom Networking Protocol (MNP) as this was written). Thus the modem-to-modem link may be synchronous even though the end user and the computer being accessed are actually responding to asynchronous communications. The result of the error-correcting protocol used by the modems, plus the protocol used by the file-transfer mechanisms on each end, may restrict throughput on a noisy line.

Several such protocols have been developed over the years and are in use today, and therein lies a problem: too many unstandardized protocols. Microcomputer enthusiasts are probably familiar with the XMODEM or Christiansen protocol, which is frequently used to transfer binary and other data from bulletin board systems to micros. The XMODEM protocol has been implemented on a variety of host and minicomputer systems. Similar in concept if not in detail, is the Kermit protocol developed at Columbia University for Unix systems and now widely available on many micro, mini, and mainframe computers under a variety of operating systems. XMODEM and Kermit are designed to be used primarily with asynchronous networks, although they could be integrated into synchronous links as well; however, these protocols have not been widely adopted for commercial applications.

IBM has dealt with the problem of file transfers for years and has developed several approaches. One of the oldest is the 3780 remote batch protocol operating over a synchronous data link. 3780 software is widely available for micros and for IBM and other host systems. The difficulty is that it requires expensive synchronous data communications, although that may be appropriate in a large organizational environment. IBM's protocol designed to ease data exchange in an SDLC/SNA network is called Logical Unit (LU) 6.2 or Advanced Program-to-Program Communications (APPC).

Under APPC, an applications program running in a microcomputer can communicate interactively with data and programs in other running computers. The advantages of APPC include the ability to retrieve data from anywhere in the network, the capacity to execute programs anywhere in the network, and faster transmission speed.[33] G. Briggs, writing in *MIS Week*, has commented that non–IBM-based micro–host links currently account for only a small portion of the market. Led by LU 6.2 the situation is expected to change. The sales of APPC/LU 6.2 technology about doubled in the last half of the 1980s.[34] This is because IBM has made APPC publicly available so that it can be incorporated into third-party software.

Concluding Note

In this chapter I have provided an overview of some of the fundamental problems in providing EWC. Clearly many manufacturers are attempting to solve the problems and to confront the issues. It is true, however, that most organizations, as they confront EWC, will have to redefine some of the approaches that have traditionally been used. The current situation is chaotic and disorganized. Yet, an organization cannot wait to implement new technologies simply because all the pieces are not in place, or because not all the elements can be predicted.

Manufacturers will have to recognize that if their products are to be widely accepted, they must be designed to be flexible to a degree unknown today. Namely, they must be able to relate to a wide variety of database systems on both hosts and micros, they must be capable of running across a variety of networks, they must operate under a variety of communications access methods on the hosts, and they must work on a variety of microcomputer systems, not just IBM PCs or copies thereof.

Notwithstanding the problems of implementing a successful EWC strategy, however, it is possible within the context of currently existing technology to do a good, if not perfect, job.

Notes

1. *BusinessWeek*, June 4, 1990, cover page.
2. See, for example, Thomas W. Madron, *Local Area Networks in Large Organizations* (Hasbrouck Heights, NJ: Hayden Book Company, 1984); and James Martin, *Telematic Society* (Englewood Cliffs, NJ: Prentice-Hall, 1981).

3. Thomas W. Madron, *Micro–Mainframe Connection* (Indianapolis, IN: Howard W. Sams & Company, 1987).
4. Ibid., p. 3.
5. U.S. Congress, Office of Technology Assessment, *Critical Connections: Communication for the Future*, OTA-CIT-407 (Washington, DC: U.S. Government Printing Office, January, 1990), p. 254, n. 48.
6. As quoted by Peter Keen, "Roundtable: Can We Talk?" *CIO: The Magazine for Information Executives*, Vol. 3, No. 8, May 1990, p. 24.
7. See John Desmond, "MIS 'bad guys'," *Software Magazine*, Vol. 10, No. 4, March 15, 1990, p. 8, for example.
8. Bill Dooley, "Elephants and Enterprise-Wide Computing: View from a-top DEC," *MIS Week*, Vol. 9, No. 36, Sept. 5, 1988, p. 12.
9. The data in Figure 1 were part of the results from the 1986, 1988, and 1990 surveys of the membership of the Data Processing Management Association (DPMA), periodically sponsored by DPMA's Education Foundation. The data were used by permission of DPMA.
10. As recounted by Peter Keen, "Roundtable: Can We Talk?" *CIO: The Magazine for Information Executives*, Vol. 3, No. 8, May 1990, p. 23.
11. Anon., "Micro–Mainframe Links' Popularity Growing Rapidly," *PC Week*, Vol. 1, No. 44, Nov. 6, 1984, p. 119.
12. Ibid.
13. G. Briggs, "Firms Told: Give PC Access to Mainframe or Fail," *MIS Week*, Vol. 5, No. 45, Nov. 17, 1984, p. 43.
14. For specific organizational examples, note the following: D. Ruby, "Mainframe Data: The Missing Link," *PC Week*, Vol. 1, No. 24, June 19, 1984, p. 42; B. Freedman, "Micro-Links Boost Firm's Productivity," *PC Week*, Vol. 1, No. 51, Dec. 25, 1984, p. 89; R. Jones, "Case-Mix and Computers: Part One: A Look at Computer Delivery Modes," *Computers in Healthcare*, Vol. 5, No. 6, June 1984, pp. 42–45; R. Jones, "Case-Mix and Computers: There's a Micro–Mainframe Connection in Your Future—Part III—Effecting the Micro–Mainframe Link-up," *Computers in Healthcare*, Vol. 5, No. 10, Oct. 1984, pp. 36–37, 39.
15. Madron, p. 7.
16. D. Davies, "Execs: CPU–Micro Software Link to Grow," *MIS Week*, Vol. 4, No. 13, March 30, 1983, p. 12.
17. J. Altman, "Smarter User-Transparency Links Coming," *MIS Week*, Vol. 6, No. 3, Jan. 16, 1985, pp. 20, 22.
18. Note the report commissioned by Microsoft and Zenith Data Systems, "The Benefits of the Graphical User Interface: A Report on New Primary

Research," prepared by Temple, Barker & Sloane, Inc., 33 Hayden Avenue, Lexington, MA 02173, Spring, 1990. Although this is a marketing-based study commissioned by two corporations with a vested interest, the methodology seems acceptable. The fundamental conclusion was that people tend to work faster and better with lower levels of frustration and fatigue when using a GUI.

19. M. McEnaney, "Volume of Micro-Mainframe Links Raising MIS Demands," *ComputerWorld,* Vol. 19, No. 9, March 4, 1985, p. 22; M. McEnaney, "Links Pose Several Challenges for MIS," *ComputerWorld,* Vol. 19, No. 11, March 18, 1985, pp. 45, 54; J. Desmond, "Micro–Mainframe Links Cater to Data Downloads," *ComputerWorld,* Vol. 19, No. 15, April 15, 1985, pp. 45, 54.

20. Anon., "Micro to Mainframe Trends," *Words,* Vol. 13, No. 3, Oct.-Nov. 1984, p. 27.

21. Ibid.

22. M. McEnaney, "Volume of Micro–Mainframe Links Raising MIS Demands," *ComputerWorld,* Vol. 19, No. 9, March 4, 1985, p. 22.

23. Anon., "PC Users: Falling in On-Line," *Burroughs World,* Vol. 5, No 10, Oct. 1984, p. 41.

24. Anon., "Costs Run High to Link Micros to Data Center," *PC Week,* Vol. 2, No. 8, Feb. 28, 1985, pp. 36, 39.

25. J. Desmond, "Links Provide Quick Fix: But Problems Can Arise from Simple Data Link Solutions," Vol. 19, No. 15, April 15, 1985, pp. 45, 58.

26. Anon., "Costs Run High to Link Micros to Data Center," *PC Week,* Vol. 2, No. 8, Feb. 28, 1985, pp. 36, 39.

27. Anon., "Micro–CPU Link Tends to Stifle Micro Flexibility: Study," *ComputerWorld,* Vol. 18, No. 39, Sept. 24, 1984, p. 35.

28. T. W. Madron, "Despite Present Claims, Micro–Mainframe Links Remain Undeveloped," *ComputerWorld,* Vol. 18, No. 30, July 23, 1984, pp. 59, 64. Several of the ideas and some of the text presented in this book have been previously published in my *ComputerWorld* column, "MicroBits," published during 1984 and 1985. These are used with the permission of *ComputerWorld*.

29. Anon., "Making the Connection," *IBM User,* June 1984, pp. 37–49, 41; S. F. Bryant, "Micro-to-Mainframe Links," *Computer Decisions,* Vol. 16, No. 8, July 1984, pp. 162–163, 166ff; J. Pallatto and S. J. Getgood, "Micro–Mainframe Links: Looking for the Perfect Window into the Big System World," *PC Week,* Vol. 1, No. 44, Nov. 6, 1984, pp. 79–92; R. L. Roth, "Making Connections in the Shadow of the Mainframe,"

ComputerWorld, Vol. 18, No. 42, Oct. 1984, pp. 7, 10, 12ff; R. P. Wenig, "Five Factors Define Micro–Mainframe Links," *ComputerWorld,* Vol. 18, No. 42, Oct. 15, 1984, pp. 63, 76; and R. P. Wenig, "A Closer Look at Mainframe Links," *ComputerWorld Australia,* Vol. 7, No. 18, Nov. 2, 1984, p. 61.

30. F. X. Dzubeck, "Telecommunications," *Office Administration and Automation,* Vol. 46, No. 2, Feb. 1985, pp. 88–89.

31. J. Cortino, "Citibank Network Sparks 'Electronic Village'," *MIS Week,* Vol. 6, No. 14, April 3, 1985, pp. 2–3.

32. R. Roth, "Making Connections with the Mainframe," *ComputerWorld Australia,* Vol. 7, No. 18, Nov. 2, 1984, pp. 15–18, 20.

33. S. Polilli, " 'Dumb' PC Link Stated," *MIS Week,* Vol. 6, No. 14, April 3, 1985, pp. 1, 25. APPC is completely described in Gerard Joseph, *An Introduction to Advanced Program-to-Program Communication (APPC)* (Research Triangle, NC: International Business Machines Corporation, 1983), document number GG24-1584-0.

34. G. Briggs, "Non–IBM PC Links May Zoom," *MIS Week,* Vol. 6, No. 3, Jan. 16, 1985, pp. 20, 22.

CHAPTER 2

Features, Facilities, and Issues in Enterprise-Wide Computing

This chapter deals partly with issues surrounding the role of mainframe computers in enterprise-wide computing (EWC). For people trying to plan for EWC without mainframes the discussion may sometimes seem arcane. On the other hand, when computers, both large and small, are thought of as *peers*, a discussion of micro/mainframe issues becomes relevant to almost everyone. I make the latter assertion because even a small installation may today opt for a system that everyone uses as a file server or a system that uses some other central computer, even if it is not as large nor as expensive as the traditional mainframe. Although some of the specific hardware referenced in this chapter may not be relevant to your situation, many of the concepts will, nevertheless, be important for your consideration.

The first step in understanding and selecting the appropriate method of linking micros and mainframes is a recognition of the differences among terminal emulators; mainframe database links; mainframe application links; microcomputer application links; and generalized, intelligent micro-to-mainframe links.[1] If only transactional access is needed, a variety of easily installed terminal emulation products are available. It is, however, much more difficult to install an integrated micro-to-mainframe system. The level of difficulty expands with greater variety in mainframe or mini target computers, with the variety of micros being used, and with the amount of flexibility demanded.

The goals I typically have in designing an integrated network usually include a broad level of connectivity among a variety of devices from multiple vendors, the ability to provide transactional access in a form more or less "native" to the target mainframe (or mini), and the ability to transfer files to and from the mainframe without the user needing to be a systems programmer. Although there has been extensive media hype over the last few years, the issues of connectivity and file transfer have not been generally or satisfactorily solved except in specialized situations. If one is willing to mold the entire mainframe–communications–micro system to the demands of a single vendor—a luxury many do not have—then many of the problems inherent in the micro-to-mainframe connection can be solved—at the price of full connectivity and at the price of the user organization's freedom to define its own needs and objectives rather than having them defined by one or a few vendors.

New products, however, are appearing quickly. There is a need for a class of "open-ended" micro-to-mainframe systems that can be tailored to the needs of specific organizations. Some of those products may be in development at this writing. As E. Horwitt has pointed out, corporate computer managers who have had to settle for one vendor's proprietary solution to micro-to-mainframe problems may be looking at a new open-ended era.[2] Open-ended micro-to-mainframe products are, according to Horwitt, an improvement over their proprietary predecessors in three important ways.

1. These products enable companies to build end user querying systems using existing databases and files, software, and training and programming costs are controlled.
2. A wider choice of applications should be capable of being interfaced at both the micro and the mainframe ends.

3. Nonproprietary products facilitate an appropriate (in the user organization's terms) user interface.

When more open-ended products appear on the market, companies will likely be able to find a micro-to-mainframe link that fits their requirements on all levels: interfacing with already-existing mainframe databases as well as with end users' unique information and application requirements, and the level of end user computer literacy. This chapter will address some of the problems to be faced in achieving these objectives.

Before discussing the micro-to-mainframe link, it is necessary to review some of the more salient data communications issues that will recur throughout this book. This volume is not intended as an introduction to data communications; for that, other references should be consulted.[3] The specific problems associated with a useful micro-to-mainframe link require thinking about data communications as part of an integrated micro/mainframe application. This review discusses, first from the mainframe perspective, then from the microcomputer perspective, data communications as part of the integration process.

Mainframe Requirements

The mainframe (host) computer system is typically used as the center of corporate database systems and as a computing tool where high speed and volume are characteristic of the applications. Traditionally the mainframe was also used in a multiuser environment because there was an economy of scale in sharing the cost of expensive systems among many users. Contemporary computing conditions still favor the first two reasons for using a central system, although with the arrival of low-cost microcomputers, supermicros, minis, and superminis, the economy-of-scale argument is beginning to have significant limitations (although it is by no means a dead issue).

To perform its functions well, the mainframe system must have enough capacity and appropriate software. The "appropriate" software includes not only user applications but also the systems necessary for terminal support, transactional and batch access to data, and file-transfer facilities. Only the last function is unique to a system in which microcomputers reside alongside the host system. With the deployment of large numbers of micros, some user applications originally running on the host system can be run more appropriately on micros, thereby taking some of the load off the central system. Moreover, some functions, such as spreadsheets, have never been cost-effective on mainframe systems, although spreadsheets provide excellent reporting tools on micros. The consequence of all this is a growing need for file transfers, especially from the mainframe to the micro.

IBM versus "The Others"

Data communications can vary depending on the central system. The most common distinction is between IBM and other mainframes or minis. IBM has for many years used synchronous communications systems (bisynchronous or SDLC/SNA), although much of the rest of the computing world used asynchronous methods (see the "Synchronous" and "Asynchronous" sections in this chapter). Because of the role played by IBM in the computer marketplace, most manufacturers of computers are now vending hardware and software that allows interconnection to IBM computers via synchronous communications. Even in the minicomputer world, however, the actual use of asynchronous communications varies. Flow control—the ability of the connected computers to control the flow of data so that none will be lost—can be handled in different ways by different manufacturers. Although there are some standards concerning the way in which flow control is handled, there are several common ways to achieve data-flow control. Digital Equipment Corporation (DEC), for example, has for many years used techniques different from Hewlett-Packard (HP).

A Teleprocessing Monitor

Figure 2.1 is a simplified block diagram of a typical IBM mainframe communications environment. Under the operating system runs an "application." "Application" in this context refers to what is often termed a teleprocessing (TP) monitor. On an IBM mainframe system, a TP monitor is the interface between a user and the user's application program. Common TP monitors are associated with IMS (a database system), TSO (Time Sharing Option), or CICS. Manufacturers of other systems, such as Software AG's ADABAS, may have their own TP monitors. A user application program runs under a TP monitor. The TP monitor, in turn, communicates with the outside world through a telecommunications access method (TAM). Older access methods included BTAM (Basic Telecommunications Access Method) and TCAM (TeleCommunications Access Method), al-

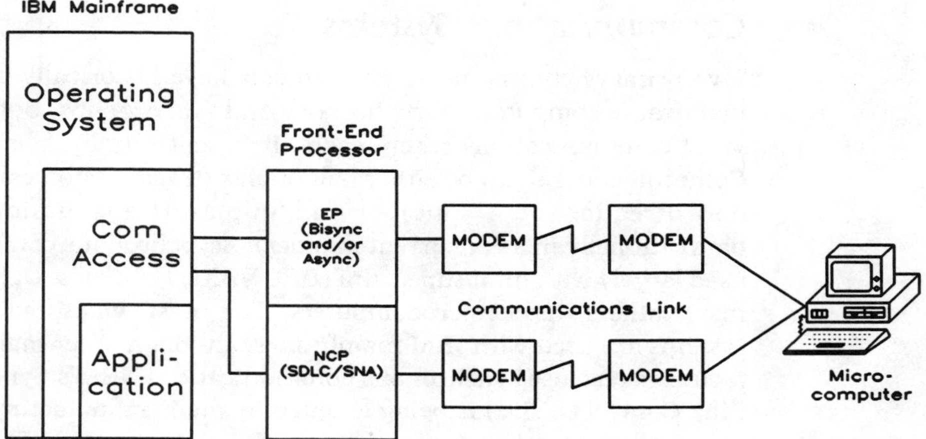

Figure 2.1. IBM Mainframe Communications Environment.

though the current IBM product is VTAM (Virtual Telecommunications Access Method). Independent manufacturers may write their own access methods, such as Software AG's CTAM (COM-PLETE Telecommunications Access Method) that operates with Software AG's TP Monitor, COM-PLETE.

Telecommunications Access Methods

The TAM is the link between the application and the channel hardware on an IBM mainframe. An IBM channel is a high-speed method for reading and writing data to peripherals. For communications purposes, the major peripheral is a Front End Processor (FEP) to which end user devices (terminals) are connected. This concept is discussed further in later chapters. The FEP is a small computer that converts data from the high-speed channel into something that can be used on a communications line, usually through a modem. IBM has marketed a series of 37xx FEPs (there was an earlier series, as well), beginning with the 3705 through the current 3745. When using older bisync or async protocols, a control program called EP governs the system and emulates an older FEP—a 2703. NCP governs the more modern SDLC/SNA system. In both cases (EP or NCP) interaction takes place between the FEP software and the TAM.

Communications Systems

Two primary communications protocols have historically been used with mainframe computers: asynchronous and synchronous. Both are forms of *serial* communications where each bit is sent serially, one after another. Communications can be either half duplex (transmission can occur in only one direction at a time) or full duplex (transmissions can occur bidirectionally in a concurrent manner). Asynchronous communications is used largely with mini/supermini (DEC VAXs, HP 3000s, Data General, and many others), and microcomputers. The most widespread synchronous systems are used with IBM mainframes, although other mainframe manufacturers also use synchronous communications. IBM's Synchronous Data Link Control (SDLC) is being adopted by many manufacturers of computers of all sizes for communications with IBM systems. The reason is, of course, IBM dominates the computer market.

Asynchronous

Asynchronous, or start-stop, communications has been around for a long time and is firmly established. It has the advantage of being easy (hence cheap) to implement in both hardware and software. With an asynchronous system data are sent one eight-bit byte at a time with a preceding (start bit) and succeeding (stop bit) bit. For every character sent, a total of 10 data bits is transmitted. In a half duplex environment, data typed at a terminal are typically echoed locally to the screen. In a full duplex system data are usually echoed from the host computer (requiring twice the amount of data transmission—once from the terminal and again from the host). Data bits are transmitted at some defined rate of speed (300, 1200, 9600, or some other number of bits per second [bps]). Because a start bit and stop bit are associated with each byte, the receiving device knows when a byte starts and stops—no synchronization between ends is necessary.

Synchronous

Synchronous data communications, in contrast, requires that the two ends of the link be synchronized through a clocking mechanism at each end. The older IBM bisynchronous protocol is byte oriented; the newer SDLC is bit oriented. In both cases data are collected into frames or packets of some defined length surrounded by information that specifies source, destination, and other information. The actual amount of "real" data, or text that can be transmitted with either bisync or SDLC, is variable and with SDLC can be of any length that is a multiple of eight bits. The actual size of text blocks used is subject to specific applications of the protocol. Synchronous systems, in general, provide greater throughput and more reliable transmission of data than asynchronous systems, but at greater cost. Bisynchronous systems are half duplex; SDLC communication is full duplex (but without host echoing).

If the synchronous packet is of some reasonable size (512, 1,024, or 2,048 bytes, for example), the overhead is less than for asynchronous transmission. Half duplex asynchronous communications always has at least a 20 percent overhead (2 bits out of every 10 transmitted). If it is operating in a full duplex, host-echoing environment, the overhead is 140 percent (20 percent on first transmission, 20 percent on host echo, plus the full 8-bit byte on host echo). Since in a full duplex system data can be transmitted both ways concurrently, the effective data rate is not cut in half, but it is significantly less than the nominal data rate. If only a single byte were sent in a synchronous block, the overhead would be high. Typically, however, the control information needed in synchronous transmission is sufficiently small to provide lower overhead than is true in asynchronous transmissions. More will be said of these issues in later chapters.

Micro Requirements

The microcomputer requirements for an adequate micro-to-mainframe link are similar to those necessary at the mainframe end. The primary difference is that most micros are single-user, single-task systems. The lack of adequate multitasking is particularly problematic (notwithstanding the availability of multitasking tools like Microsoft's Windows, Quarterdeck's DesqView, or alternative operating systems such as OS/2 or UNIX) in the micro-to-mainframe connection. Availability of an appropriate multitasking operating system would enable communications software to run in the background when other tasks were being executed. IBM's sponsorship of OS/2 is, in large part, a recognition of this problem and it does provide the basis for one solution. In addition to desirable operating-system features such as multitasking, there are communications hardware and software requirements that must be met for implementing the micro-to-mainframe connection.

Operating System Features

In the context of large organizations the primary microcomputer is the IBM PC family and compatibles running under PC/MS-DOS from Microsoft, just as Apple holds the majority position in elementary and secondary schools. Most of what is said in this book, will, therefore, assume a reference to PC/MS-DOS, unless otherwise specified. DOS 3.x provided system interrupts (system calls) for supporting LANs. In particular, beginning with DOS 3.1, were system calls supporting Netbios, the IBM PC Network's controlling software that, along with an appropriate user interface, can provide access to a remote node through an extended path. The same concept, incorporated into PC software operating with a communications link to a mainframe (as well as appropriate mainframe software), could provide a virtual disk on the central system. This form of the client–host link would be almost transparent to the end user.

In a more prosaic software system the operating system provides access to attached communications hardware. That access may be through system calls or by directly addressing communications ports. If software manufacturers confine themselves to using standard operating system facilities, then programs should be able to run on any MS/PC-DOS machine, even if the machine is not fully compatible with the IBM PC. To improve the performance of the software, however, many manufacturers program around the operating system, limiting the software to machines similar to the IBM PC. In any event, access must be provided to serial communications ports for either asynchronous or synchronous networks. Other network protocols require specialized software and hardware.

Communications Hardware Facilities

Depending on the communications environment and on the particular PC, a variety of communications hardware may be needed. For either asynchronous or synchronous communications it is necessary to have the circuitry, often on plug-in boards, that translates ASCII data into the electrical signals required for transmission and reception on some communications medium. The most common standard communications port for this purpose is an RS-232-C interface. A cable may then connect the interface to a modem. Alternatives might include a combined RS-232-C interface and a modem on an internal board, a board that emulates a 3x78/9 IBM terminal that is linked to a cluster controller with a coaxial cable carrying a high speed baseband SDLC signal, or various LAN cards that handle Ethernet or other signals. All this hardware takes data internal to the PC and converts it into a form capable of being transmitted on a communications channel over some medium.

Terminal Emulation

The issue here is simply making the micro function as a terminal. There are many terminal-emulation programs or combinations of software and hardware on the market. By many I mean more than 150, with new ones being announced all the time. A terminal-emulation program makes the micro act like it is some "standard" or popular terminal. Two important terminal emulations are those that make the micro act like DEC's VT100 (VT200, VT300, X3.64, etc.) family of asynchronous terminals and those that make the micro act like one of IBM's family of 3270-type synchronous terminals. To have adequate response time for transactional processing 9600 bits per second (bps) is the minimum required communications speed.

In a mixed vendor or mixed protocol computing environment—a single user having to access both IBM/PCM machines and asynchronous minis, for example—an asynchronous terminal emulator and a protocol converter on the IBM/PCM will make the asynchronous "terminal" act like a 3270 terminal. There are many VT100 emulators available. At the IBM/PCM end a protocol converter is plugged into the Communications Processor or is channel attached. The protocol converter appears to the IBM/PCM as a 3274* or 3174 terminal controller. Every protocol converter I have seen supports many terminals, but always a VT100.

Another approach is to emulate some variety of 3270 directly on the micro. This approach, even using the same line speed, frequently produces better response time since the overhead of protocol conversion takes place at the micro, not at some remote point. In one sense the least expensive way to go is to buy a software/hardware package that emulates a combination display station and controller (such as a 3x76). Communications is via a

---

*The 3274 controller and 327x terminals have now been superceded by the 3174 and 317x terminals. The entire system is still often referred to as the 3270 Display System, however. There are many 327xs still in use and 327x compatible controllers are still produced by manufacturers other than IBM.

synchronous RS-232-C connection with the communications processor at the mainframe. The disadvantage of this approach is that one micro workstation will take one synchronous port that otherwise could support up to 32 display stations working through a terminal controller. Some operating-system software may have limitations on the number of synchronous lines that may be supported or the cost of additional synchronous lines on the communications processor may not be warranted.

The alternative 3270 solution is a combination of software and hardware in an add-on board that contains the necessary circuitry for making the micro communicate with a terminal controller (a 3x74, for example) via coaxial cable and software to drive the hardware. IBM's PC 3270 took this approach to its maximum extent by integrating the hardware into the design of the PC. In this configuration the micro appears to the user almost exactly like a 3270-type terminal, with equivalent speed. The disadvantage can be the cost, which, when calculated, must include the port on the terminal controller, the PC hardware, and software—the resulting price may not be much different from a 3270-type terminal. The advantage is that this solution precludes the necessity of *both* a micro and a 3270 terminal on a user's desk.

A LAN-based modification of the 3270 approach can be found in IBM's broadband PC local area network (LAN) and its Token Ring LAN. One product available is a 3270 Emulator Program that turns one PC into a communications server emulating a 3x74 terminal controller, and a 3x78 or 3x79 display station. Up to 32 of the PCs on the LAN can operate through the server concurrently, acting as individual 3270 display stations to the mainframe. Other manufacturers have followed IBM into the marketplace with similar devices. The importance of this approach is that it illustrates one method of integrating a LAN into a micro-to-mainframe link. To the extent that the 3270 Display System will continue to play a major role in IBM's mainframe networking strategy, 3x7x emulator programs can be one way of integrating LANs and mainframes. The 3270 Display System has been enhanced in recent years with IBM's introduction of the 3174 cluster controller that allows the insertion of a LAN Network Interface Card (NIC), specifically a Token Ring card, which means that a Token Ring LAN can be directly linked through a 3174 to a larger SNA network. The problem with all this is that the relationship between the LAN and the mainframe is not a peer relationship—it is still largely a master/slave relationship.

Functional Requirements

To achieve an appropriate micro-to-mainframe connection in a cost-effective manner, several issues must be taken into account. The overriding requirement is that an end user be able to download data from the mainframe to the micro, or, where appropriate, to upload from the micro to the mainframe, without the intervention of a technical support team. If the manner in which the micro-to-mainframe link is established requires external intervention, then the end user will be dissatisfied, and the cost will be too high. The cost will be high because of the additional personnel needed to intervene in the process. Clearly, some user support personnel will almost always be required in any organization, but the need for such a staff should be minimized by providing systems end users can deal with themselves.

The ideal data communications environment would be one in which the user of the system does not have to know or recognize that a communications system is in use. In the special case of the micro-to-mainframe link, this means that there are three fundamental elements that must be addressed, primarily by software, for the connection to be satisfactory. First, data must be extracted from the mainframe database environment. Second, once those data have been extracted, they must be passed from the mainframe to the micro. Third, something must happen to those data on the micro. If each of these elements are kept entirely separate from one another, the tools necessary to transfer data from one system to another can easily be created. Unfortunately, this "simple" approach to the problem is only simple from the perspective of the central planners—it is definitely not transparent from the perspective of the end user. To integrate these three elements requires a consistent and user-friendly integration that limits end user involvements in the process.

Mainframe Data Extraction

Mainframe data extraction is the process by which appropriate data are made available for downloading to a microcomputer. To some, this may appear to be a trivial problem. After all, micro enthusiasts have been downloading data (programs, source listings, and so forth) from bulletin board systems and information utilities (CompuServe, Prodigy, and others) for years. Providing the data communications environment is acceptable, it is true that simple flat files can be downloaded with some ease—many terminal-emulation programs allow that to happen. A flat file, by the way, is one organized by records with each record containing one or more fields. A flat file is usually rectangular—that is, each record has the same number of fields. If no subsetting of data, either by field or record is necessary, then downloading a flat file is straightforward—it is simply a special case of listing the dataset.

In a corporate, governmental, or educational database environment, however, files are rarely organized as flat files. Database systems such as IBM's IMS, Software AG's ADABAS, or others may have more complex structures: relational, hierarchical, or whatever. Specific information is typically located with keys processed through data dictionaries. If a formal database system is not used, methods such as IBM's ISAM (Indexed Sequential Access Method) or the newer VSAM (Virtual Sequential Access Method) require special programming for access. Even with flat rectangular files it may not be appropriate for everyone to have access to all fields of every record in the file. The consequence of these various means of storing data on the mainframe is that downloading is no longer a simple analogue of listing a flat file and capturing the results on a micro. It is now necessary to have a mainframe application program that will allow the user to select fields and records in a manner appropriate to the data of interest.

There are several approaches that might be used to solve this problem. The need to subset data has a history that predates microcomputers by many years. The traditional technique used in mainframe programming environments is for a programmer to write a custom program to extract the data and place it in a flat file for a user. From a user's perspective this is not convenient, is usually slow, and can be expensive. To be readily available to an end user, a more general extraction program might be purchased or written. Several commercially available systems come to mind and can be effective tools: Statistical Analysis System (SAS), FOCUS, Statistical Package for the Social Sciences (SPSS), and others.

It should be noted that packages like SAS and SPSS, although written originally as statistical packages, have developed into generalized data management systems often available on large computers. Specialized query and reporting tools, like FOCUS, are becoming prevalent. With tools like those just noted, or through a generalized query written for a particular environment, an end user can write a few simple statements and produce an intermediate file that can then be downloaded with simple downloading programs. The key criteria for extraction programs are:

- Generalized—capable of being used by many people with differing extraction problems.
- Keyword or menu driven—in other words, user-friendly.
- Output in a form that generally conforms with the organization required by the target microcomputer:
  - Flat files organized with short physical records.
  - Specialized files, such as the Data Interchange Format (DIF) structure accepted by many microcomputer-based spreadsheets.

If the extraction subsystem is part of an integrated transfer system, then the output of the extraction module on the mainframe might be one or more records to a memory buffer rather than all the data to an intermediate dataset. In other words, in an integrated system the extraction program would pull some data, then make it available to the communications line through a memory buffer containing the current data.

Micro–Mainframe Communications

Once data have been extracted and staged for downloading from the mainframe, the communications process must begin. This is a long-winded way of introducing the basic problem confronting anyone trying to build an integrated file-transfer system between micros and mainframes. Similar problems occur with systems other than IBM, although the IBM environment is often the most complicated. To provide a truly general system, a manufacturer will have to provide software that operates under a variety of IBM and non–IBM TP monitors and TAMs, as well as asynchronous, bisynchronous, and SDLC protocols—not to mention the micro end of the connection. If an organization wishes to economize, it should not operate multiple TP monitors, multiple TAMs, or multiple-line protocols. The cost of using multiple systems can be high, with software leases, maintenance, and personnel time. Given the current marketplace, however, an organization will probably have to maintain multiple systems to provide effective, user-oriented file transfers, unless it is willing to go 100 percent with IBM's conception of systems integration—something often not possible.

Similar issues are almost as complicated on the micro end of the connection. Again, unless one is willing to standardize on an IBM PC or a close facsimile, it may be difficult or impossible to acquire all the hardware and software necessary to provide an integrated system. (It should be noted, however, that Apple's Macintosh computers are gaining increasing support in integrated environments.) At the micro the hardware and software must support the appropriate line protocol, must be capable of capturing the data to memory and disk as it comes down the line, and must make sense of the data when it arrives. An integrated system should also be capable of working on micros from a wide variety of manufacturers. Clearly there is a demand for standardizing the micro-to-mainframe link, but standardization does not currently exist.

There is some hope, however, providing that software manufacturers head the pleas of user organizations. On the IBM mainframe end, products that interact directly with VTAM will be more flexible than those that are limited to specific TP monitors. On the micro end, software that confines itself to working through standard operating system calls will be more general than software that interacts directly with the hardware. These are really the micro and mainframe ends of the same issue.

Micro Data Format Conversions

Finally, even if the data can be transferred from the mainframe to a micro, it may not be (probably won't be) in the format needed for a particular micro-based application. It seems like every manufacturer of micro-based software tries to outdo every other manufacturer by ensuring that one product never uses data in the same format as another product. Today, however, many software products that can read a variety of data formats and put them into the form required by the specific application have been developed. As on their mainframe predecessors, however, it often turns out that the time spent managing one's micro data is much greater than the time spent producing a report or analyzing the data.

In an integrated micro/mainframe environment, file transfer would take place in an automatic manner from within the micro application, or from within the mainframe user application. A micro-based spreadsheet, for example, should allow users to specify some mainframe data, then the software should go out, interact with a host program, obtain the data, and present it in the spreadsheet. Manufacturers of some microcomputer and/or mainframe software are attempting to provide some of these facilities. One major problem in the way of effective integrated links is a lack of any standards governing the connection, although such standards, either formal or *de facto*, may emerge.

Single-Vendor/Multivendor Environments

As ubiquitous as IBM is in the mainframe arena, or DEC in the supermini market, these manufacturers do not have all the solutions for the problems faced by user organizations. Even when they have solutions, they may not have the best solutions for a given organization. The result is a multivendor software and hardware environment in data processing shops of any significant size. According to a study by International Resource Development, companies in the past were often forced to design custom software for micro communications. The future of the data communications will be the emergence of Very Large Systems Integration.[4]

Multivendor environments exist in many large organizations. As K. Burton has pointed out, system integration is becoming both inevitable and necessary among Fortune 1000 companies.[5] Burton identified two benefits for integrated systems: the capability to share resources and information and the elimination of barriers to the free flow of information. It is clear to many that the integrated system of the future will be dependent on the operating system. This is true at both the micro and mainframe end of the connection. These developments will allow increasingly sophisticated micro-to-mainframe links throughout the 1990s.

What is a multivendor environment? Simply a mixture of software and hardware from more than one vendor. An IBM or DEC salesperson will often try to offer a "complete" data processing solution to an organization—a package of software and hardware from a single vendor. The easy way out—but often not the most economical—is to accept the premise that a single vendor can provide everything required. Computer vendors, however, generally know less about an organization's computing needs than does the organization itself. One way out of the babel of competing products is through the adoption of national and international standards. Many manufacturers are gradually coming to see the wisdom of standards, but progress is slow because the establishment of standards is a combined political, economic, and technical process.

Observers of the scene not only point to standards as a way out, but also to the expanded use of old and new technologies. Local area networks and intermediate minicomputers have been suggested as means for overcoming the problems of multivendor environments consisting of mainframes, minis, and micros.[6] The development of OSI network and IEEE 802 LAN standards has greatly enhanced the viability of LAN technology as a primary integration tool. Mini manufacturers are also providing sophisticated access to IBM mainframes, making IBM SDLC/SNA communications a *de facto* standard.

Services

The micro-to-mainframe link is established to provide *services* to users. A service is often delivered through a *server*. The term server has been widely used and accepted in the context of LANs, although it is an appropriate concept in any network environment. A server contains the hardware, and at least part of the software, necessary to produce the service. Servers include print servers, file servers, and gateway or bridge servers. Servers usually operate at some point remote from the end user and are designed for multiuser access to expensive, complicated, or infrequently used services. Services might also include processes, software, or hardware other than servers, such as support for full-screen applications (such as editing).

Remote Full-Screen Functions

The ability to use full-screen functions on a remote host will often determine the terminal emulation selected within an organization. If an organization has confined its communications network to a standard IBM bisynchronous or SDLC/SNA system, then most likely it will use 3270 terminal emulation on its PCs. If the host computer is a DEC VAX then it is likely to adopt a VT100 terminal emulator. In a mixed system, where users need to access either central system with a single terminal, then some form of protocol conversion will be needed. That terminal emulation might be on any of the machines, or a combination of them, but some protocol conversion technique will have to be used. Structuring the network in an appropriate fashion can preclude the necessity for multiple communications boards in the PCs and the consequent learning curve involved in dealing with different communications software.

Servers

File and print servers were among the original enticements of LANs. The servers allowed multiple users to access expensive peripherals and to maintain common databases. Added-value services, such as electronic mail, are an outgrowth of file serving. Electronic mail, however, can be implemented in a completely distributed environment, although it is often accomplished in a more straightforward fashion if common file servers are available. As the cost of high-capacity hard disks and quality printers has declined, however, the emphasis has moved to the issue of common database systems and more exotic or expensive peripherals, such as large plotters or other devices. What is true of LANs is even more true of the capabilities available on large mainframe computers.

In one sense mainframe and large minicomputers constitute the ultimate in high-performance file and printer servers. High-speed high-quality laser printing is frequently available, and the corporate database is accessible. If the organization's network is large, then a corporate-wide electronic mail system may be possible only through the central computer. In these contexts, the mainframe acts as a big peripheral to the micro. File servers on either a LAN or a WAN can also be used as archival devices for micros, and used in this manner they are, indeed, microcomputer peripherals. On the other hand, micros as target nodes on a large network provide distribution points for reports or other information the organization deems necessary for its proper operation. Because data can be extracted from the corporate database, however, the issue of data-transfer integrity must be confronted.

Concluding Notes

The purpose of this chapter has been to provide an overview of features and facilities necessary for a successful micro-to-mainframe link. Success in this endeavor will depend on how well the link is planned and executed: It can happen systematically or it can happen haphazardly. Regardless of how it happens, however, it will. As J. Y. Bryce has contended, MIS managers who attempt to avoid the trend towards micro–mainframe communication are doomed to failure. A more intelligent strategy is to accept the opportunity to change with the new technology. When establishing micro–mainframe links, there are several factors to consider: physical connections, software, security, auditing, and data integrity.[7]

Notes

1. See, for example, the discussion in Anon., "Careful Product Evaluation Provides Link to Success," *Data Management*, Vol. 23, No. 4, April 1985, p. 19.

2. E. Horwitt, "New Solutions of the micro-to-mainframe puzzle," *Business Computer Systems,* Vol. 4, No. 4, April 1985, pp. 42–48.

3. This is by no means a definitive list of sources, but several of James Martin's books are still used as introductions to the field. See, for example, James Martin, *Teleprocessing Network Organization* (Englewood Cliffs, NJ: Prentice-Hall, 1970), and more recently, *Design and Strategy for Distributed Data Processing* (Englewood Cliffs, NJ: Prentice-Hall, Inc., 1981). Many books dealing with communications for micros have appeared, including Larry E. Jordan and Bruce Churchill, *Communications and Networks for the IBM PC* (Bowie, MD: Robert J. Brady Company, 1983). Local Area Networks are now important in the process, as well: Thomas W. Madron, *Local Area Networks in Large Organizations* (Hasbrouck Heights, NJ: Hayden Book Company, 1984).

4. Anon., "Users Seen Biased against Emerging Link Products," *PC Week,* Vol. 1, No. 36, Sept. 11, 1984, p. 65. Since 1984 Very Large Systems Integration has come under the umbrella of Enterprise-Wide Computing.

5. K. Burton, "System Integration Vital to Role of MIS Exec," *ComputerWorld,* Vol. 18, No. 48, Nov. 26, 1984, p. 32.

6. Cf., G. Briggs, "Firm: PC-Mainframe Link will Shift to PC Net Tie," *MIS Week,* Vol 5, No. 39, Sept. 26, 1984, p. 35; and E. Warner, "Minis to Act as Hosts: Larger Role Predicted as Departmental CPU," *ComputerWorld,* Vol. 18, No. 50, Dec. 10, 1984, pp. 107, 128.

7. J. Y. Bryce, "MIS Managers Must Go with Micro Network Flow," *ComputerWorld,* Vol. 19, No. 1.

CHAPTER 3

Micros, Mainframes, and Networks

The micro-to-mainframe connection cannot work without a network![1] Chapter 2 alluded to a variety of networks without describing them in any detail: Local Area Networks (LANs), Wide Area Networks (WANs), SDLC/SNA networks, and asynchronous networks. In large organizations, and increasingly in all organizations, the bottom line in doing work effectively is often *communications*: the generic process of transferring information from one individual to another. That information may be intelligible to people or intelligible to computers. Several computing devices (computers, terminals, or other devices) connected by an electronic communications system is a computer network. In general, communications networks (such as the telephone system) can exist (or could in the past) without computers, but computer networks cannot exist without communications systems.

Computer networks can be organized in a variety of ways, and some of these are described in later pages. By the early 1980s it was possible to distinguish between what have been called "local" networks and what I shall call (solely to distinguish them from local networks) "global" networks. Local networks are sometimes described as those that "cover a limited geographical area . . .," where every "node on the network can communicate with every other node, and . . . requires no central node or processor."[2] A supplementary definition, such as Lee A. Bertman's, suggests that a LAN "is a communications network capable of providing an intrafacility internal exchange of voice, computer data, word processing, facsimile, video conferencing, video broadcasting, telemetry and other forms of electronic messaging."[3] A more restrictive definition frequently seen has been repeated by Robert Bowerman: LANs "are designed for sharing data between single-user workstations."[4] In many LANs, all the nodes are microcomputers, although there is nothing that requires such a condition inherent in the technology, albeit the existence of large numbers of microcomputers have probably been a major factor in the development of LANs.

Local area networks are to be distinguished from global networks (or WANs) in that global networks often have at least one or more computer nodes central to the operation of the network. The central node is at least a time-sharing minicomputer and is frequently a large mainframe computer. In a global network microcomputers are often used as intelligent terminals within the network. Local area networks may be attached to one another or may themselves be nodes in a global network. Local area networks can have radii that range from a few hundred meters to several kilometers. Global networks can be extended worldwide, if needed.

Local area networks and WANs do not meet all networking needs, however. There is a need for a high-speed network that will extend beyond the area covered by a LAN, but not restricted to the normal methods of wide area networking. The IEEE 802.6 committee has provided standards for a Metropolitan Area Network (MAN). A MAN is defined as a network with a diameter of not more than 50 Km. Such a network clearly meets a need for an intermediate size data communications system that could have benefits beyond those offered by either LANs or WANs.

A Network Vocabulary

Before networks and communications can be discussed with any degree of success it is necessary to define some terms. Although computer jargon can often be arcane, the language of communications and computers can be downright unintelligible. Most of the terms needed to understand networks are simply extensions of ordinary English, although there are several coined terms as well as acronyms. Even if you have an understanding of networking vocabulary, this section will at least indicate how terms are being used in this book.

Computers can be said to process transactions of one form or another. Most computers through the early 1970s processed transactions in batches.

Throughout the earlier days of computing it was common to talk about batch processing as meaning the processing of groups of punched cards. Each card was a transaction and the computer read the batch of cards and acted upon them. During the 1960s, *interactive* computing became popular. With interactive computing, programs can be structured so that transactions are acted upon individually, rather than in batches. Interactive processing generally originates from data-entry devices, much like typewriters, called terminals. Computing literature sometimes refers to batch terminals as well as interactive terminals. Batch terminals, which read cards or tapes or disks, and then send data to a computer in batches, are often called *Remote Job Entry* (RJE) terminals or *Remote Batch Terminals* (RBT). A general term sometimes used to reference terminals is "remote." Hence, a remote site, a remote terminal, or simply a remote. A remote is any device that works remotely from the central computing facility.

Whether the processing is batch or interactive, it can take place in centralized or distributed networks. A centralized network depends entirely on a central computing facility (of one or more computers). Alternately, a distributed network assumes that some tasks will take place on one computer and other tasks will take place on another computer. Sometimes the two computers must talk to one another to transfer information. Each intelligent entity on a network is called a *node*. Some nodes are computers, others are terminals, and still others may be communications devices of one form or another. When networks became important to computing during the early 1970s, they were centralized. As the 1970s came to a close, however, because of declining prices of computers and because the need for more local and regional computing in large organizations, distributed systems were discussed extensively. Even by the early 1980s, although there was a good bit of talk about distributed processing, it was still more of a dream than a reality in most organizations.

Within a network environment there must be some specialized communications equipment. A *modem* (an acronym for MOdulator/DEModulator) is a device that enables data to be transmitted over long distances without error. Some modems are "hard-wired" to leased telephone lines or to other cables. Some modems are used with dial-up telephone lines. Some are originate only—they must begin the communications process—while others have originate and answer modes (allowing another device to originate the communications link). An auto-dial modem can be used with a program (on a computer) to automatically call another address, whereas an auto-answer modem can automatically answer the call.

The speed at which a modem (and associated lines) can transmit data is measured in *bits per second* or *baud* rates. (Note that baud is the same as bits per second (b/s) only if each signal event represents exactly one bit [not always the case], although the two terms are often incorrectly used interchangeably.) The bit-rate often exceeds the baud-rate where data are being transmitted over dial-up lines at speeds in excess of 2400 b/s (that is, 4.8, 9.6, 19.2, and 56 kb/s). Sometimes it is useful or necessary to have several low-speed (low baud-rate) channels share a single high-speed line. This is accomplished by placing a pair of *multiplexors* between the modem and terminals on one end of the line and a computer at the other end. There is often a cost savings in using a single channel that can be shared by several independent data paths.

Through the early 1980s, most data were transmitted over telephone lines or their equivalent. Since then, however, *broadband* systems, using coaxial cables, have come into use. Broadband systems use the same technology as cable television systems and can transmit data reliably at high speeds. *Fiber optics*, a system for transmitting data with high-intensity light, was just becoming commercially feasible in the early 1980s, but is rapidly becoming the technology of the nineties. The advantage of fiber optics over standard telephone lines or broadband systems is that they are unaffected by most environmental problems, although the notion that water will not affect fiber performance is often misunderstood. The performance of optical fiber is seriously degraded if water is introduced around the fiber. It is easier, however, to produce a submarine fiber-optic cable than a copper cable since the fiber bundle itself takes up so little physical space that effective sealing technologies may be employed.

Data transmitted on standard telephone circuits use *voice-grade* lines—lines designed primarily for voice communications. Broadband systems use very high or ultrahigh radio frequencies as the communications medium. Modems are essentially devices for modulating and demodulating the electrical pulses carrying data on voice-grade lines, although the literature also talks about radio frequency (RF) modems. *Baseband* systems use frequencies equal to those originally generated by the original equipment without using of modems to manage frequency shifts.

When data are transmitted, it is done either *asynchronously* or *synchronously*. Asynchronous transmission is often called *start-stop*. With synchronous transmission characters are sent in a continuous bit stream. With asynchronous transmission one character at a time is sent preceded by a "start" signal and terminated by a "stop" signal. Each time a key on an asynchronous terminal is pressed, a character is sent, another key must be pressed for a second character to be transmitted. Such machines are generally less expensive than are synchronous terminals.

In contrast to asynchronous machines, which usually use one character as the unit of transmission, synchronous devices use a block of characters as the unit of transmission. When machines transmit to each other continuously, with regular timing, synchronous transmission can provide the most efficient use of the communications lines. To permit synchronous communications, however, devices must have buffers (some memory at least equal to one block of data), which along with timing mechanisms, result in higher production costs. IBM has used two forms of synchronous communications: The older binary synchronous (or bisync) system, and the newer, synchronous Data-Link Control with Systems Network Architecture (SDLC/SNA). The actual manner in which data are organized and transmitted, within the context of either asynchronous or synchronous communications, is called a protocol.

Connectivity, a central concept in LANs means that any device on the LAN may be individually addressed as an individual connection. For a large computer with many ports, each port is a connection, and a single-user terminal or microcomputer is also a connection. *Sessions* take place when a circuit is established between or among connections. Some LANs have the capacity to allow multicast or broadcast sessions—transmissions to a subset of all connections or to all connections. Network nodes are intelligent devices on a network and may support one or more connections. Networks of similar or different characteristics may be connected to each other through gateways, which, in principle, allow a user/connection on one network to communicate with a user/connection on another network.

Once a session is established between two network connections, data are often transmitted in a packet. A packet contains control information, such as the source and destination addresses of the data to be transferred (called "header-control information"), as well as one or more bytes of user data. In a packet-switched system, the header-control information is necessary to initially establish the session, but a *virtual circuit* is frequently structured once the session is in operation, which reduces the need to effectively reestablish the session addresses on each transmission of data, thereby reducing network overhead. A specialized packet called a datagram is also used by some networks (see pp. 74–75).

Network Topologies

There are a variety of ways in which networks might be organized, and most networks are in a constant state of change and growth. If the computer network has only a main-site or host computer that does all data processing from one or more remotes, it is a centralized network. A network with remote computers processing jobs for end users, as well as a main-site computer (which is itself optional), is the beginning of a distributed network. A distributed network can be either centralized or dispersed, but a network that does not involve distributed processing can only be centralized since all data processing is done on a main-site computer.

It is possible for a single communications system to provide communications for two or more concurrently operating computer networks. The following sections will review several characteristic (although oversimplified) network configurations: point-to-point, multipoint, star (centralized), ring (distributed), bus structure (distributed), and hierarchical (distributed). In addition, the following sections contain expanded discussions of LANs. Figure 3.1 contains diagrammatic representations of the various network configurations or topologies.

Point-to-Point

A point-to-point network is undoubtedly the simplest network, for it has only a computer, a communications line (direct or through the telephone system), and one terminal at the other end of the wire. The terminal can be either an RBT or interactive. This was the earliest form of networking, and many networks still begin in this fashion and gradually develop into more complex entities. In such a system the central computer need not be large. A microcomputer can act as a host computer for one or more terminals. Normally, however, such systems have a large computer as the host system.

Multipoint

Multipoint networks constitute a straightforward extension of point-to-point systems in that instead of a single remote station, there are multiple remote stations dropped off the same communications line. Those remote stations are RBTs, interactive, or both. The remote stations may be connected via independent communications lines to the computer or may be multiplexed over a single line. In either a point-to-point or a multipoint

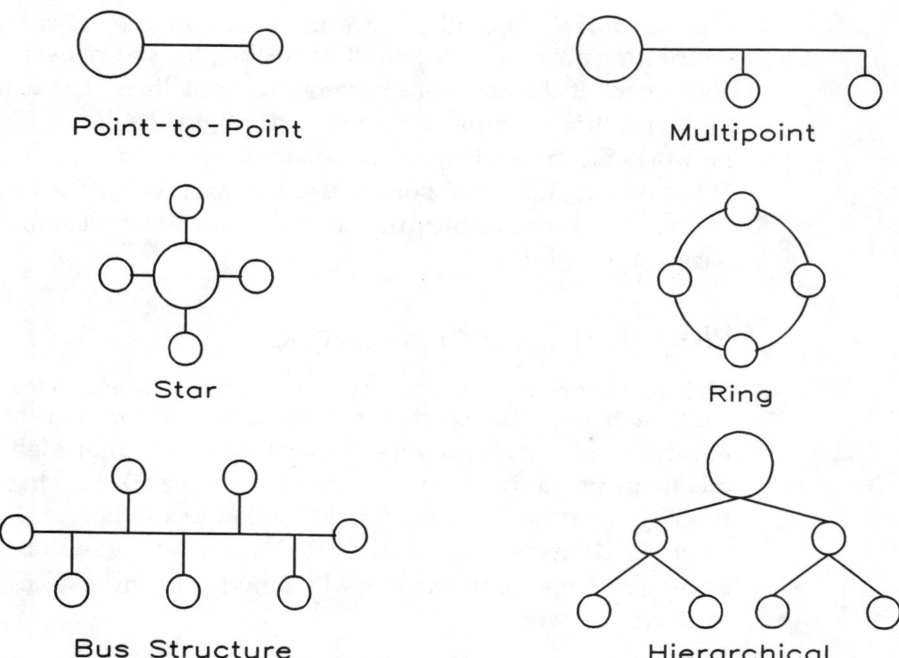

Figure 3.1. Network Topologies.

system, the characteristics of the remote workstations are a function of the work to be accomplished at the remote site. Local area networks, in some of their manifestations, are expansions of the multipoint concept. In its original context, a multipoint system contained only one node with "intelligence"—it had only one computer on the system. A LAN will normally have intelligence at all or most points on the system without the necessity for any central system.

Star (Centralized) Networks

To reiterate, a star or centralized network is one in which primary computing is accomplished at a single site with all remote stations feeding into that site. Often, each remote site enters the central system via a single communications line, although point-to-point and the classical multipoint systems are also centralized networks and are directly incorporated into star networks. Typically, however, a multipoint network does not have distributed processing capabilities, although a star network may have other computers at the end of its communications lines. The computer supporting a traditional multipoint network might, itself, be linked into a star network. Electronic Private Automatic Branch Exchange (EPABX) systems, based on telephone technology, use a star topology. The computer that acts as the switch constitutes the central node since all information must be passed through it.

Ring (Distributed) Networks

A ring network is organized by connecting network nodes in a closed loop with each node linked to those adjacent on the right and the left. The advantage of a ring network is that it can be run at high speeds, and the mechanisms for avoiding collisions are simple. As Saal has noted, the "ring topology does not have the flexibility that bus structures have, yet it forces more regularity into the system. . . ."[5] Ring networks sometimes use *token-passing* schemes to determine which node may have access to the communications system.

Bus Structures (Distributed)

The bus network depicted in Figure 3.1 is configured, at least logically, with taps (arms, branches, et cetera) extending off a central backbone. As a signal traverses the bus—normally coaxial, fiber-optic, or twisted-pair cables—a connection listens for the signal, which carries an address designation. Bus systems such as Ethernet or most broadband (cable television) systems use either a single cable with forward and return paths on the same wire, or a two-cable system—one for forward signals and one for return signals. With systems based on cable television (CATV), a signal processor, which takes a low incoming signal from a device on the bus and upconverts it for retransmission on a higher frequency channel, exists at the *headend*.

Hierarchical (Distributed) Networks

A hierarchical network represents a fully distributed network in which computers feed into computers that feed into computers. The computers used for remote devices may have independent processing capabilities and draw upon the resources at higher or lower levels as information or other resources are required. A hierarchical network is one form of completely distributed networking. The classical model of a hierarchical distributed network is that used by Texas Instruments in which there are several IBM 3090s at the top; IBM 4381s or similar machines in the mid-range; and a combination of minis (such as the TI990), micros, and other machines at the bottom. The TI990s may function at a fourth level and the micros (or intelligent terminals) at a fifth level.

Distributed Data Processing (DDP)

This discussion has spoken of centralized and distributed processing as if the two concepts in networks were at opposite ends of some continuum, although this is not the case. Nor can distributed processing be thought of simply as decentralized computing. One definition, suggested by Data 100, states that distributed computing places "a substantial part of the pre- and post-processing of data, and access to data at the places where the data originates and is used . . . while maintaining central control of the network."[6] It is not uncommon for networks that start as simple centralized systems to migrate to distributed systems without conscious design. As often as not, a typical RBT in a network may be replaced with a mini- or micro-processor-based device providing local file storage and processing capabilities as well as the capacity to generate batch jobs (or interactive jobs, for that matter).

The decision to acquire a terminal with intelligence may be the decision of the end user, not the decision of the network analysts. If there is the possibility of communicating with the central system with some intelligent device (such as a microcomputer), an end user may make the decision to do distributed data processing. The decision to turn a centralized network into a distributed processing network, therefore, may be removed from decisions made by analysts at the central site. The key point is that if a network migrates into a distributed system, it is unlikely that there will be the element of central control desirable for many functions, particularly access to central databases (or to distributed databases).

Both local and global networks may be distributed networks, but they perform somewhat different functions for an organization. As has been noted, the cost of computing hardware has been declining, the cost for communications has been on the rise. This has led some industry analysts to "sense that the traditional concept of linking many company locations into a common network to utilize centralized facilities was waning in its desirability."[7] Yet it is also clear that the "'gurus of the future' are correct when they forecast a pivotal role for networking in future information distribution solutions."[8] The networks of the 1990s will tend to be decentralized because data processing and databases will become increasingly distributed. The organizational implications of such a situation are manifold, but one major implication is the decentralization of responsibility (within the organization) for network maintenance and function. On a global scale, networks may be established when needed instead of being hard-wired (with leased telephone lines, for example).

On the other hand, LANs will themselves distribute processing among many intelligent nodes, probably (though not necessarily) hard-wired together. Such a LAN can then become an intelligent node of a global network. The LAN can participate in what Paul Truax, of Truax & Associates Inc., calls the "four corporate information disciplines." These four "disciplines" are office automation, data processing, database administration, and telecommunications.[9]

Network Standards

To understand some of the issues involved in network planning and to lend credibility to networking itself, it is useful to take a quick look at some of the relevant standards available. There are several standards organizations in North America and Europe, which seek to rationalize electronic systems. Among those organizations are the International Standards Organization (ISO) and the Institute of Electrical and Electronics Engineers (IEEE). Network standards of any kind are of recent origin, which has led to an almost chaotic array of network products.

In 1977 the ISO chartered a committee to study the compatibility of network equipment, a development that eventually led to the publication of the Open System Interconnection Reference Model (OSI Reference Model). In this context, "open system" refers to a network model open to equipment from competing manufacturers. As Frank Derfler and William Stallings have noted, the OSI "reference model is useful for anyone involved in purchasing or managing a local network because it provides a theoretical framework . . ." by which networking problems and opportunities may be understood.[10] The OSI Reference Model divides networking issues into functions or layers. These layers are depicted in Figure 3.2.

ISO/OSI Reference Model

Open System Interconnection

Layer	Function
Layer 7 Application	End-user and end-application functions such as file transfer (FTAM), virtual terminal service (VTP), and electronic mail (X.400).
Layer 6 Presentation	Data translation for use by Layer 7, such as protocol conversion, data unpacking, encryption, and expansion of graphics commands.
Layer 5 Session	Provides for the establishing of a session connection between two presentation entities to support orderly data exchange.
Layer 4 Transport	Transparent transfer of data between session entities, relieving the session layer of concerns for data reliability and integrity.
Layer 3 Network	Contributes the means to establish, maintain, and terminate network connections among open systems, particularly routing fucntions across multiple network.
Layer 2 Data Link	Defines the access strategy for sharing the physical medium, including data link and media access issues.
Layer 1 Physical	Definition of the electrical and mechanical characteristics of the network.

Figure 3.2. OSI Reference Model.

Each layer in the OSI Reference Model defines a functional level. Equipment compatibility can be defined within a layer, or lower level implementations can be hidden to achieve compatibility at some higher level. The OSI Reference Model's dual purposes are to ensure information flow among systems and at the same time permit variation in basic communications technology. Moreover, in any given organization, it might be possible to have one network service the lower levels and another network service the higher levels, using gateways among the networks.

In the OSI Reference Model, Layer 1 is the hardware base for the network. Layers 2 through 7 are implemented in software. The Application Layer (Layer 7) provides services for network users. The responsibility for the initiation and reliability of data transfers takes place in Layer 7. General network access, flow control, and error recovery are, in part, a function of this layer. Tasks are performed at the Layer 7 level and all lower levels are designed to support the applications. Electronic message systems, terminal-emulation capabilities, and file-transfer programs are illustrative of the software operating at Layer 7.

Translating information for use by Layer 7 is accomplished in the Presentation Layer (Layer 6). Such services as protocol conversion, data unpacking, translation, encryption, character set changes or conversions, and the expansion of graphics commands take place in Layer 6.

Layer 5 (the Session Level) is of particular importance to LANs. Recall that one major reason for implementing a LAN is connectivity—the ability for any two (or more) devices to connect with one another. When a link is made between two devices a session is established. In a somewhat more technical sense, the Session Layer provides for the establishment and termination of streams of data from two or more LAN connections, or nodes. When a network maps network addresses on specific connections, a Level 5 function is taking place.

The purpose of the Transport Layer (Layer 4) is to provide an additional, yet lower level, of connection than the Session Layer. The Transport Layer confronts the fundamental reliability in data transfer, which includes flow control, error handling, and problems involved with the transmission and reception of packets. A more detailed discussion of packets appears in a later chapter, so suffice it to say that a packet is composed of user-originated data plus information the network needs to transport user data from one network node to another.

In many LANs a functional Layer 3 (Network Layer) is not needed. Networks that require routing mechanisms among nodes require Layer 3. Local area networks, however, in some implementations, have data broadcast to every node, and a particular connection collects those packets properly addressed to it. Baseband LANs, such as Ethernet, typically broadcast on only a single channel and require no routing. Broadband systems, however, are frequently designed with frequency agility (the ability to use more than a single channel) and therefore require some bridging mechanism—that mechanism requires some routing technique.[11] When LANs are connected via gateways to one another, however, a functional Layer 3 is required.

The Data-Link Layer (Layer 2) defines the access strategy for sharing the physical medium (the cable of whatever variety). Such access strategies are discussed at greater length later in this chapter, but common LAN techniques include Carrier Sense Multiple Access/Collision Detection (CSMA/CD) and token-passing schemes. Techniques for network specific information in data packets, such as a node address, are functions of Layer 2.

Layer 1 is the Physical Layer—the layer that defines the electrical and mechanical characteristics of the network. Modulation techniques, frequencies at which the network operates, and the voltages employed are all characteristic of Layer 1. Because all networks must implement layers 1 and 2, they have received the most attention from network vendors. If the attention paid to these layers results in compatible components, then the concept of standards will prove useful. Standards are often less a technical accomplishment than they are the illustration of some vendors' ability to lobby a standard to success.

The development and implementation of OSI standards promises to make new and expanding networks easier and less expensive in multivendor enivronments. With increasing frequency OSI is the model being followed by manufacturers and by requirements of goverments and user organizations worldwide. In the United States OSI standards have been incorporated into the National Institute for Standards and Technology (NIST, formerly the National Bureau of Standards [NBS]) "Federal Information Processing Standards." The OSI Reference Model is a key factor in the development of the Manufacturing Automation Protocol (MAP), developed by General Motors. And the U.S. Department of Defense (DoD) has reviewed OSI protocols for suitability for its requirements, although it supports its own Transport Control Protocol (TCP). Other standards, such as those of the IEEE (see Chapter 4) are integrated into the OSI scheme.[12]

The Nature and Character of Standards

Lest I wax too enthusiastic concerning the standards movement, let me hasten to add that standards will not and should not end debate over what is "best" concerning some specific technology. Standards committees are typically composed of computer scientists from universities and representatives of manufacturers with special interests concerning the technology being considered. A final draft of a standard is likely to be a compromise among a variety of special interests, mediated by the need for technical definitions that make some sense. Nor are contemporary standards designed to be chiseled in stone. Rather, they are designed to be enlarged and modified so that new technologies can coexist with older devices.

In a book dealing with enterprise-wide computing it will be necessary to reference standards across all the layers of the OSI Reference Model. The OSI standards are those that have been adopted internationally, while those of national standards organizations, such as the IEEE in the United States, pertain only to specific nations. Selected national standards sometimes will be adopted by the ISO. Thus, the IEEE 802 LAN standards have become international standards. For the 1990s, however, it is the international standards movement that will be important for data communications.

Overview of OSI

The OSI Reference Model was devised to allow "standardized procedures to be defined enabling the interconnection and subsequent effective exchange of information between users."[13] "Users," in this sense, means systems consisting of one or more computers, associated software, peripherals, terminals, human operators, physical processes, information-transfer mechanisms, and related elements. These elements together must be capable of "performing information processing and/or information transfer."[14] The importance of the OSI Reference Model is that it will permit various networks of the same or different types to easily communicate with one another as if they constituted a single network.

At the outset it is important to keep in mind that conformance with the OSI Reference Model does not imply any particular implementation or technology. It does not, in other words, specify a medium (such as fiber-optic cable, twisted pair, or coax), nor a specific set of recommendations (such as the IEEE 802.3, 802.4, or 802.5 networks in the United States). The OSI Reference Model is designed to support standardized information exchange procedures but provides neither details, definitions, or interconnection protocols.[15] The OSI Reference Model, therefore, is a frame of reference for open systems with implementation details being left to other standards. Because the OSI Reference Model is a frame of reference, it provides the framework for the definition of services and protocols that fit within the boundaries established.

Scope and Field of Application

The development of the OSI Reference Model has been led by the International Telegraph and Telephone Consultative Committee (CCITT) and those recommendations have been adopted by ISO. The scope of the OSI Reference Model is relatively broad and may be summarized in the following five points:[16]

1. To specify a universally applicable logical structure encompassing broad communications applications, especially those of CCITT.
2. To act as a reference during the development of new communications services.

3. To enable different users to communicate with each other by encouraging the compatible implementation of communication features.
4. To enable the steady evolution of communications applications, particularly those of the CCITT, by allowing sufficient flexibility so that advancements in technology and the evolving needs of users can be accommodated.
5. To allow new user requirements to be satisfied in a manner compatible with existing services consistent with OSI.

The OSI Reference Model is designed to be applied in the development of interconnection protocols for communications services as follows:

1. A new requirement is first expressed in user oriented terms, then analyzed to allow the requirement to be grouped into appropriate functional subsets;
2. A formal description technique (FDT) may be required for the specification of a requirement although narrative text will also be used for clarification;
3. A set of service definitions and protocol specifications is evolving for each of the seven layers, thus extending the application of OSI;
4. New functions will be incorporated into the Reference Model to enhance future applicability;
5. For new uses and applications of OSI where no appropriate protocol is contained in the Recommendations, new protocols, particularly for the application layer, will be needed—and, we might add, are in the process of being written.

OSI Environment

It is important to understand that the OSI Reference Model is concerned with the exchange of information among open systems—not with the internal functioning of each individual "real" open system. This concept is depicted in Figure 3.3. A "real system" in this context is one that complies with the requirements of the OSI Reference Model in its communications with other real systems. A real system is, therefore, a set of "one or more computers, associated software, peripherals, terminals, human operators, physical processes, information transfer means, etc., that forms an autono-

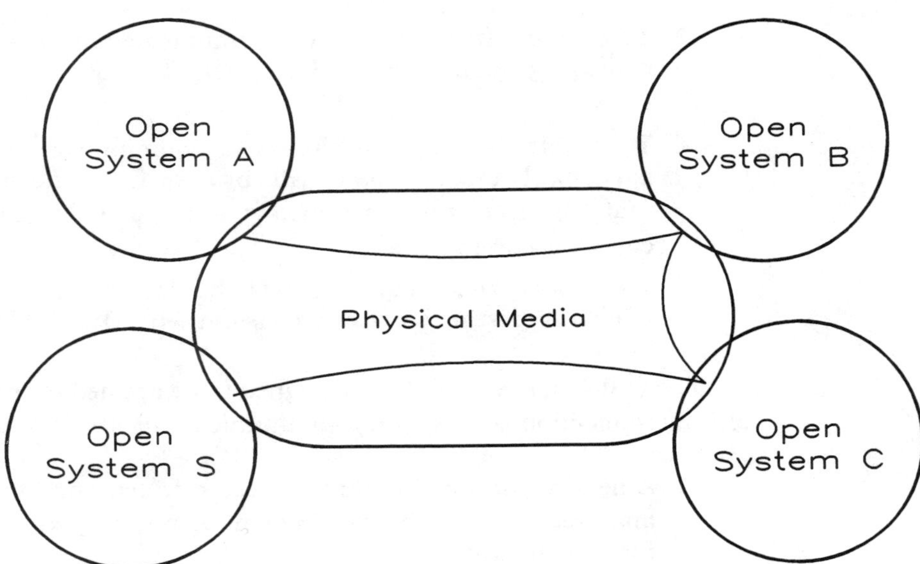

Figure 3.3. Open Systems Connected by Physical Media.
Source: International Telegraph and Telephone Consultative Committee (CCITT), Recommendation X.200, Reference Model of Open Systems Interconnection for CCITT Applications, Fascicle VIII.5-Rec. X.200 (1984), p. 5.

mous whole capable of performing information processing and/or information transfer."[17] Within an open system, an application–process performs the information processing for a particular application.

Aspects of systems not related to interconnection are outside the scope of OSI. This still leaves broad scope for OSI for it is concerned not only with the transfer of information among systems, but also with their ability to interwork to achieve a common or distributed task. This is implied by the expression, "systems interconnection." The fundamental objective of the OSI Reference Model is to define a set of recommendations to enable open systems to cooperate. Cooperation involves a broad range of activities:

1. Interprocess communication: the exchange of information and the synchronization of activity among OSI application–processes.
2. Concern with all aspects of the creation and maintenance of data descriptions and data transformations for reformatting data exchanged among open systems.

3. Concern with storage media and file and database systems for managing and providing access to data stored on the media.
4. Process and resource management by which OSI application–processes are declared, initiated, and controlled and the means by which they acquire OSI resources.
5. Integrity and security of data during the operation of open systems.
6. Program support for comprehensive access to the programs executed by OSI application–processes.

Since some of these activities may imply exchange of information among the interconnected open systems, they may be of concern to OSI.

Concepts of a Layered Architecture

In a layered architecture each open system is viewed as logically composed of an ordered set of subsystems.[18] The seven subsystem layers of the OSI Reference Model have been depicted in Figure 3.2. Subsystems that are adjacent to one another in the vertical hierarchy communicate through their common boundary. Within each subsystem or layer are *entities*. Entities in the same layer, but in different open systems, are termed *peer-entities*. Some conventional definitions have been developed to refer to the components of the layered architecture:

(N)-subsystem. An element in a hierarchical division of an open system that interacts directly only with elements in the next higher division or the next lower division of that open system.

(N)-layer. A subdivision of the OSI architecture, constituted by subsystems of the same rank (N).

(N)-entity. An active element within an (N)-subsystem.

peer-entities. Entities within the same layer.

sublayer. A subdivision within a layer.

(N)-service. A capability of the (N)-layer and the layers beneath it that is provided to (N + 1)-entities at the boundary between the (N)-layer and the (N + 1)-layer.

(N)-facility. A part of the (N)-service.

(N)-function. A part of the activity of (N)-entities.

(N)-service-access-point. The point at which (N)-services are provided by an (N)-entity to an (N + 1)-entity.

(N)-protocol. A set of rules and formats (semantic and syntactic) that determines the communication behavior of (N)-entities in the performance of (N)-functions.

Layering and the method for referring to each layer (N, N+1, N–1, et cetera) are depicted in Figure 3.4. The highest layer does not have an (N+1)-layer above it and the lowest layer does not have an (N–1)-layer below it. The physical medium is not a part of the layered architecture.

When an entity communicates, it does so with a peer at the same layer at another open system; however, not all peer (N)-entities need or even can communicate. Conditions that prevent such communication include the possibility that they are not in interconnected open systems or that they do not support the same protocol subsets. A distinction is made between the *type* of some object and an *instance* of that object. A type is a description of a class of objects, while an instance of this type is any object that conforms to this description. The instances of the same type constitute a class. A

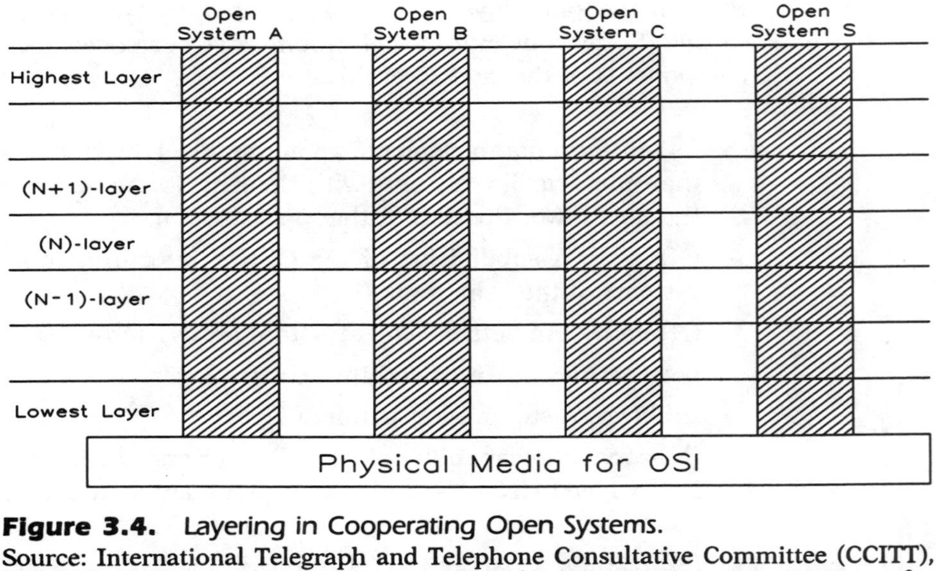

Figure 3.4. Layering in Cooperating Open Systems.
Source: International Telegraph and Telephone Consultative Committee (CCITT), Recommendation X.200, Reference Model of Open Systems Interconnection for CCITT Applications, Rascicle VIII.5-Rec. X.200 (1984), p. 8.

computer program, for example, is a type of something and each copy of that program (running perhaps on different machines or concurrently on the same machine) are instances of the type. In the OSI Reference Model communication occurs only between (N)-entity instances at all layers. Connections are always made to specific (N)-entity instances.

As previously noted, a layer may have sublayers. Sublayers are small substructures that extend the layering technique to cover other dimensions of OSI. A sublayer, therefore, is a grouping of functions in a layer that may be bypassed, although the bypassing of *all* the sublayers of a layer is not allowed. A sublayer uses the entities and connections of its layer. The discussion of the IEEE 802 standards, which follows, will address sublayering, particularly the Logical Link Control (LLC) and Media Access Control (MAC), which are sublayers of the Data-Link Layer (Layer 2). Except for the highest layer, each (N)-layer provides (N+1)-entities in the (N+1)-layer with (N)-services. The highest layer represents all possible uses of the services provided by the lower layers.

It is important to understand that an open system can be OSI compatible without providing the initial source or final destination of data. In other words, an open system need not contain the higher layers of the architecture. The IEEE 802 standards, for example, apply only to the lowest two layers, Data Link and Physical. This is often the source of significant confusion since references to 802.3 (commonly called Ethernet) or 802.5 (token ring) sometimes lead to commentaries on Transmission Control Protocol/Internet Protocol (TCP/IP) or XNS or some other "protocol." Transmission Control Protocol/Internet Protocol and XNS exist at layers beyond the Physical and Data-Link (although TCP/IP and XNS are not OSI standard protocols). Peer entities communicate through peer protocols at the appropriate layer of the OSI Reference Model architecture as seen in Figure 3.5.

A commonly misunderstood issue relates to error detection and notification. In a fully elaborated set of interconnected open systems, using a number of peer protocols at some or all of the layers of the OSI Reference Model, each (N)-protocol may require its own error-detection and notification functions to provide a higher probability of both protocol–data–unit error detection and data-corruption detection than is provided by the (N–1) service. Thus multiple levels of error detection and notification exist. Error detection itself is a management function of which there are three major categories: (1) application-management, (2) systems-management, and (3) layer-management.

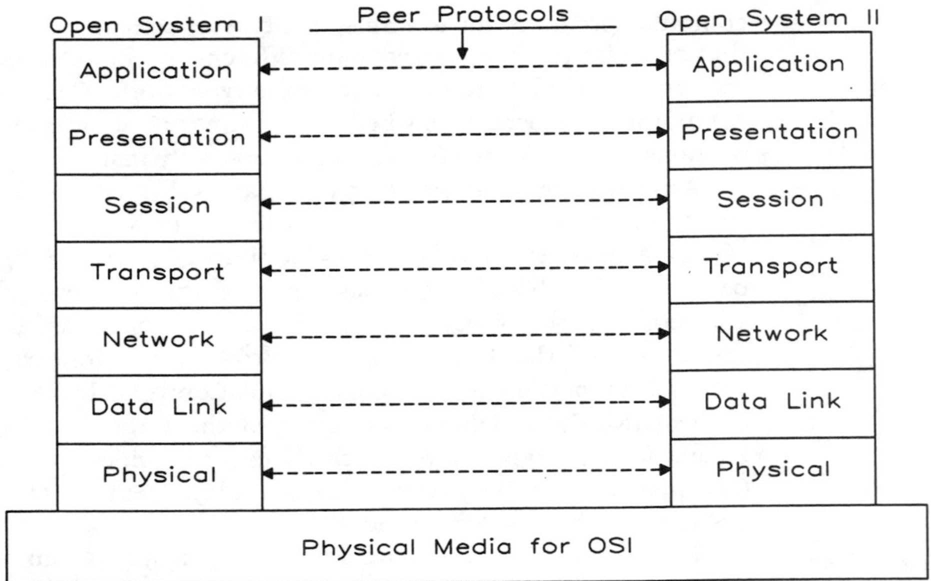

Figure 3.5. Seven-Layer OSI Reference Model and Peer Protocols.
Source: International Telegraph and Telephone Consultative Committee (CCITT) Recommendation X.200, Reference Model of Open Systems Interconnection for CCITT Applications, Fascicle VIII.5-Rec. X.200 (1984), p. 26.

Not all open systems provide the initial source or final destination of data. The physical media for OSI may not link all open systems directly. Some open systems, therefore, may act only as relay systems, passing data to other open systems. A related concept is *routing*. A routing function within the (N)-layer enables communication to be relayed by a chain of (N)-entities. Neither lower nor upper layers know that a communication is being routed by an intermediate (N)-entity. An (N)-entity participating in a routing function may have a routing table. The functions and protocols that support the data forwarding are provided in the lower layers: Physical, Data-Link, and Network. This forwarding function is illustrated in Figure 3.6.

There are a number of layered data-communications architectures available, but architectures other than those in the OSI Reference Model are often proprietary and not designed to promote the interoperability of networks. The two best known examples are IBM's SNA and DEC's DNA. It is possible, therefore, to formulate alternative layering strategies. In the

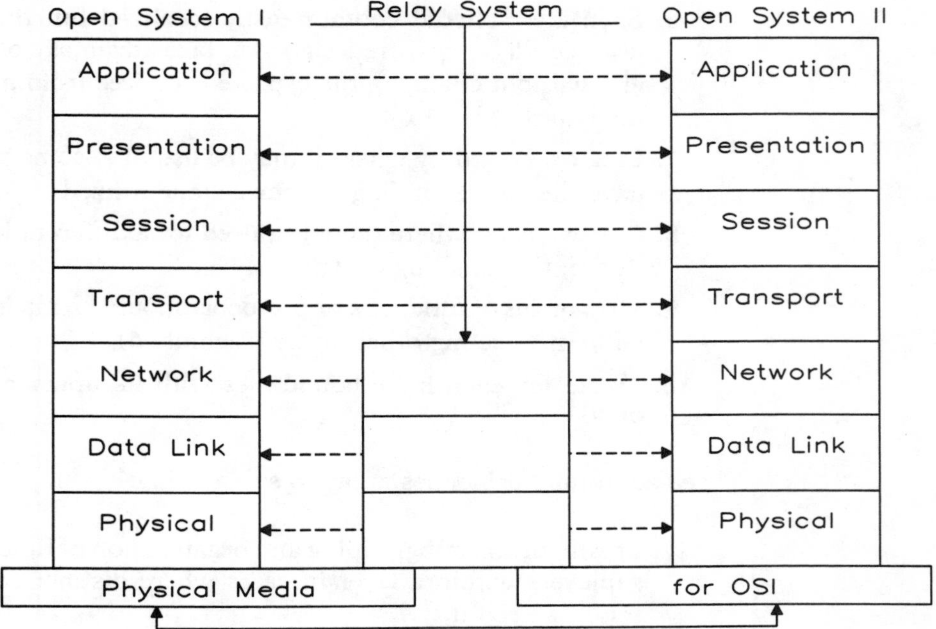

Figure 3.6. Communication Involving Relay Open Systems.
Source: International Telegraph and Telephone Consultative Committee (CCITT) Recommendation X.200, Reference Model of Open Systems Interconnection for CCITT Applications, Fascicle VIII.5-Rec. X.200 (1984), p. 26.

construction of the OSI Reference Model, however, some general principles were developed to guide the process. In closing this section it may be useful to review those principles:

1. Do not create too many layers since excessive numbers lead to excessive complexity.
2. Create a boundary between layers at a point where the description of services can be small and the number of cross-boundary interactions are minimized.
3. Create separate layers to handle functions that are manifestly different.
4. Collect similar functions in the same layer.
5. Select boundaries at a point that past experience has demonstrated to be successful.

6. Each layer should contain easily localized functions so that the layer could be easily redesigned to take advantage of new technologies without changing the expected services from and provided to the adjacent layers.
7. Create a boundary where it may be useful at some point in time to have the corresponding interface standardized.
8. Create a layer where there is a need for a different level of abstraction in the handling of data.
9. All changes of functions or protocols should be made within a layer without affecting other layers (see note 6).
10. Create for each layer boundaries with its upper and lower layer only.

Three additional principles apply to sublayering:

11. Create further subgrouping and organization of functions that form sublayers within a layer in cases where distinct communications services need it.
12. Create, where needed, two or more sublayers with a common, and therefore minimal functionality to allow interface operation with adjacent layers.
13. All bypassing of sublayers.

With respect to principle 7, note that OSI does not require interfaces within open systems to be standardized. There was, when that principle was written, some disagreement over the usefulness of standards for internal interfaces. Moreover, even when standards for such interfaces are defined, the Recommendation is clear in rejecting adherence to such a standard as a condition of openness.

The Seven Layers of the OSI Reference Model

Following the principles enunciated in the previous section, the seven-layer OSI Reference Model has evolved. It might be useful to review Figure 3.2. Layers 1–6, together with the physical media for OSI, provide a step-by-step enhancement of communication services. In the OSI Reference Model, Layer 1 is the hardware base for the network but does not include the physical communication media. Layers 2 through 7 are implemented in software. In Table 3.1 I have attempted to list by layer some of the standards

TABLE 3.1. OSI Intra-Layer Standards

Layer	*Standard Name*	*Number*
Application:	Office Document Architecture (ODA)	ISO 8613
	File Transfer, Access, and Management (FTAM)	ISO 8571
	Virtual Terminal	ISO 9040
	Network Management	ISO 9595/96
	Manufacturing Message Spec.	ISO 9506
	Distributed Transaction Proc.	ISO 10026
	Document Filing and Retrieval	SC 18N 1264/5
	Remote Database Access Protocol	ISO 9576
	Job Transfer and Manipulation	ISO 8832/33
	Document Transfer, Access, and Manipulation Protocol	CCITT T.431/433
	The Directory	CCITT X.500, ISO 9594
	Message Handling Service	CCITT X.400, ISO 10020/21
	Common Service Elements:	
	Association Control Service Elements (ACSE)	ISO 8649/50
	Reliable Transfer Service Elements (RTSE)	ISO 9066
	Remote Operations Service Elements (ROSE)	ISO 9072
Presentation:	Connection-Oriented Presentation Protocol	ISO 8823
	Connectionless Protocol	ISO 9576
Session:	Connection-Oriented Session Protocol	ISO 8327
	Connectionless Protocol	ISO 9548
Transport:	Connection-Oriented Transport Protocol	ISO 8073
	Connectionless Protocol	ISO 8602
Network:	Connectionless Protocol	ISO 8473
	X.25	ISO 8208
	End System to Intermediate System Exchange Protocol	ISO 9542
	Proposal on how to use ISDN in OSI and OSI in ISDN	ISO 9574
Data Link:	Logical Link Control	IEEE 802.2, ISO 8802/2
	Media Access Control:	
	CSMA/CD	IEEE 802.3, ISO 8802/3
	Token Bus	IEEE 802.4, ISO 8802/4
	Token Ring	IEEE 802.5, ISO 8802/5
	Fiber Distributed Data Interface	ISO 9314
Physical:	CSMA/CD	IEEE 802.3, ISO 8802/3
	Token Bus	IEEE 802.4, ISO 8802/4
	Token Ring	IEEE 802.5, ISO 8802/5

TABLE 3.1. (continued)

Layer	*Standard Name*	*Number*
	Fiber Distributed Data Interface	ISO 9314
	Slotted Ring	ISO 8802/7
OSI Model Related:	Application Layer Structure	ISO 9545
	Procedures for OSI Registration Authorities	ISO 9834
	Security Architecture	ISO 7498-2
	Naming and Addressing	ISO 7498-3
	Management Framework	ISO 7498-4

Note: While several of these standards are completed, some were still undergoing development at the time of writing. Enhancements were also being made to existing standards (such as the 8802 LAN standards and to modem standards) and these are not separately listed.

either adopted or in the process of development. Several of those standards—the LAN standards emanating from IEEE—are part of the primary focus of this book and will be explored in detail. They represent much of the work that has been done for layers 1 and 2. Other illustrations will be given in this chapter.

Throughout the set of standards discussed in this book two concepts recur and need to be defined here: *connectionless* and *connection-oriented* services. These are also sometimes referred to as *datagram* and *virtual-circuit* services, respectively. Generally, a datagram may be defined as a finite-length packet with sufficient information to be independently routed from source to destination without reliance on previous transmissions. Datagram transmission typically does not involve end-to-end session establishment and may or may not entail delivery-confirmation acknowledgment. A connection-oriented service establishes a virtual connection that gives the appearance to the user of an actual end-to-end circuit. The virtual connection contrasts with a physical circuit in that it is a dynamically variable connection where sequential user data packets may be routed differently during the course of a virtual connection. A connectionless service does not set up a virtual or logical connection between hosts and does not guarantee that all data units will be delivered or that they will be delivered in the proper order. The advantages of connectionless service are flexibility, robustness, and connectionless-application support.

Connectionless applications are those that require routing services but do not require connection-oriented services.

A datagram service, such as that provided by the DoD IP, is a connectionless service. Likewise, in the context of the OSI Reference Model, some protocols provide connection-oriented services while others provide connectionless services. Moreover, both these services can exist at several levels. The ISO 8473 standard, for example, is a connectionless protocol for the Network Layer and functions similarly to IP, while ISO 8073 is a connection-oriented protocol at the Transport Layer. As will be seen in Chapter 4, the IEEE Std 802.2 (ISO 8802/2) Logical Link Control standard can be implemented as either a connectionless or connection-oriented service in the DATA-Link Layer. Typically, if a network is configured to handle connection-oriented services at say, the Transport Layer, the protocols at the Network and Data-Link layers would likely be implemented as connectionless services.

The DoD's IP has already been mentioned, and the DoD has also defined TCP. A significant literature is developing concerning the relationship between TCP/IP and OSI because a great deal of internetworking, in the United States, is currently being accomplished through the use of TCP/IP. The DoD, along with the U.S. government generally, has committed itself to moving from TCP/IP to the OSI Reference Model standards. That movement will likely take until into the 21st century to accomplish, but it requires that the relationship of TCP/IP to OSI be well understood. To describe completely the OSI structure, standards at every level from the Network Layer through the Application Layer would have to be described, thus providing sufficient material for an entire book. Some parallel comment on OSI and TCP/IP standards is necessary because already networks in the United States, including both those of the DoD and the National Science Foundation, explicitly project migration from TCP/IP to OSI standards. It is important, therefore, to understand where parallel protocols fit and how to get from one standard to the other.

Compared with TCP and IP, OSI Reference Model standards provide equivalent or superior functionality. X.400, the international message transfer standard, provides significantly greater capability than the Simple Mail Transfer Protocol (SMTP). A standard since 1984, X.400 is gaining significantly in vendor support. The international standards corresponding to TCP/IP's File Transfer Protocol (FTP) and virtual terminal services (TELNET) are FTAM and VTP, respectively. These were not yet widely available at this writing, but will provide much greater capability when implemented. A report issued in 1985 by the National Research Council (NRC, U.S.) detailed many of the reasons for migration from TCP/IP to OSI Reference Model standards.[19] With respect to the DoD, the NRC study produced three findings:[20]

1. DoD objectives can be met by international standards.
2. TCP and OSI transport are functionally equivalent.
3. There are significant benefits for DoD in using standard commercial products.

In the long run the cost of OSI products should be lower than corresponding TCP/IP products. There are, however, some functional benefits in addition to lower cost:

1. The variety of commercial products integrated with OSI-related standards will continue to grow and expand.
2. OSI counterparts to FTP, SMTP, and TELNET do not suffer from the same limitations.
3. OSI-related standards extend far beyond the DoD standards in areas such as document architecture, network management, and transaction processing.

During the period of transition it will be necessary for many TCP/IP networks to operate in parallel with OSI networks, using Application Layer gateways that map between TCP/IP and OSI applications. As networking becomes more global and as TCP/IP runs out of addresses, the OSI Reference Model will become the dominant internetworking standard. With these notes in mind, the discussion now turn to the seven layers of the OSI Reference Model.

The Complexity of Standards

The task of establishing standards is complex and not easily achieved. In fact, part of the problem is political rather than technical, since for any given technology there may be one or more special interests that may have a great deal to lose depending on the adopted standards. This problem is reflected in the IEEE 802 committee's decision to support both bus and ring topologies and two media (baseband and broadband). The committee decided to standardize virtually all serious proposals rather than just one. This was likely a compromise based on the recognition of the need for broad acceptance of the standards if they were to make a difference.

The complexity issue can be illustrated by comparing a "local network reference model" to the OSI Reference Model. Two sublayers within the Data Link Layer and the Physical Layer comprise the local network model:[21]

- Physical. Deals with the nature of the transmission medium, electrical signaling, and device attachment.
- Medium Access Control. Since many devices share a single medium, some method for regulating access to that medium is necessary.
- Logical Link Control. The establishment, maintenance, and termination of the logical link between devices.

The relationship between the OSI Reference Model and local network models is depicted in Figure 3.7. The long-term advantage of acceptable standards is that many different manufacturers will be able to produce compatible devices, and this will, in the long run, be a boon to purchasers of such systems.

The strategy being pursued by the IEEE's 802 committee is to provide a flexible framework for LANs. At least part of the reason for this approach has likely been the inability to impose single standards on a wide range of special interests. In addition, however, there is an implicit recognition that user needs differ as well as demands of LAN manufacturers. The 802 standards committee is actually producing a family of standards for LANs. Those most frequently discussed as of this writing were the following:

1. ANSI/IEEE Std 802.3 (ISO DIS 8802/3), a bus using CSMA/CD (discussion follows) as the access method.
2. ANSI/IEEE Std 802.4 (ISO DIS 8802/4), a bus using token passing (discussion follows) as the access method.
3. ANSI/IEEE Std 802.5, a ring using token passing as the access method.

ANSI/IEEE Std 802.2 (ISO DIS 8802/2) specifies the IEEE Standard Logical Link Control protocol and is used in conjunction with the medium access

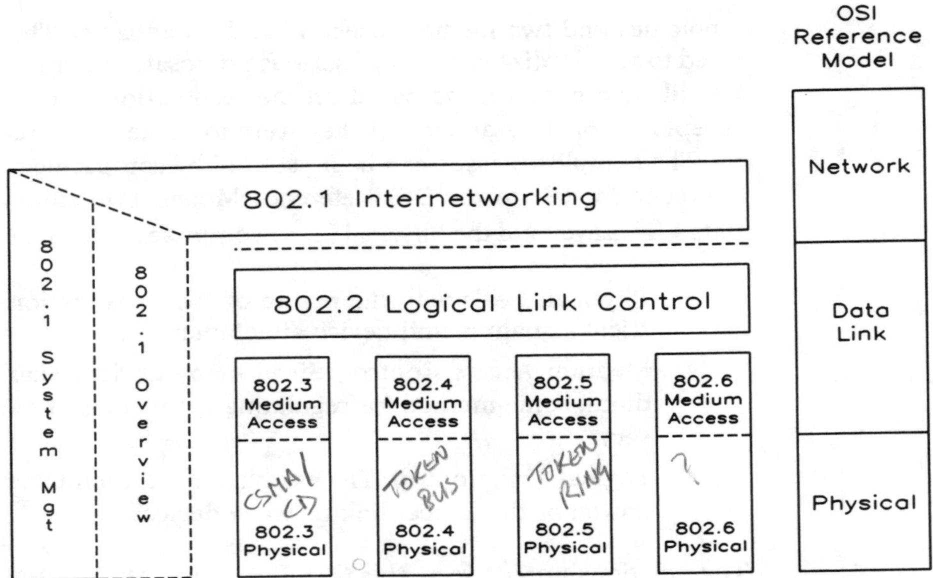

Figure 3.7. Relationship of IEEE Standards and the OSI Reference Model. Source: Based on IEEE P802.1, Draft E, July 1, 1987. "Overview, Internetworking, and Systems Management," unapproved draft published for comment only, by permission of the IEEE. All rights reserved by The Institute of Electrical and Electronics Engineers, Inc., p. 7.

standards. The relationship among these standards and their relationship to the OSI Reference Model is specified in greater detail in a document entitled IEEE 802.1. Other access methods were under investigation or recently adopted as of this writing, particularly, 802.6 (MANs).

Networks Determine the Micro-to-Mainframe Link

The manner in which networks are organized, and the protocols they use, determine the way in which the micro-to-mainframe connection can work. Some LANs are designed primarily for microcomputers and have few, if any, micro-to-mainframe gateways. On the other hand, general-purpose asynchronous or synchronous networks are often slow and not user-friendly. The way in which various devices interact with the communications system can also limit the micro–mainframe link. Consider some of the problems involved with that link.

Assume that in an organizational context a mainframe might be used as a peripheral to micros. The mainframe may need to be a secure, large-scale file server for a network consisting mostly of micro-based workstations. Steps must be taken to connect to the mainframe system. Those steps can always be done by "hand" through a terminal emulator, but a more elegant approach would be to have the mainframe simply appear as a virtual disk on the micro. To make the process completely automatic something like the following steps would have to be taken:

- A session must be established over the communications system with the mainframe.
- A login sequence on the mainframe would have to be generated, which should include a requirement for a user identification number and a password
- A mainframe program that interacts with the micro-based software might be needed to ensure correct and appropriate file transfers.

Connective Versus Dedicated Networks

The distinction I am trying to make here is between those networks that are designed to provide full connectivity among a wide variety of devices and applications, and those networks that are essentially terminal-to-mainframe systems. The classic concepts of networking were the latter; the more modern approach involves a high degree of connectivity. Even IBM, a primary architect and defender of dedicated networks, has admitted that highly connective approaches are desirable, although within the IBM sphere of influence the potential for connectivity remains wedded to at least IBM's SNA (see later chapters).

Asynchronous Versus Synchronous Data Communications

Chapter 2 discussed the differences between synchronous and asynchronous data communications, and further discussion will appear in later chapters. Under current circumstances the primary approach to ensure global connectivity is through an asynchronous communications system because almost every manufacturer supports asynchronous communications using either the RS-232-C hardware standard, or its CCITT equivalent. As newer networking techniques become more widely deployed, and as gateways and bridges among different networks become more common, it will not be necessary to rely on asynchronous systems for broad connectivity. The down side to the use of multiple networking methods is, however, that the difficulty of maintaining the network increases. Recognizing the need for connectivity, IBM is attempting to redefine aspects of SNA to provide the connectivity being demanded by user organizations.

Flow Control and Speed Matching

In a data communications environment it is frequently necessary during data transfers to regulate the flow of data between two connections. The process by which that regulation takes place is called flow control. Some form of flow control is required to ensure the integrity of the data transmitted and received, otherwise data might be lost during transmission. Flow control prevents the receiving device from being overwhelmed by the transmitting device. Flow control can be implemented in either software or hardware or some combination of both. An understanding of flow control is essential because the implementation of flow control can have a direct impact on the cost of the system.

Data are transmitted and received in either a serial or parallel mode. Each byte or character of information is commonly composed of eight bits of data. In parallel transmission systems, each bit of a byte (or word) is transmitted concurrently across individual wires. In serial systems (which may be either asynchronous or synchronous), a byte is transmitted one bit at a time, one after the other. With serial communications, data are transferred in either half-duplex or full-duplex. Two-way communications can be implemented in either half- or full-duplex. In half-duplex, data can be sent in only one direction at a time. In full-duplex, data can be sent in both directions concurrently. To have flow control, however, it is necessary to operate in full-duplex. If the network devices have some memory (buffer) and are flow controlled independently from user devices, then the two connections of a session may run at different speeds (bits per second), enhancing the flexibility of the system.

In systems using parallel data transfers, flow control is a hardware function. Two electrical control signals are present on the parallel cable (often called "strobe" and "ready") which allow "handshaking" between the source and destination devices on a character-by-character basis. More important in the general LAN environment, however, are serial data transfers (although there are some small LANs implemented with parallel buses).

The most widely applicable serial standard, available on almost all computer systems, is RS-232-C.

RS-232-C is a standard promulgated by the Electronics Industries Association (EIA) in the United States and is one of a series prefaced with the "RS" designation. There are ISO standards that are essentially the same as several of the EIA standards. International Standards Organization 2110 is equivalent to RS-232-C and ISO 4902 is compatible with EIA RS-449. RS-449 is a newer standard than RS-232-C and represents a major enhancement of the RS-232-C standard. The RS-232-C standard supports both asynchronous data transfers and synchronous systems of data exchange. The method of data exchange is called a protocol.

Although asynchronous serial communications are important to individuals and to some commercial information utilities, in large organizations synchronous systems are probably more important. The protocols for data transmission are implemented in the Data-Link Layer (Layer 2) of the OSI Reference Model supplemented by some hardware control signals. Common synchronous standards include Bisync (Binary Synchronous Communications from IBM); SDLC (Synchronous Data-Link Control from IBM); HDLC (High-Level Data-Link Control from ISO); and X.25 (Recommendation from the X.25 CCITT). Other standards organizations or manufacturers have proposed other synchronous standards.

With serial data transfers the transmissions between source and destination devices must be synchronized. With asynchronous transfers data are synchronized on a byte-by-byte basis using a start and stop bit before and after the eight bits of the byte transmitted. Synchronous transmissions are synchronized by timing signals. Flow control in asynchronous, full duplex systems takes place using one of three possible approaches: XON/XOFF, ETX/ACK (End of TeXt/ACKnowledge), or EIA Reverse Channel signal method.

The XON/XOFF and ETX/ACK methods both use special characters in the ASCII (American Standard Code for Information Interchange) character set and are implemented in software. The Reverse Channel signal method implements an electrical signal for flow control. The RS-232-C standard defines 23 signals (out of 25 possible signals) normally implemented with a connector called a DB-25 (a 25 pin connector) in the United States. Two of the 25 lines are unassigned and used by manufacturers to implement device-specific signals. As few as three of the lines and signals (the minimum number necessary for data exchange) may be implemented or as many as 25 may be present.

XON is the ASCII control (nonprinting) character with a hex value of 11 (decimal 17). This character is also called DC1 (Data Control 1). XOFF is an ASCII control character with a hex value of 13 (decimal 19) and is called DC3 (Data Control 3). The End of TeXt character is an ASCII control character with a hex value of 3 (decimal 3). The ACKnowledge message has a hex value 6 (decimal 6). With an ASCII keyboard on a terminal or microcomputer, these characters may be generated by typing Control Q (XON), Control S (XOFF), Control C (ETX), and Control F (ACK).

With XON/XOFF, which is the most common flow-control technique, when a destination device senses that a data overrun is about to occur, it transmits an XOFF character to the source device. When the source device receives the XOFF message it suspends sending until it receives an XON character. Less common is ETX/ACK in which a block of data is transmitted by the source device, followed by an ETX. The destination device then disposes of the data and returns an ACK to the sending device, and transmission proceeds. The reverse channel method uses logic similar to XON/XOFF except that stop and resume control messages are implemented by using separate electrical signals on the RS-232-C cable.[22]

Flow control is an essential attribute of any LAN if it is to work with a wide variety of devices and if data transfers are to take place reliably. Non-flow-controlled devices can sometimes be used at slow data-transfer rates, although this is not the preferred approach. The difficulty that confronts managers in a large organization is that not all devices implement flow control. The major source of irritation in this regard is IBM. IBM has never been fond of asynchronous data communications, yet its synchronous communications systems are incompatible with other industry elements, and IBM's networking standards have not been appropriate for LANs. To confront the LAN market, IBM announced its first LAN in 1983, a broadband system, and in 1985 a Token Ring, baseband system. Other computer manufacturers have also failed to implement full flow control. The old Hewlett-Packard (HP) 2000, for example, although using a full duplex system, had no flow control except for some specialized block mode terminals from HP, although that problem has long since been remedied in the newer HP series, including the HP/3000 family.

In a large organization, however, the IBM problem is particularly vexing given the overwhelming market position of IBM. IBM implemented asynchronous serial communications in half-duplex mode using its series of 37x5 front end processors (FEPs) on its large mainframes. If the LAN an organization wishes to implement requires full duplex, flow-controlled, asynchronous communications with an IBM system, then there are two non-LAN solutions available. First, an FEP from a manufacturer other than IBM can be purchased. NCR/COMTEN, for example, sells an FEP designated as the 1270, which can be configured with both asynchronous and synchronous ports. The asynchronous ports can run at up to 9600 b/s (or higher), full-duplex, using XON/XOFF flow control. This has an obvious economic effect but the solution works. Other FEP manufacturers also offer full-duplex, flow-controlled systems as special request items, although at this writing none can run as fast as 9600 b/s.

A second, and in some ways more desirable, alternative is the use of protocol converters. Protocol converters became widely and economically available in the early 1980s and on IBM systems allow IBM's 3270-type synchronous terminals to be emulated on low-cost ASCII terminals or microcomputers. The protocol converter is plugged into a synchronous port on an FEP (a 37x5, COM-TEN, et cetera). Protocol converters can typically be configured with from 8 to 32 asynchronous ports and will support a wide variety of ASCII terminals. The asynchronous ports on the protocol converter can typically run up to 9600 (or even 19.2K) b/s and are fully flow controlled. By emulating an IBM 3270 terminal, all full-screen capabilities are available to the end user. If a terminal such as DEC's VT100 (DEC's original smart ASCII terminal, now superceded by the VT200, VT300, and ANSI X3.64) is chosen, then full-screen capabilities will be available on such machines as DEC's VAX superminis, other DEC machines, IBM and IBM-compatible systems, and machines from other manufacturers. The point is that with this configuration, flow control can be implemented for the LAN and result in better user support, including generally available full-screen capabilities.

Micros, Mainframes, and Networks: An Assessment

Microcomputers and mainframes (including minis) are clearly more useful to users if they are networked. A large organization may have several different networks, each connected to one another. A small organization may need only one LAN. The organizational purpose of a network is to improve the way in which people work together. Since most processing today is transactional, networks are necessary to make that processing available to those who need it; however, different organizations have different networking problems. Individual departments may need LANs, while the total institution may need a very large LAN or a WAN. An objective in network design should be to make the network transparent to the user, although current technology has far to go in making this objective a reality.

Networking micros, mainframes, and minis can ultimately reduce paper costs, improve business communications, and expand the quality and quantity of human networks within an organization. But the networks must be *connective*. That is, they must be designed to encompass devices from many different manufacturers connected to potentially different networks. A need exists, therefore, for gateways and bridges from one network to another, along with a common "backbone" transport system. The "best" network for any given organization is one that will not only accomplish the general objectives just listed, but also accomplish the specific goals and objectives of a particular company or other institution.

Notes

1. Much of the material in this chapter has been drawn from T. W. Madron, *Local Area Networks in Large Organizations* (Rochelle Park, NJ: Hayden Book Co., 1984), Chapters 1 and 2.
2. H. J. Saal, "Local-Area Networks," *Byte*, Oct. 1981 (6, 10), pp. 96–97.
3. L. A. Bertman, "Exploring the Capabilities of Local Area Networks," *The Office*, May 1983, p. 104.
4. Robert Bowerman, "Choosing a Local Area Network," *Interface Age*, July 1983, p. 55.
5. Harry Saal, "Local Area Networks: An Update on Microcomputers in the Office," *Byte*, May 1983, p. 62.
6. As reported by John M. Lusa, et al., "Distributed Processing: Alive and Well," *Infosystems*, Nov. 1976, pp. 35–41.
7. Dale G. Mullen, "Is your telecommunications network obsolete?" *Telematics*, Vol. 1, No. 4, Sept. 1981, pp. 17–19.
8. Ibid., p. 18.
9. From an address to the 1980 DPMA international conference, as quoted by Wayne L. Rhodes, Jr., "Office of the Future: Light Years Away?" *Infosystems*, Vol. 28, No. 3, March 1981, pp. 40–50.
10. Frank Derfler, Jr. and William Stallings, *A Manager's Guide to Local Networks* (Englewood Cliffs, NJ: Prentice-Hall, 1983), p. 79.
11. Note Gregory Ennis, "Routing Tables Locate Resources in Bridged Broadband Networks," *Systems & Software*, March 1983.
12. The state of OSI development can be followed in various places. See, for example, Jean Bartik, "OSI: From Model to Prototype as Commerce

Tries to Keep Pace," *Data Communications*, March 1984, pp. 307–319; Jerrold S. Foley, "The Status and Direction of Open Systems Interconnection," *Data Communications*, Feb. 1985, pp. 177–193; Sunil Joshi and Venkatraman Iyer, "New Standards for Local Networks Push Upper Limits for Lightwave Data," *Data Communications*, July 1984, pp. 127–138; and Kevin L. Mills, "Testing OSI Protocols: NBS Advances the State of the Art," *Data Communications*, March 1984, pp. 277–285.

13. The actual text of standards is sometimes difficult to obtain. An easily accessible compilation of many of the more important standards can be found in Harold C. Folts, ed., *McGraw-Hill's Compilation of Data Communications Standards*, Edition III (New York: McGraw-Hill, 1986), 3 volumes. The ISO 7498 standard (OSI) was adopted from the CCITT Recommendation X.200. X.200 has been used as the basis for the discussion in this chapter and references are made to that document, designated as *Fascicle VIII.5–Rec. X.200*. In references following the identification of the actual standard, volume, and page references to the standard are found in *McGraw-Hill's Compilation of Data Communications Standards*. *Fascicle VIII.5 - Rec. X.200*, p. 3 (Vol. 2, p. 2235).

14. Ibid.

15. Ibid., p. 3 (Vol. 2, p. 2235).

16. Ibid. Both the listing that designates the scope of OSI as well as the listing of points concerning the application of the OSI Reference Model follow either identically or very closely the wording in the "Introduction" to the OSI Reference Model.

17. Ibid., p. 4 (Vol. 2, p. 2236).

18. The concepts of a layered architecture are given in p. 40, ibid., pp. 6ff (Vol. 2, pp. 2238ff), Section 5.

19. National Research Council, *Transport Protocols for Department of Defense Data Networks*, Feb. 1985.

20. As summarized by William Stallings, et al., *Handbook of Computer–Communications Standards*, Vol. 3, "Department of Defense (DoD) Protocol Standards (New York: Macmillan Publishing Company, 1988), p. 22.

21. William Stallings, "A Tutorial on the IEEE 802 Local Network Standard," in Raymond L. Pickholtz (ed.), *Local Area & Multiple Access Networks* (Rockville, MD: Computer Science Press, Inc., 1986), pp. 2–3.

22. Greater technical detail on these flow-control techniques may be found in Elizabeth A. Nichols, Joseph C. Nichols, and Keith R. Musson, *Data Communications for Microcomputers* (New York: McGraw-Hill Book Company, 1982), pp. 161–170.

CHAPTER 4

Network Security Issues

Since the inception of computer networks, security has been an often discussed topic. While most discussions of network security have been limited to the data processing community, the discussions sometimes surfaced in the public press. By 1983, however, the issue of computer network security had become the topic of a popular motion picture (*War Games*), and the problem received widespread comment in the popular press. That computer networks are vulnerable and security breeches are costly is illustrated by a U.S. Justice Department survey taken in 1988 that reported "the average take for today's computer thief is $883,279, compared with only $6,100 for an old-fashioned bank robber."[1] Consequently, as Thomas L. Davidson and Clinton E. White, Jr., have observed, "measures must be taken by the network security system to identify legitimate users for authorized purposes while denying unauthorized access or use of sensitive data."[2]

Davidson and White suggest security systems be thought of "as a series of concentric circles forming layers of protection around computer data and resources."[3] The outer rings represent the least security, the inner rings the most security. The real difficulty with the concept presented by Davidson and White is that it is too simplistic in light of modern technology. Some similar approach is, however, probably useful in gaining an understanding of the security issue. Rather than concentric circles, think instead of security as a series of layers with the topmost layer representing the tightest security, and the bottom layer the least secure. This approach is depicted in Figure 4.1.

Two of the major trends in computing and networking over the past decade or so have contributed mightily to the problems surrounding security: The demands for connectivity and easy access (user-friendliness) to computing and network resources. A third element entered in the early 1980s, as well: The wide deployment of microcomputers. Successful implementation of a highly connective system tends to thwart some methods of security and control. One of the primary objectives of computer networks, and especially of local area networks (LANs), is to provide easy and convenient access to computer systems within an organization, and that very ease of use can sometimes conflict with security needs. The various layers

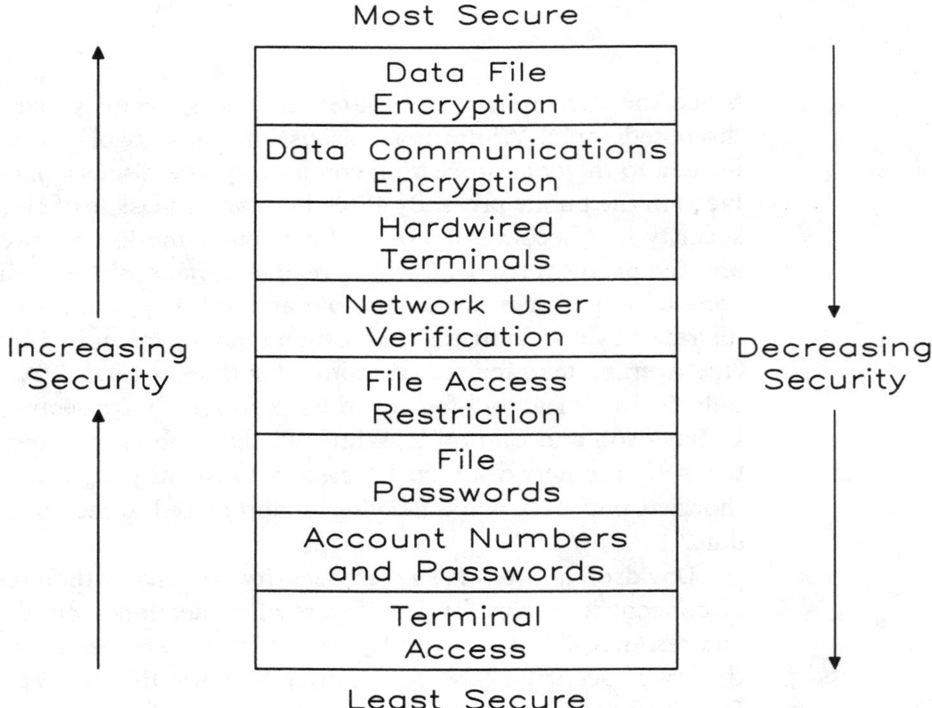

Figure 4.1. Layers of Security.

of security are designed to prevent unauthorized access and herein lies a major issue of security: At what point is the maintenance of security more costly than a security breach? That question must be answered within each organization.

What Is Network Security?

It may seem trivial to ask the question, but the fact is that there is no universal agreement on what constitutes security—or at least appropriate security—in a computing and communications environment. Indeed, in many organizations there is debate over whether security is needed at all or whether the level of security provided is too high or too low. The layers of security addressed in Figure 4.1 relate to only one kind of security: information security. At the very least there are three broad areas of security: information security, physical security, and disaster recovery.[4] A somewhat broader list of concerns would include security issues revolving around the data center, distributed processing, mini- and microcomputer controls, and end user access. A more extensive security list might include physical, personnel, data, application software, system software, telecommunications, and operations.[5] S. Rao Valabhaneni has suggested that in order to implement necessary security it is important to activate five types of controls: directive, preventive, detective, corrective, and recovery.[6] To this list might be added two more ephemeral and often overlooked controls: legal and ethical.

The rapid and widespread deployment of microcomputers during the 1980s, as much as anything, got the attention of those in industry and government concerned with security. Even as late as 1985 it was common to find a significant amount of confusion concerning what constituted security issues. There was, for example, an attempt to distinguish between terms like *integrity* and *security*. Writing in *Micro Communications* in 1985, M. Durr noted that the increase in the number of microcomputers was intensifying the problem of data integrity.[7] Durr made a distinction between integrity and security by suggesting that "data integrity" referred to errors introduced into data while "data security" involved protection of the data from outright loss, theft, or malicious change. Data integrity referred to unintentional data losses from lost or damaged bits or erroneous manipulation such as electrical interference on the transmission medium. Error-checking protocols can largely overcome (at the cost of degrading throughput) the problem of transmission-line interference. The erroneous manipulation of data relates to off-line processing at the micro. People, according to Durr, are the bottom line on data integrity. As will become clear in the discussion on the *OSI Security Architecture*, later in this chapter, integrity is now thought of as a subdivision of security. Durr was quite correct, however, in identifying *people* as the fundamental source of both the problems relating to information security as well as the opportunities available in solving those problems.

Security in information processing is required because information can be compromised through ignorance, inadvertence, accident, or malice. Note that the fundamental objective is to preserve the information that has been flowing through the system, although other aspects of physical and personnel security are also very important. Because information can be compromised these controls become important. Management produces *directive controls* when actions, policies, procedures, directives, or guidelines are issued that cause or encourage a desirable event to occur. Required standards, guidelines, methods, practices, and manual or automated techniques that are designed to result in high-quality, reliable systems are *preventive controls*. *Detective controls* produce feedback regarding whether the preventive controls have or are working. When problems occur or have been detected, then *corrective controls*, both manual and automated, provide procedures for correcting errors, irregularities, or omissions. *Recovery controls* provide for backup and recovery after a system failure. While all five of these controls are considerably more complicated than the summary just given, they are extraordinarily important even in the smallest organization, assuming of course, that the information being processed is important to the well-being of that organization.[8]

The five controls just described are those typically addressed by auditors and are of concern to computer professionals responsible for systems integrity. Such controls are necessary regardless of whether a failure is the result of accident or malice. The problem of malice can and should also be attacked from other perspectives. There is serious concern regarding informaton security at the state and federal governmental levels. Congress and state legislatures are continuing to pass laws that criminalize computer fraud and theft. That development is coupled to a growing understanding that the inappropriate use of computers and communications systems reflect ethical failures. From an ethical perspective robbing someone of information is as much of a theft as robbing a bank of money. Sabotage of a computer/communications system is no less a moral failure than sabotaging an airplane. Increasingly such acts are being legally defined as criminal activities. An example of sabotage is the widely reported case of Robert Morris' "worm" program that "infected" many computers (perhaps as many as 6,000 in 500–700 organizations) on the national Internet in November, 1988. Morris was convicted and sentenced in May, 1990, the first such conviction under the Federal Computer Fraud and Abuse Act of 1986.[9] Although many computer professionals and others believe that Morris' punishment was far too light to appropriately fit his crime, it was indicative of the growing concern with information system failures because of either malice or stupidity.

Computer/communications security extends far beyond user identification codes and passwords. It comprises a comprehensive set of rules and practices that helps ensure that the information on which our businesses and our society is based will not be compromised. *Information security* consists of a combination of *data security* and *communications security*. Data security is the procedures and actions designed to prevent the unauthorized disclosure, transfer, modification, or destruction, whether accidental or intentional, of data. Communications security (COMSEC) is the protection resulting from the application of *cryptosecurity*, *transmission security*, and *emission security* measures to telecommunications and from the application of *physical security* measures to communications security information.[10] These measures are taken to deny unauthorized persons information of value that might be derived from the possession and study of such telecommunications and may be defined as follows:

- Cryptosecurity. The COMSEC component that results from providing technically sound cryptosystems and their proper use.
- Transmission Security. The COMSEC component that results from all measures designed to protect transmissions from interception and exploitation by means other than cryptanalysis.
- Emission Security. The COMSEC component that results from all measures taken to deny unauthorized persons information of value that might be derived from intercepting and analyzing compromising emanations from cryptoequipment and telecommunications systems.
- Physical Security. The COMSEC component that results from all physical measures necessary to safeguard classified equipment, material, and documents from access thereto or observation thereof by unauthorized persons.

It is easy to see from Figure 4.1 why technical definitions of security are ultimately concerned with encryption techniques, since encryption is the most effective method for securing information. It must also be recognized that security from an auditor's perspective must include procedures that go beyond the technical definitions, since the auditor's concern is to safeguard the organization's fiscal integrity to the extent that the fiscal integrity is a function of information processing. Finally, society at large has a stake in information security, since every year the national well-being is more dependent on information flows. Hence at a societal level, law and ethics become elements of a total information-security program.

How Much Security Is Enough?

A subsidiary question is, how much is your information worth to the operation of your organization? Or even, how much of the worth of your organization is dependent on your information? Rear Admiral Grace Murray Hopper, until recently one of the oldest persons on active duty with the United States Navy, has an appropriate answer to that question. She was, in her words, the "third programmer on the first computer," and was one of the original authors of COBOL. Admiral Hopper, in a speech a few years ago, made the point that information processors have frequently placed emphasis on "processing" information to the exclusion of understanding the worth of the information itself.[11]

With the deployment of microcomputers as workstations in large organizations, the value-of-information issue has become more apparent than it was previously. Micros have proved to be catalysts for this issue because people want micro-based workstations to download subsets of organizational data for further local processing, analysis, and reporting. Database administrators concerned about the integrity of their data, as a result of these changes in the way data are used, have had to learn new practices. It is becoming more apparent than ever that if information is to be used as the basis of organizational decision making that information must be "timely" and "accurate." Part of an assessment of the value of information is how much it costs to ensure that it is timely and accurate.

Even though timeliness and accuracy have always been an objective of data processors, in the old days that often meant generating the data in machine-readable batches (cards or something equivalent), producing an initial report, checking the report for accuracy, making corrections, then producing a final report—a process that could take days or weeks. In today's environment, where the end user may control much of the process, a file or record may be updated one moment from some terminal, and downloaded to a micro by some other user the next moment, massaged, and a report generated in an hour. Technology has provided timeliness—people still provide accuracy.[12] The result of the differences in timeliness between development and/or report-generation time on a mainframe and on a micro is not solely one of easier-to-use technology on the micro, nor of the obtuseness of mainframe-systems developers. At least some of the difference is that over the years mainframe-development people have been required to adhere to a greater degree of corporate accountability than is typically true of so-called end user computing.

In a mainframe environment procedures have often been established over a period of years in cooperation with all sorts of interests within an organization. Such procedures are usually absent with micro-based computing. Furthermore, many of the procedures required in a mainframe environment are tied directly to security concerns—something that is only superficially recognized, if ever, with micro-based computing. An illustration of this is the question of how data is stored after it has been massaged on micros. If the analysis is done on the mainframe, all the standard security measures typical of large systems are taken to ensure that the analysis is not lost or at least the data on which the analysis was based is not lost. The analysis can be replicated if necessary because standard backup procedures ensure that the data will always be available. Not everybody, however, has standard backup procedures for micros. Therein lies the problem. A way of looking at the mainframe as a microcomputer peripheral is to regard it as a secure and cost-effective file server for backing up microcomputer files. If the files generated on the micro are important means for making organizational decisions, then those data are every bit as important to the organization as any generated on the mainframe. Yet they are not as secure and are not usually in any audit trail anyone can find.

The effort to answer the question of how much security is enough has led to the development of various techniques, both quantitative and qualitative, to assess the risk involved in *not* establishing appropriate security. In general, as the risk of a security failure increases, and as the cost of the system increases, the cost of doing damage control increases. This is illustrated in Figure 4.2. The general answer to the question is, therefore, to establish sufficient security procedures so that both security and corrective costs are minimized. A low-cost low-risk system is less in need of heavy-duty security than is a high-cost high-risk system. Yet, these are still relative

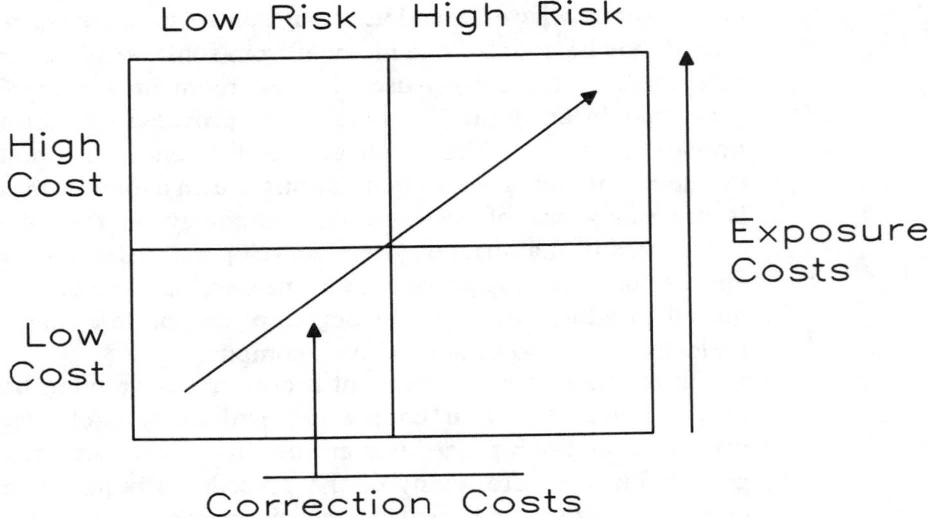

Figure 4.2. Security Costs Versus Risks.

terms, since a \$5,000 system for IBM or AT&T or the federal government may be trivial, while a \$5,000 system for an independent consultant, an author, or a one-person law firm may be catastrophic.

In any event, it is still useful for an organization to attempt to assess the risk involved in security or the lack thereof. Credit for the first application of quantitative risk-analysis techniques probably goes to Robert Courtney. In 1977 Courtney, then with IBM, first presented the technique. In this context risk is defined in terms of probable loss dollars per year according to the relationship:

$$R = P \times E$$

where R is risk, P is the probability that a security threat will occur a given number of times per year, and E is the exposure cost attributed to any such loss. The difficulty with this formulation is that the assignment of probabilities is subjective and costs are often difficult to determine. The exercise itself is instructive, however, for it forces the members of an organization to think through their risk exposure.

P is not a simple statistical probability estimate. The probable exposure is known as the Loss Multiplier (P_L) which annualizes the rate of occurrence of a given risk. For example, if something happened once every 300 years, then the P_L would be .00333 (365/109500, not counting leap days during leap years). If it happened once a day, the P_L would be 365 (365/1), and if it happened 100 times per day the P_L would be 3,650 (365/.1). In other words, the P_L is calculated as follows:

Loss Multiplier = (Number of Days per Year) / (Number of Days Between Events)

For example, a given piece of equipment might have a Mean Time Between Failures (MTBF) of 10,000 hours. If that item operated 24 hours per day, then the number of days between events would be 10,000/24 = 416.67 days per event. One year = 365 days, so the P_L for this device is 365/416.67 = .876. Some other device has a failure rate of two per day: 1 (day) / 2 = .5 days per event. P_L = 365/.5 = 730. Something that fails about once every three months (90 days) would produce P_L = 365 / (90/1) = 4.06. There are other techniques available for estimating rates of occurrence, but where possible those estimates should be based on hard data rather than on subjective estimates.

Just as it can be difficult to estimate the Loss Multiplier, it is also difficult to precisely calculate the costs of expected losses. Losses are not simply a function of equipment replacement cost. Many other factors can increase costs because of a computer/communications system failure. Some of the factors to be considered are:[13]

1. Personnel productivity time resulting from an outage. This includes the salary per hour of the employees concerned, as well as the cost of fringe benefits for those hours lost but paid. Employees here include anyone whose job is dependent on the existence of the system, whether technical support or end user.
2. Personnel time required to correct the outage, including direct salary and benefits.
3. Value of business lost because of the outage.
4. Cost of using alternative methods if that is at all possible.
5. Legal liability costs.
6. The hazard-protection and business-interruption insurance costs.
7. The backup and recovery capabilities costs, including annual-testing costs.

8. Equipment-replacement costs, including ordering and shipping, installation, and testing and startup processing time.
9. Damage-repair costs less insurance recoveries.
10. The current replacement cost of the asset.

A simple example will suffice. Suppose that a data entry operator, using a microcomputer, has an equipment failure. It takes one full day to get the failing device fixed or replaced. The costs would be something like the following:

1. Cost of operator's time including fringes: \$12.30/hour x 8 = \$98.40
2. Repair costs (personnel): \$30.00/hour x 4 = \$120.00
3. Lost business (operator billed at \$20/hour): \$20.00 x 6.8 = \$136.00. The 6.8 hours is the maximum amount of billable time an operator is likely to have in a normal eight-hour day. That is calculated by excluding coffee breaks and providing a time for backing up at the end of the day.
4. No alternative methods available.
5. No legal liabilities in this case.
6. Some small proportionate share of insurance overhead costs (?).
7. Backup and recovery costs: \$22.30.
8. The hard drive failed; replacement cost: \$800.00 (including ordering, installation, and startup time).
9. No other damage costs.
10. Cost of replacement of asset covered in (8).

When these costs are totaled the cost of expected losses comes to \$1,056.70. The P_L for this problem is .876. The risk, or annualized probable loss is, therefore, \$1,056.70 x .876 = \$925.67. There are limits to the usefulness of this kind of risk analysis, but it is probably the most valuable of the techniques available. Obviously doing a risk analysis for a network would be more difficult and network failure could cause very large probable losses.

The list of ten factors used to calculate the "actual" costs of expected losses could also be applied to problems caused through malice. When Robert Morris sent his virus across the Internet the cost of expected losses probably looked something like the following.

Assumptions:

1. Several hundred computer systems were involved. Assume the number was 500.
2. Assume an average of 10 users per system were precluded from using those systems for 24 hours, at an average personnel cost of $50.00 per hour at a maximum pay of 8 hours for each 24-hour period = $400.00/person x 10 x 500 = $2,000,000.
3. An average of two technical people per installation to clean up the system affected at $800.00/day for one day = $800 x 500 = $400,000.
4. Cost of lost revenue from connect-time charges at $10.00 per hour for an average of $800.00/day per installation for the average of 10 users = $800 x 500 = $400,000.

The cost of losses caused by Morris were, using these assumptions, about $2,800,000. The foregoing calculations are very conservative, since as noted earlier, Morris' worm may have hit as many as 6,000 computer systems across 500–700 institutions. Jay Bloombecker, director of the National Center for Computer Crime Data, estimates that the cost to the Los Alamos National Laboratory alone was about $250,000. It required two days to restore service at NASA's Ames Research Center in Mountain View, California—a facility that services 52,000 on-line users.[14] These are the reasons why many computer professionals thought that the fine of $10,000 and some community service was an inadequate punishment. Just because most of the institutions involved were government or university systems does not reduce the loss calculations. Because of the nature of Morris' virus there was no permanent damage to software systems or data, thus minimizing the losses, but substantial losses were nevertheless incurred even though they may not be exactly the numbers presented.

The answer to the question, "how much security is enough?" is dependent on the cost of potential loss to the organization. Spending nothing on security is too little, while spending sufficient to ensure total redundancy is likely too much for most purposes. An automobile assembly plant employing several hundred workers and manufacturing a large number of automobiles per day, with a factory floor controlled by a MAP (Manufacturing Automation Protocol) network, may require very substantial security systems to preclude unscheduled outages. A bank would clearly require substantial security to preclude unwanted intrusions for the purpose of electronically misappropriating funds. In these cases substantial expenditures for security would be warranted.

How much damage can occur if there were unauthorized disclosure or alteration of sensitive data, and how much is an institution willing to pay to protect the information? These are the critical questions in designing a security system. One answer is to keep a truly sensitive processor and its data off a network under the assumption that the only secure computer system is one that is electrically and physically isolated. Even in such an isolated system, however, issues of physical security exist. Some networks can be made more secure than others, but total security may not be possible.[15] It is also increasingly difficult to maintain a computer system not connected or networked to another system, particularly in organizations of any substantial size.

Other issues also intrude into the discussion of security. The size of a network may preclude problems of security or may increase those problems. A small LAN, totally contained in a single office, probably has different security problems than a large LAN spread across a campus environment. In a small LAN, data integrity may be compromised more as a result of inadvertence than of malice, and relatively simple techniques might be appropriate. In a large LAN encryption or call-back techniques might be needed. With a small LAN it may be possible to control what is attached to a system, in a large LAN such control may be more difficult. In a large, highly connective system, for example, an individual with a LAN connection may simply plug in a cheap auto-answer modem and a new point of semipublic access is created, which would be difficult to detect even if rules against such connections were in effect.

OSI Security Architecture

As part of its set of Open System Interconnect (OSI) standards, the International Organization for Standardization (ISO) has produced a standards document (DIS 7498-2, *OSI Reference Model Part 2: Security Architecture*) that can provide significant guidance for security.[16] Among the things DIS 7498-2 contains are the following:

- A checklist of important security features.
- Assistance for organizing the task of providing security.
- Guidance for implementors and purchasers.
- A means for standardizing security implementations.

Two fundamental purposes served by the ISO standard are:

- To provide a functional assignment of security features to OSI layers that will guide future enhancements of OSI-based standards.
- To provide a structured framework within which vendors and customers can evaluate security products.

Within the OSI framework the standard also defines security services and mechanisms. In order to understand the approach taken by the ISO three concepts must be addressed: *security threat*, *security service*, and *security mechanism*.

Security Threat

Any action that compromises the security of information owned by an organization or individual is a security threat. Two types of threats have been identified—*passive* and *active*—and are dealt with in somewhat different ways.

Passive Threats

Passive threats do not, in general, alter any data in the system. Rather, these threats involve reading information for the purpose of profiting from knowledge of the information. Because there is no tampering with the information, audit trails of access are often sparse or nonexistent. Passive threats, are, therefore, difficult to detect. Passive threats, however, can often be prevented, and prevention is fundamental to fighting such hazards.[17]

In a network, passive threats consist of releasing message contents to an attacker, or allowing the attacker to read a packet header (traffic analysis) in order to determine the location and identity of either the communications source or destination. If a message has already been filed on a host system, of course, access to that system can result in an attack on the system in order to obtain information already stored.

A primary method used to thwart passive threats is the use of encryption techniques to make the information unusable without the key necessary for decoding the data. Encryption is accomplished by using either a code or a cipher. With a code, a predefined table substitutes a meaningless word or phrase for each message or part of a message. In contrast, a cipher uses a computable algorithm that translates a bit stream into an indecipherable cryptogram. Cipher techniques can often be more readily automated and are, therefore, used more frequently in computer and network security systems. With conventional encryption, the original data, or "plaintext," is converted into an unintelligible "ciphertext." The conversion is accomplished using an algorithm and a key composed of a bit string that controls the algorithm. Both the sender and receiver must possess the key, so key management becomes an issue. The algorithm must be sufficiently powerful to preclude decipherment of the message based solely on the ciphertext.

From a network perspective there are two fundamental types of encryption: link and end-to-end. Link encryption implies that data are encrypted independently on each vulnerable communication link, which for a simple network may be end-to-end, but for a more extended network may be from packet switch (router, bridge, et cetera) to packet switch. In this situation the data are vulnerable at each packet switch, so there is a separate problem of node security over which the user may have little or no control. The advantage of this scheme, however, is that the entire packet, including the header information, can be encrypted. End-to-end encryption, as the name suggests, takes place at the source and destination addresses of the packet. While this eliminates data vulnerability at intermediate nodes, the header is in the clear. A hybrid system that employs both approaches is the most secure. The header is vulnerable only at end and intermediate nodes, and the substantive information is never vulnerable. A slight variation of the end-to-end scheme is permanently storing data in encrypted files that might be used in place of or in addition to the other two approaches to encryption.

The task of key management is to control of key selection and key distribution in a cryptographic system. A key is a piece of digital information that interacts with encryption algorithms to control encryption of information and, thus, must be protected from disclosure. With conventional encryption systems, both ends of the communication link must have a copy of the key, thus potentially compromising security. This is mitigated to some extent by frequent key changes. An alternative is a public key cryptosystem. This is an encryption methodology that depends on two keys. A public key is made available to anyone who wants to encrypt information and is used for the encryption process. A private key—known only to the owner—is used for the decryption process.

The classical approach to encryption/decryption is to use a *symmetric* algorithm for which both the sender and receiver of an encrypted message are required to have the same key. The disadvantage of symmetric algorithms is that, for security, the algroithm and the key must be kept secret. Moreover, the key must be communicated from one person to another, thus creating a security threat. A major advantage, however, is that some authentication system can be established so that problems involving bogus information can be reduced. The newer alternative methodology uses an *asymmetric* system first reported in 1976.[18] Public-key encryption is the outgrowth of this development. The advantage of an asymmetric system is that the second, private key, is known only to the receiver who calculates it. In such a system, the encryption/decryption algorithms and the encryption (public) key may be made public. The decipherment key is related to the encipherment key, but is actually a random sample from a large universe of potential key values.[19]

While there are proprietary encryption algorithms in use, one of the most widely used algorithms is the data encryption standard (DES) supported by the National Institute of Standards and Technology (NIST) of the U.S. government, formerly (prior to 1988) the National Bureau of Standards (NBS). The DES is an algorithm to be implemented in electronic hardware devices and used for the cryptographic protection of digital, binary-coded information. At one time computer security systems in the United States were certified by the National Security Agency (NSA). The data encryption standard was scheduled for decertification by NSA in 1988, although public outcry kept that from happening. The NSA's perspective was that DES, while very good, was not secure enough for many national security applications. In the meantime, however, NSA did get out of the DES and commercial certification business. Today it certifies security products only for the U.S. Department of Defense (DoD) or other classified and/or sensitive systems. The result of all this is that the fate of DES in the future is in the hands of NIST rather than NSA. At this writing (mid-1990), however, DES was alive and well.[20] It might be noted that while encryption frequently takes place at the Physical Layer (of the OSI Reference Model), it could be employed at any or all of the layers as packet assembly takes place.[21]

As previously noted, a second form of passive threat revolved around traffic-analysis security. If an attacker can read the packet header, then the source and destination of the message is known even when the message is encrypted. When link encryption is employed, however, that possibility is decreased or eliminated. Encryption can limit only the reading of header information and messages. Considerable information can be inferred from traffic analysis itself—the total volume and the amount of traffic entering and leaving selected nodes. Encryption cannot address this issue. One possible countermeasure would be to pad the communications link by generating a continuous stream of random data or ciphertext. An attacker would, therefore, find it difficult to distinguish between usable data flow and noise, thus making it difficult or impossible to count the amount of real traffic. If there is fear concerning an active threat, then a message-authentication procedure can be used.

Active Threats

As might be anticipated, active threats are often thought to be more serious than passive threats because active threats are often designed to alter or to generate spurious data or control signals rather than to simply read the content of those signals. Loss can obviously be caused when the information flow is seriously altered, but whether an active threat is more serious than a passive threat is a function of cost of the harm caused by whatever threat occurs. Stealing trade secrets or national defense secrets, even when no alteration takes place, can turn out to be very costly. In any event, the active threats that are cause for concern include *denial of message service*, *masquerading*, and *message stream modification*.

Keep in mind that active attacks can occur almost anywhere across the communications route: cable, microwave links, satellite channels, routing nodes, host or client computer systems—anywhere. Unless a very large amount of money is available for security, as in a military establishment for example, it is unlikely that extensively guarded physical facilities along an entire route is feasible. In fact, even for military organizations 100 percent coverage is probably impossible. In some way, however, an active threat can only be made if "physical" access is achieved. In this case physical may mean, somewhat metaphorically, access through a terminal hundreds of miles away from the target, or through radio channels also distant from the target. Even active wiretapping—the unauthorized attachment of a device to a communications circuit in order to obtain illegitimate access to data—may not physically require a device spliced into a cable. As might be imagined, preventing active attacks can prove to be very difficult, and the security goal might well be to detect active attacks quickly and recover from any disruption or delays caused by such attacks.

Perhaps the most obvious active threat faced by a communications system is an attack that can destroy or delay most or all messages. In a modern, information-based society, such an occurrence could easily lead to the loss of large sums of money or worse. Such a threat need not even arise as a conscious plot of a gang of terrorists. If a major switching node on a switched network, such as telephone systems, were to go out of service, telephone service could be jeopardized for hours or even days (as happened with AT&T as recently as 1989). Unless there is sufficient redundancy in the switch, it is unlikely that the device will never crash. Consequently, neglecting a system by not providing redundant alternatives can be the source of an active threat. This concept can be expanded to include physical attacks by hostile forces that can have similar results. An example of a somewhat different physical attack on a system was that by Robert Morris with his Worm on Internet in 1987. Perhaps the most important contemporary example is the theft of money by infiltrating electronic funds transfers and/or bank accounting systems. Any activity that can potentially destroy or substantially delay most or all messages constitutes an active threat.

A more subtle approach to active interference with a network is through masquerading. Masquerading is the attempt to gain access to a system by posing as an authorized client or host. In this scenario an attacker poses as an authentic host, switch, router, or similar device in order to communicate with a peer to acquire data or services. Anyone who has ever been around a university knows that students (and sometimes faculty) share user IDs and passwords even when cautioned against the practice. That is the most benign form of masquerading because it is usually not done to damage anyone else. As any university computing center director can attest, however, there are always some people who will willfully destroy what others have built. Another classic example from a university environment is the occasional attempt to access administrative systems to alter grade records. This is sometimes accomplished by simply noting user IDs and passwords staff members have pasted to their terminals as a memory aid (but also as a security breach). The effort, in other words, to masquerade as an authentic user is an old, if not honored, pastime. The effort to make a target system actually believe it is communicating with the desired host or client system, however, requires far more sophistication but is not beyond the technical capabilities of many. Masquerading, as a technique, may be used for either passive or active purposes, but has been described under active threats because the objective is often interventionist in character.

Active threats might also occur through message stream modification. Here an attacker might selectively modify, delete, delay, reorder, and/or duplicate real messages or insert counterfeit messages. Even encrypted messages can be damaged in transit in ways that will not thwart cyclic redundancy check (CRC) error-checking codes in transport packets. As a packet for transmission is formed by the protocol software (see "Concepts of a Layered Architecture" in Chapter 3, and figures 7.5 and 7.6 in Chapter 7), it acquires one or more cyclic redundancy checksums calculated by the sender and recalculated by the receiver. If those checksums are different, then a retransmission of the packet is usually requested. In a similar way, a manipulation detection code (MDC) can be generated on only the plaintext of the message contents prior to encipherment. Doing so may ensure that even if a packet is manipulated so that it is changed but passes the error-correction tests, the actual encipherment of the plaintext will be altered sufficiently to produce a different checksum.[22] The MDC is one method of detecting message-stream modification, and there are several different checksums used for the purpose. The ISO version of this approach is contained in the international standard ISO 8731-2, known as MAA (message authenticator algorithm).[23]

Security Service

A *security service* is an activity or provision of an activity that enhances the security of information systems and an organization's information transfer. In the OSI Reference Model the defined services consist of five groups: confidentiality, authentication, integrity, nonrepudiation, and access control. In a layered communications architecture, such as the OSI Reference Model, security could be built in almost anywhere. The OSI security architecture is more explicit, however, in that it specifies the layers in which specific services are to be provided. The relationship between security services and OSI layers is found in Table 4.1.

Confidentiality or *data confidentiality* guarantees that information is not made available or disclosed to unauthorized individuals, entities, or processes. This service category provides mechanisms that, in general, protect transmitted data from passive attacks. The concept of confidentiality can be applied to an entire message or to fields within a message. The latter case is often called *selective field confidentiality*. Data confidentiality is affected by whether the communications protocols use connection-oriented or connectionless services. A connection-oriented service is one that establishes a virtual connection that appears to the user as an actual end-to-end circuit and is sometimes called a virtual circuit or virtual connection. Contrasted to a connection-oriented service is a connectionless service, which is a class of service that does not establish a virtual or logical

TABLE 4.1. Location of Security Services in OSI Layers

	Security Services					
OSI Layer	*Confidentiality*	*Traffic Flow Confidentiality*	*Authentication*	*Integrity*	*Nonrepudiation*	*Access Control*
Application	Y	Y	Y	Y	Y	Y
Presentation	Y	Y	Y	—	—	—
Session	—	—	—	—	—	—
Transport	Y	—	Y	Y	—	Y
Network	Y	Y	Y	Y	—	Y
Data Link	Y	—	—	—	—	—
Physical	Y	Y	—	—	—	—

TABLE 4.2. Security Services and Mechanisms

	Mechanisms							
Services	*Encryption*	*Digital Signature*	*Access Control*	*Data Integrity*	*Authen-tication*	*Traffic Padding*	*Routing Control*	*Notarization*
Confidentiality	✓	✖	✖	✖	✖	✓	✓	✖
Integrity	✓	✓	✖	✓	✖	✖	✖	✖
Authentication	✓	✓	✖	✖	✓	✖	✖	✖
Access Control	✖	✖	✓	✖	✖	✖	✖	✖
Nonrepudiation	✖	✓	✖	✓	✖	✖	✖	✓

✓ Considered Appropriate ✖ Not Considered Appropriate

connection and does not guarantee that data-units will be delivered or be delivered in the proper order. Connectionless services are flexible, robust, and provide connectionless application support. Connectionless applications are those applications that require routing services but do not require connection-oriented services.

Authentication ensures that a message is genuine, has arrived exactly as it was sent, and came from the stated source. It may also involve verifying an individual's identity, such as a person at a remote terminal or the sender of a message. *Data-origin authentication* is corroboration that the source of data received is as claimed. *Peer-entity authentication* is corroboration that a peer entity in an association is the one claimed. The emphasis in the OSI Reference Model is more explicit than in other contexts in that authentication refers especially to the certainty that the data received comes from the stated source. Data-origin authentication operates in conjunction with connectionless service, whereas peer-entity authentication usual refers to operation with connection-oriented services. In other contexts the idea of authentication might be made synonymous with data integrity, but in the OSI Reference Model, the two are clearly separated and distinct.

Data integrity ensures that data have not been altered or destroyed in an unauthorized manner. The two concepts of data integrity and authentication remain, however, closely allied even within the OSI Reference Model. This alliance extends to the mechanisms used to support the services. Note from Table 4.2 that the same mechanisms apply to both services. Moreover, they are usually required together. Both data integrity and authentication rely heavily on encryption as a primary security mechanism. Just as with authentication, data-integrity services can be applied to the entire message or only to selected fields. Integrity issues vary somewhat depending on whether the message is being transmitted in the context of a connection-oriented or a connectionless service. If it is being used with a connection-oriented protocol, the data-integrity mechanism can be provided with a form of recovery mechanism.

Repudiation is when one of the entities involved in a communication denies or repudiates participation in whole or in part of that communication. The security service defined by the OSI architecture, called *nonrepudiation*, is the precise opposite of repudiation and can be provided in two forms: with proof of origin or with proof of delivery. One of the mechanisms by which these forms of nonrepudiation can be provided is through the use of a digital signature. A digital signature is a number depending on all the bits of a message and also on a secret key. Its correctness can be verified by using a public key (unlike an authenticator, which needs a secret key for its verification). A second mechanism for providing proof of origin or with proof of delivery is through notarization by a trusted third party.

Finally, *access control* can be applied at either the source or destination of a communication or somewhere along the route. Access control protects a network against deliberate saturation by an opponent or unauthorized access to an information service. Access control typically takes place in the application layer but may also be accomplished in the transport or network layers. Sometimes it is desirable to provide protection for a subnetwork by allowing only authorized entities access to it. Access-control services in the transport layer can handle such a problem.

Security Mechanisms

Many of the standard *security mechanisms* were encountered during the preceding discussion of security services. Security mechanisms are operating procedures, hardware and software features, management procedures, and any combinations of these that are designed to detect and prevent either passive or active threats on any component of an information system. Security mechanisms are related to security services in that the mechanisms are the procedures used to implement a security service. The relationship between OSI-defined services and selected mechanisms may be clearly seen in Table 4.2. The service "Confidentiality," for example, can be implemented through the use of encryption, traffic padding, and/or routing control. "Encryption," on the other hand, can be a component of the implementation not only of confidentiality, but also of integrity and authentication services.

The preceding section explored the encryption issue rather extensively. Of all the security mechanisms noted in Table 4.2, encryption and digital signature have the broadest application and provides the greatest degree of security. The primary use of encryption mechanisms is to prevent breaches of confidentiality, integrity, and authenticity. One encryption method is the NIST's DES. It is intended that DES be implemented in hardware rather than simply as free-running software in a computer's main memory. In a communications environment, DES allows conclusive identification of the person using the password and the actual personal computer or terminal being linked to a host. Such a system can provide a high degree of security even on dial-up lines. The data-encryption device for a personal computer is a plug-in board completely encased in epoxy, which is inside ametal box so that the encryption chip cannot be removed.[24] Considerable effort has been expended creating encryption systems for data transmission and storage. Those without the key to the encrypted information cannot access the contents of the data, although the files themselves might be vulnerable.[25]

There are a number of authentication techniques available for network security. The scope of *authentication* in network security can be very wide. When a unit of information (a message, file, or document) is genuine and came from its reputed source, it is said to be *authentic*. Some questions to be asked might include the following:

- Did the source have the authority to issue the unit of information?
- Does a payment correspond to a genuine invoice?
- Is the sender who he/she/it claims to be?

Authentication extends from data entry through the safe arrival of information at its destination.

Data entry is sometimes checked through the use of checksums, a summation of a set of data items for error detection, or a bit more narrowly, a sum of digits or bits used to verify the integrity of data. Cyclic redundancy checks are often used to identify when there have been accidential errors in data transmission. A CRC is an algorithm designed to generate a check field used to guard against errors that may occur in data transmission. The check field is often generated by taking the remainder after dividing all the serialized bits in a block of data by a predetermined binary number. Greater security is often needed, however, and that is the function of systems designed to check data integrity through the use of secret parameters. The ISO has recognized the need for more than one type of authenticator, and this has led to several authenticator algorithms or methods including the Decimal Shift and Add (DSA) and the MAA.

An increasingly important technique for authentication is the digital signature. A digital signature is a number depending on all the bits of a message and also on a secret key. Its correctness can be verified by using a public key (unlike an authenticator, which needs a secret key for verification). While digital signatures are used for authentication, they are also used to implement integrity and nonrepudiation services as well. When used for nonrepudiation, digital signatures may be used in conjunction with notarization, which is the verification (authentication) of a message by a trusted third party similar in logic to classic notarization procedures, although in this context it is normally an automated procedure.

The most common security experience of network end users is access control through the use of passwords. A password is a unique word or string of characters used to authenticate an identity. A programmer, computer operator, or user may be required to submit a password to meet security requirements before gaining access to data. The password is confidential, as opposed to the user identification, which like telephone numbers, is often known to many. An alternative to a password might be a passphrase, which is a phrase used instead of a password to control user access. Unfortunately, password systems can often be circumvented. Closely akin to the use of passwords are questionnaires. A *questionnaire* is a method of identity verification that makes use of information known to the authorized user but is unlikely to be known by others. A common and widely used example is to request the user's grandmother's maiden name. The advantage of the questionnaire is that it uses memorable information. The disadvantage is that it may involve a rather lengthy dialogue.

There are a variety of products that allow identity verification by more esoteric means than those described thus far. It is possible, for example, to design a system using smart cards (credit-card sized cards with at least some memory and circuity apart from the ability to record data), or cards with magnetic strips (such as credit cards) for verification by token, for example. It is also possible to design systems requiring comparisons with file copies of voice, handwritten signatures, fingerprints, and/or retinal patterns. These various technologies all find some use but can be expensive to implement. Before embarking on a security program requiring such techniques, it would be well to do the analyses suggested earlier in this chapter and some careful cost accounting.

A better approach might be to isolate sensitive data and its access on "private" concurrent networks, using an alternative communications protocol along with encryption and call-back techniques. A call-back system can often be implemented in a straightforward fashion. Such systems use either a specialized modem or the computer to break the connection to a user, after the user has properly logged on an application, then call the user back at one or more authorized terminals from which the application might be accessed. Like many other security systems, however, call-back techniques are vulnerable to determined efforts to undermine them. Even advances in related communications technology, such as call forwarding in telephone systems, have implications for security systems.

Network Security Systems

Part of the problem in assessing how to respond to network security needs is in deciding where the network begins and ends. Unfortunately, the common definitions of what constitute networks do not help much. A communications network, it will be recalled, may be defined as the total network of devices and transmission media (radio, cables, et cetera.) necessary to transmit and receive intelligence or a series of points connected by communications channels. A computer network is one or more computers linked with users or each other via a communications network, or a system of interconnected computer systems and terminals. A glance at Figure 4.3 will suggest that the foregoing definitions are too hardware oriented; therefore, a modified definition of an *information network* is necessary. An information network is a series of points connected by communications channels for the purpose of transmitting and receiving intelligence through a consistent protocol stack.

The network depicted in Figure 4.3 is a simplified OSI network consisting of three points: two full open systems and a relay. A full open system may be a normal, general-purpose computer, or it may be a specialized control device. The key in this model is, however, that the network does not end at a modem between the physical medium and the computer but at the Application Layer of the OSI protocol stack. The physical medium may be part of a LAN, a WAN, or a combination of the two. There will be an operating system (OS) for each open system, an OSI protocol stack, and a user program supported by both the OS and the OSI protocol stack. In a similar vein, in an IBM SNA network there will be not only the physical medium plus 3270 devices, but also an appropriate Front End Processor (FEP) with its software, access method software such as VTAM, and a teleprocessing (TP) monitor that actually allows a remote user to do something. The hardware plus the SNA protocol suite to the TP monitor is properly part of the network. Mainframe shops are not often organized following the logic that has just been described, but the description is accurate.

In an OSI network, all security services can be handled in Layer 7

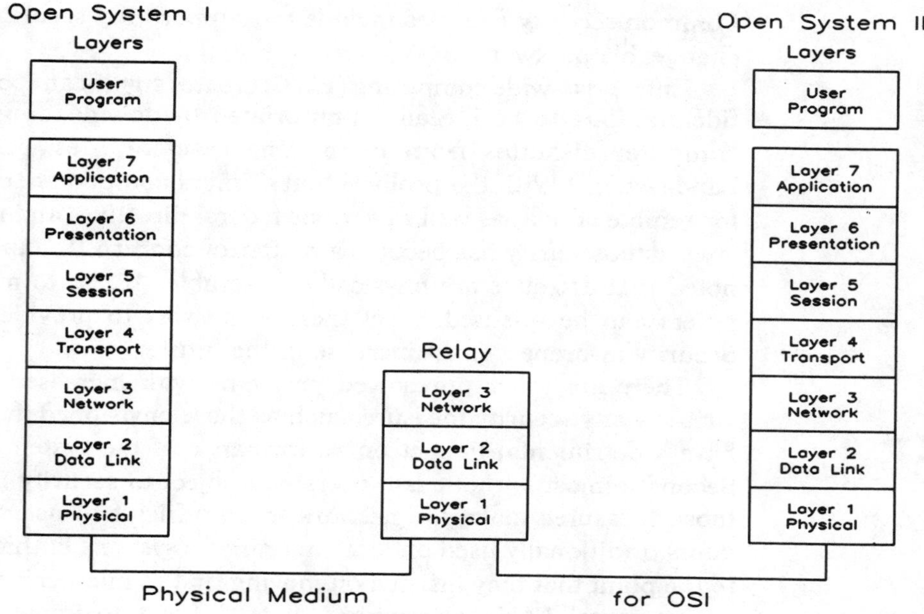

Figure 4.3. OSI Standard Network.

(Application), although, as illustrated in Table 4.1, some security services can be offered at almost all layers of the OSI Reference Model. Information encryption and decryption takes place largely at the Presentation Layer, and the identification and authentication of the intended communications partners take place in the Application Layer, although they can take place in other layers, as well.

The Impact of Security Measures

The lack of information security has become a serious risk in networking in general and is widely discussed in the data processing trade press.[26] Several link vendors are selling systems to control user access to micro and mainframe applications. D. Boyd has suggested that when purchasing a micro–mainframe software package, users should be aware of the available security options.[27] According to Boyd, an adequate package will provide security at both the database level and the terminal or microcomputer level.

Common security facilities include the support of a security log and user-changeable passwords.

Enterprise-wide computing (EWC) creates significant potential for confidential data to be illegally appropriated by downloading it to personal computer diskettes from mainframe resident files, according to H. Landgarten.[28] With the proliferation of microcomputers and the potential for remote access, as well as various federal directives and right-to-privacy laws, data security has become a matter of concern. J. Van der Hoven has noted that diskettes are physically vulnerable. Access to mainframe computers can be misused.[29] Yet there is no way to provide total security. Security awareness must increase in the future.

There are other unresolved problems with increased security. First, virtually any security measure, such as those envisioned in Figure 4.1, will have a detrimental impact on performance of the system being secured. Second, almost without fail, users will object to security measures, since those measures make the network more difficult to use. Security procedures traditionally used on large mainframe systems bothered many users to the point that they insisted on moving first to microcomputers then to a departmental LAN environment. It is difficult to imagine user-friendly security, since security features are designed primarily to keep people out—not make it easier to get in. Yet, as LANs become linked in regional, national, and international networks, it behooves corporations and governments to pay attention to security.

It is difficult to overemphasize the negative side of security systems, since they, in turn, will affect productivity, morale, and even budgetary considerations. Moreover, the ultimate success of security systems requires the cooperation of those using the systems. If users don't take security seriously, then it will be even more difficult to apply successful security measures. The importance of personnel in the security process was underscored in an analysis of the distribution of security budgets when, in mid-1990, *ComputerWorld* reported that "to prevent damaging accidents as well as calculated offenses, most of a company's security budget is spent on educating its personnel."[30] Specifically, *ComputerWorld*'s data suggested that on average 68 percent of a company's security budget is spent on personnel. Although the *ComputerWorld* report is somewhat difficult to interpret because they did not define the meaning of "personnel" or other categories, it nevertheless clearly demonstrates the need for employee compliance in the security process.

Closing the Barn Door

Backup and other operational problems are closely related to the issues of data integrity and security in a large organization. If your data are important to you and your organization, then data should be protected from inadvertent loss or damage as well as from theft or inappropriate change. In a central data processing facility these issues are confronted by regular daily, weekly, monthly, quarterly, and yearly backups; storing the backup tapes in secure locations, and storing backup tape in multiple locations. In a well-run system the absolute loss of data is a rare occurrence. Micro users know, however, that even if they understand all the admonitions about the need for backup, it rarely occurs in the single-user environment. If the mainframe is used as an archival machine for micro-based data, then proper backup and recovery are possible through normal mainframe channels.

Conclusions

Security is important and problems of security should be heeded; however, an excessive concern for security will ensure a certain amount of paranoia on the part of network managers. Some security problems exist because some data may be essential to national security or to the economic well-being of a corporation. Other security issues exist because there are "hackers" (computer enthusiasts given to tinkering) and vandals all around us. Better laws that protect data, as legislation has traditionally protected other property, might be one way to deal with computer network security, although such laws are likely to be only marginally effective. Individuals and organizations have made, are making, and will make enormous, investments in information, and security systems are necessary to protect that investment.

Notes

1. As reported by J. B. Miles, "Government Makes Network Security a Big Business," *Government Computer News*, Oct. 2, 1989, Vol. 8, No. 20, p. 29.
2. Thomas L. Davidson and Clinton E. White, Jr., "How to Improve Network Security," *Infosystems* (June 1983), p. 110. See also T. W. Madron, *Local Area Networks in Large Organizations*, p. 98.

3. Ibid.
4. Robert R. Moeller, *Computer Audit, Control, and Security* (New York: John Wiley, 1989), pp. 353–500.
5. S. Rao Vallabhaneni, *Auditing Computer Security* (New York: John Wiley, 1989), Parts III and IV.
6. Ibid., pp. 57–93.
7. M. Durr, "Ins and Outs of Data Integrity," *Micro Communications*, Vol. 2, No. 1, Jan. 1985, pp. 18–22.
8. These definitions are taken from Vallabhaneni, *Auditing Computer Security*, pp. 57–58.
9. Note John Markoff, "Computer Intruder Is Put on Probation and Fined $10,000," *The New York Times National*, Saturday, May 5, 1990, pp. 1, 9. For detailed background on this case see the following: Eugene H. Spafford, "The Internet Worm: Crisis and Aftermath," *Communications of the ACM*, Vol. 32, No. 6, June 1989, pp. 678–687; Jon A. Rochlis and Mark W. Eichin, "With Microscope and Tweezers: The Worm from MIT's Perspective," *Communications of the ACM*, Vol. 32, No. 6, June 1989, pp. 689–698; and Ted Eisenberg, et al., "The Cornell Commission: On Morris and the Worm," *Communications of the ACM*, Vol. 32, No. 6, June 1989, pp. 706–709. This event also triggered new interest in codes of ethics. See, for example, *Communications of the ACM*, Vol. 32, No. 6, June 1989, pp. 688 (David J. Farber, Chair, DNCRI, DAP, National Science Foundation), 699 (Gary Chapman, Computer Professionals for Social Responsibility), and 710 (Vint Cerf, Internet Activities Board).
10. These particular definitions are from Federal Standard 1037 (FED-STD-1037), *Glossary of Telecommunication Terms*, which, in turn, is based on MIL STD 188–120.
11. For a more complete account, see T. W. Madron, "Just A Reminder: Data Is Priceless," *ComputerWorld*, July 16, 1985.
12. A discussion of this issue as applied to the contemporary trend to move software development from mainframes to high-performance micros may be found in Steven W. Mann, "The Art of Building Computer Programs," *PCToday*, Vol. 4, No. 10, Oct. 1990, pp. 29–34.
13. This list goes beyond, but is based on, Moeller, *Computer Audit, Control, and Security*, p. 371.
14. As reported by Dave Powell, "Fighting Network Infection," *Networking Management*, Vol. 7, No. 9, Sept. 1989, pp. 38ff. (8 pages).
15. Ibid.

16. This section loosely follows William Stallings, "A Network Security Primer," *ComputerWorld,* Vol. 24, Jan. 29, 1990, pp. 63–66, 70. Stallings piece was also reprinted in *Datapro Reports on Information Security* (Delran, NJ: McGraw-Hill, 1990), Vol. 2, IS35-110-101 through IS35-110-107.

17. For an interesting, more-or-less popular account of a serious "passive" threat, yet one that was tracked down, see Clifford Stoll, *The Cuckoo's Egg: Tracking a Spy Through the Maze of Computer Espionage* (New York: Doubleday, 1989).

18. W. Diffie and M. E. Hellman, "New Directions in Cryptography," *Transactions of the IEEE on Information Theory,* IT-22, No. 6, Nov. 1976, pp. 644–654.

19. See Chapter 8 in D. W. Davies and W. L. Price, *Security for Computer Networks,* 2nd Edition (Chichester, UK: John Wiley & Sons, 1989) for a more detailed description of how key systems operate. For an applied approach to cryption algorithms, see Rick Grehan, "Cloak and Data," *Byte,* Vol. 15, No. 6, June 1990, pp. 311ff.

20. For the relevant publications see "Data Encryption Standard," *Federal Information Processing Standard (FIPS) Publication 46,* Jan. 15, 1977, also published as *American National Standard Data Encryption Algorithm,* American National Standards Institute, Inc., Dec. 30, 1980, and supplemented with "DES Modes of Operation," *Federal Information Processing Standard (FIPS) Publication 81,* Dec. 2, 1980; "Telecommunications: Interoperability and Security Requirements for Use of the Data Encryption Standard in the Physical Layer of Data Communications," *Federal Standard of the General Services Administration,* Aug. 3, 1983, FED-STD-1026; "Telecommunications: General Security Requirements for Equipment Using the Data Encryption Standard," *Federal Standard of the General Services Administration,* April 14, 1982, FED-STD-1027; and "Telecommunications: Interoperability and Security Requirements for Use of the Data Encryption Standard with CCITT Group 3 Facsimile Equipment," *Federal Standard of the General Services Administration,* April 4, 1985, FED-STD-1028.

21. For a recent applied description of DES in which there is C code for doing encryption and decryption, see Al Stevens, "Hacks, Spooks, and Data Encryption," *Dr. Dobbs Journal,* Vol. 15, No. 9, Sept. 1990, pp. 127ff. For an explanation of DES see Asael Dror, *Byte,* Vol. 14, No. 6, June 1989, pp. 267ff.

22. See Davies and Price, *Security for Computer Networks,* pp. 123–125.

23. *Banking — Approved Algorithms for Message Authentication Part 2: Message Authenticator Algorithm,* International Standard ISO 8731-2, International Organization for Standardization, Geneva, 1987.

24. H. Landgarten, "Beware of Security Risks when Implementing Micro–Mainframe Links," *Data Management,* Vol. 23, No. 4, April 1985, pp. 16–18.

25. Madron, p. 99.

26. Security discussions have been taking place for some time. Cf. Anon. "DP Fears for Data Security Risk from PC," *ComputerWorld Australia,* Vol. 7, No. 18, Nov. 2, 1984, p. 61; and Anon., "Controlling Micro Links," *Computer Decisions,* Vol. 16, No. 11, Sept. 1984, p. 50. The concern for security has been increasing at a substantial rate as is evidenced in the trade press and in other citations in this chapter.

27. D. Boyd, "Micro-Mainframe Links Pose Array of Security Risks," *ComputerWorld,* Vol. 18, No. 51, Dec. 17, 1984, pp. 41, 48.

28. Landgarten, "Beware of Security Risks . . ." pp. 16–18.

29. J. Van der Hoven and D. Grey, "The Growing Need for Security in Automated Offices," *Computing Canada,* Fall 1984, pp. 27–28, 32–33.

30. "Trends," *ComputerWorld,* Aug. 5, 1990, p. 114.

CHAPTER 5

LAN Technology in Enterprise-Wide Computing

The growth of local area networks (LANs) in the mid-1980s helped shift thinking from computers *qua* computers to the way in which computers communicate and why. There are many different kinds of LANs, having different implications for Enterprise-Wide Computing (EWC). This chapter will review some of the technology associated with LANs and attempt to show what a LAN is and what it does. This discussion will lay the foundation for later analyses of the role of LANs in the EWC connection. Local Area Networks are particularly important because many workstations will be connected to a LAN as the first stage in a distributed networking and computing environment.

When IBM entered the LAN market back in the mid-1980s it was passingly thought that some of the disarray would disappear. Similarly, the adoption of LAN standards, it was hoped, would bring order out of chaos. The former did not happen because IBM has not been able to dominate LAN technology or sales. The adoption of IEEE 802 standards helped, but the standards process is slower than technological growth. Consequently, battle lines continue to be drawn over four major issues:

1. Access methods (Carrier Sense Multiple Access/Collision Detection [CSMA/CD] token passing, or neither).
2. Bandwidth (how fast or how much data can pass).
3. Broadband versus baseband (with telephony as a slow third).
4. Physical medium or cable plant (coaxial or twisted pair, as a starting oversimplification).

LANs—What Are They?

In Chapter 3 (pp. 51–52) we offered a preliminary definition of local area networks that suggested that they were networks that (1) cover a limited geographical area; (2) require no central node or processor;[1] (3) provide intrafacility internal exchange of voice, computer data, word processing facsimile, video conferencing, video broadcasting, telemetry, and other forms of electronic messaging;[2] and/or (4) are designed for sharing data among single-user workstations.[3] These attempts at defining LAN failed to recognize (except, perhaps, number 3) the potentials inherent in a networking concept that assumes most of the nodes to be peers of one another. A local area network must be *local* in geographic scope, although the term "local" might mean anything from a single office to a large building to a multi-building educational or industrial campus. One clear attribute of a LAN, however, is connectivity—the ability for any given point (node, connection) to communicate with any other point.

It is clear that there is currently no precise and commonly accepted definition of a LAN. One good summary attempt to describe LANs was provided by the IEEE 802 standards committee in 1982.[4] The Institute of Electrical and Electronics Engineers (IEEE) characterization of a LAN was conveniently summarized in the widely quoted Datapro *EDP Solutions*.[5] The attempt to define the meaning of "local area network" closely follows Datapro's summary, although some modifications have been made. According to the IEEE 802 committee, "A Local Network is a data communications system which allows a number of independent devices to communicate with each other." A LAN can be further characterized as follows:

- Intrainstitutional, privately owned, user administered, and not subject to FCC regulation. Excluded from this are common-carrier facilities, including both public telephone systems and commercial cable television (CATV) systems.

- Integrated through interconnection by a continuous structural medium. Multiple services may operate on a single set of cabling.
- Capable of providing full connectivity.
- Supportive of both low-speed and high-speed data communications. Local Area Networks are not subject to speed limitations imposed by traditional common-carrier facilities and can be designed to support devices ranging in speed from 75 bps (bits per second) based on almost any technology to about 140 Mbps (Mega [million] bits per second) for commercially available fiber-optic LANs.
- Commercially available (off-the-shelf). The LAN market is still volatile, notwithstanding IBM's standards movement and the LAN offerings of major manufacturers, and many systems are still custom designed. Even announced products may still be in beta-test. Since LAN is as much a concept as a product, the term "commercially available" should be taken to mean that the components for the LAN that provide device connections to a physical medium such as a CATV system are commercially available.

These are the characteristics that make LANs attractive to large and small organizations. For large organizations the realization that much computing takes place close to the source of computing power was an important but not necessarily overwhelming reason for LANs. Xerox, an early leader in LAN development (and the inventors of Ethernet), found in one study that as much as 80 percent of all data processing requirements take place within 200 feet of the host computer, and an additional 10 percent are satisfied by resources within a half mile.[6] While that finding was and is widely reported, it is useful primarily as marketing information rather than as the driving force behind the deployment of LANs, even in large organizations. Further, the Xerox study is inapplicable in small organizations where LANs provide the only information-processing environment.

The Uniqueness of LAN

Local area networks are unique because they are useful to organizations: They simplify social processes. Global networks were implemented to make more cost-effective use of computers. Local area networks are implemented to make more cost-effective use of people. Connectivity is the driving concept behind LANs in a manner unknown to global networks. Local area networks are a recognition of the need for people to use data and, as a byproduct, to pass data from one person to another.

One key to the interest in LANs is that those who govern large organizations have recognized that "organization" implies social interaction. Computers do not run organizations, people do. Computers do not make decisions, people do. Computers, no matter how smart, assist people in running organizations. Since an organization is primarily a social process, it will operate most efficiently when decision-assisting tools are available to the people who populate it. This means that the people who use computing in an organization do not do so as isolated hermits but as social beings engaged in commerce and conversation.

Many different computing facilities have been introduced into the organizational milieu: microcomputers, terminals, intelligent copiers, large computers, small computers. Yet an empty computer is like an empty mind—of little or no use to anyone, including its owner. If each computer facility must be filled anew, by hand, then work is made less, not more efficient. In the developing information age it is important that technology assist people to reduce the amount of information to manageable levels and to improve the quality of that information. In an organizational context, networks provide the means for allowing the available computing power to be used to its most complete extent.

LANs for Organizational Needs

In the first edition of this book there was a distinction made between *general purpose or micro-based LANs*, and another discussion of *hybrid LANs*. Those characterizations are no longer truly necessary, although the issues they posed still need clarification. The original dichotomy was established between those LANs that supported thousands of connections—provided low-speed (asynchronous, RS-232-C support) access as well as high-speed access—and those that were designed primarily to connect micros. Even today, to the uninitiated, LAN means only those networks that link microcomputers. Yet, as is implied in Figure 5.1, LAN technology has gone far beyond these simple distinctions.

General-purpose LANs were originally conceived as those produced by manufacturers such as Sytek, Inc., Ungermann-Bass, Bridge Communications, and others that provide LANs using several different media but consisting primarily of terminal servers to which devices are attached for

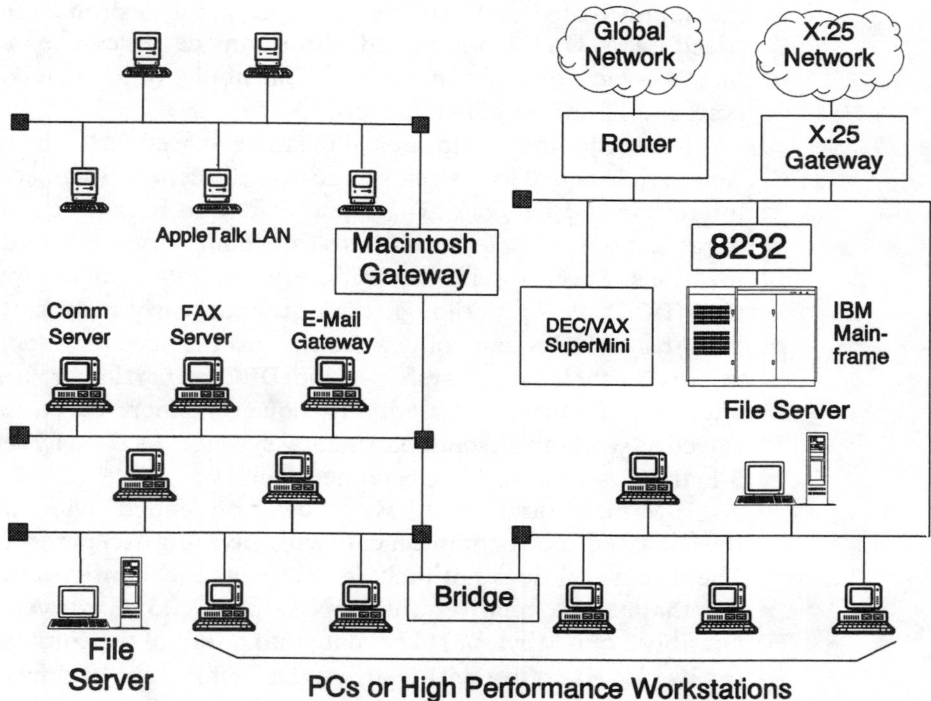

Figure 5.1. LAN Connectivity.

asynchronous, RS-232-C communications. This approach, which was almost the only viable one in the early 1980s, allows a variety of dumb terminals and micros to communicate primarily (although not excusively since any node can address any other node) with a multiuser system. If that multiuser system was an IBM-type mainframe, then it was also necessary to have an asynchronous communications front end processor (FEP) attached to the computer, as is still necessary for an System Network Architecture (SNA) network (see Figure 5.1). All of this was costly, to say the least, but coupled with a general-purpose communications medium, such as a broadband CATV system, it provided a level of connectivity previously unattainable. It is still frequently useful to be able to communicate over a LAN with asynchronous devices, but the options have grown immensely. The disadvantage of such an approach is that data communications is typically limited to 9.6 Kb/s or 19.2 Kb/s and they do not support most of the sophisticated end user services that are a desirable feature of micro-based LANs. On the other hand, almost any device can be made to communicate asynchronously, and without the ability to do so, a communications system will not be fully connective.

The earlier manifestations of the micro-based LANs, by way of contrast, were not designed to provide connectivity except to a file server and to other micros on the network. This approach soon became a problem in large organizations, although that is still the configuration found in small organizations. Several manufacturers, especially Digital Equipment Corporation (DEC), Wang (although Wang was an early manufacturer of broadband-based LANs), and others quickly saw the need for attaching more than micros to their larger systems, and DEC in particular, became a strong advocate of Ethernet. Essentially, however, micro-based LANs were conceived as work-group or departmental systems. As is easily seen from Figure 5.1, the possibilities have become much broader.

IBM mainframes still have to be "front-ended" with something, since they do not directly communicate with anything except through "channels." The discussion does not include S/370 channel configuration; suffice it to say that it is a relatively high-speed path (1.5 Mbytes/s, 3 Mbytes/s, or possibly 5 or 6 Mbytes/s) to get data into or out of the computer. A 37xx FEP (or its cloned equivalent) is an expensive machine and has never been an ideal means for communicating with the mainframe, except for SNA connectivity with 3270 display systems and related communications. In 1988 IBM introduced the 8232 LAN controller, which was originally an industrial strength 80286 microcomputer with a mainframe channel interface. Any of IBM's microcomputer LAN boards or selected third-party Ethernet boards can be inserted into the 8232. The cost of an 8232 is but a fraction of the cost of an FEP. Combined with software running under VM or MVS (IBM mainframe operating systems) this connection provides high-speed access as directly as possible to a LAN.

Terminal servers also continue to play a role and will continue to do so until asynchronous devices disappear—a possibility that was predicted a few years ago but has proven to be false in recent years. Although in principle any IEEE standard LAN can function in such an environment, products were most widely available for 802.3 (Ethernet). In Figure 5.1 the router implies connectivity with Open System Interconnection (OSI) or Transport Control Protocol/Internet Protocol (TCP/IP) global networks, as does the X.25 gateway. A number of other possibilities exist for routing, gatewaying, or bridging to other networks as well. A VAX can be plugged (with an appropriate interface board) directly into the Ethernet, as can a number of other devices. In other words, it is now possible to use a LAN as a front-end to a variety of devices, and at the same time, use it as a micro-based system with micros and their associated servers. The technologies of the general-purpose and the micro-based LANs are rapidly converging and for a number of purposes have already done so.

The "gotcha" in all this is the paucity of good, reliable network-operating-environment software to make everything work smoothly and effectively. As late as 1989, in order to have everything depicted in Figure 5.1 communicate with everything else, it was necessary to run TCP/IP protocols over the LAN to provide a "real" system. The reason for this is that DEC wants their customers to run DECNet, IBM wants to use proprietary software, and the micro-based network operating systems (NOSs) manufacturers were, at the end of the 1980s, just coming to recognize the need to support micro-link protocols beyond what they had produced. While the entire environment can and should come together using TCP/IP, it leaves something to be desired from the standpoint of user interaction. By 1989, however, and clearly into the 1990s, manufacturers such as Novell and Banyan were clearly promoting their NOSs as the basis for enterprise-wide computing (EWC). They positioned themselves, both from a marketing and technical perspective, to become EWC systems.

Services and Servers

A service is often delivered through a server. The term has been widely used and accepted in the context of LANs, although it is an appropriate concept in any network environment. A server contains the hardware, and at least part of the software, necessary to produce the service. Servers include print servers, file servers, communications servers, and others. Servers usually operate at some point remote from the end user and are designed for multiuser access to expensive, complicated, or infrequently used services. Services might also include processes, software, or hardware other than servers, such as support for specialized terminal emulations in a LAN-to-mainframe link.

File and Print Servers

File and print servers were among LANs' original enticements. The servers allowed multiple users to access expensive peripherals and to maintain common databases. Added-value services, such as electronic mail were an outgrowth of file serving. Electronic mail, however, can be implemented in a completely distributed environment, although it is often accomplished in a more straightforward fashion if common file servers are available. As the cost of high-capacity hard disks and quality printers has declined, however, the emphasis has moved to the issue of common database systems and more exotic or expensive peripherals, such as large plotters or other devices. What is true of LANs is even more true of the capabilities available on large mainframe computers.

In one sense mainframe and large minicomputers constitute the ultimate in high performance file and printer servers. High-speed high-quality laser printing is frequently available, and the corporate database is accessible. If the organization's network is large, then a corporate-wide electronic mail system may be possible only through the central computer. In these contexts, the mainframe acts as a big peripheral to the micro. File servers on either a LAN or a WAN can also be used as archival devices for micros, and used in this manner they are, indeed, microcomputer peripherals. On the other hand, micros as target nodes on a large network provide distribution points for reports or other information the organization deems necessary for its proper operation. Because data can be extracted from the corporate database, however, the issue of data-transfer integrity must be confronted.

An important distinction between LANs and multiuser computer systems that must be clearly understood is that, in a micro-based LAN, actual processing is distributed out to users' workstations. With a multiuser computer environment, however, processing is centralized at the multiuser system. This is a very important distinction for some of the reasons already cited. It is also an important distinction because of the increasing power of file servers. When micro-based LANs were introduced in the early 1980s, file servers were typically just another machine of the same variety as the workstations. This meant that there was a major roadblock to increasing the performance of the LAN. Almost from the beginning the data rates of even the slowest LAN technology were faster than the access rates of the hard-disk drives supported by the servers. Moreover, micros designed as single-user devices were pressed into multiuser service, a fact that also degraded performance.

The problems just noted have resulted in a search for better, faster computers to be used as file servers. Because of the relatively high cost of even small minicomputers, the search has usually been directed toward improving micro technology, machines based on Intel's 80386 or 80486 processors. That approach is changing, however, as a by-product of major computer manufacturers, such as DEC, IBM, Hewlett-Packard, Data General, and others who have recognized the market demand for LANs as a method for delivering multiuser services at low cost and the development of relatively inexpensive multiuser minicomputers. Virtually all the major minicomputer manufacturers, plus IBM, now support Ethernet, and several support IBM's Token Ring. As noted, there were some holdouts with respect to Ethernet, and there are still concerns about Token Ring, but it is becoming increasingly clear that for a manufacturer to continue selling its wares, it must support the major LAN systems. The basic LAN technologies to support are those specified by the various standards organizations: IEEE in the United States and the International Organization for Standardization (ISO) in Europe. In both cases this means the IEEE 802 LAN standards.

Getting 802.3/Ethernet or 802.5/Token Ring cards for a few micros does not, however, make a network. An additional item of software is also required: a NOS. The NOS brings the LAN environment together so that it can actually be used for something useful. Suffice it to say at this point that the NOSs commercially available are becoming better all the time and somewhat lower level (or more primitive, depending on one's point of view) network operating environments, such as TCP/IP-based software, are available.

Gateways and Bridges

Because most LANs operate within the context of larger networks, and because in large organizations several or many departmental LANs may have to communicate with one another, gateways and bridges have been manufactured. Related to gateways and bridges are communication servers that provide some specialized access to the LAN, such as terminal servers supporting remote access or dumb terminals. Unfortunately these two terms—gateways and bridges—are used with great imprecision in many trade journals and computer magazines. It has become reasonably common, however, to distinguish between the two, and the definitions that follow will be used consistently in this book. A "gateway" consists of the hardware and software necessary for two technologically *different* networks to communicate with one another. A LAN is linked to a WAN, for example, through a gateway.

In contrast to a gateway, a "bridge" is used to link to technologically *similar* networks to one another. Two Ethernets, for example, would be linked with a bridge rather than a gateway. Both gateways and bridges are necessary to expand connectivity and to allow people to communicate with one another or with network resources not located on the LAN of which one is a primary member. If all networks being linked use the same NOS, such as Novell's Netware, the use of gateways and bridges may be quite simple—at least from the end user's perspective. If different NOSs are being used, or if different network architectures are being used, the bridges or gateways may become complicated both technically and from a user's perspective.

Let me hasten to one or two or several caveats about the distinction between gateways and bridges. First, the issue of what is technologically similar or different is more apparent than real. Part of the reason for this lies in the fact that networks can be defined in terms of hardware or software or a combinatin of the two. Chapter 2 discussed the OSI protocol stack, which is a layered network architecture. Regardless of hardware differences among several networks, and regardless of the base protocols of those networks (Ethernet and X.25, for example), if those networks all use the same layered protocol stack, it is possible to have bridging between the same layer on two electrically and mechanically dissimilar networks. Likewise, the IEEE 802 committee has defined a "MAC layer bridge" where the Media Access Control (MAC) sublayer of the OSI Data-Link Layer is the point at which bridging can take place between or among IEEE standard networks. An 802.5 Token Ring network, therefore, could be *bridged*, not *gatewayed*, to an 802.3 (CSMA/CD, Ethernet) network, thus obviating a statement to the contrary made in the previous paragraph. In other words, in a network premissed on a layered architecture, if control for the bridging mechanism takes place in layer *n*, then lower layers need not be the same or similar in the networks being bridged. Bridging at the electro/mechanical level requires electro/mechanical equivalence; bridging at the MAC sublayer requires MAC equivalence; bridging at the OSI Network Layer requires Network Layer equivalence. Otherwise gateways will be required, since in gateways *protocol conversion* takes place.

FAX Servers

The parent of this book, as well as other books I have written concerning LANs, did not addressed specialized servers and services that are just becoming popular in the early 1990s. An example of such a service is the ability for users of a LAN or other EWC to send a facsimile (FAX) without either having a FAX machine in their office or physically going to a FAX machine somewhere on the premises. Because of increasing demand for such a service, the marketplace in the United States has responded with an increasing number of products designed to provide both incoming and outgong FAX capabilities generated from a FAX server on a LAN or from a mini or mainframe central computer system. The typical FAX machine is a device consisting of three basic components—an image scanner, a FAX modem, and a printer—often integrated in a single unit with each FAX file treated as a cohesive image (rather than character data).[7] It should be noted that FAX technology is essentially telephone oriented. Most of the LAN/FAX products, therefore, are designed to get a FAX sent over the telephone system from a LAN rather than directly over the LAN between two LAN addresses. A bit more will be said of this later.

There are at least four server/service issues of which it is important to be aware:

- Multiuser, LAN-based FAX servers;
- Mainframe-based transaction-processing servers;
- Value-added network FAX services; and
- Application-based FAX services.

Two metaphors are used to describe FAX operations and around which FAX software is designed: FAX as printer and FAX as EMail (electronic mail). This means that, depending on the manufacturer, the FAX software and hardware may appear as a peculiar kind of printer, or it may appear as a specialized kind of Email. *Application-based* FAX services are those that allow an end user to send a FAX from within an application program, such as a word processor or spreadsheet. In this case the printer metaphor is usually operative and allows the user to write a memo, for example, and simply print it to the FAX board. The FAX as EMail metaphor conceives of FAX as a simple message-transfer system between two or more people. If no other needs exist, then an EMail service may be more cost-effective. A brief comparison between EMail and FAX may be seen in Table 5.1.

The LAN-based FAX has the same components as the standalone FAX machine, but they may be distributed across the network. The server consists of a FAX-board, which contains the FAX modem, perhaps an independent graphics processor to speed up the process and whatever software is necessary to drive the device. The FAX-board may be placed in a worksta-

TABLE 5.1. FAX Versus EMail

EMail	*FAX*
Character/Text Based	Image/Graphics Based
Resource Conservative	Resource Intensive
May Reduce Use of Paper	May Encourage/Increase Use of Paper
Sent to Individual Addresses	Often Sent to General Delivery
Must Have EMail Address	Must Have Telephone Number

tion, in the main LAN file server, or in a dedicated microcomputer acting as a FAX server. All of these solutions imply cost considerations, but the objective should be the best cost/reliability/convenience performance. Users may access FAX services through a scanner, the local EMail, some word processors, or perhaps by designating an ASCII file for transmission. For incoming FAXs, distribution to specific network users (addresses) is problematic, since good and standardized rerouting mechanisms do not exist.

In a mainframe environment the printer metaphor is the normal approach. Frequently the FAX device in an IBM mainframe system will appear to be a 3770 remote job entry (RJE) terminal. Consequently, any application that can print to such a printer can print to the FAX and can be, therefore, sent to wherever. Links can be established to a 3x74 cluster controller, an FEP, or a LAN. The FAX server is typically an AT class microcomputer containing the appropriate interface cards and software and is plugged into the telephone system. Many such systems are outgoing only, although IBM itself markets a receive/send version of this product for systems running with SNA. With the mainframe server the user interface resides in the mainframe, but the communications hardware and software may still reside elsewhere in a modified and/or dedicated microcomputer. A value-added network FAX service, sponsored by common carriers such as AT&T, MCI, and U.S. Sprint, or by value-added network providers such as CompuServe or GE Information Services, supply a variety of FAX services. These services include broadcast FAX, delayed delivery to ensure off-peak pricing, support for graphics and corporate logos, and EMail and binary-file transfers. These services are essentially a service bureau approach to mainframe-style FAXing and normally include send-only services.

There are some FAX-server issues to be considered in setting up a network-based FAX system. These issues include at least the following:

- Standards.
- Distribution/routing of incoming FAXs.
- Security for the incoming documents.
- The implications of integrating FAX into an electronic communications environment.

World FAX standards follow the recommendations of the International Telegraph and Telephone Consultative Committee (CCITT). Current FAX equipment adheres to standards set in 1981 by Study Group XIV of the CCITT. It was the adoption of this standard that led to the enormous growth in FAX sales over the last few years. The standards address three primary machine groups: I, II, and III, although Group III has superseded other machine groups. The standards include specifications for the direction of scanning; the size of the scan line; the number of scan lines per millimeter; and phasing, sychronization, and modulation techniques. Group III FAXs support grayscale images, encoding an average of 16 gradations between black and white. Significant limitations for Group III FAXs include both resolution and transmission speed, which are being addressed by both a proposed new Group IV standard as well as an enhanced Group III standard. Group IV has been proposed to define high-resolution digital equipment operating in the range of 56 Kb/s, with resolution at least as fine as 240 x 240 "lines per inch (lpi)."

The most difficult of the problems facing the acceptance of multiuser FAX use is the lack of routing standards for incoming FAXs. Without a routing standard, multiuser FAX will have limited marketability. The current standards for FAX have been developed by the CCITT and are limited primarily to a definition of the graphics file to which a FAX document is translated and to the modem standard to be used to transmit and receive that file. More comprehensive standards are being considered and suggested, however, including TR.29 from the Telecommunications Industry Association, which will include additional standards for an applications programming interface (API), binary-file transfer (BFT), FAX DCE/DTE control, high-resolution Group III, high-speed Group III, and *FAX routing*. The routing project is designated ANSI Project 2731. The purposes of Project 2731 are to explore and define the content of routing address information, to provide a communications or computer system with the information necessary for directing an incoming FAX message to a specific user, and to work with unmodified existing Group III FAX machine technology to tranmist the required routing information.

In the meantime, however, the only methods for routing messages after initial receipt, apart from printing and hand delivery, or manual notification, are the use of direct inward dialing (DID), dual-tone multifrequency decoding (DTMF), or Optical Character Reader (OCR) techniques. The first two require reliance on the local telephone system to accomplish the addressing. In the case of DTMF, the sender must manually enter a network address, which is then converted from DTMF to a real address that can be used to deposit the fax into the recipients "mailbox." There is, however, weak international support for DTMF: It compels the cumbersome entry of alpha information, it requires some manual intervention with existing equipment, and it necessitates hardware modifications for the receiver. With DID the FAX server/gateway converts DID routing information into a network address and then deposits the FAX file into the recipient's mailbox. The advantage of DID is that it is an existing standard technology. The great disadvantage for this purpose, however, is that it requires the fairly costly DID service for the receiver, requires additional costly hardware, and is not available internationally. The third method may require reading a network address from a specific location on a cover sheet with the use of OCR software, often resulting in high error rates, high cost for receiver, and requirements for user training and a standardized cover sheet. The result of all this is that most LAN FAX server systems, as of this writing, require manual routing and distribution of either printed or electronic FAXs, just as in the case of a standard FAX machine.

Not only is routing received FAXs problematic, so also is the security of the transmitted document. The need for essentially manual methods for the distribution of received FAXs means that those documents may be handled by several people between sender and receiver. On a LAN, even when the FAX files simply reside on a file server and are picked up by the end receiver, they are available for anyone to read. Encryption schemes are probably the ultimate answer to FAX security, but there are operational issues involved there, as well. Presently, whether an incoming FAX comes to a standalone FAX machine or to a multiuser FAX server, a FAXed document must be considered a "public" document. Like routing, FAX security needs some attention from standards organizations as well as an operational overview by those using FAX services.

In order to integrate FAX into EWC there are some services that should be the goal of the project. Those services should include at least the following:

- FAX-to-FAX (send/receive) communications.
- PC-to-FAX (may be send only) communications.

- EMail-to-FAX (ideally, send/receive) communications. (Related to EMail is the general problem of distribution of FAXed documents to end users).
- Broadcast FAX (send only) communications.
- The ability to transmit graphics without rerouting to additional scanning devices—onced scanned always scanned.

LAN Access Methods—Collision Avoidance or Detection?

A LAN configured with either a bus or a ring topology needs a single cable, or possibly two (one for forward, the other for reverse signals), to carry all messages. This means that on a well-used system more than one node will usually be attempting to get a message on the cable at the same time. The manner in which access to the cable is gained then becomes important for the LAN. Two primary methods are used to control access: CSMA/CD and token passing. The IEEE 802 Committee (Local Area Networks) has proposed standards for both access methods. The 802.3 standard addresses CSMA/CD;[8] 802.4 deals with the token bus;[9] and 802.5 with the token ring.[10] The 802.3 standard is almost identical with Ethernet; 802.4 specifies token passing on a bus topology; and 802.5 with token passing on a ring topology.

Collisions are assumed to be a normal operational occurrence in CSMA/CD systems. The most frequently used analogy is the comparison of a CSMA/CD-based LAN with a group discussion. In such a discussion each member of the group listens for an opportunity to be heard. On some occasions, however, two or more members will attempt to speak at the same time with the result that other members will hear only partial messages. Each network device in a CSMA/CD-based LAN listens all the time but defers transmitting if the cable is in use. In a highly loaded CSMA/CD network the periods of silence may be short. The consequence of short periods of silence is that several devices may attempt to transmit at the same time, resulting in collisions. Large numbers of collisions will result in lower network throughput since many retransmissions will have to take place.

Token passing, which was originally used for ring topologies, became available on general-purpose (rather than proprietary) systems using bus structures in 1983. A "token" simply designates the location "of the poll on a distributed polling list."[11] Each network device must be polled, and as that polling is done each station has an opportunity to transmit. The consequence is that there can be no collisions. Polling need not take place in a centralized fashion because each station can pass on the token following a transmission. Because there is no collision detection (and no collisions) the capacity of a token-passing system may be accurately calculated, although a token-passing scheme relies on all devices being serially polled, which implies its own set of problems.

Both CSMA/CD and token-passing systems have advantages and disadvantages. For the potential consumer of LAN products, however, the issue between the two schemes is used in marketing efforts. With appropriate network management techniques, either system will provide adequate access. Until 1983 it was not even possible to obtain token passing on broadband systems, and even then the offerings were limited. From a managerial perspective—and this will not be a universally accepted statement—the issue is not so much whether CSMA/CD is better/worse than token passing, but will the design philosophy of the LAN vendor meet the system needs of the buyer? At this writing neither system was clearly superior to the other, although proponents of the two systems would deny that fact.

Not long ago an acquaintance approached me to discuss the LAN I was attempting to implement. The first question was, "How does that system handle collisions and access?" I quickly replied that it used CSMA/CD. "I really prefer token passing," the acquaintance commented. My friend missed a significant point: Regardless of which access method is technically superior, no one makes decisions based on such issues. Rather, decisions are made—and should be made—based on what currently available products will meet user needs.

As the remainder of this chapter is read, please bear in mind that the relevant question is not "What networking scheme do I like?" but "What problems do I need to solve?"[12] Unfortunately the battle is still joined in technical terms, and it is important to understand enough of those terms to place them in the proper perspective. The remainder of this chapter, therefore, will be devoted to a clarification of media issues.

Bandwidth

Bandwidth is the range of frequencies assigned to a channel or system. It is the difference, expressed in Hertz (cycles), between the highest and lowest frequencies of a band. The wider the bandwidth the faster data can flow through the channel, or, alternatively, the more data can flow through the channel. The capacity of a channel, which dictates the information rate, is in part dependent on the bandwidth available to it, although the technological ability to use the bandwidth can also limit the capacity. Bandwidth is measured in Hertz (Hz), the number of cycles supported per second. Analog telephone systems, for example, have a restricted bandwidth (about 3,000 Hz) and often suffer from certain technical mandates, such as channel nonlinearities. These combine to require the use of advanced technology modems employing extensive coding and adaptive-equalization to effect even moderate data transmission rates (that is, up to 56-64 kb/s) with cost-effective devices. A more important limitation of telephone systems—even modern digital Private Branch eXchanges (PBXs)—are the number of concurrent circuits or sessions that can be economically supported—usually less than 1,000. By way of contrast, a broadband (CATV) system can range from a bandwidth of 6 MHz (a single television channel) to 300 or 400 MHz (the entire CATV spectrum), providing very great capacity, and resulting in possible data-rate ranges from very low rates to the large megabit range. This bandwidth can also provide for thousands of concurrent sessions.

The immediate management issue, however, is not bandwidth, but how many devices may be connected to a given system running at what data rate. If the network is being designed to directly support users sitting at terminals, a reasonable requirement is that each session be capable of communicating at 9.6 Kbps and that the number of potential connections be at least the maximum number of potential users, plus computer or device ports expected over some appropriate period of future time. If a LAN vendor can demonstrate the ability to meet those requirements, then, in a managerial sense, bandwidth is a moot issue. Depending on the specific LAN involved, the number of connections may range from some small number (about 64) to some large number in the tens of thousands.

Broadband, Baseband, and Telephony

Although there are a number of architectures currently being marketed, which claim to be the last word in LANs, for a LAN capable of spanning the floors of a large high-rise, or the many buildings of a campus facility, only two contenders are technologically feasible: broadband and telephony. Baseband systems are available for more restricted circumstances and for medium-sized buildings because baseband systems are typically limited and do not normally extend beyond about two kilometers. Baseband and broadband are frequently contrasted with one another, while telephone technology represents a considerably different concept.

Broadband LANs

Broadband systems transmit data, voice, and video signals through the use of CATV technology and components. Broadband is a communications medium using a channel having a bandwidth characterized by high data-transmission rates. Like telephone technology, CATV is a general-purpose technology that can be used by, but is not restricted to, LANs. The CATV system can be constructed with off-the-shelf components using a mature technology.

Any broadband system requires two channels on which data must move. An "outbound" channel is used for traffic leaving the "headend," and an "inbound" channel is used for traffic directed to the headend. The headend of the system is simply a signal processor that takes an inbound signal and upconverts it to an outbound channel. A device transmits on the inbound channel and receives on an outbound channel. Both channels can reside on a single cable or can, like Wang's broadband system, use two physical cables—one for inbound traffic, the other for outbound traffic.

Cable television systems operate with either a 300 MHz or 400 MHz spectrum divided into 39 to 58 television channels of 6 MHz each. The spectrum is organized in a subsplit, midsplit, or highsplit system. The "split" refers to the placement of the "guard-band" in the spectrum. The guard-band is a range of frequencies that divides the forward and return channels of the system and is a required dividing line. This organization is illustrated in Figure 5.2.

The original CATV systems, and most of those used for commercial television transmission, use a subsplit scheme. The reason should be obvious: A commercial operator makes money by transmitting entertainment. Consequently, a commercial operator has traditionally wanted the maximum number of outbound channels. In a full two-way environment, however, it is likely that more inbound channels are necessary than are required for normal commercial operations. A high-split system simply provides even more return paths, although in the early 1980s CATV component manufacturers were not regularly manufacturing or delivering high-split equipment. Even though most commercial operations do not currently have

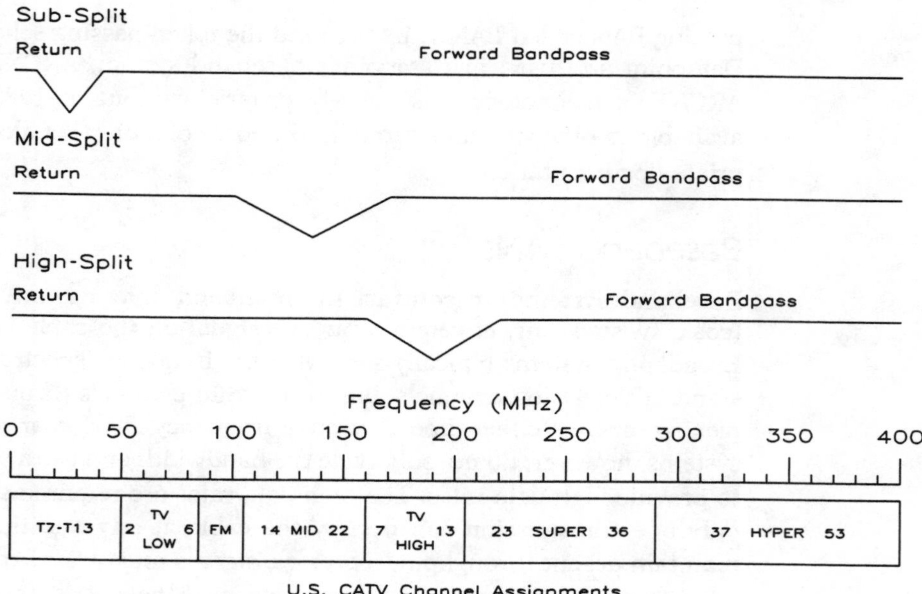

Figure 5.2. Single-Frequency Cable Allocations (U.S. CATV Standards).

two-way capacity, the conversion to a two-way system is not necessarily expensive (around $300 per mile of trunkline).[13] A 400 MHz sub-split system provides 4 return (inbound) channels and 54 forward (outbound) channels, while the midsplit system divides the spectrum into 14 return channels and 38 forward channels.

When implementing a CATV system the organization of that system affects the selection and spacing of amplifiers on the trunkline and perhaps within buildings. The system requires amplifiers to periodically boost the signal strength along the cable. Amplifiers are uni-directional in dual-cable systems and bidirectional in single-cable systems. Broadband CATV systems use 75 Ohm coaxial cable. Digital signals, in order to make use of CATV, must be converted to analog signals through the use of an RF (Radio Frequency) modem. Thus, broadband always uses modulated signals.

Most of the broadband LANs use a CSMA/CD access method similar to that used by Ethernet. Part of the reason for the choice is undoubtedly the fact that CSMA/CD has typically been used in a bus-oriented network, while token-passing schemes have been the access method for ring topologies. In mid-1983, however, 3M announced a broadband, bus topology, token-passing LAN called LAN/1. LAN/1 used the token-passing scheme devised by Datapoint and used in Datapoint's baseband system, ARCNET. Until 1982 ARCNET's technology was entirely proprietary, but in 1982 it was made available to other manufacturers in the form of a chip-set along with appropriate documentation.

Baseband LANs

Baseband systems, in contrast to broadband, may use any physical cable (coax, twisted pair, et cetera.), but the signal on the cable is unmodulated. Broadband systems typically subdivide the frequency spectrum, not only by standard television channels, but also within channels through some multiplexing scheme (either time division or frequency division or both). Baseband systems, however, do not subdivide the bandwidth and use a wide bandwidth to provide high data rates. The high data rates are required since essentially only one transmission can occupy the cable at any one time. In order to maintain decent throughput, therefore, signals must travel very fast.

Access to a baseband system such as Ethernet is accomplished not through a modem but through a transceiver. The transceiver simply transmits the signal received from the device to which it is attached and forms the data into usable chunks. Those usable chunks are frequently packets that consist of a source address, a destination address, and a small quantity of user data. Since baseband systems are designed only for LANs, somewhat more work has been done with providing office automation products and server mechanisms than is the case with broadband or telephonic systems (although WangNet, a broadband system, has some servers available and other manufacturers have announced or are developing such servers). On the other hand, voice and video products are generally unavailable for baseband systems.

During the mid-1980s Ethernet received the lion's share of the baseband publicity. With IBM's announcement of its Token Ring LAN, however, Token Ring started acquiring a significantly large press. By the late 1980s IBM and others were suggesting that Token Ring would replace Ethernet in the early 1990s. However, as late as mid-1991, Ethernet network interface cards (NICs) were outselling Token Ring cards by about 3 to 2. The reasons for this were numerous, but cost was certainly a factor as well as significant diversity in wiring options for Ethernet.

The Telephonic LAN

The term "telephonic LAN" is used in this book to describe the products based on telephone technology sold in competition to LANs. Specifically, telephonic LANs are structured around a PBX or a Private Automatic Branch eXchange (PABX), different names for the same technology. These systems are also known as Electronic Automatic Private Branch Exchanges or EPABXs. The acronyms, PBX and PABX, will be used interchangeably. Since a PBX is basically a private telephone system, now available from a number of vendors, a PBX can encompass both standard voice communications as well as data, although commercial grade, full-color, fast-scan television is unavailable. Note that it is now possible to send fast-scan monochrome video over telephone lines, but the ability to do so does not mean that telephone lines can be used for high-volume broadcast television services any more than the fact that two-way audio circuits on a CATV system will turn a cable television facility into a telephone system.

The modern PBX is a digital device with extensive redundancy to ensure minimum downtime. Following the telephone model, however, PBX is fundamentally a switching device. Companies manufacturing PBXs for data and voice traffic include some of the traditional telephone systems as well as companies that previously sold data switches as a means of managing the ports on large mainframe computers.

Like the true LAN industry, standards are developing for digital uses of telphone systems. The CCITT Study Group XVIII has proposed the Integrated Services Digital Network (ISDN). Part of the purpose of ISDN is to standardize the PBX-to-computer interface. The ISDN is the international telephone industry's response to the need for better digital data communications, and it is evolving from the public-switched telephone network. One objective of ISDN is to offer standard end-to-end connections and simultaneous support of voice and nonvoice services through a single access. Emphasis is on the integration of voice, data, and video, although the video capabilities of most real telephone products are very limited.[14]

In the ISDN construct, two channels are available for high-speed communications. The B-channel (basic-access channel) carries circuit-switched voice and circuit- or packet-switched data at 64 Kb/s or less. Out-of-band signaling for the B-channel is provided by the D-channel. It is a packet-switched channel that will operate at 16 Kb/s. When the D-channel is not signaling for the B-channel it can be used for low-speed data transmission. The ISDN subscriber may obtain multiple B-channels and a D-channel on either a switched or nonswitched basis. Wiring requirements are somewhat more stringent than for standard telephone systems in that a balanced, metallic, four-wire transmission medium is necessary since it must have the capability of bidirectional transmission at 192 Kb/s. Full deployment of ISDN capabilities will take place over the remainder of the twentieth century.[15]

While the PBX will provide connectivity equivalent to a broadband LAN, the PBX approach tends to be slower than either broadband or baseband. Under normal operating conditions, however, data rates are often limited to around 2,400 b/s for asynchronous data (although this is rapidly changing) as compared with 9,600 or 19,200 b/s for broadband and baseband systems. The adoption of ISDN-based equipment will, of course, increase these transmission rates. Then, too, although the process of making connections can be automatic, devices are addressed in precisely the same manner a telephone call is made, and that can take a number of seconds to complete.

The Physical Medium

Many media are used to provide LAN services. The most common are twisted-pair copper cables and coaxial cable (for either baseband or broadband). As the engineering problems involved in using fiber optics disappear, this technology will become more important, possibly overtaking coax sometime in the 1990s. Flat, multiconductor "ribbon" cables, infrared light transmitters and receivers, and microwave and other radio systems are also used for some LAN applications.

A decision concerning the medium to be used can be considered in several different ways. In one sense, that decision may be of no real consequence to network or subnetwork buyers since the medium used may simply be the by-product of equipment needs. On the other hand, many network and network-products vendors promote the medium they have chosen as part of their marketing technique. If some system uses twisted copper wire, such as that used for telephone installations, the marketing ploy may be to suggest that at least some existing wiring can be used, even when this is almost never possible. Cost is also often used to suggest one medium over the other. When installing a network, however, the key question is, "Can the medium handle all my needs now?" Therein lies a problem.

Twisted Pair

For many years electrical and electronic communications were accomplished using paired copper wires, hence the term, twisted pair. Although modern telephone systems use many different forms of media, telephone technology is still logically based on the twisted pair (usually two pair), and the cabling within buildings for telephone systems always uses two pairs of copper wires. Copper wire has some limitations for data transmissions over distances of any magnitude. The electrical characteristics of copper wire introduce distortion, which increases with speed and distance. At high speed, bandwidth is also a problem. These limitations are being somewhat overcome by the use of shielded copper wire, but the addition of shielding also increases the cost of the cable.

Coaxial Cable

For broadband systems and for many baseband systems the practical alternative to twisted pairs is coaxial cable. Coax has a single center conductor, surrounded by an insulator, surrounded by a wire-mesh shield. Coax can handle much greater bandwidth, and in particular can handle electrical signals running at radio frequencies. The center conductor and the wire-mesh shield share a common geometric axis and are, therefore, "coaxial" to one another. Coax comes in a number of standard sizes, up to about .75 inches. The larger sizes handle more like pipe than like wire.

Coaxial cable is classed not only by its physical size, but also by its impedance (measured in Ohms), and coax of different impedance is used for different purposes. For example, IBM 3270-type terminals are connected to their controllers by coax that has an impedance of 90 Ohms, while CATV systems use coax with an impedance of 75 Ohms. While coax is not noise free, it can operate in electrically noisy environments that would defeat twisted pair. The CATV industry has popularized the use of coax and has created specialized contractors capable of designing and installing systems. Many new buildings, at least for large organizations, are prewired for CATV just at they are prewired for telephone. Hardware is readily available for making splices and taps for the distribution of information via CATV coaxial systems.

Fiber-Optic Cable

By 1990 fiber-optic cable provided a feasible alternative to twisted pair and coax for many applications. While twisted pair and coax must be placed in locations free of overt environmental problems (either physical or electrical), fiber-optic cable does not have that drawback. It cannot be accidentally grounded, and it is not troubled by electrical noise. Fiber-optic cables are made of nonconducting glass and information is transmitted via optical techniques. Many of the problems inherent in twisted pair and coax are avoided with fiber optics, although the optical properties of the cable can be affected by kinks or similar damage. The potential transmission speed of fiber-optic cable is higher than coax, and coax is higher than twisted pair.

Fiber-optic technology originated in 1970 when Corning Glass Works introduced the first communications-grade fibers. Two previously unrelated disciplines were merged to produce fiber optics: Semiconductor technology, which produced the light sources and detectors, and optical waveguide technology, which produced the cable. To some, fiber optics has come to symbolize the future of data communications. This point of view has resulted from several important advantages over copper wire (either twisted pair or coax):[16]

- Broad bandwidth. Not even coaxial cable, which has a very high bandwidth, has the potential of fiber-optic cable.
- Fiber is immune from electromagnetic interference (EMI) and radio frequency interference (RFI) and is durable in harsh physical environments.
- Optical cable carries no current, and is not, therefore, a fire hazard. Some types of optical cable bundles, however, have a metalic carrier that may carry current, especially where repeaters are employed, thus obviating this advantage.
- Even the highest capacity fiber cable is small and lightweight, which reduces installation problems.
- The immunity of fiber to environmental problems results in a very high rate of reliability, with bit-error rates as low as one error in every billion bits transmitted.
- Optical fiber is more difficult to tap, without detection, than most other physical media and therefore is more secure for many applications.

Through the mid-1980s the primary use for fiber optics was long-haul telephone communications. AT&T was aggressively marketing fiber as a general-purpose backbone for voice/data systems within organizations. Because of its ease of use in point-to-point applications, fiber is finding an increasing role as a medium for bypassing the local telephone subscriber loop. Some LAN manufacturers are also offering fiber-optic links for LANs. In the past, fiber cable has been both costly and difficult to handle in the field. By 1990, however, prices were falling, and improved tools for making field connnections were making fiber more competitive with copper wire. With increasing sales of fiber, therefore, it is only a matter of time until fiber-optic LANs become cost-competitive with other technologies.

In the mid-1980s the primary problem with fiber optics was that devices for splicing and tapping the cable were expensive and difficult to use. This meant that while fiber-optic cables could be used for point-to-point high-speed communications with considerable success or for limited connection LANs, it was not yet possible to use it for extended distribution wiring. Many estimates suggested that the engineering problems with the use of fiber optics in a LAN would be overcome by the late 1980s or early 1990s, and these estimates have proven to be quite accurate. Certainly fiber optics can be used for heavy-use, short-run requirements or long-haul applications. Also, unlike the use of coax, connecting devices have not been standardized for fiber-optic cable. The lasers used for transmitting information still have relatively high prices, although prices are falling.[17] The ability to use fiber economically was changing rapidly by the end of the 1980s. This is perhaps best illustrated in the use of fiber by telephone companies as a *home* wiring technology. As early as 1986 Southern Bell experimented with the use of fiber for wiring homes. By 1988 a few more telephone companies had also started to experiment. By 1989, however, this movement seemed to mushroom. In late 1989, when practically no American homes were wired with fiber, one forecast estimated that some 225,000 American homes would be wired with fiber by 1992.[18] Even 225,000 homes is still a long way from covering the 60 or 70 million homes in the United States, but considering the potential cost of replacing the existing copper wire, this seems like an enormous and very fast leap.

There is no one best transmission medium. The selection of a medium is dependent on the use to which it is to be put. To build a CATV system, for example, economics may still dictate the use of coax, although this is rapidly changing. It is quite likely that during the 1990s fiber will replace coax for many of the applications for which coax was once used. In a similar vein, a flat copper ribbon cable might be most appropriate for a given application rather than coax, as might twisted pair. The fundamental question is not, "What medium shall I use?", but "What do I want to accomplish?" In a practical sense, the question of medium is not usually, even for a large organization, an open option. A PBX system requires a large amount of twisted pair; CATV or baseband systems requires a large amount of coax.

Reliability

An assessment of network reliability is difficult at best. Virtually all networks have high reliability, but for somewhat different reasons. If a LAN's vendor were to produce a network with questionable reliability, it would not stay in business very long. As we noted in Chapter 2, that reliability can be defined in several ways. A number of factors relate to network reliability. This section is concerned primarily with component (hardware) reliability rather than with the integrity of data transfers.

The issue of component reliability can be further subdivided between the reliability of the communications medium (PBX/twisted pair or the coaxial cable system) and LAN components that do not impact the entire network. The most common measure of reliability is mean time between failures (MTBF). The reliability of the network as a whole is the MTBF in which the entire network is out of operation. The reliability of a component is the MTBF of the specific item of equipment. The two may not be correlated with one another because potential single points of failure in a network are typically served by redundant systems.

In a PBX/twisted pair LAN, the single point of failure is the PBX itself. Since a PBX-based system has a centralized star topology, the complete failure of the PBX switch will take out the entire network. Private automatic branch exchange manufacturers address this problem by extensive equipment redundancy within the digital switch. The failure of a single circuit on a PBX system will not result in a complete failure of the system. For the transmission medium an MTBF of 175,000 hours (about 20 years) is reasonable, and for "intelligent network devices, such as switches or interface units for attaching devices, an MTBF of 30,000 hours is a good goal."[19] Thirty thousand is about 3.5 years. With a PBX-based system, since the PBX switch is the primary part of the network, 3.5 years MTBF is not good enough, hence the redundancy built into the PBX. Makers of PBX equipment claim reliabilities in the order of 99.9 percent uptime,[20] although PBXs can go down.

With broadband systems the claims for reliability are equally impressive. A 30-to-40-year MTBF has been established for passive CATV components (such as directional taps) and an 18-year MTBF has been established for amplifiers.[21] Although there are very few single points of failure in a broadband system, one occurs at the headend. The headend of a broadband system is a signal processor (sometimes called a frequency translator) regardless of whether the CATV medium is used for data or for television. Consequently, headend reliability is handled through redundant signal processors, often equipped with automatic switches. The power supplies used in broadband systems, used to power the amplifiers, while not usually a single point of failure, are frequently backed up with batteries.

Unlike PBX or broadband systems, which have reliability data available from telephone installations or from commercial CATV systems, baseband LANs have too short a history to provide much MTBF data, although it can be assumed that the manufacturers of such systems have a concern for component reliability equal to that of broadband or PBX manufacturers. In general, bus topologies should be more reliable than stars or rings. A token-passing ring structure can be stopped if any one node is out of operation unless redundant data paths have been provided (including the ability of the token system to ignore nonexisting addresses).

IEEE LAN Standards Overview

This chapter has blithely discussed bits and pieces of various IEEE LAN standards without describing those standards. Subsequent chapters will make use of the information provided here. The IEEE 802 standards provide the basis for the important LAN development in the 1990s. Because of the importance to the future development of LAN, an understanding of the 802 standards is essential. It may be helpful to look at Figure 5.3 and the manner in which the IEEE standards fit into the OSI Reference Model. The overview and internetworking issues are treated in 802.1 while 802.2 deals with Logical Link Control (LLC). 802.3 deals with CSMA/CD. A token-passing bus standard is described by the 802.4 standard. Finally, 802.5 defines a token ring system. The primary issues of 802.3, 802.4, and 802.5 revolve around the MAC definition. Also described in this chapter is the metropolitan area network (MAN) standard adopted as 802.6. For further information on 802.6 and further detail on all the 802 standards, read Thomas W. Madron, *LANS: Applications of IEEE/ANSI 802 Standards* (John Wiley & Sons, 1989).

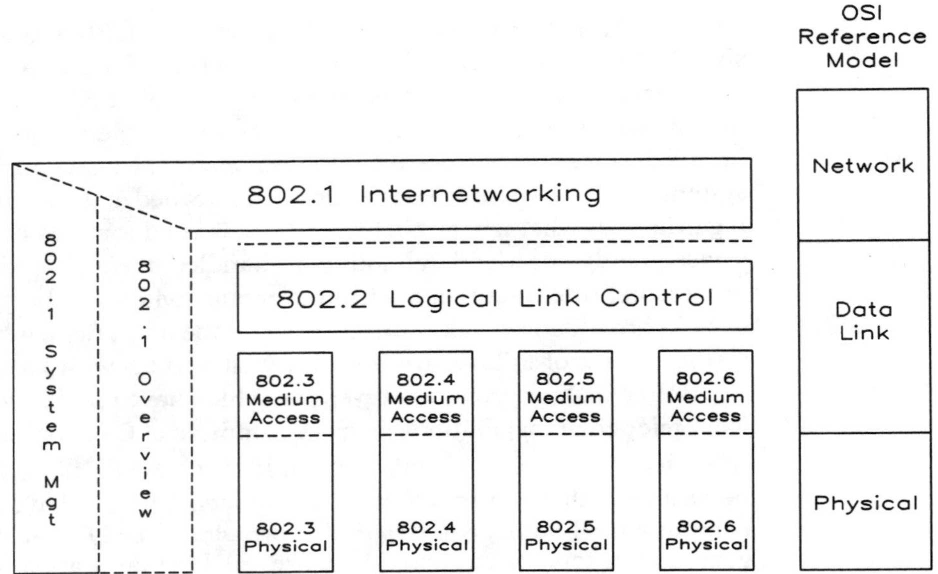

Figure 5.3. Relationship of IEEE Standards and the OSI Reference Model. Source: Based on IEEE P802.1, Draft E, July 1, 1987, Overview, Internetworking, and Systems Management, unapproved draft published for comment only, by permission of the IEEE. All rights reserved by the Institute of Electrical and Electronics Engineers, Inc., p. 7.

LLC Standards

As can be seen in Figure 5.3, with the IEEE 802 standards the LLC and MAC sublayers correspond to the Data-Link Layer of the OSI Reference Model while the physical layer of 802 corresponds roughly to OSI's physical layer. The LLC is that part of a data station that supports the logical link functions of one or more logical links. The LLC generates command packets, or frames (called "protocol data units" or PDUs), or interprets such PDUs. In particular, the responsibilities assigned to a LLC include the following:[22]

1. Initiation of control signal interchange.
2. Organization of data flow.
3. Interpretation of received command PDU's and generation of appropriate response PDU's.
4. Error control and recovery functions in the LLC.

In addition to the basic functions just noted, two primary services are specified: unacknowledged connectionless service and connection-oriented services. The first is a datagram-style that allows sending and receiving LLC frames with no acknowledgment for assured delivery.[23] All forms of connection, point-to-point, multipoint, broadcast, and multiplexed, are supported.

In contrast to unacknowledged service is the connection-oriented service. The latter provides a virtual circuit form of connection between service-access points. In other words, this service provides the means by which a network node (entity), in the words of the IEEE 802.2 Standard, "can request, or be notified of, the establishment of Data-Link Layer connections." The result of this service is that sequencing, flow control, and error recovery can be provided for the Data-Link Layer. In order to reset a session, a reset service is provided by which established connections can be returned to the initial state. The connection-oriented services are summarized as follows:

1. Connection establishment. The means by which a network entity can request or be notified of the establishment of Data-Link Layer connections.
2. Connection reset. Return to the initial state of an established connection.
3. Connection termination. The request or notification of the termination of Data-Link Layer connection.
4. Connection flow control. The means to control the flow of data across the Network Layer/Data-Link Layer interface for a specified connection.

Standards for MAC

Standards for MAC in LANs deal with the methods for allowing a particular node to transmit on the data-transmission channel available to it. Common sense dictates that if LAN manufacturers were left to develop MAC systems they would likely be proprietary and would not communicate from one to another. This is not to say that a single preferred standard will develop in the near future, but with the promulgation of the IEEE 802.3 (CSMA/CD), 802.4 (Token Bus), and 802.5 (Token Ring) standards, the proliferation of techniques was limited. Furthermore, since the standards are public, all possible manufacturers can build to those specifications. This means it is likely that hardware from different manufacturers may be mixed in a single network, providing competitive pricing for the consumer. Even with multiple standards, the developments are "starting to bring the industry closer together."[24]

The IEEE 802 Committee (Local Area Networks) has proposed standards for both CSMA/CD and token-passing MACs. The 802.3 standard addresses CSMA/CD while 802.4 deals with token passing.[25] The 802.3 standard is almost identical with Ethernet although 802.4 uses a token-passing scheme.

CSMA/CD (802.3)

The first of the 802 standards dealing with MAC is CSMA/CD. The original baseband version of this technique was developed by Xerox[26] as part of its Ethernet local network.[27] During the mid-to-late 1970s, as Xerox was working on Ethernet, MITRE was developing a broadband-based system also based on CSMA/CD. By 1980 other companies were busily at work on other CSMA/CD systems. Although the 802.3 standard is often referred to in the industry press as "Ethernet," the standard as it was adopted did not follow precisely the Xerox definitions, although there was great similarity. Most of the 802.3-compatible hardware being produced will not work on older Ethernet systems, although some manufacturers support both. The broadband 802.3 standard attempted to define the rules for placing the earlier baseband protocols on broadband. It should be noted that there are some LANs on the market that use CSMA without collision detection, although these will likely pass by the wayside as buyers insist on 802.3 compatible equipment. A typical baseband, coax-wired, 802.3 LAN is illustrated in Figure 5.4.

As this book was being written there were five subsidiary 802.3 standards in place. A means of identifying each implementation is with a simple, three field, type notation for the physical layer:

<data rate in Mb/s><medium type><max segment length (*100 m)>

The IEEE Std 802.3-1985 standard, for example, defined a 10 Mb/s baseband system with a maximum segment length of 500 meters. This is identified as "TYPE 10BASE5". This notation will occasionally be used in this discussion. Those standards are:

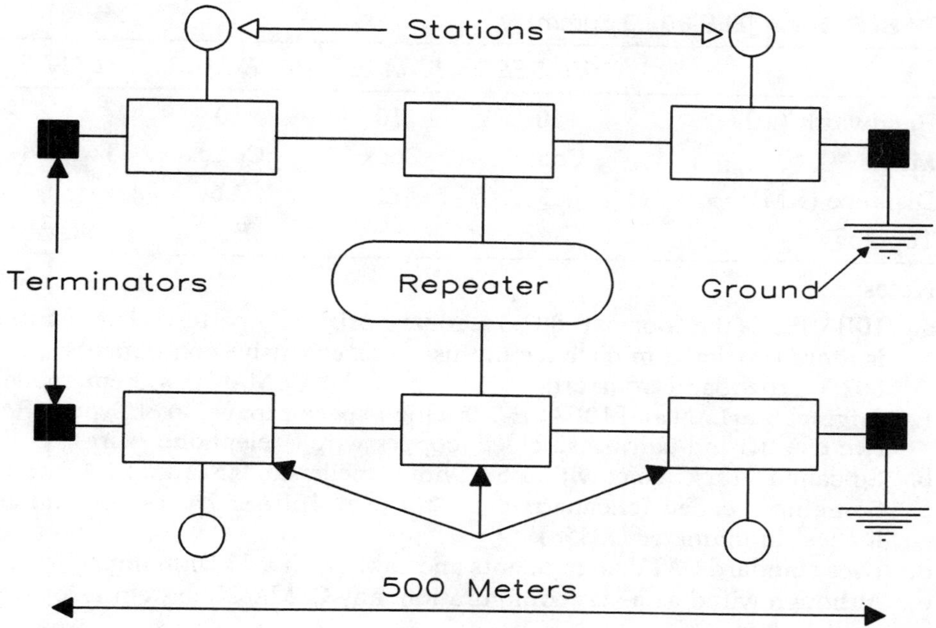

Figure 5.4. Baseband Coax 802.3 (Ethernet) LAN.

- ANSI/IEEE 802.3—1985, Type 10BASE5, 10 Mb/s, maximum length of 500 meters, baseband, thick wire (coax); the "original" 802.3 (Ethernet) specification.
- ANSI/IEEE 802.3—1988a, Type 10BASE2, 10 Mb/s, maximum length of 200 meters, baseband, thin wire (RG58 coax).
- ANSI/IEEE 802.3—1988b, Type 10BROAD36, 10 Mb/s, maximum length of 3600 meters, broadband.
- ANSI/IEEE 802.3—1988e, Type 1BASE5, 1 Mb/s, maximum length of 500 meters, baseband, twisted pair wiring.
- ANSI/IEEE 802.3—199x, Type 10BASE-T (10BASE1), 10 Mb/s, maximum length of 100 meters, baseband, twisted pair wiring.

The characteristics of these standards are summarized in Table 5.2.

In baseband CSMA/CD systems, such as Ethernet, collisions are detected by adding a DC (Direct Current) bias to the signal and having all stations look for a DC level greater than that of a single transmitter. On a

TABLE 5.2. IEEE 802.3 Summary

	10BASE5[a]	*10BASE2*	*10BROAD36*	*1BASE5*	*10BASE-T*
Bandwidth (Mb/s)	10	10	10	1	10
Media	Coax[b]	Coax[c]	Coax[d]	Twisted	Twisted
Distance (KM)	.5	.2	3.6	.5	.1
Topology	Bus	Bus	Bus	Star[e]	Star[e]

Notes:

a. 10BASE5 is the "normal" 802.3 standard originally patterned after Ethernet. 10BASE2 is more restricted in distance but uses less expensive components. 10BROAD36 is the 802.3 broadband standards. 1BASE5 is the CSMA/CD system modeled on AT&T's original StarLAN and 10BASE-T is a high-speed expansion of Type 10BASE1. The latter two use twisted-pair, unshielded, copper wire ("telephone" wire).

b. So-called "thick" coax with a 50 Ohm impedence, 9.525 mm (.4 inches) in diameter.

c. Sometimes called "cheapernet" or "thinnet" 10BASE2 uses 50 Ohm coax 4.8 mm (.2 inches) in diameter (RG58).

d. Uses standard CATV components and cable with a 75 Ohm impedence in various sizes.

e. Although wired as a star configuration, any CSMA/CD system is logically and conceptually a bus.

broadband system (since it cannot pass DC signals), when the transmitter receives the reflection of what was sent (a result of full-duplex mode) a bit-by-bit comparison is accomplished, and any discrepancy is assumed to be the result of a collision and the signal is retransmitted. Systems that implement Ethernet on broadband, such as those manufactured by DEC, Chipcom, and others, are examples of broadband CSMA/CD systems.

Any CSMA system must deal with collisions, and the manner in which collisions are handled will determine other characteristics of the network. Without collision detection the typical approach is to transmit when the medium is idle, then if the medium is busy, wait an amount of time determined by a probability distribution and try again. This is called a *non persistent* protocol. Modifications to this approach include 1-persistent and p-persistent protocols. Collisions are determined by a lack of acknowledgment from the receiving station. The objective to reduce the likelihood of collisions to the bare minimum. With CSMA, however, there will be collisions, especially as the traffic increases and the various wait states associated with busy detection will decrease throughput of the network.

Consequently, it is necessary for a system of any substantial size to provide collision detection.

In the IEEE CSMA/CD specification, the persistence algorithm used is 1-persistence. Therefore, for any given node, if the medium is idle, transmit; if the medium is busy, continue to listen until the channel is sensed idle, then transmit immediately; if there is a collision, wait a random amount of time and start over. Collision detection, in general, is accomplished by having the node continue to listen to the medium during transmission. For packets of the correct length, a collision can be detected before the entire packet is sent. In that case, the transmitting node stops transmitting immediately and sends a short jamming signal to signal all stations that a collision has occurred. Following the jamming signal the node waits a random amount of time and then attempts to transmit again. Wasted bandwidth is now reduced to the amount of time it takes to detect a collision.

How long does it take to detect a collision? Generally, on a baseband system, the delay is twice the propagation delay. The propagation delay is the amount of time necessary for a signal to travel from one point on a circuit to another. In a broadband system the delay is four times the propagation delay because if two nodes were in the same room, with a session between them, the signal would have to move from one node to the headend and them back an equal distance. On a baseband system, the signal has to travel only half the distance. The result of these facts is that in a baseband system the frame or packet length must be at least twice the propagation delay and with broadband systems at least four times the propagation delay. This also means that there is a limit on the end-to-end length of a CSMA/CD network—if the cable is too long, collisions will never be detected properly.

Token Passing (802.4 and 802.5)

The IEEE 802.5 standard defines a token ring while the 802.4 standard defines a token bus. IBM's Token Ring generally follows the 802.5 standards. Just as CSMA/CD can result in lower throughput under conditions where large numbers of collisions occur, so too a token-passing scheme can degenerate under heavy loads measured in terms of the number of connections on the system, since the token must pass every node before returning to any given connection.

Token Bus (802.4)[28]

Although the nodes on a token bus may be physically connected in a bus—as on a broadband CATV system, for example—they form a *logical* ring. Each node is assigned logical positions in an ordered sequence. The last member of the sequence is followed by the first. Each station must know the identity of the nodes preceding and following it. The physical configuration of the bus is irrelevant and independent of the logical ordering. The "token" in a token bus system is a control frame or packet that regulates the right of access to the medium. Among other things, the token frame contains a destination address. The target station, when the token has been received, is granted control of the medium for a specified length of time. A token bus is illustrated in Figure 5.5.

During the time a station has control over the medium, it may transmit one or more frames and may poll stations and receive responses. When the time expires, or when the node has completed its transmissions, it passes the token to the next logical station. Transmissions, therefore, consist of alternating token and data-transfer sequences. A token bus may also allow non-token-using stations that can respond only to polls or requests for

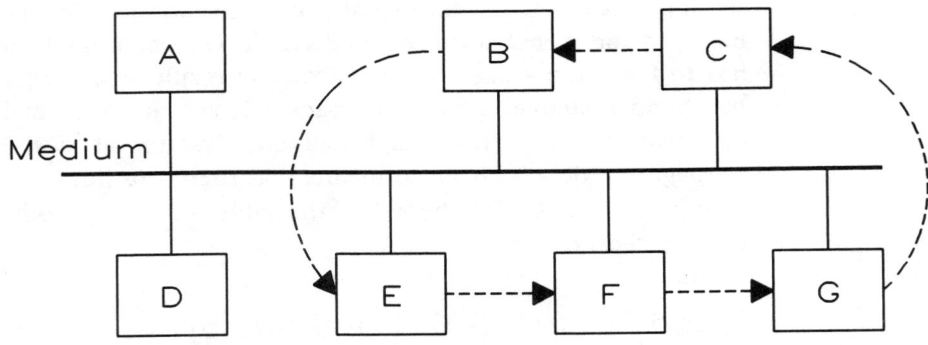

LAN Stations A-G
Logical Ring: Stations B, C, E, F, and G

Figure 5.5. Logical Ring on Physical Bus.
Source: Based on ANSI/IEEE Std 802.4-1985. *TOKEN-PASSING BUS ACCESS METHOD AND PHYSICAL LAYER SPECIFICATIONS,* © 1985 by the Institute of Electrical and Electronics Engineers, Inc., by permission of the IEEE. All rights reserved by the Institute of Electrical and Electronics Engineers, Inc., p. 19.

acknowledgment. Management functions are more extensive for a token bus than for a CSMA/CD LAN. One or more stations must perform *ring initialization*, *additions to the ring*, *deletions from the ring*, and *error recovery*.

Ring initialization is the procedure used to determine which node goes first, second, and so forth. When the logical ring is started, or after it has broken down, it must be reinitialized. There must be some method available to add either new or nonparticipating nodes to the ring. Similarly there must be a method for a node to be removed from the ring, either arbitrarily or voluntarily. If two or more stations try to transmit at the same time, duplicate ring addresses exist, and an error condition occurs. Similarly, when no station thinks it can transmit, the ring has been broken, and an error condition occurs. There must, therefore, be an error-recovery mechanism available.

Under 802.4 specifications, the physical connections use 75 Ohm CATV coaxial cable and analog (RF) signaling. There are actually three forms of physical connection specified. Two of the three use "single-channel" signaling, which means that the transmitters do not have a tight bandwidth and frequency-division multiplexing—like that used for CATV systems—cannot be used. In other words, this is intended essentially for a cable system dedicated only to the LAN, not as part of a general broadband installation that might use the cable system for multiple purposes, including video. The third option uses a full, commercial quality, broadband system that can carry multiple data and video channels. The simplest, most restricted, and cheapest option operates at 1 Mb/s. The second option operates at 5 or 10 Mb/s, and, unlike the first option, allows the use of splitters to achieve a tree topology. The full broadband option provides three data rates: 1 Mb/s occupying a 1.5 MHz channel; 5 Mb/s using a standard CATV 6 MHz channel; and 10 Mb/s absorbing a 12 MHz channel. Note that in the full broadband system, two data paths are required (to and from the headend translator), and the full bandwidth needed is actually twice the figures quoted (3, 10, and 24 MHz, respectively).

Token Ring (802.5)

Although the token bus must ultimately run over a logical ring, the token ring is a physical ring. It consists of a set of stations serially connected by a transmission medium. Information is transferred sequentially, bit by bit, from one active node to the next. Each node or station serves as the means for attaching one or more devices (such as terminals and workstations) to the ring. Each station regenerates and repeats each bit. The station that has access to the medium transfers information onto the ring, thereby allowing it to be read by subsequent stations. Those stations addressed copy the information as it passes. The originator of the information finally removes the information from the ring.[29] Figure 5.6 is a diagram of the IBM implementation of 802.5. In order to allow the physical wiring to be accomplished as a star network, IBM has used concentrators that, in effect, contain the physical ring.

The token is defined by a unique signaling sequence that circulates on the medium following each information transfer. After detection, any station may capture the token by modifying it. There are two basic formats in token rings: tokens and frames. The token consists of three eight-bit sequences or "octets." The first octet is the starting delimiter (SD), the second access control (AC), and the third the ending delimiter (ED). When the token is captured, the station modifies it to a start-of-frame sequence and appends additional fields, making it a complete frame. When the information transfer is complete, the sending station generates a new token.

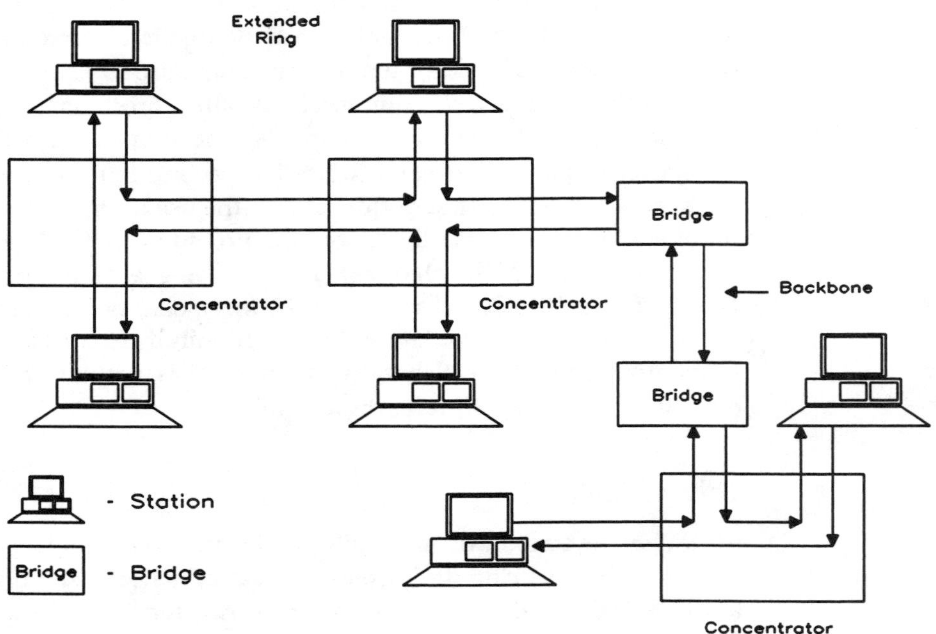

Figure 5.6. Extended IBM Token Ring.

The token ring was originally proposed in 1969[30] and was known as the Newhall ring after one of its developers. The 802.5 standard was an outgrowth of research conducted by IBM.[31] IBM's Token Ring Network as developed by Texas Instruments, is an implementation of the standard. In IBM's implementation of the Token Ring Network for PCs, the token-ring logic and MAC is contained on a board inserted into the micro. The connection on the board is then wired (using shielded twisted pair) to a wiring concentrator. Multiple concentrators can be daisy-chained in a ring to provide access for a fairly large number of stations. Although IBM's Token Ring Network uses a ring topology, the ring itself is contained in the wiring concentrator(s). Consequently, the physical wiring of an IBM Token Ring Network is actually done as a star.

The marketplace and manufacturing milieu for 802.3 (Ethernet) is well established and thriving. 802.4 token bus networks have found less general applicability. In both those standards there was a high degree of concern for the interoperability of devices made by different manufacturers, and at least for 802.3 standard devices interoperability is more or less a reality. A reading of Std 802.5-1985 does not evidence this same broad concern. The differences may lie in the fact that 802.3 was originally sponsored by a consortium of manufacturers that had developed Ethernet, although Xerox was its original driving force. 802.4 was pushed by companies who were not computer manufacturers, most notably, General Motors, to support MAP.

802.5, however, was sponsored primarily by IBM. The result of IBM's sponsorship seems to be a standard that is not entirely consistent in its approach with the other standards either in operational details or definitions (which could have been much the same across protocols), and which—at least originally—had a number of holes. Other manufacturers are now supporting the 802.5 standard in a variety of ways. IBM is attempting to capitalize on the popularity of TCP/IP among some market segements by producing TCP/IP software for the Token Ring. This will help introduce the Token Ring into some organizations that heretofore have relied exclusively on 802.3.

MANs (802.6)

In recognition of the need for standards beyond the LANs, yet less than standard WANs, the Metropolitan Area Network Working Group IEEE 802.6 was established in 1981. Unlike LANs, which are designed for data transmission, the emerging MAN standards support data, voice, and video transmission. Since MANs are designed for networks spanning distances greater than five kilometers, and since MANs are viewed as integrated information networks, LAN access methods have serious deficiencies. Consequently, the working group has adopted the Distributed Queue Double Bus (DQDB) architecture and protocols.[32] One way to think about a MAN is as a network of LANs. While the emerging MAN standards are not limited to linking LANs, that is certainly one major possibility. While standards for networks less than WANs, but more than LANs, are desirable, it remains to be seen whether this effort by the IEEE will prove to be successful. Note that the term "metropolitan" is used somewhat generically to include areas up to city size, but could also mean large campus environments. As a general-purpose, high-speed, information communications utility, however, a MAN could have wide use, particularly if the protocol could make use of existing transmission media, such as CATV systems and existing twisted pair or fiber-optic telephone lines.

IBM's Impact on Microcomputer LANs

A recurrent theme of this book is the impact of IBM on the entire computer and communications industry. The ubiquitous presence of IBM is not necessarily good for the industry, but it is certainly a fact of life. In the early 1980s, IBM made some noise about future developments of LANs and suggested that they would ultimately introduce four (depending on how one counts LANs). The four were a broadband system, a token ring, a token bus, and LAN services operating in the context of a new 3x74 terminal controller. In 1984 IBM introduced its first LAN product, the broadband PC Network originally manufactured by Sytek, Inc., of Mountain View, California. A year or so later, in 1985, the IBM Token Ring Network, using technology developed by Texas Instruments, was announced. Since that time IBM has extended support of at least the Token Ring to some varieties of the 3174 cluster controller, is manufacturing an 802.4-based industrial network, and will sell Ethernet (802.3 from Ungermann-Bass) if pressed. In addition, again in partnership with Texas Instruments, IBM has brought out a 16 Mb/s version of the Token Ring designed to actually provide the product with the throughput they claimed earlier for the 4 Mb/s system. While IBM's game plan might seem to be all things to all people, its central effort is to focus on providing its existing (mainframe) customer base with a wide variety of options and to support its overall SNA network architecture. Notwithstanding its public statements, concerning the fall of Ethernet in the 1990s, Token Ring pricing is not yet (in 1990) competitive with 802.3 products, and only with the introduction of the 16 Mb/s system does its throughput match that of CSMA/CD systems in large LANs.

Choosing a Technology

In most organizational environments the choice of an appropriate LAN technology is not a value-free technical decision. The first question should always be, however, "What problems do I wish to solve with the LAN?" An answer to this should be as comprehensive as possible, or no solution will be especially cost-effective. In particular, "I" may not know what all the problems are. Part of the problem identification must, of course, deal with the geographical attributes of the system.

A LAN in a single office on a single floor will work with almost any technology, although some will afford better services than others. In a multibuilding campus environment, however, few of the baseband systems will suffice. Even in a single, large building, when the actual lengths of cable trays and wiring paths are calculated, baseband may be inadequate, and conduit systems never even approximate the path of a bird between buildings.

A second major issue concerns the devices to be attached to the LAN. Is there control over the acquisition of those devices, or is an attempt being made to provide connectivity to a random selection of digital devices? Are mainframe computers as well as micros and terminals to be connected to the LAN? At what speed do users need to communicate? Are server mechanisms, such as those for file sharing required? These, and related issues, form the basis for the decision on the appropriate LAN. Finally, of course, the issue of cost must be confronted, although it is extremely difficult to get more than a very general picture of the true cost of any large system.

A third major issue is the requirement for auxiliary services, such as voice or video, which may also influence the decision. If high-quality, fast-scan video is required, then neither a PBX nor a baseband system will work. The only alternative is broadband. If it is necessary to link the data system with a fully connective, telephone-type voice communications system, then perhaps only a PBX will suffice.

Finally, management in a large organization is most easily sold on a LAN if the individuals involved can be convinced that a new and esoteric technology is not being foisted on them. None of the widely selling LAN systems use esoteric technologies. It is particularly vexing, when explaining the use of CATV, for people to see CATV as an esoteric system. Cable television technology is a mature technology, even though it is rapidly developing. Many people are still not acquainted with two-way cable, and the fact that CATV is most frequently used by the entertainment industry implies that it might be frivolous.

When these questions have been answered it will be possible to at least stipulate the broad outlines of the system. Should it be broadband, baseband, or PBX? And one should not overlook the possibility of using some baseband systems connected together with a broadband or PBX system, assuming the appropriate gateways are available.

Notes

1. H. J. Saal, "Local-Area Networks," *Byte*, Oct. 1981 (6, 10), pp. 96–97.
2. L. A. Bertman, "Exploring the Capabilities of Local Area Networks," *The Office*, May 1983, p. 55.
3. Robert Bowerman, "Choosing a Local Area Network," *Interface Age*, July 1983, p. 55.
4. IEEE Project 802, "Local Network Standards: Introduction," Draft C, May 17, 1982.
5. Datapro Research Corporation, *EDP Solutions*, Dec. 1982, pp. CS10-650-101, 102.
6. The study by Xerox has been widely quoted. See Linda B. Drumheller and Nicholas A. Lombardo, "LANs: Here to Stay?" *Small Systems World*, May 1983, pp. 25–29.
7. The following sources provide recent and easily found information on LAN/FAX technology: Doug Allinger, "LANs & FAX Get Hitched," *LAN Technology*, Vol. 6, No. 9, Sept. 1990, pp. 55ff; DataPro Research. "Facsimile (9)," *Office Products Evaluation Service* (Delran, NJ, 1990); John Bush, "FAX and High-Speed Modem Users Face ADPCM Woes," *Data Communications*, Vol. 18, No. 16, Dec. 1989, pp. 45–48; David Greenfield, "Those Fabulous Fax Boards," *Data Communications*, Vol. 19, No. 1, Jan. 1990, pp. 89ff; Bonny Hinners, "FAX or Opinions: Netware Compatible FAX Servers," *LAN Magazine*, Vol. 5, No. 6, June 1990, pp. 130ff; Mary Jander and Paul R. Strauss, "Affordable Fax/Data Gear on Way," *Data Communications*, Vol. 19, No. 3, March 1990, pp. 43ff; John T. Mulqueen, "Global FAX Frenzy Sparks Interest from Carriers," *Data Communications*, Vol. 19, No. 9, July 1990, pp. 70ff; Jon Pepper, "PC FAX Delivers Greater Power, More Flexibility," *Personal*

Computing, Vol. 14, No. 1, Jan. 1990, pp. 124ff; David M. Stone, "PC to Paper: FAX Grows Up," *PC Magazine,* Vol. 8, No. 7, April 11, 1989, 94ff.

8. Technical Committee on Computer Communications of the IEEE Computer Society, *Carrier Sense Multiple Access with Collision Detection (CSMA/CD) Access Method and Physical Layer Specifications*, Std 802.3-1985 (New York: IEEE, 1985).
9. Technical Committee on Computer Communications of the IEEE Computer Society, *Token-Passing Bus Access Method and Physical Layer Specification*, Draft Std 802.4-1985 (New York: IEEE, 1985).
10. Technical Committee on Computer Communications of the IEEE Computer Society, *Token Ring Access Method and Physical Layer Specifications*, Draft Std 802.5-1985 (New York: IEEE, 1985).
11. C. Kenneth Miller and Robert H. Douglas, "Local Area Networks: A Comparison of Standard Bus Access Methods," *Digital Design,* June 1983, pp. 125–128.
12. Much of the substance and text of this chapter was taken from Thomas W. Madron, *Local Area Networks in Large Organizations* (Hasbrouck Hts., NJ: Hayden Book Co., 1984), Chapter 3. For comment on the early LAN battles, see Kenneth Klee, John W. Verity, and Jan Johnson, "Battle of the Networkers," *Datamation*, March 1982, p. 116.
13. Edward B. Cooper and Philip K. Edholm, "Design Issues in Broadband local networks," *Data Communications,* Feb. 1983.
14. For background on ISDN, see Marc H. Rudov, "Marketing ISDNs: Reach Out and Touch Someone's Pocketbook," *Data Communications,* June 1984, pp. 239–245; Timothy C. Shafer, "Packing Data for the ISDN Migration, and Avoiding Costly Baggage," *Data Communications,* Nov. 1984, pp. 233–236; and Edward I. Kay, "ISDN Follow-Up: Opportunities in the Global Information Village," *Data Communications,* Oct. 1984, pp. 223–232.
15. Marc H. Rudov, "Wanted: Concerned Users to Join ISDN (R)Evolution," *Data Communications,* June 1985, pp. 229–236.
16. This list is based on *Datapro Reports on Data Communications*, "An Overview of Fiber Optics" (Delran, NJ: Datapro Research Corporation, 1986), May 1985, pp. C05-010-151ff. See also *Datapro Management of Data Communications*, "Optical Fiber System Economics" (Delran, NJ: Datapro Research Corporation, 1986), April 1984, pp. CS25-850-101ff.
17. Charles L. Howe, "Still Only a Glimmer: Optical Fiber in U.S. LANs," *Data Communications*, Vol. 16, No. 1, Jan. 1987, pp. 66, 68, 70.
18. John Markoff, "Here Comes the Fiber-Optic Home," *The New York Times*, Section 3 (Business), Nov. 5, 1989, pp. 1, 15.

19. Derfler and Stallings, p. 120.

20. Ed Yasaki, "Is There a PBX in Your Future?" *Datamation*, March 1983, p. 102.

21. Edward Cooper, "13 Often-Asked Questions About Broadband," *Data Communications*, April 1982.

22. IEEE Standards Board, *IEEE Standards for Local Area Networks: Logical Link Control*, ANSI/IEEE Std 802.2-1985 (New York: The Institute of the Electrical and Electronics Engineers, Inc., 1984), pp. 20, 21.

23. Stallings, p. 7.

24. M. Edwards, "Standards Chart Direction of Local-Area Network Advances," *Communications News*, Vol. 22, No.10, Oct. 1985, pp. 60–64, 66.

25. IEEE Standards Board, *IEEE Standards for Local Area Networks: Carrier Sense Multiple Access with Collision Detection (CSMA/CD)* (New York: The Institute of Electrical and Electronic Engineers, Inc., 1985); IEEE Standards Board, *IEEE Standards for Local Area Networks: Token-Passing Bus Access Method and Physical Layer Specifications* (New York: The Institute of Electrical and Electronic Engineers, Inc., 1985).

26. See, for example, the following: R. Metcalfe, D. Boggs, C. Thacher, and B. Lampon, "Multipoint Data Communication System with Collision Detection," U.S. Patent 4,063,220, 1977; R. Metcalfe and D. Boggs, "Ethernet: Distributed Packet Switching for Local Computer Networks," *Communications of the ACM*, July 1976; and J. Shoch, Y. Dala, and D. Redell, "Evolution of the Ethernet Local Computer Network," *Computer*, Aug. 1982.

27. G. Hopkins and P. Wagner, "Multiple Access Digital Communications System," U.S. Patent 4,210,780, 1980; and G. Hopkins, "Multimode Communications on the MITRENET," *Proceedings of the Local Area Communications Network Symposium*, May 1979.

28. IEEE Standards Board, *IEEE Standards for Local Area Networks: Token-Passing Bus Access Method and Physical Layer Specifications* (New York: The Institute of Electrical and Electronics Engineers, Inc., 1985).

29. IEEE Standards Board, *IEEE Standards for Local Area Networks: Token Ring Access Method and Physical Layer Specifications* (New York: The Institute of Electrical and Electronics Engineers, Inc., 1985), p. 23.

30. W. Farmer and E. Newhall, "An Experimental Distributed Switching System to Handle Bursty Computer Traffic," *Proceedings of the ACM Symposium on Problems in the Optimization of Data Communications*, 1969.

31. N. Strole, "A Local Communications Network Based on Interconnected

Token Access Rings: A Tutorial," *IBM Journal of Research and Development,* Vol. 27, Sept. 1983; and R. Dixon, N. Strole, and J. Markov, "A Token-Ring Network for Local Data Communications," *IBM Systems Journal,* Vol. 22, No. 1, June 1983, pp. 47–62.

32. See Chapter 7, "LANs and WANS," for more detail on MANs. For some of the technical background, see William E. Bracker, Benn R. Konsynski III, and Timothy W. Smith, "Metropolitan Area Networking: Past, Present, and Future," *Data Communications,* Vol. 16, No. 1, Jan. 1987, pp. 151–159. See also, IEEE 802.6 Working Group on Metropolitan Area Networks, *Draft IEEE Standard 802.6: Metropolitan Area Network* (New York: IEEE, 1986).

CHAPTER 6

Micros as Mainframe Peripherals: Mainframes as Micro Peripherals

In July 1984, I wrote, "claims that all the products for appropriate micro to mainframe connections are already on the market are clearly premature."[1] That comment was in response to claims that by the mid-1980s products provided terminal emulation, electronic mail, access to third-party databases, reduction of mainframe data processing, and use of data by different applications.[2] Unfortunately, the connection is still underdeveloped, although the situation is changing rapidly. In many, if not most, large organizations, those five "reasons" just listed for the micro-to-mainframe connection are probably not even the most important issues that need to be confronted.

In large organizations some of the objectives for using micros as workstations are as follows:[3]

1. The ability to extract data from the corporate database, download it, massage it, and produce reports locally.
2. The composition of documents locally, then transmit them to some other target system which might be an electronic mail system, an automated composition machine in the print shop, or some other expensive (or esoteric) device.
3. The use of the mainframe as an archival peripheral for the micro.
4. The effort to make the use of the mainframe more "user friendly" with an off-line transaction set-up system which presumably would lead to a reduced effect on mainframe resources.
5. The ability to act as an intelligent node in a distributed processing environment.

Even today not all the products are in place to accomplish all these tasks successfully and to the satisfaction of specific organizations.

Fundamental to some of the functions listed is the ability to emulate some terminal. Many products are available that provide emulations of popular asynchronous devices, and a growing number of products emulate IBM's 3270-type synchronous terminals. This chapter will describe the use of micros as mainframe peripherals, the sometimes misunderstood use of mainframes as micro peripherals, and the general issue of terminal emulation. The entire issue of 3270-type terminal emulation in a synchronous network is important enough to devote a separate chapter and will only be referenced here.

Micros as Mainframe Peripherals

Almost from the beginning of microcomputing personal computers have been used as peripherals to larger machines. Popular thinking about peripherals—or at least the classical way of thinking—usually dictates that the smaller machine is always a peripheral to the larger system. That this concept of peripherals no longer applies will be discussed later in this chapter. This section will view microcomputers as peripheral devices to a mainframe or mini computer. The vast majority of communications software products for micros are designed to make the micro appear to a larger machine as a terminal—a standard peripheral device.

Having said that micros can be used as terminals, note the variety of terminals in the marketplace and in use in organizations. Even when used only as tools to do transactions on a central system, not all terminals (or terminal emulators) are equal.

Micros as Terminals

S. Austin, in "In Search of the Missing Link (Terminal Emulators),"[4] has pointed out that terminal emulators, those add-on boards and software products that allow microcomputers to act like dedicated terminals, present both welcome solutions and new problems for two groups of people—data processing (DP) managers and corporate end users. Notwithstanding the apparent claims of terminal emulator manufacturers, terminal emulators do not and cannot provide a complete micro-to-mainframe link. As Austin points out, with terminal emulators corporate end users can access mainframe data, reduce workloads for DP managers, and lay the groundwork for a full-scale micro-to-mainframe link.

Terminal Emulators and What They Do

There is a wide variety of asynchronous, ASCII terminal emulators from which to choose. The simplest asynchronous communications program is sometimes called a "dumb" terminal program. Such a program gives the user access to the asynchronous communications hardware and acts like a simple teletype machine—it will not have the capacity to transfer files, to address the screen, or to provide other services. On the other hand, for organizations that need only to communicate with large mainframe systems, a simple terminal-emulation program is effective and inexpensive.

The better, more intelligent programs provide a wide variety of services in addition to simple communications. They often provide file-transfer capabilities—an important function—full control of the hardware, the ability to access the operating system (OS) of the micro and its software, and other features. Examples of such programs are ASCOM (Dynamic Microprocessor Associates, Inc.), CrossTalk (MicroStuff, Inc.), PROCOMM Plus (DataStorm Technologies), TELETERM (Telexpress, Inc.), and others. Some of these programs are available for a wide variety of micro systems. In addition, these programs also "emulate" one or more standard terminals, such as Digital Equipment Corporation's (DEC's) VT100 or Lear-Siegler's ADM3A terminals. While the VT100 and the ADM3A are no longer produced, the VT100 screen addressing system became the basis for the ANSI X3.64 standard, and the ADM3A screen addressing system was used in a wide variety of terminals from other manufacturers and in micro software. Consequently, the names VT100 and ADM3A have long outlived the original products. An increasing number of programs emulate some common graphics terminals, such as the Tektronix 4010 or the DEC VT240. A variety of software and hardware requires terminal-emulation capabilities.

Terminal Protocols

Terminal emulators make a micro work like some standard terminal or terminal definition. In general, that means using the protocols designed to address the screen and providing other features of the original terminal. Many terminals, when provided with a specific character string from the host, are able to perform a variety of screen functions. All or part of the screen can be cleared, the cursor can be placed at a precise location on the screen, or other screen control can be effected. This ability is important to perform full-screen functions, such as editing. The older TTY (Teletype) terminals were not able to address the screen and editing was limited to a line at a time. Modern terminals, to aid in full-screen applications, typically have some memory—a "buffer"—that allows greater control over the information placed on the screen.

Although many terminal protocols have arisen, two have become predominant: IBM's synchronous 3270-type and an outgrowth of DEC's asynchronous VT100. Much of DEC's VT100 protocol has found its way into an ANSI standard (X3.64) for screen addressing. That standard is now almost universally available on the 8086 family of microcomputers using MS-DOS (from Microsoft). When a VT100 terminal or emulator receives certain character strings, the screen should behave in a well-defined way.

The character strings are often called "escape" sequences because they begin with the ASCII escape character (decimal 27, hex 1B), which will be symbolized as <ESC>. When a terminal using the ANSI standard receives the sequence "<ESC>[2J", for example, the screen is cleared. To place the cursor at a particular spot on the screen to make the display more pleasing, or because a mainframe editor needed to control the screen, the sequence "<ESC>[Pn;PnH" would be issued. The left bracket ([), semicolon (;) and character "H" are all literals in the string. The first "Pn" represents the screen line number, and the second "Pn" represents the screen column number. The line and column numbers (parameters) are character literals of the appropriate numbers, not the ASCII codes for the numbers. To place the cursor at the 10th row and the 15th column, issue the string

"<ESC>[10;15H". This string, in hexadecimal notation, would be: 1B 5B 31 30 3B 31 35 48.

The ability to do enterprise-wide computing (EWC) through a highly connective network is affected by the terminals accessing the system. In such an environment it is probably not possible to control the terminal types. A host may not even know anything about the type of terminal attempting to gain access, yet it would be desirable to provide all terminal capabilities, including access to full-screen applications. In order to make this possible, it is necessary to have a *virtual-terminal protocol* intercede between the "real" terminal and the host by providing an intermediate language common to both. Virtual terminal protocols, which include Internet's TELNET (see Chapter 7) and the OSI Reference Model's VTP (see Chapter 3), function by providing a common protocol for access to lower layers even when the two host sytems are quite different or the terminals being used by end users are quite different. The virtual terminal, therefore, consists of a well-defined set of functional characteristics. The virtual-terminal protocol takes input from either the physical terminal, or the host, in whatever constitutes the native code; translates the information into the virtual-terminal protocol's terms; and in Internet at least, passes that information to the Transport Control Protocol (TCP), the Internet Protocol (IP), and on to the network access protocol (NAP). Virtual-terminal protocols are designed to support interactive, terminal-oriented (terminal-to-process) traffic, although they sometimes may also support process-to-process and terminal-to-terminal communication. Although all virtual-terminal protocols provide these general services, they differ in the manner in which the services are defined and the transfer protocol is supported.

Choosing the Appropriate Terminal to Emulate

The difference between choosing a terminal-emulation program for individual use—as between micros, for example—and for corporate use is that organizations typically establish standards either by choice or default. Transactions on a mainframe computer system, to function correctly, frequently require terminals of a particular type. An application written for use with IBM's 3270 family of terminals will not function with a terminal not emulating a 3x78/79. Similarly, DEC's standard editors on VAX systems will not function in full-screen mode unless a terminal that looks like a VT100 is connected. The communications protocol (asynchronous or synchronous) used by the network may also dictate the required terminal.

Corporate Standards

An organization might standardize on a VT100-compatible terminal and terminal emulator. In a multivendor DP shop, there may be both IBM-compatible mainframes and DEC's VAX 11/780 super minicomputers. A VT100-type terminal can access IBM-compatible systems through protocol converters that make VT100s, among other terminals, look like IBM 3270-type terminals. This means that users can have full-screen editing and other capabilities on either the IBM-type systems or on the VAXs *from the same terminal*.

Within an organization, other communications standards can also be important. In an asynchronous network operating at higher speeds—9,600 b/s or 19.2 Kb/s, for example—flow-control standards are essential. Until the mid-1980s some terminal-emulation software manufacturers did not deal adequately with flow-control issues. By "adequately" I mean the ability to flow control listings to the screen so that data are not lost. This ability is essential to a large organization where the slow speeds of 300 to 1,200 b/s are inadequate for a production environment. If file-transfer capabilities are part of the package, then flow control is also required.

Why standardization? Standardization of at least elements of the communications system has many advantages in an organizational environment. Some of those advantages are as follows:

1. Allows large-scale, mass purchases of equipment and software.
2. Reduces end user training costs in that users need not learn how to use many different emulators or machines.
3. Improves the speed and reduces the cost of problem solving since user services personnel can more effectively address user equipment and software problems.
4. The network itself can be configured to deal with only limited terminal types, reducing communication problems.
5. A common user interface can be structured.

Communications Protocols

In any EWC environment, the first problem is simply connecting the two or more machines so that they will be able to meaningfully interface. Many writers and software manufacturers have taken the oversimplified position that this is usually done through a serial communications line on the mainframe and an RS-232 serial interface on the micro.[5] Many large organizations, however, use IBM's bisync or Synchronous Data Link Control/System Network Architecture (SDLC/SNA) synchronous networks. Under such circumstances it is necessary to provide 3270 emulation or to provide protocol converters that allow asynchronous terminals to behave as if they were 3270 devices. Increasingly, these communications take place over a LAN.

OTHER NETWORK REQUIREMENTS

The choice of the appropriate terminal to emulate finally comes down to a combination of other choices made by the organization. Those choices involve both the communications system and the central computers being used. These decisions are not made by isolated individuals, but by corporate policy—either knowingly or by default. One issue avoided in this chapter is whether the micros are connected to the central systems through gateways from a micro-based local area network (LAN). Local Area Networks present a somewhat different response to the problem of terminal emulation in that the gateway server will probably provide the appropriate terminal emulation for the connected micro. A 3174 server will provide 3270-type emulation, and an asynchronous server will likely provide some other emulation, such as VT100. With LANs, the end user typically will have no choice other than what is provided, since the emulator will have to interact appropriately with the LAN. A primarily terminal network, however, will interface with a broader range of off-the-shelf software and hardware.

Making the Emulator Smarter

No matter how good the emulator software, terminal emulation is no better—if no worse—than the terminal it is emulating. What microcomputer terminal emulators can do, however, is provide added-value services that go beyond the capabilities of a standard terminal. Many software manufacturers attempt to provide a range of these extra services—an effort to make the emulator smarter. Of any possible list of added services, probably the most widespread, and perhaps the most important, is the ability to transfer files.

Added Features and Facilities

What are the added value services that are available with at least some terminal-emulation programs? The file-transfer issue will be addressed further. This section will look at other added features and facilities. Some of the added features found in one package or another are the following:

1. Automated features:
   a. Session Establishment. In a telephone-based dial-access network, this means the ability to automatically dial a remote system. In other networks it means interacting with the access device to establish a session with the remote system. Many programs handle the telephone system adequately but do poorly with systems like Sytek's LocalNet/20, or Ungermann-Bass' Net/One.
   b. Automatic Logon. Once a session has been established, it is normally necessary for the user to provide a user identification code and password to the remote system. Many software packages allow this basic logon to be automated, although the ability to work through multiple levels of systems and/or passwords is limited or nonexistent. To access an IBM mainframe, for example, running under VM (Virtual Machine Facility), users may have to access another operating system using the VM "dial" command. Once their ID is established, users may need to log on to an application (such as a database system) with one or more additional passwords. This more complicated operating environment is beyond most current terminal emulators. Automated logon systems may also have some security implications.
   c. Remote control of the micro "terminal" by the host system.
2. Provision of a "script" language to serve as the basis for automated processing. This is essentially a command language that can be placed in a file with the program automatically executing the commands in sequence.
3. Sufficient variety in the available commands to completely define the communications environment.
4. Availability of a full-screen text editor, or access to an existing editor, to deal with documents while remaining on-line.
5. The ability to operate in the background of the microsystem concurrently with one or more other programs.

The last point, the ability to operate in the background, is sufficiently important to require further comment. In an organizational environment, microcomputer-based workstations are provided to improve the productivity of the affected employees. This means that at least some communications processes need not be, and indeed, should not be, the primary application on the micro. Historically, however, most micros could run only one program at a time—they were (and are) single-task machines. Part of the reason for single tasking is that most micros, through the mid-1980s, were too slow to adequately support multitasking—the ability to run more than one program concurrently. Consequently, multitasking OS's were slow to develop.

In response to the need for multitasking software, Microsoft (Windows), Quarterdeck (Desqview), and others have produced operating environments that run under MS-DOS. Both products[6] were designed to give background priority to communications.[7] These multitasking products allow multiple applications to run concurrently as do multiuser OS's such as AT&T's Unix, Concurrent PC-DOS from DRI, and OS/2 from IBM. Unix, OS/2, and Concurrent PC-DOS are the most ambitious products since they are full OS replacements for MS-DOS. Depending on what concurrent applications are doing, all these products slow down programs operating under them. With the 80386-class machines, however, that disadvantage has diminished—but not disappeared. While the PC/AT using an Intel 80286 processor does not have the speed and power to support a fast multiprocessing environment, the faster 80386 machines can be used for effective multitasking.

Why should a communications program be running in the background? In an organization there are many reasons, including building a distributed electronic mail (EMail) and document distribution system. One major task of many corporate data centers is running and printing lengthy reports that are used only occasionally, but must be distributed to end users in a timely fashion. Many of those reports need not be on paper so long as there are efficient means for finding information when it is needed. One alternative to the distribution of paper copies of such reports is to deliver the documents electronically to appropriate microcomputers, let the micro record them on disk, and then provide a means for browsing the file. Some high-cost office-automation systems are designed to let this happen in a fairly automatic fashion. Allowing a communications program to run in the background of a PC, however, would be a strong first step in further automating the process at a low cost.

File-Transfer Add-Ons: What They Can and Cannot Do

The most popular add-on to terminal emulators is the ability to transfer files from and to the host computer. There are several vexing problems relating to file transfer, including the need for an error-free file transfer protocol, a simple and straightforward user interface, data format conversion, and the ability to extract data from the central database in a reliable and secure manner. Of these issues, file-transfer add-ons to terminal emulators tend to take care of the file transfer protocol and sometimes a usable human interface, but rarely do they provide the means for host data extraction or data-format conversion. Moreover, the file transfer protocols implemented with most terminal emulators tend to be those developed for microcomputers, not those designed primarily for a mainframe environment. File-transfer issues will be discussed in greater detail in Chapter 8.

Mainframes as Micro Peripherals

The use of a mainframe computer or supermini as a microcomputer peripheral has become a reality, thanks to some innovative new PC–mainframe software. Imagine having a gigabyte or more of mass storage no further than an E: away. Better yet, how would you like to be able to work productively with mainframe applications that are invoked from the DOS prompt?

The previous section of this chapter discussed terminal-emulation programs that make micros work like smart terminals when accessing a mini or mainframe computer. The best of the emulators provide powerful tools for interacting with central computer systems. No matter how good the emulator, however, the micro still appears to the user as if it were a terminal. Operations that should be simple—such as transferring files between micros and mainframes—are often arduous even at data transmission rates of 9,600 or 19,200 b/s.

A new class of communications software is slowly becoming available for those people in organizations with appropriate access to large mainframe systems: Software that allows the micro user to use the disk storage capacity of the mainframe as a virtual-disk peripheral. Such software can be referred to as a "generic micro-to-mainframe link," making the mainframe into a large network file server. Generic micro-to-mainframe links do not depend on a specific application or vendor. They work with a standard OS such as VMS on DEC's VAXs, or MVS on IBM mainframe systems, and provide an integrated link between a host program and a companion program running on a PC. Datability's Remote Access Facility (RAF)—as well as other similar products—makes the mainframe or supermini into a virtual disk for the PC, thus allowing the PC user to manipulate and transfer files between the mainframe and the PC by using standard DOS file commands. The mainframe acts as a file server for any number of remote PCs.

Mainframes as Network File and Print Servers

The concept of a server is most closely associated with the recent proliferation of LANs. In one sense, however, server mechanisms have always existed on computer networks: They were called mainframes or minis. Computer professionals have recently become more self-conscious about the way they think about server mechanisms and about the way end users should access those systems. There are three kinds of services that exist on mainframes, providing data can be transferred from the micro to the big machines in a fast and economical fashion: large-scale, high-speed disk storage; high-speed, high-quality printers; and high-speed, large-capacity computational capabilities. Providing a "friendly" way to move data from the micro to the mainframe and to route files to the appropriate devices is the basis for using mainframes as micro peripherals.

The Mainframe as a Virtual Disk

There are several examples of currently available software that allow mainframe mass storage devices to appear to the user as if they were disks on the micro. Virtual Disk Access Method (VDAM) accesses mainframe files as if they were on a floppy or hard-disk drive attached to the PC. Tempus-Link is based on the virtual floppy concept: It uses a data-compression algorithm, can work on an asynchronous dial-up basis, and will support formatting into both ASCII and Data Interchange Format (DIF) files. iLINK encodes and decodes data files into usable formats. Mobius, from FEL Computing, is a software system that fully integrates the DEC VAX as well as the old DEC System-10, and DEC System-20 host computers with CP/M and MS-DOS microcomputers. Mobius is designed for use by large corporations and universities. It allows any microcomputer spreadsheet program to use host files in the same way it uses files on the micro's own disk drive.

A companion product to Tempus-Link is Tempus-Data, described by

Micro Tempus Inc., as "an open-ended data management system that allows non-technical users to select, extract and update mainframe data from the familiar micro-computer environment." A strength of Tempus-Link is read/only access to several popular IBM mainframe database systems: IMS/DL1, IDMS, RAPID, TOTAL, ADABAS, and MODEL 204.

A major disadvantage of the system is that it runs only under CICS, Time Sharing Option (TSO), and (in the future) VM/CMS. These are commonly used IBM mainframe software products that provide 3270-based access to the IBM or IBM-compatible mainframe (sometimes called teleprocessing [TP] monitors). Unfortunately, although these are the products pushed by IBM, some of the independent database systems, such as ADABAS (from Software, AG) and MODEL 204 (from Computer Corporation of America) can be purchased with their own TP monitors. COM-PLETE, which is a companion product for ADABAS, is a powerful monitor with its own set of data-management utilities.

CICS, TSO, and COM-PLETE operate under OS/MVS. Micro Tempus Inc., and other producers of similar products, would be well advised to produce a simple, straightforward TP monitor or be prepared to interface Tempus-Link with a wider variety of monitors. The managers of many IBM and IBM-compatible mainframe systems choose not to use the IBM products largely because of performance problems or cost. The problem with producing a small, simple TP monitor, possibly with direct system calls to BTAM (Basic Telecommunications Access Method) or VTAM (Virtual Telecommunications Access Method), is that the user may then be precluded from accessing database files organized under a more extensive TP monitor like COM-PLETE or CICS. It is unreasonable to expect potential users to acquire CICS only for using Tempus-Link, and many installations actively discourage TSO use because of the negative performance implications of the system.

Similar in concept is V-Drive from Virtual Microsystems (Berkeley, CA), which allows IBM-PC's and compatible to easily use VAX/VMS and MicroVAX/VMS systems as file servers. V-Drive makes the host appear to the PC user as a large, DOS-formatted volume like any other disk drive physically attached to the PC. The user can run DOS applications directly on the PC using data files stored on "virtual disks" on the host.

Linkware Corp. has introduced a software package that allows different types of computers to communicate with each other in a strictly controlled, secure environment. Linkware: Information Server is a network application that resides on host mainframe computers or personal computers. The software functions as a virtual server capable of porting or transferring information to various types of hardware and transforming files to the appropriate format. It is now available for the IBM VM/SP environment and several personal computer environments. Arbiter, from Tangram Systems, is a virtual disk product allowing access to an IBM mainframe through VTAM and obviates the need for a "standard" TP monitor. When a file is written to or read from or to that "virtual" disk, however, the data go up a communications line to the mainframe.

On the mainframe end, the data are captured and saved in a format apparently compatible with the micro's OS. Some additional mainframe utilities, which allow the transfer of information from the mainframe's database system to the micro's virtual disk, or vice versa, may be available. The advantage of this arrangement is that the mainframe system will have large amounts of disk space but, even more importantly, will have standard procedures to back up and protect the data—a constant problem for microcomputer users. Such a product cannot be casually acquired and demands the active cooperation of the central computing facility.

One problem faced by many users is the need to transfer data to and from the mainframe. There are many possibilities concerning the uses of such facilities. During the past few years many people have suggested that programmers, for example, should develop code on micros, including substantial testing, before moving it to a target mainframe. Mainframes and superminis are operated in environments that ensure proper backup and data security. Consequently, micro-based data stored temporarily on a mainframe will probably be there when needed—quite unlike some PC environments. Another problem faced in organizations is the need for an individual to alternate use of micros, mainframes, and minis to accomplish some task. This may require knowledge of several computer operating environments—a task not very easy for novice users. The ideal situation would be one where people dealt with a single operating environment or user interface, thus limiting the learning overhead necessary to be a productive employee. One product that seems to work as advertised is Datability's RAF, which runs on a DEC VAX supermini running under the VMS OS.[8]

In order to better demonstrate the utility of such software it may be instructive to look at one product—Datability's RAF—in detail. Remote Access Facility was chosen because it is a good example of the genre and because I have had the opportunity to evaluate the product in detail. Remote Access Facility is designed to meet at least three objectives: (1) To provide a micro-to-mainframe file transfer and manipulation facility through the use of a microcomputer virtual disk on a DEC VAX computer system; (2) To allow execution of VAX applications in an MS-DOS user environment; and (3) To provide a tightly integrated microcomputer front-end to program modules on the VAX for computational purposes not within a PC's scope. Remote Access Facility can communicate with a VAX over a standard RS-232 serial connection at speeds up to 19,200 bps, or through an Ethernet link, which is one of DEC's standard access techniques. In pursuit of these objectives, RAF enables PCs to perform five different and distinct micro-to-mainframe interactions:

- Automatic contact and login to a remote VAX.
- Direct PC access to VAX files.
- PC execution of entire VAX computer programs.
- PC calling of remote VAX subroutines.
- Access to multiple VAXs in a cluster environment.

Because users will sometimes have to directly interact with the target VAX, RAF also provides a full VT100 terminal-emulation mode, which maintains the screen image of the PC and remote computer when switching from terminal mode to DOS to provide user continuity. The VT100 is a DEC terminal standard, much like 3270 display stations are a standard in IBM mainframe environments. In a RAF or RAF-like environment the PC user may not even know where the information is coming from.

Automatic login is accomplished through the use of a "conversation" or script file. Conversation files contain a series of control statements that allow virtually transparent access to a VAX. These files vary in complexity according to the nature of the computing environment and the degree of automation desired. An example of a conversation file can be seen in Listing 6.1. A conversation file can be executed in several ways. Two standard utilities provided with RAF are LOGIN.COM and LOGOUT.COM. These programs execute those parts of a script file that start with a LOGIN: label or a LOGOUT: label. Each segment must terminate with a DONE statement. The sample conversation file assumes asynchronous serial communications access through a Sytek LocalNet/20 broadband LAN, but similar files can be configured for access through intelligent modems. Remote Access Facility responds to the VAX "Login" prompt and to the "Password" prompt and then executes the VAX program RAFPC which sets up the RAF server.

```
! LOGIN PROCEDURE FOR RAF OVER A SYTEK LOCAL AREA NETWORK
LOGIN:      !remote monitor
            TIMER 10
            SEND /<13>/
            WAIT /#/
CALL:       SENDcr /LOC 1/
            WAIT /#/ /UNKNOWN COMMAND/
            IF 2 GOTO CALL
ECHO:       SENDCR /ECHO OFF/
            WAIT /#/
            SENDCR /CALL DEC/
            WAIT /CALL COMPLETED/
            IF TIMEOUT GOTO E1
            SEND /<13>/
            WAIT /Username:/
            SENDCR /USER/
            WAIT /Password:/
            SENDCR /PWD/
            WAIT /$/
            SENDCR /RUN RAF:RAFPC/
            WAIT /RAF/
            DONE

E1:         PRINT /* * * * * * * * * * * * * * * */
            PRINT /           LAN PORT ON VAX/
            PRINT /NOT AVAILABLE AT THIS TIME/
            PRINT /* * * * * * * * * * * * * * * */
            DONE

LOGOUT:     send /<03><03><03><03><03><03><03>/
            wait /$/
            SENDCR /LOG/
            wait /#/
            sendcr /loc 17/
            DONE
```

Listing 6.1. LAN Login Procedure.

When the conversation file is completed, the user has access to virtual disks D: through S:. With the use of the MS-DOS Change Directory (CD) command, the user can change the directory associated with a specific RAF remote device (virtual disks D: through S:). From the C: (hard disk) PC root directory, for example, one could issue the following commands:

```
C>CD D:USER:[ACCOUNT1]<CR>
C>CD E:USER:[ACCOUNT2]<CR>
```

where "USER:[ACCOUNT1]" and "USER:[ACCOUNT2]" are VAX directories. From that point on, all that would be necessary to use MS-DOS commands like "TYPE" or "COPY" would be to refer to "disks" D: or E:. For example, to list a text file in a remote directory one would issue the standard DOS-type command:

```
C>TYPE E:XYZ.TXT<CR>
```

To copy a VAX file from the VAX to the PC for further processing one could enter:

```
C>COPY E:XYZ.TXT C:\TEXTFILE\XYZ.TXT<CR>,
```

which would place the file XYZ.TXT in the DOS directory \TEXTFILE on the local hard disk, drive C:. Remote Access Facility communicates via a proprietary full-duplex, error-correcting protocol that includes compression algorithms. Thus, while copying files at 9,600 b/s is slow compared to local copy commands, RAF offers significant performance enhancements when compared to other error-correcting file transfer protocols. For example, transferring a 15,938-byte text file to the VAX using Kermit took 60 seconds. Copying the same file with RAF took only 20 seconds. Transferring a 15,047-byte binary file with Kermit took 126 seconds; with RAF, the same transfer took only 33 seconds. A card image file of about 207,000 bytes of character data took only 2 minutes 22 seconds to transfer to a VAX, but with a more standard file-transfer technique embedded in a terminal emulator, transfer to an IBM (compatible) mainframe took 22 minutes.

Once the RAF virtual drive has been defined, applications can access VAX files and write files directly to VAX directories. A word processing file or a spreadsheet file can be saved directly to the VAX from WordStar or Lotus simply by saving to drives D: or E:. Utilities such as Sidekick can edit VAX text files directly. Of course, programs such as the Norton Utilities, which act directly on the hardware, cannot be used on RAF virtual drives. MS-DOS file utilities, such as FFM by Bill Neidert, can be executed. The VAX directory appears on the left half of the screen, and a DOS subdirectory appears on the right. All of FFM's utilities (Copy, Rename, Delete, Show) can be performed on the files in the VAX directly, just as if it was a DOS directory.

A major advantage of using a product like RAF is that end users are able to access VAX applications *as if they were local PC programs*. It is possible, therefore, to execute an instruction like "VTX" (the DEC/VAX videotex system) on the PC and be placed immediately in VTX on the VAX. Remote Access Facility has two methods for accomplishing this task. First, the RAF utility "REMOTE" can be used to produce a small ".com" file that automatically submits a command to the VAX, providing that the RAF link is active. The REMOTE command is straightforward:

```
C>REMOTE filename "VAX_command"<CR>
```

To make videotex appear as a local application, even though it is running on the VAX, issue the following REMOTE MS-DOS command:

```
C>REMOTE VTX "VTX"<CR>
```

If the resulting VTX.COM file is placed in a directory with a path defined through DOS, executing VTX from any DOS directory will result in the VAX Videotex program appearing on the screen, just as if it were a DOS application. In order to see a directory on the VAX, a COM file named VDIR might be created using the RAF command REMOTE VDIR "DIR." When VDIR is executed on the PC, RAF executes the command "DIR" on the VAX. Alternatively, one can also enter the command DIR D: through DOS, and RAF will translate the VAX "DIR" command so that the directory listing appears in DOS format.

The REMOTE utility provides a very simple method for executing a VAX command or program from the PC's prompt. There are some things it does not do smoothly enough, however, including checking the communications line to ensure that RAF is active. Datability provides a set of subroutines in a library called RAFLIB.LIB, which allows specialized programs that can access VAX facilities to be written on the PC. The programming languages supported as of this writing were Fortran (Microsoft), C (Lifeboat, Lattice), Pascal (Microsoft), and BASIC (Microsoft basic compiler, IBM basic compiler, and Microsoft Business Basic). There are a number of things these subroutines can do, including checking the communications line to ensure that RAF is active, and, if it is not, to login to a VAX using a predefined conversation file. An example of a program that does this checking and then executes the VAX/VMS "DIR"ectory command is shown in Listing 6.2.

A third major feature that facilitates a user-transparent micro-to-mainframe link is RAF's ability to call subroutines running on the VAX from a main program running on the PC. One reason this feature is important is that access to many mainframe and supermini database systems is organized through the use of subroutine calls from a calling program that provides the user interface. This is an approach quite different from the database packages typically found on micros. With the ability to call sub-

```
      program rtest
c
      character file*20, param*50, prog*50, sys*50
c
c     Initialize the program for RAF
c
      call raffor
c
c     check for a RAF link
c
10    call rafok(iflag)
c
c     if the RAF link is not active, then login using the
c        'conversation' file 'lan.cnv'.
c
      if (iflag .ne. 1) then
         file = 'c:\raf\lan.cnv'
         param = ' '
         call raflgi (file,iflag,param)
      endif
c
c     execute a VAX command (in this case, DIR)
c
      sys = 'DIR '
      call rafrun (iflag, prog, sys)
      if (iflag .ne. 1) then
         write (*,'('' Remote program/command'',
     *                ''  ended in Error'')')
         go to 20
      endif
c
      write (*,'('' VAX application finished'')')
c
c     End this program's link with RAF
c
20    call rafend
      end
```

Listing 6.2. PC Fortran Program to Perform Remote Process Execution.

routines executing on the VAX from a PC main program, it is possible to write very user-friendly front-ends to large-scale corporate databases. Similarly, computational problems too complex for today's generation of micros can have calculations performed on the VAX, and the results can be passed to the main program running on a PC. Listings 6.3 and 6.4 illustrate this approach with a fairly trivial example.

To make the remote execution of VAX subroutines work, it is first necessary to compile both programs. On the VAX end the following commands are executed in order to compile XYZ and place its object file in a subroutine library called TESTLIB (the dollar sign is the VAX/VMS prompt):

```
$ fortran xyz
$ library/insert testlib xyz
```

On the PC, the program RAFTEST is compiled with the Microsoft Fortran compiler and then linked with the MS-DOS LINK.EXE in the normal way; however, RAFLIB.LIB must be part of the linking procedure, as well as any user libraries and the FORTRAN and MATH libraries along with a local object file produced by a RAF utility, RAFSL. RAFSL allows the user to define to RAF what and where the remote and local subroutines are, producing a local subroutine of the same name as the remote subroutine

```
      PROGRAM RAFTEST
C
C     TEST RAF REMOTE SUBROUTINE FACILITY
C
      CHARACTER A*1, PROG*10, SYS*10
      INTEGER*2 N
C
C     Initialize the RAF Interface
C
      CALL RAFFOR
C
C     Clear the Screen and Write first notice
C
      CALL CLS
      CALL LOCATE (1,1)
      WRITE (*,'(''This is the MAIN Program'',
     1  '' Running on the PC'')')
C
C     The character variable "A" is initialized with an "I"
C         to tell RAF that the "real" argument in XYZ (N) is
C         an Integer variable.
C
      A = 'I'
C
C     Call Subroutine XYZ which exists on the VAX
C
      CALL XYZ(N, A)
C
C     Write the final notices on the screen
C
      WRITE (*,5)
5     FORMAT (' The VAX Task has Completed and',
     1  ' We''re back on the PC')
      WRITE (*,10)
10    FORMAT (' TASK COMPLETED, N ='\)
      WRITE (*,'(I4)') N
C
C     Deinitialize RAF
C
      CALL RAFEND
      END
```

Listing 6.3. PC Fortran Program to Call a VAX Subroutine (XYZ).

```
        SUBROUTINE XYZ(N)
C       THIS IS A TEST
C
C       TEST RAF REMOTE SUBROUTINE FACILITY
C
        INTEGER*2 N
        N = 0
        DO 10 I=1,50
           N = N + 1
10      CONTINUE
C
        RETURN
        END
```

Listing 6.4. VAX Fortran Subroutine to Accumulate N=50.

(XYZ in the examples) and the necessary code for the program to actually access the VAX when RAF is active. RAFSL also has an option to produce the final version of the VAX subroutine by requesting the name of the subroutine and the name of the library in which it resides. The resulting file on the VAX is XYZ.EXE. This is the equivalent of the linking procedure usually required on the VAX for a VAX program to run. RAFSL is completely menu driven and is easy to use. The result is a finished program that runs partly on the PC and partly on the VAX, doing whatever the programmer wishes it to do.

Although there are many compelling reasons to view the mainframe as a file server for micros, there are some compelling reasons not to do so. First among these reasons is the line speed at which most micros communicate with mainframe systems. In general, most micros connected to mainframes through the mid-1980s were linked as terminals of some kind: Either asynchronous terminals or as 3270-type synchronous terminals. When operating in a terminal-emulation mode on a dedicated network, the typical line speed for asynchronous devices is 9,600 b/s. Transferring a 100K binary file to the VAX with RAF takes well over three minutes.

"I can live with that," you say? Try backing up a 20 Mbyte hard disk at 9,600 b/s with RAF. It would take about 10 hours! If the PC were put on automatic and this activity accomplished in the dead of night, individual users might not see a problem. Remember, however, that there may be hundreds of users attempting to do PC-to-mainframe backups, placing a considerable load on both the mainframe and the communications system, possibly slowing down the transfer rate even further.

One solution to this problem is to use higher speed communications—directly coupling the mainframe into a high-speed LAN, such as Ethernet.

Remote Access Facility, in fact, approaches this issue through an implementation that can use Ethernet, since that is DEC's preferred method of linking several VAXs and peripherals (such as terminal servers). With an Ethernet board installed in a PC, connected to a DECNet Ethernet, transfer speeds from VAX to PC would provide performance better than or equal to the speed at which a PC accesses a floppy disk. Even using slower serial communications, the concept remains viable for some situations. By the mid-1990s it is likely that most connections will be via a LAN.

Early versions of RAF had some operational anomalies that should be or have been changed. For example, it preempted all device names from the last physical device through device name S:. Especially with DOS 3.1 and later, this greatly detracts from the utility of the DOS SUBSTitute command to specify paths as virtual disks or to add physical drives on XT, AT, or 80386 class machines. This is also a major inconvenience to users working in a LAN, which may also need some of those drive identifiers. This is a major problem in the increasingly complex workstation configurations people are now finding necessary. Datability should, we think, allow the user to place a limit on the number of virtual disks defined rather than arbitrarily insisting on all device names through S:. We say this notwithstanding the fact that limited use can be made of "devices" named beyond Z: using some of the keyboard's special characters as drive names. Datability is moving toward a Microsoft Windows version that may help this situation.

RAF and products like it are designed to assist with cooperative computing. Cooperative computing requires not only facilities for having parts of a task run on more than one machine, it also means timely establishment of the links among the machines. Typical of the kinds of things that can happen is illustrated when the REMOTE procedure is submitted without an active RAF connection. The RAF system, after a relatively long time (2 minutes or more), times out. RAF indicates the link is not active and then asks for (A)bort or (R)etry. The DOS prompt often does not come back, depending on what response is made. Rather, a reboot of the system may be necessary. Sometimes this can entail turning the PC off and doing a hard cold start. These REMOTE procedures should first check the connection, then gracefully provide an exit back to MS-DOS. Of course, this problem can be averted by programming one's own procedures, but this limits RAF's flexibility somewhat for the end-user.

For a system with the features provided by RAF, the product is relatively easy to use, seems to be stable, and certainly lives up to the claims of its developers. It is an example of a class of products essential to EWC. When a mainframe is present, the mainframe will be regarded as a peripheral to the micro, rather than the reverse. This, and other products like it, promise the end-user of computing a simple and flexible interface to large super-mini and mainframe systems. In a computing environment in which distributed processing is becoming well established, RAF-like products will likely become the means for highly sophisticated systems of micro/mainframe integration.

The Mainframe Print Server

Closely related to the use of the mainframe as a file server is its use as a print server. Like the file-server concept, using the mainframe as a PC print server means providing the ability to print a file, generated on the micro, on the mainframe's printing facilities. This might be desirable because of the availability of high-quality, high-speed printing on the mainframe. As the prices for letter-quality printers, especially small laser printers, has fallen, this may be less attractive than in previous times. It remains true, however, that many large laser printers have much more capability than some of the smaller lasers. The networking issues remain about the same, however, for both print and file serving, since the problem of transferring a file to the mainframe, then routing to a printer, still exists. The principal objective of implementing such a system would again be to make the facility appear to the user as an extension of the micro. Ideally, users could print from a microcomputer-based word processing package to a virtual printer on the mainframe.

Although it is possible to simply send a file to a mainframe system, then use a mainframe utility to print the file, it is often a complicated process. Moreover, if the mainframe's printers are heavily used, the turnaround time might be excessive. The major reason for using the mainframe as a print server would be if the mainframe's printer had features and facilities not available locally. Notwithstanding the disadvantages of using the mainframe's facilities in this fashion, situations are bound to arise in which the integration of mainframe printing facilities and microcomputers would be advantageous to both the organization and the micro users.

User-Transparent Micro–Mainframe File Transfers

One common theme of this chapter has been the issue of how to transfer "bulk" data between the micro and the mainframe. Much of the focus has been on making those data transfers transparent to the user. Over the past few years many people have suggested that programmers, for example, should develop code on micros (which includes substantial testing) before moving it to a target mainframe. A batch job-submission facility is similar in concept. It would be helpful to completely set up a mainframe job on a micro and submit it directly to the mainframe's OS. IBM has produced several versions of the IBM PC designed to operate in a mainframe environment. These have included the XT/370 and AT/370 systems.

The AT/370 system operates under IBM's VM/PC operating system. Features available under the VM/PC include the text editor XEDIT, which is the same as the XEDIT product on VM/CMS on IBM mainframes, VMPCSERV (a mainframe link program), the OS/VS COBOL compiler, and a 370 assembler. Installations using VM/CMS on the mainframe can use VMPCSERV to control communications. Mainframe CMS (conversational monitor system) minidisks can be used as local PC minidisks as well as VM printers are used as VM/PC printers. For those central systems using TSO running under OS/MVS, TSOSERV can be used in a manner analogous to VMPCSERV, which includes executing TSO commands from a local VM/PC session and file spooling to the mainframe for printing.

Third-party (non-IBM) support for IBM environments are now coming to market, such as Unicorn Systems' MicroCICS.[9] Customer information control system (CICS) provides a transactional environment for many IBM mainframe users. With MicroCICS, programmers can generate BMS (basic mapping support) maps; define, load, and edit VSAM (Virtual Sequential Access Method) files; and modify system table information. MicroCICS reportedly provides almost full compatibility with recent CICS releases. XEDIT is distributed by IBM with VM/PC, although experienced TSO users and programmers will be more familiar with TSO's SPF editor. Another third-party software developer has generated a PC-based version of the SPF editor called SPF/PC (from Command Technology Corporation).

All these things can be done, of course, but they typically require the user to go through several discrete steps—hardly a transparent process. Moreover, appropriate communications software and hardware is frequently not designed with these objectives in mind, so the capabilities may not be universally available within an organization. Cost, too, may keep many organizations from providing some or all the services discussed. The AT/370 PCs are expensive high-end machines, not typically used for end user workstations. There are, however, some things that can be accomplished with low cost. For example, if a user is a frequent user of both micros and mainframes, it might be appropriate to equip that person with a text editor on the micro that looks like the one used on the mainframe, or vice versa.

A development that is picking up steam is the use of minicomputers as intermediaries between micros and mainframes. This hierarchical approach to computing is not new, of course, but computer prices are now approaching the point where organizations other than the wealthiest corporations can consider such possibilities. It is also apparent that "supermicros" (or perhaps "mini-minis") such as DEC's MicroVAX, AT&T's various UNIX systems, IBM's AS/400, and others on the market will play an important role in this hierarchical structure. A MicroVAX is far more powerful than a PC/AT, for example. It is also more expensive. These machines can support a true multiprocessing environment and are capable of supporting multiple users. Writing in *ComputerWorld*, G. Villapiano has suggested that, when establishing micro-to-mainframe links, many DP departments overlook a viable alternative—using a minicomputer as an interface between the mainframe and the micros.[10] Such an approach, according to Villapiano, can reduce systems cost, maintenance, and complexity. Minicomputers can be used for presorting, prequalification, and other preprocessing tasks, thereby unburdening the mainframe. Among other things, minis can act as gatekeepers for access to mainframe resources and as additional ports to the network. Finally, because many minis are UNIX-based and fault-tolerant, system standardization, control, and reliability are enhanced.

IBM has recognized the possibilities inherent in a micro–mini–mainframe link in several products now available for its AS/400 minicomputer.[11] Software with EMail and a database server that allows micro and minicomputers to exchange editable documents is offered for IBM PCs. Using the AS/400 in a micro-to-mainframe setup reportedly provides security, faster response time, less mainframe degradation, and cost efficiency.

Some manufacturers nominally in the "office automation" business are recognizing the potential of the micro–mini–mainframe link and they are almost universally providing direct micro support through a minicomputer (often with a LAN add-on to the mini system). The minicomputer can link to IBM or other mainframes. Even DEC, which has for years attempted to avoid buckling under to IBM's "standards," is now offering a full line of support for linking VAX superminis to IBM mainframes and is supporting IBM-style micros.

Whether one thinks of the micro as a mainframe peripheral or the mainframe as a micro peripheral, the interaction between the two must clearly become simpler for the end user. Ideally, the user would have to confront only a single computing environment. For computers to become better information tools, people must use them in much the same manner as pencils and paper—without much educational overhead. This can be accomplished only by designing *integrated* micro-to-mainframe links that allow the user to easily use whichever computing environment is most appropriate to the problem at hand. Many of the tools are, or should soon be, available to do this task, but it will also take some organizational will, specifically the DP divisions within large organizations, to recognize the demand.

Notes

1. T. W. Madron, "Despite Claims, Micro–Mainframe Links Remain Undeveloped," *ComputerWorld*, July 23, 1984.
2. As quoted in *ComputerWorld*, June 11, 1984, p. 127.
3. T. W. Madron, "Despite Claims, Micro–Mainframe Links Remain Undeveloped," *ComputerWorld*, July 23, 1984.
4. S. Austin, "In Search of the Missing Link (Terminal Emulators)," *Business Computer Systems*, Vol. 4, July 1985, pp. 83–96.
5. G. Wheelwright, "Micro–Mainframe Links," *Communications* (GB), Vol. 2, No. 4, April 1985, pp. 19–21.
6. An early entry into this arena was IBM's TopView. See T. W. Madron, "Is TopView Worth the Investment?" *ComputerWorld*, May 13, 1985.
7. Lee Thé, "How to Automate Your Communications," *Personal Computing*, Vol. 9, No. 9, Sept. 1985, pp. 91–97.
8. This review of RAF was published in a somewhat different version in T. W. Madron and D. J. Molta, "PCs Teach the VAX New Tricks," *PC World*, Vol. 5, No. 1, Jan. 1987, pp. 230ff. Since 1987 Datability has continued to enhance RAF. See, for example, R. Rupp, "New Tools for PC LAN-to-VAX Integration," *NewWare Technical Journal*, July 1990, pp. 21ff; and Anon., "A PC-VAX Fusion," *Digital Review*, July 24, 1989.
9. Brandy C. De Shazo, "Personal CICS," *PC Tech Journal*, Vol. 3, No. 12, Dec. 1985, pp. 171ff.
10. G. Villapiano, "Links: Micro to Mini," *Computerworld*, Vol. 18, No. 46A, Nov. 14, 1984, pp. 29, 32.

11. Although IBM's System 36 and System 38 have now been supplanted by the AS/400, a helpful older article is E. Horwitt, "IBM's Beautiful Baby: New System 36 Developments Provide Greater Micro-to-Mainframe Capabilities," *Business Computer Systems*, Vol. 4, No. 4, April 1985, p. 35.

CHAPTER 7

LANs and WANs

Earlier chapters alluded to the importance of IBM-style synchronous data communications. This chapter will delve more deeply into the "hows" and "whys" and will introduce methods for integrating micros into these networks. Later chapters will cover specific methods for micro integration in asynchronous networks. Although many newcomers to computing—those who have learned about computing through microcomputers—seem to believe that computing was born with the IBM PC, this is not the case. IBM has, of course, been a dominant manufacturer in the mainframe computer business for decades. With the coming of Remote Job Entry Terminals (RJE), in the 1960s, it became apparent that reliable methods of transferring files were necessary—Data-Link Control protocols became necessary.

Through the 1960s, most of IBM's mainframe computing was batch oriented, characterized by running a job consisting of a group, or batch, of punched cards. Reports were then printed on heavy-duty printers. Because large organizations often needed to read cards and print reports at sites other than at the computing center, RJE devices were developed. As originally conceived, an RJE terminal made it possible to pass large batches of data from the remote end and receive processed data back from the host. Data were input from cards to a card reader and received back as printed reports or punched cards. Today the functions of the card reader/punch and printer have been taken over by transaction terminals and, increasingly, microcomputers.

Many microcomputer applications still engage in batch processing, not transaction processing, even though the use of punched cards is virtually dead. Using keyboards does not necessarily imply transaction or interactive processing. Batch computing is a technique in which many data transactions are collected over a period of time and aggregated for sequential processing. A batch system is to be distinguished from transaction or interactive computing. In a transaction environment, files are updated and results are generated immediately as a result of data entry. In an interactive environment, transactions are processed one at a time, often eliciting a response from a user before proceeding. An interactive system may be conversational, implying continuous dialogue between the user and the system.

Because data processing (DP) was batch oriented, and because remote computing originally took place over dedicated pairs of copper wire (either dedicated phone lines or privately owned cables), a reliable and efficient method for transferring data had to be developed. Twisted-pair wire is electrically "noisy," which introduces the possibility of data errors, especially when large quantities are sent at one time. It is important to note, however, that a data communications protocol is *not* a "cable-and-controller" system, but a means for organizing data for transfer between or among computers and/or terminals. As shall be seen, however, hardware organization does interact with the protocols in important ways. This chapter will, therefore, discuss hardware organization from time to time.

Perhaps the most important alternative to LANs for organizing enterprise-wide computing (EWC), even in the 1990s and for large systems, is IBM's System Network Architecture (SNA). System Network Architecture is a layered network architecture originally designed to provide a wide range of networking capabilities, and it can accommodate functions associated with both LANs and wide area networks (WANs), although it is often thought of as an architecture for WANs rather than for LANs. In the late 1970s, when Xerox realized that most users were within a short distance of the central computer, Ethernet was developed, and LANs were thrust into the mainstream of the computing enterprise. Digital Equipment Corporation (DEC) responded to SNA with its own layered architecture, Digital Network Architecture (DNA). Unlike IBM, which continues to promote SNA, with some modifications, DEC, in Phase V, has moved DNA to an OSI Reference Model-compliant architecture. On a more general level, generic Transport Control Protocol/Internet Protocol (TCP/IP) systems, or eventually, generic OSI (Open System Interconnection) networks, can also be structured to provide an overarching network architecture for environments in which LANs and WANs coexist.

Distributed Processing and LANs

There are, according to James Martin, two main reasons why one might wish to perform a transaction on a distant machine.[1] First, local equipment may have insufficient power to perform the task at hand. Second, the data needed may be stored elsewhere. The first reason is often seen in scientific and research institutions where sheer number-crunching power is required. The second is often seen in commercial or governmental environments where the *corporate database* is kept and maintained. The two functions are not mutually exclusive, of course. A large, powerful, database-management system may need additional computing power in order to meet response-time objectives. It may also be necessary to maintain large amounts of data that are subject to extensive scientific analysis by multiple researchers.

Accessing a remote computer may not necessarily mean engaging in distributed processing. Computer networks consisting of a central computer and a number of terminals linked by a data-communications system have been around for a long time. For distributed processing to take place, the "system" must consist of more than one processor. A by-product of this definition's generality is that a very large number of configurations are possible. These definitions can be made more specific by insisting that the processors be in different locations, that they be linked by communications systems, that they serve one organization, that they serve a coherent set of objectives, and/or that the processors are linked in an integrated fashion. These and other possible constraints to distributed processing are probably violated more often than observed in any real organization. Moreover, with the advent of the microcomputer's wide distribution, a distributed processing environment may grow without the explicit knowledge or acquiescence of the owners of the parent machines.

Distributed Computing

There are other terms and concepts helpful in understanding distributed processing. Two concepts are particularly useful: distributed data processing (DDP) and distributed intelligence. A DDP system employs more than one geographically separate processor linked by telecommunications. Distributed intelligence involves the use of processors in terminals, controllers, or peripheral machines to execute functions that individually do not perform the complete processing of a transaction. Local Area Networks have become important elements in distributed processing environments. A simplified diagram of LANs in a traditional hierarchical distributed processing system may be found in Figure 7.1.

Among the various network topologies discussed in Chapter 3, and graphically depicted in Figure 3.1, was a hierarchical system. When a LAN—which may be a bus, a ring, or a star—is a node in a distributed system, a hierarchical structure is at least implicitly established. As shown in Figure 7.1, the mainframe is tied to the LAN through a data-communications line of some sort—later discussion will center on the options for that line—in one of several ways: Through a gateway or communications server on the LAN, or through a more direct attachment such as a board in a VAX or an 8232 channel-attached LAN controller for an IBM mainframe. A file server may be attached to either LAN. A specific example may be helpful.

In a university, for example, a central file of alumni is likely maintained

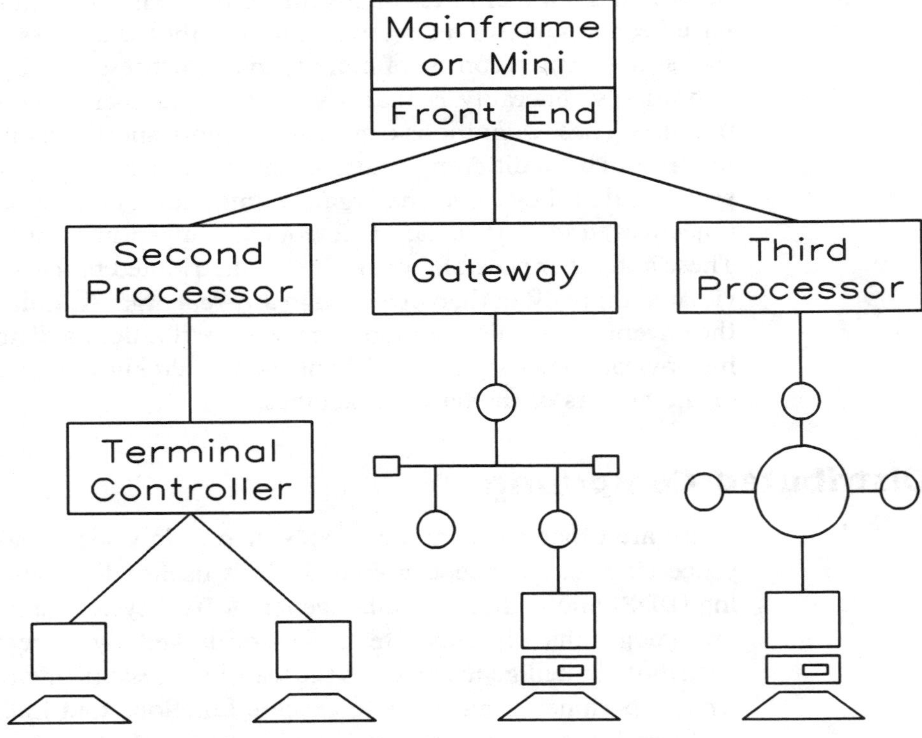

Figure 7.1. LANs in a Traditional Distributed System.

for access by several departments, including an Alumni Office, the Athletics Department, the President's Office, and perhaps the Registrar's Office, as well as individual academic departments. The Alumni Office produces not only many general mailings during the year but also mailings to specific subsets of the complete alumni file. Each year specific class reunions are organized for five, ten, and twenty year intervals. In 1990, therefore, there were reunions for the classes of 1985, 1980, and 1970.

The staff members of the Alumni Office are bound together in a PC-based LAN as depicted in Figure 7.1, which also has several laser printers attached to the file server. Transactions are generated that access the mainframe's database system to separately subset and download the alums for the classes of 1970, 1980, and 1985 to the file server. Three staff members might be assigned as project managers for the three class reunions. Each of those people, from their own workstations, write "personalized" letters of invitation to the alums for the years individually assigned, merge the respective mailing lists now on the file server, and print the letters and envelopes. There were follow-up mailings, of course, so they kept the files until 1990's round of reunions were completed.

The process just described has many advantages and virtually no disadvantages from the standpoint of project management. First, to complete the entire project there need be no direct intervention by the central computing center staff—the projects are under the complete control of the Alumni Office. Second, only a single database of alumni is kept, thereby conserving computer resources whether at the local or central level, even though it is shared by many departments. Third, the actual work of processing the projects is accomplished at the most convenient (and user-friendly) level of the computing environment without placing stress on the central mainframe for doing what is, in reality, trivial computer processing. In essence, all processing on this particular project has been accomplished at the most appropriate computing level. The several project managers have maintained complete control over their projects and are, therefore, completely accountable for the success or failure of the projects. By the mid-1980s it was possible to structure systems that worked precisely as described, although I will hasten to add that few worked as smoothly (most failures could probably be laid at the doorstep of organizational, rather than technical, constraints). Unfortunately, in many, if not most, organizations, intraorganizational "glitches" often prevent the deployment of truly integrated distributed processing.

Bear in mind that I have, thus far, described only one possible network environment out of many available. In a smaller organization without a central mainframe, there might be a network of LANs, for example, with each LAN being the peer of all others. Likewise, there might be a network of multiple mainframes or superminis, some of which might have local hierarchical structures, others might be organized as equal peers in a high-speed LAN. Then, too, the mainframe or supermini might be tightly integrated into the LAN to serve as the LAN's file server. The precise details of a particular configuration will depend on a number of technical, political, and other organizational factors, but cost-effective technology is available for such distributed processing. Increasingly, LANs will be nodes in a distributed system rather than terminal controllers with dumb terminals (or PCs acting as dumb terminals) at the end of the line.

This section has attempted to demonstrate the viability of LANs as nodes in a larger, distributed network without discussing specific WAN architectures. In most real situations, however, it will not be possible to start from scratch and devise the "best" solution. For most installations it will be necessary to integrate LANs into an existing network of some kind. Two of the most important network architectures—sponsored by large computer manufacturers—are IBM's SNA and DEC's DNA. In addition, LANs will be integrated into Metropolitan Area Networks (MANs). Local area network NOSs (Network Operating Systems) also constitute network architectures, which will be considered in a later chapter. At that point it will be important to understand how LANs fit into the overall OSI scheme of things, and that will be illustrated by reference to MAP, the Manufacturing Automation Protocol. Finally, this chapter will look at LANs in the context of the Internet, the TCP/IP national network in the United States (important to the public sector, but with growing importance for the private sector as well).

Three of the networks discussed in the following pages are full-fledged network architectures: TCP/IP, SNA, and DNA. They are all layered architectures, although none is OSI standard. The MAP, by way of contrast, is a self-contained NOS since MAP assumes a LAN as the primary Physical and Data-Link Layer communications medium: An IEEE 802.4 token bus system. The other architectures can and do use a wide variety of physical media and are not linked to IEEE's Media Access Control (MAC) standards. Each subsequent section will explicity compare the architectures with the OSI Reference Model in an effort to demonstrate selected architectural details; however, do not be misled by this method of presentation. System Network Architecture, DNA, and TCP/IP are not OSI standards. Clearly, both SNA and DNA are proprietary standards adopted by IBM and DEC, respectively. Even TCP/IP, although usually thought of as a standard, was devised by the U.S. Department of Defense (DoD) for its own proprietary use. The brief comments on MANs point up the differences between fully elaborated network architectures and the IEEE standards in that the IEEE 802.6 (MAN) standard, like its LAN standards, deal only with the Physical and Data-Link layers of the OSI Reference Model. Note, however, that in the move from DNA Phase IV to DNA Phase V, DEC is moving to OSI compliance.

LANs and MANs

Although the IEEE has adopted a MAN standard, there are relatively few examples of what might be called MANs available, and these do not conform to the proposed IEEE standards. Those MAN networks that do exist are largely based on CATV and are often called Institutional Networks, or I-Nets. For several years I-Nets have been part of the franchising requirements of many community cable systems, but most cable companies have yet to fulfill the promises of the franchises. Moreover, recent Congressional legislation has reduced the role of local government in governing and regulating cable companies, leading to a further decrease in implementation of I-Nets. Finally, cities have been remiss in following up on franchise requirements. These failures, coupled with somewhat confused legal relationships between services reserved to telephone companies and cable systems, have meant that companies, local governments, school systems, and the like have continued to build their own networks based on leased telephone lines, private short-haul microwave, and occasionally on cable systems.

Cable operators, when they have attempted to provide data-communications services, have had very mixed results at best. Part of the problem has been that they have inappropriately marketed such services. Sammons Cable, Warner Communications, and others, have attempted to market consumer-based data services that include the distribution of various data and videotex systems. Market studies over the past fifteen years have indicated that in the United States (unlike Europe) consumers are not yet ready to pay for videotex services. On the other hand, in markets where clear data-communications services are needed, cable companies have been rather myopic in their evaluation of the need. In almost any university community, for example, there are hundreds or thousands of people (students, faculty, and staff) that need high-speed access to university computer facilities. Typically that access is through dial-up telephone service, which has been mediocre at best and relatively slow (300, 1,200, or 2,400 b/s).

With the development of higher speed (2,400 and 9,600 b/s), reasonably priced telephone modems, this situation is changing. Because analog telephone service is electronically noisy, required error-correction techniques often make the throughput of high-speed dial-access service unpredictable. Cable companies, by way of contrast, could offer high-quality, high-speed (9,600 or 19,200 b/s) services in a cost-effective manner without having to support any computer facilities of their own. For a cost approaching that of added-value consumer services, such as pay TV (HBO, Cinemax, Showtime, and similar services), cable companies could provide good quality data-communications services. Yet cable companies have failed to take advantage of these possibilities. Because of recent decisions of the Federal Communications Commission (FCC), the Bell Operating Companies (BOCs) may soon be able to compete with the CATV systems using the BOC's fiber plant, and ISDN (Integrated Services Digital Networks) is only a few years off.

In Figure 7.2 some possible options may be seen for LAN to MAN connectivity. Early in the work of 802.6, it considered a slotted ring proposal put forth by Burroughs, Plessey, and National Semiconductor. Although 802.6 dropped consideration of the earlier slotted ring, that topology has continued to be developed in Japan. In November 1987, 802.6 adopted Queued Packet and Synchronous Exchange (QPSX) as the sole MAN standard—at least for the present. Almost immediately the name of QPSX was changed to the Distributed Queue Double Bus (DQDB) because the Australian group that promoted the standard set up a firm with the QPSX name to sell products. The competing proposal, the multiplexed slot and token ring (MST), was withdrawn as a draft standard and is being sold as a proprietary network.[2] At this writing the MAN 802.6 manifestation is cloudy because modifications are still under consideration. Multiplexed slot and token ring, for example, may, in fact, be the bridge to FDDI-II since both are based on the same FDDI technology.

The MAN, an evolutionary step beyond the LAN, promises high-speed communications at distances greater than any LAN can handle. But in another sense, the MAN is what standards groups will make it. Just what standards will define a MAN is being hammered out by the IEEE's 802.6 committee. The committee outlined several goals for a MAN standard: It should accommodate fast and robust signaling schemes; it should guarantee security and privacy and permit establishment of virtual private net-

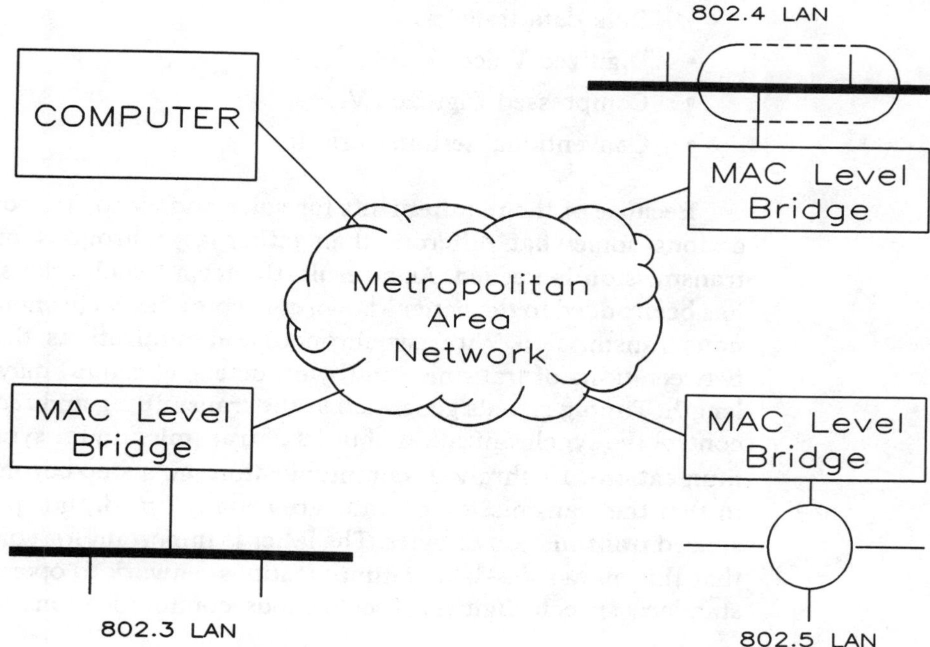

Figure 7.2. MAN to Other Connectivity.

works within MANs; it must ensure high network reliability, availability, and maintainability; and it should promote efficiency for MANs regardless of their size. The DQDB dual-bus MAN proposal, sponsored by Telecom Australia, was adopted because it meets or exceeds those requirements.[3] The DQDB architecture is illustrated in Figure 7.3. It is conceived as a system that will likely run on either a broadband CATV system or on fiber-optic cable at 150 Mb/s or greater.

The difficulty in describing MAN standards is that the standards are still being developed. As John L. Hullett and Peter Evans have noted, however, a "good standard is crucial to MAN development, since interoperability between computer and telecommunications networks is a prerequisite to a successful launch of the new technology."[4] Unlike the 802 LANs, a MAN is expected to carry voice and video information in addition to data. Typical MAN traffic is expected to include:[5]

- LAN interconnection.
- Graphics and digital images.

- Bulk data transfer.
- Digitized Voice.
- Compressed Digitized Video.
- Conventional terminal traffic.

Because of the requirements for voice and video, a mode of communications somewhat different than either asynchronous or synchronous transmission is needed. As a result, the term "isochronous" transmission has been added to the better known concepts of asynchronous and synchronous transmission. With asynchronous communications, the time intervals between units of transmission (bytes, octets, et cetera) may be of unequal length. Timing signals generated at the transmitting and receiving stations control the synchronization of units of transmission for synchronous communications. Isochronous communications go a step beyond synchronous in that the transmission of units are equally timed, thus providing evenly spaced transmission of bytes. The latter is important for voice and video in that this allows the data communications network to operate much like a standard speech digitizer. Isochronous communications would generate

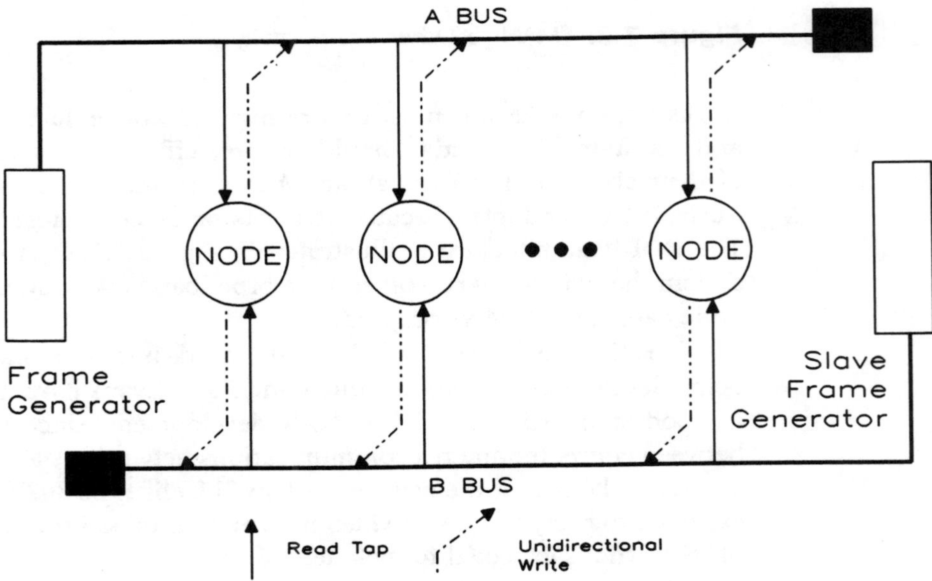

Figure 7.3. Dual-Bus Architecture.

voice signals, thereby eliminating the need for buffering mechanisms. These developments might be summarized by noting the important trend toward the use of packetized data and the services required for the delivery of those data.

The way in which LANs will be connected to MANs is through a MAC Layer bridge (see Chapter 6 for more detail). Bridges can operate several OSI Reference Model layers, although typically bridges will exist in either the Data-Link Layer or in the Network Layer. In the IEEE LAN standards, interoperability is typically achieved through a device that contains a MAC Layer specific for the LAN technology of the two networks being bridged. As will be shown in subsequent chapters, the output of the MAC sublayers are consistent with one another. Consequently, data moving in and out of the MAC sublayer is standardized in order to work with Logical Link Control (LLC).

LANs and the Internet: TCP/IP

Both TCP/IP and OSI are layered protocol stacks. The TCP/IP protocol set consists of four layers that might be labeled as Physical, Routing, Service, and Application.[6] The OSI protocol is, of course, structured around the seven-layer OSI Reference Model. The Physical Layer is not actually specified by TCP/IP. The user is free to use any physical transmission including WANs, MANs, and LANs. The most common networking systems at this writing were X.25 and IEEE 802.3 (Ethernet), both of which are explicit parts of the OSI framework. Remember in the discussions of the IEEE 802.x networks the 802 specifications dealt only with the OSI Physical and Data-Link layers, with the LLC sublayer providing a standardized access to the Network Layer. The TCP/IP begins at the rough equivalent of the OSI Network Layer.

The IP is more-or-less equivalent to the Network Layer of the OSI Reference Model, while TCP corresponds to at least the Transport Layer, and in some ways to the Transport (4) through the Presentation (6) layers. The comparable international protocols are the Connectionless-Mode Network Service (OSI 8473) for the Network Layer and the Connection Oriented Transport Protocol Specification (OSI 8073) for the Transport Layer. The other TCP/IP-related protocols are related to the Application Layer and include the File Transfer Protocol (FTP), the Simple Mail Transfer Protocol (SMTP), and the Terminal Emulation protocols (TELNET). Approximately equivalent international standards include File Transfer, Access and Management (FTAM, OSI DIS 8571), the Message Handling System (X.400), and the Virtual Terminal Protocol (VTP, OSI DIS 9041). In general, the OSI protocols are richer than those of TCP/IP. Moreover, related international protocols that support a wide variety of services exist in the layers between Transport and Application .

The Relationship of TCP/IP and OSI

Before going further with the discussion of the relationship of OSI and TCP/IP, it is necessary to clarify the use of the abbreviation "OSI," which is sometimes used to refer to the Open Systems Interconnection Reference Model, described in Chapter 3. The abbreviation OSI is also used to designate a more detailed set of protocols to be used as guidelines for configuring a real OSI network. It is used in the latter sense in this chapter. When OSI means the Reference Model, it will be modified appropriately. In Figure 7.4, I have attempted to display the relationship among the layers of TCP/IP, the OSI Reference Model, and the actual component standards for guiding the development of real systems.[7]

The seven layers of the OSI Reference Model are displayed on the right side of Figure 7.4. The boxes on the right contain names or numbers for some ISO standards for each layer. Some layer names for the four TCP/IP levels are on the left side of Figure 7.4, and the names of the TCP/IP components at those levels are in the boxes on the left. The TCP/IP protocol stack has been equated to the appropriate layers of the OSI Reference Model, but bear in mind that it is easier to draw such figures than to make their components equivalent. In general, the OSI standards are much richer both in number and in functionality than the TCP/IP standards. One of the challenges for users of TCP/IP networks, over the next few years, will be to migrate to OSI standards.

Migration from TCP/IP to OSI

The purpose of both TCP/IP and OSI is to provide a set of manufacturer-independent communications protocols. The DoD's motive, when it started developing TCP/IP in the late 1970s, was to broaden the base of hardware and software from which it had to choose for purposes of competitive bidding, rather than to be stuck with a proprietary networking system. With the development of international standards, however, it has become clear that far greater numbers of manufacturers will support international stan-

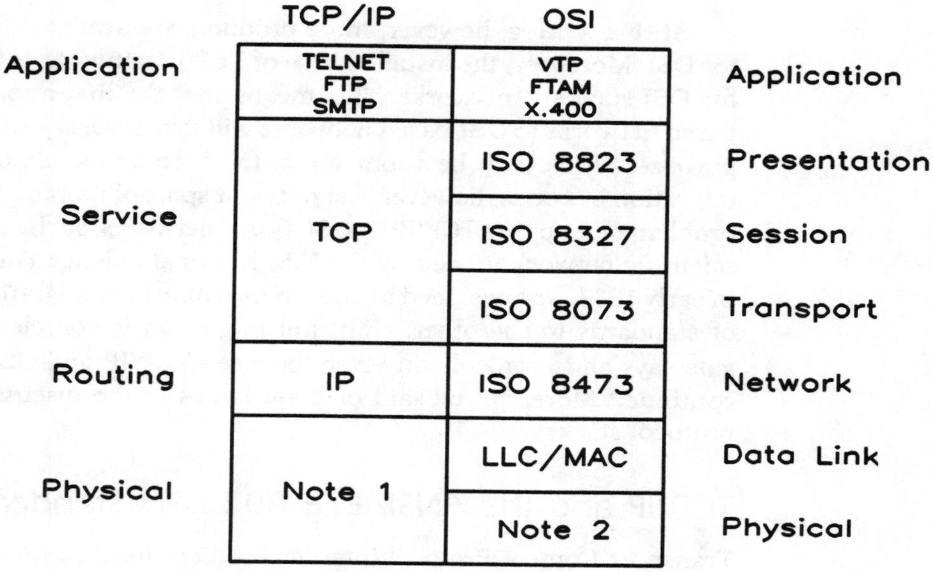

	TCP/IP	OSI	
Application	TELNET FTP SMTP	VTP FTAM X.400	Application
Service	TCP	ISO 8823	Presentation
		ISO 8327	Session
		ISO 8073	Transport
Routing	IP	ISO 8473	Network
Physical	Note 1	LLC/MAC	Data Link
		Note 2	Physical

X.400 = Message handling service.
ISO 8823 = Connection-oriented presentation protocol.
ISO 8327 = Connection-oriented session protocol.
ISO 8073 = Connection-oriented transport protocol.
ISO 8473 = Connectionless protocol.
LLC = Logical link control.
MAC = Media access control.

NOTES:

1. Some writers suggest that "Ethernet" and X.25 are the normal standards for TCP/IP. X.25 actually exists at the Network Layer while using HDLC as a Data Link protocol. X.25 and 802.3, therefore,are used only to deliver TCP/IP packets to IP (rotuing).
2. The Physical Layer in OSI parlance includes various modem standards, IEEE 802.x LANs, and the 8802/7 slotted ring standard.

Figure 7.4. TCP/IP–OSI Architectures.

dards than will support TCP/IP. International standards also have the support of most of the governments of Western Europe as well as the support of standards organizations. These factors, coupled with the richer functionality and more extensive protocol stack of the international standards, have led U.S. governmental organizations, including DoD, to announce that they too will move to OSI over the next decade.

At this writing, however, more products are available for TCP/IP than for OSI. Moreover, the installed base of TCP/IP networks is far greater than for OSI-standard networks. This means that the migration from TCP/IP-based networks to OSI-based networks will take several years, and for some purposes there may be room for both. A consequence of the need for migration has been, however, a significant spurt of literature discussing the problem of mapping TCP/IP to OSI. Some networks, such as the high-speed scientific network funded by the U.S. National Science Foundation (NSF) in early 1987, was designed to allow reasonably easy migration from one set of standards to the other. Until full migration is complete, products for gateways and protocol converters between TCP/IP and OSI networks will continue.[8] More will be said of these issues in the discussion of the two protocol stacks.

TCP/IP and the ANSI/IEEE 802 LAN Standards

Transport Control Protocol/Internet Protocol itself is independent of the Physical Layer. The most commonly used protocol suites below TCP/IP, however, are IEEE 802.3 (Ethernet) and X.25. The U.S. Air Force has recently been working on the definition of a Unified Local Area Network Architecture (ULANA) that seeks to formalize the relationship between the two protocol suites to provide user-transparent communications, especially for linking dedicated workstations and shared database capabilities.[9] Therefore, ULANA is one example of the way in which TCP/IP and IEEE 802.3 can work together. In the ULANA scheme, the IEEE MAC sublayer and the IEEE Physical Layer underlie the IP without making use of the IEEE LLC. The IP, of course, feeds TCP, and TCP, in turn, supplies services to TELNET, FTP, and SMTP. This formal use of IEEE standards will, ultimately, enhance the ability of the Air Force to migrate to OSI standards.

An Introduction to TCP/IP

Unfortunately, some authors occasionally mislead the unwary into the belief that there is some automatic relationship among certain standard protocol stacks. This is especially apparent in discussing LANs. I will, therefore, reiterate that although TCP/IP has been frequently implemented on 802.3 standard LANs, TCP/IP is a set of protocols unrelated to the Physical and Data-Link layers as described in the OSI Reference Model. The TCP/IP can be implemented on top of virtually any physical data-communications medium and related Physical and Data-Link layer protocols.

One other caveat should be noted. The classification of TCP and IP into different network layers is not accidental. Transport Control Protocol can reside on a single, integrated network and not require IP. That is, if node A on network Y wishes to communicate with node B on network Y, routing functions that exist within IP are typically not required. If network Y is an IEEE 802.3 LAN, for example, the 802.3 standard implementation will take care of getting a frame from node A to node B. If, however, node A on network Y wishes to send a message to node C on network X, and network X is, perhaps, an X.25 network, then IP is required. Transport Control Protocol provides packet sequencing, error control, and other services required to provide reliable end-to-end communications, while IP will take the packet from TCP, pass it through whatever gateways are needed for delivery to the remote TCP layer through the remote IP layer.[10] Some networks, in fact, may use IP but not TCP, preferring instead to use some alternate protocol at the Transport Layer.

Although I have been using, and will continue to use, the term "TCP/IP" to refer to several different protocols, the set of protocols is often termed the "Internet protocol suite" or the "Internet protocol stack." At this writing the term "protocol stack" seemed to be the catch-term of choice by the data-communications industry and will continue to be used herein. The Internet stack consists, as previously implied, not only of TCP and IP, but also of some Application Layer protocols. "TCP/IP" will continue to be used herein to refer to the entire internet stack.[11]

Much of the impetus for the development of TCP/IP was the need for internetworking services—the ability of an end user to communicate through a local machine to some remote machine or remote end user. The "traditional" TCP/IP services are supported by the appropriate protocols, which are described in this chapter. Those protocols are as follows:

- The FTP, which allows file transfers from one computer on the Internet to any other computer on the Internet.
- The TELNET, which provides a means for allowing a user on the Internet to log on to any other computer on the network.
- The SMTP, which allows users to send messages to one another on the Internet.

Each of the services implied by these protocols should generally be present in any TCP/IP implementation, although SMTP is not always supported by microcomputer-based systems.

Transport Control Protocol/Internet Protocol was designed before the widespread deployment of microcomputers and high-performance workstations. It was conceived in an era when users communicated through minicomputers and mainframes. With the changing nature of both computer technology and data communications technology, however, a need has developed for some computers on the Internet to perform specialized services, leading to a "server/client" model for the delivery of services. A server system provides specific services for network users, while a client system is a user of those services. Server and client may be on the same or different computers. Additional services provided within the scope of TCP/IP are as follows:[12]

- Network file systems;
- Remote printing;
- Remote execution;
- Name servers;
- Terminal servers; and
- Network-oriented window systems.

Not all the protocols that support these services, however, are a part of the official TCP/IP protocol stack.

The process by which a *packet* is constructed may be seen in Figure 7.5. The way in which information is transferred from one node to another in a TCP/IP network is illustrated in Figure 7.6. Transport Control Protocol communicates with applications through specific "ports," and each port has its own local number or address. If a process on Node A, associated with Port 1, must send a message to Port 2, Node B, that process transmits the message to its own Service Layer TCP with appropriate instructions to get it to its intended destination (Node and Port). TCP hands the message to IP with instructions to get it to the appropriate Node. In turn, IP transmits to the Physical Layer with instructions to get the message to the gateway, which is the first *hop* to Node B. This sequence of events is regulated by adding control information to user data at the various layers and may be clearly seen in figures 7.5 and 7.6. Transport Control Protocol segments user data into manageable units, then appends a TCP header, which includes the *destination port*, *segment sequence number*, and *checksum* to test for errors in transmission. This unit is called a *TCP segment*.

Once the TCP segment has been assembled, it is passed to IP, where an

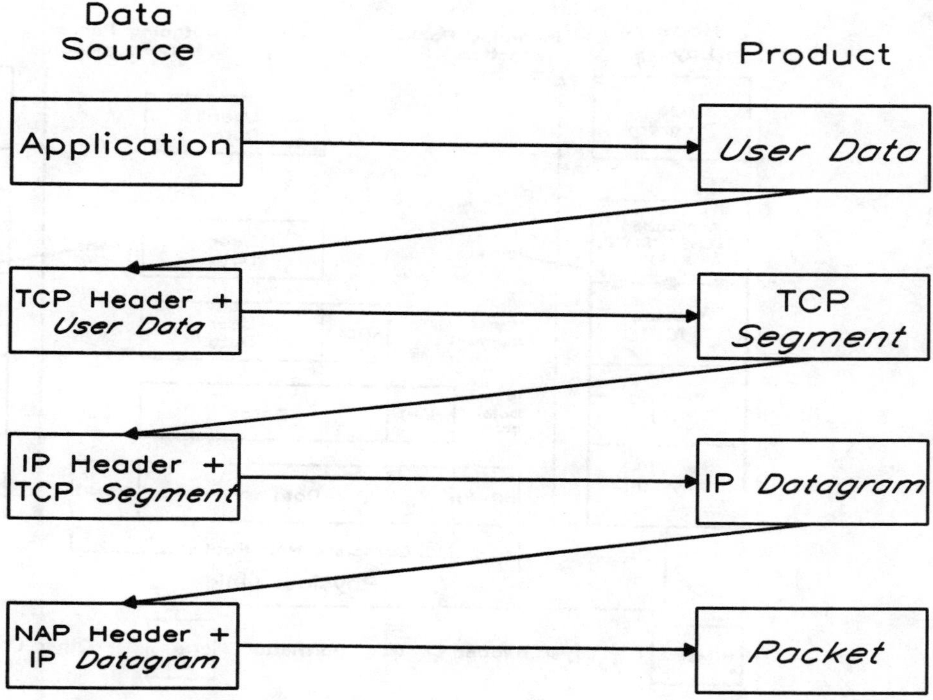

Figure 7.5. Packet Assembly.

IP header is appended. A major item stored in the IP header is the destination Host/Node address. The resulting unit is an *IP datagram*. Generally, a datagram may be defined as a finite-length packet with sufficient information to be independently routed from source to destination without reliance on previous transmissions. Datagram transmission typically does not involve end-to-end session establishment and may or may not entail delivery confirmation acknowledgment. The IP datagram is then given to the Physical Layer, where the network access protocol appends its own control information, thus creating a *packet*. The packet is then sent out on the physical medium. The packet header contains sufficient information to get the entire packet from Node A to at least the gateway and perhaps beyond. In the case of an IEEE 802.3 network, for example, the packet would be an 802.3 frame that encapsulates the TCP/IP data and control information. Note that error correction is likely to take place at several levels. As will be seen in chapters 7, 8, and 9, the 802.3, 802.4, and 802.5 protocols do their

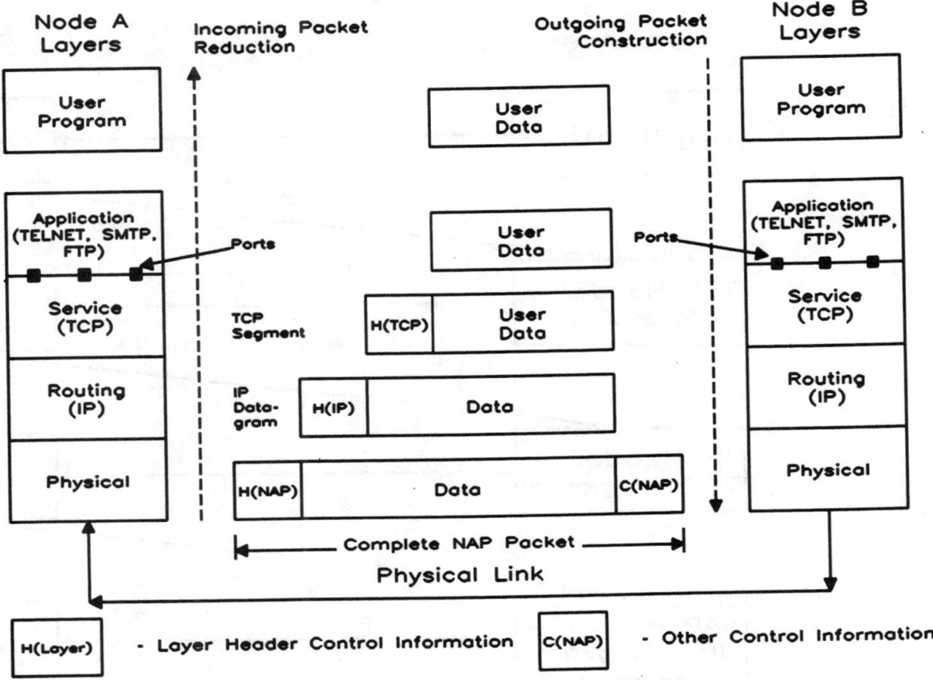

Figure 7.6. Nesting of Internet Layer Protocols.
Notes: H(Layer) Denotes Layer Header Control Information [H(TCP), H(IP), H(NAP)]; C(NAP) Denotes Other Control Information.

own error correction. The IP header also contains a checksum, as does the TCP header. At the receiving end, the reverse process takes place.

In Figure 7.6 the "layer" labeled "Physical" is intended to contain both the functions of the OSI Data Link and Physical layers. All nodes of a TCP/IP network might reside on a single LAN, such as an Ethernet. In such a case, TCP/IP would be operating as a LAN NOS. The original concept behind TCP/IP was, however, that it would provide a common standard for linking many remote machines, and more recently, many remote networks. Consequently, some router/gateway/bridge system must be used.

IBM and EWC

In many respects it may be impossible to briefly characterize IBM's approach to networks and networking simply because the task is so large.

Quite simply, IBM has, for many years, tried with varying degrees of success to provide something for everyone. A continuing and fundamental cornerstone of the IBM concept is their SNA, particularly as that has been enhanced by Advanced Program-to-Program Communications (APPC). The latter contains IBM's approach to peer computing so characteristic of concepts found in OSI and in TCP/IP. Local Area Networks, especially the Token Ring, have also developed into a major component of the strategy, although these two are being integrated into the broader SNA architecture and most recently into the Enterprise Systems Connection (ESCON) Architecture, using wideband, high-speed fiber-optic channels that allow customers to interconnect their computer systems over miles instead of a few hundred feet.[13] ESCON is designed to provide a cooperative, high-speed network environment for a wide range of IBM's computer systems. At the heart of the ESCON approach is a fiber-optic cabling system capable of delivering data at up to 10 megabytes (that is correct, megabytes not megabits). Interfaces are available that support the newer IBM computer series directly, the 3745 FEP, and FDDI 100 Mb/s rings, thus providing access to LANs as well. Conceptually, and this is key, ESCON is an extension of IBM's mainframe channel architecture—the system by which high-speed peripheral devices and mainframe computers have interfaced for many years. Thus, with ESCON, customers are no longer bound to a single computer room someplace but may provide high-speed, cooperative computing almost anywhere in a campus environment. It should be noted that this approach is an expansion of IBM's understanding of networking as revolving around their mainframe computer systems.

Local Area Networks have become of strategic importance to IBM if for no other reason than because the marketplace is demanding them. The primary technology supported by IBM is, as noted elsewhere, the Token Ring; however, IBM still supports the PC Network (a broadband system), its first entry into LANs. Moreover, notwithstanding the IBM propaganda against Ethernet, it resells Ungermann-Bass' Ethernet interface cards. In addition, IBM also sells an industrial LAN, its entry into the MAP market, based on 802.4 technology. The 8232 LAN controller will support Token Ring, Ethernet, and PC Network cards for channel attachment to an IBM 370/390 architecture mainframe. It also supports these same cards (including Ethernet) as attachments to other computers and devices. Connectivity between the 3270 Display System and the Token Ring has been established through one model of the 3174 cluster controller capable of accepting a Token Ring network interface card. Bear in mind as well that both the

PS/2 personal computers and the OS/2 operating system were structured as productivity tools within a networking environment. Unlike the manufacturers of LAN-based NOSs, IBM has not attempted to refocus EWC or networking on LANs. It should be remembered that LANs were first marketed by IBM in support of their mainframe systems, not as a replacement for them. For that reason it is possible to contend that IBM is not even in direct competition with Novell or Banyan, for example, in the LAN NOS competition. Where they do compete, however, is in IBM mainframe environments, and there Novell, Banyan, and others must go head-to-head with IBM.

SNA

SNA *is not* a data-communications protocol. It is a set of rules, procedures, and structures that encompasses IBM's data-communications design philosophy. Nor is SNA an OSI standard network, although it, like DEC's DNA, is a layered architecture. As the impact of OSI standards gathers strength, IBM is trying to come to terms with the two networking models. It remains to be seen how IBM's efforts in this arena will turn out. It, SNA, is also part of an IBM corporate strategy since it is the framework for future IBM data-communications development. New IBM products will have the SNA guidelines imposed on them.

The scope of SNA is broad. As a result, none of IBM's products implement the entire architecture. Conversely, IBM's individual products implement only those SNA elements that pertain to the function of the specific product. System network architecture is often confused with various explicit or implicit components of the architecture. System network architecture *is not* a Data-Link Control System such as SDLC (Synchronous Data Link Control), although SDLC is the most common protocol used; SNA is not a communications access method (not VTAM [Virtual Telecommunications Access Method]); and SNA is not a standard like X.25. Because of IBM's market position, however, SNA might be called a de facto communications architecture standard.[14] From a competitive perspective, DEC and others have had to come to terms with SNA.

System Network Architecture is a layered architecture similar to the OSI Reference Model described in Chapter 3. The relationship of the scope of OSI, SNA, SDLC, and BSC (Binary Synchronous Communications) models may be seen in Figure 7.7. Figure 7.7 is neater than reality, but the effort is useful, nevertheless. SNA proper is divided into only five (not seven)

OSI	SNA	SDLC	BSC
Application	End-User		
Presentation	Function Management		
Session	Data Flow Control		
	Transmission Control	Data Link Protocols Only	
Transport	Path Control		
Network			
Data Link	Data Link	Data Link	Data Link
Physical	Physical		

Figure 7.7. Scope of OSI, SNA, SDLC, and BSC Models.

layers—"End User" and "Physical" are not part of the formal scope of SNA. The "Data-Link" layer is marginal to SNA. The remaining four layers do not neatly fit the OSI model. On the other hand, the OSI model, not SNA, is the standard, and IBM and others have found the relationship of the two helpful.[15] Clearly, SDLC and BSC are concerned only with Data-Link Control and have limited scope. SDLC is clearly the Data-Link Control method most frequently used with SNA.

After the foregoing introduction to SNA, it is necessary to add a caveat. SNA is undergoing extensive renovation—an activity that started in the 1980s[16]—partly because computing preferences, even among IBM's largest mainframe customers, are changing with the impact of microcomputers, departmental LANs, true distributed processing, non-IBM multiprotocol bridges and routers, the acceptance of non-IBM LAN system software (such as Novell's NetWare), and related technology. In some of these areas IBM lags behind the marketplace. By 1990, Advanced Program-to-Program Communications (APPC) had been extended to include virtually all IBM computing environments from the MVS host operating system to micros.

Even as production on this book was being completed, IBM announced the Advanced Peer-to-Peer Networking (APPN) architecture as an enhancement to SNA.[17] The point is, it is not possible to cover all the latest details of something like SNA in a single book. This book does, however, attempt to provide a broad sweep of pertinent issues concerning IBM's SNA. Be warned that it is necessary to ask detailed questions of IBM concerning their current SNA position at the time of purchase.

Synchronous Protocols

IBM's two synchronous Data-Link Control protocols are Binary Synchronous Communications (BSC or Bisync) and SDLC. The former is byte oriented and the latter is bit structured. Binary Synchronous Communications has been in use since 1968 for data transmission between IBM computers and batch and transaction terminals. At this writing BSC is being rapidly displaced by SDLC/SNA, introduced in 1974, as IBM's strategic objectives for networking change, although many IBM mainframe installations still use BSC, and mixed systems are common.

One issue in data communications is the physical line's efficiency. Under circumstances in which machines transmit and receive continuously, with standard timing, synchronous transmission is more efficient than asynchronous transmission. A start/stop asynchronous protocol has the constant overhead of a start and stop bit as well as delays between characters, for a minimum of a 20 percent overhead (2 of every 10 bits). With synchronous communications, every bit follows one after the other without extra start-stop bits or delays. As a practical matter, this means that in a given period of time, at a comparable line speed (9,600 b/s, for example), more data can be transferred synchronously than asynchronously. Because synchronous communications is always organized into a block structure for transmission, extensive error checking has always been part of synchronous protocols, something that has only come recently to asynchronous communications.

Regardless of transmission mode, three levels of synchronization are needed: *bit synchronization*, *character synchronization*, and *message synchronization*.[18] The receiving machine must know when a bit starts and stops, when a character starts and stops, and when a message starts and stops. Bit synchronization is largely a function of hardware and establishes initial timing between the two ends of a communications session. Modems or other communications devices will contain a clock for automatically establishing a "bit phase." At the beginning of a synchronous data block, a special bit pattern is transmitted to establish character synchronization. With BSC, for example, the synchronization character is 01010101. This character is sent continuously during idle periods, and at least two transmissions are required to establish synchronization. If a block or packet structure is used, message synchronization will be necessary on either start-stop or synchronous systems. Messages will be framed by *start-of-header*, *start-of-text*, *end-of-record*, *end-of-block*, and *end-of-transmission* characters.

To standardize this discussion of BSC and SDLC, as well as other communications protocols in later chapters, the following issues will be considered:[19]

- Data Transfer Control. How the messages are organized and synchronized.
- Error Checking and Recovery. The method used to ensure that the data transmitted are the same as those received.
- Information Coding. The data coding supported by the protocol such as the American Standard Code for Information Interchange (ASCII), or IBM's Extended Binary Coded Decimal Interchange Code (EBCDIC).
- Information Transparency. The ability to transmit any character, including Data-Link Control characters, as data, especially important when transferring binary files over modern data communications networks.
- Line Characteristics. Are either half- or full-duplex or other line characteristics required?
- Synchronization Methods. How are blocks or packets synchronized?

Binary Synchronous Communications (BSC)

Since its introduction in 1968, BSC came to dominate IBM-oriented data communications. It became a well-known, well-understood, and stable method for transferring data between IBM or IBM-compatible devices. Even in the 1980s, when it became clear that most of IBM's data communications support would center on SDLC/SNA, the installed base of BSC systems was so great that it remained a major force in the marketplace.[20]

Data Transfer and Control

A BSC message or transmission block is divided into several standard fields, some of which may vary in length. Selected bit patterns (characters) have been reserved for communications control:

SOH: Start of Header.

STX: Start of Text.

ETX: End of Text.

ITB: Intermediate Text Block.

ETB: End of Transmission of Blocks Preceding the Last Block Multiple Block Transmission.

EOT: End of Transmission.

NAK: Not Acknowledged.

DLE: Data Link Escape to Extend the Set of Control Characters.

ENQ: Inquiry to Solicit Response from Receiving Station.

In addition, there is the synchronization character (SYN), noted earlier, as well as some two-character control sequences.

The message format for a BSC transmission block may be seen in Figure 7.8. Fields are delimited with selected control characters, and "user data" (text) may be preceded by an optional header. If a header is used, it begins with an SOH and is terminated when an STX is sent. The header is

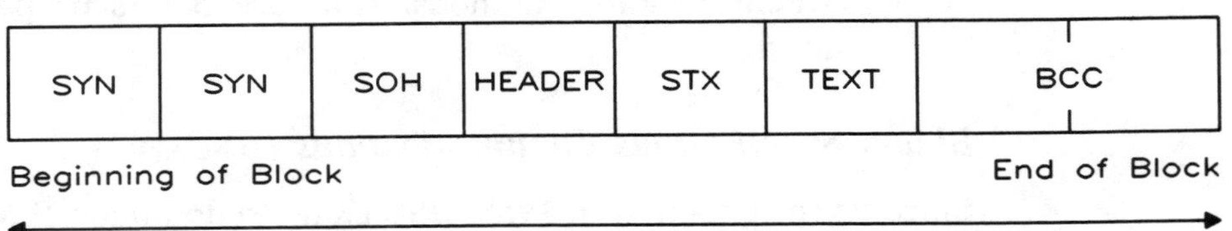

Figure 7.8. BSC Message Format.

defined by the software of the managing system. In a network, polling and addressing information are also required but are sent as separate control messages. The text field is of variable length and may contain transparent information. If data are defined as transparent, they are delimited by DLE STX and DLE ETX (or ETB) in addition to STX and ETX (or ETB). A trailer section consisting of only a block character check (BCC) is used for error checking and recovery.

Error Checking and Recovery

As microcomputers become increasingly popular, error checking and recovery are widely recognized as engendering significant problems. As noted earlier, these problems have been recognized from the inception of BSC. Binary Synchronous Communications can use various forms of redundancy checks: Vertical Redundancy Check (VRC), Longitudinal Redundancy Check (LRC), and Cyclical Redundancy Check (CRC). Vertical Redundancy Check is often called parity checking. Parity can be designated as (among other things) Odd, Even, or None. If no parity checking takes place, a full eight-bit ASCII or EBCDIC character can be transmitted. If Odd parity checking is taking place, then for each seven-bit character either a zero (0) or a one (1) is added to ensure an odd number of ones in the bit stream. Odd parity checking takes place, with BSC, only when ASCII characters are being sent. This is a very unusual condition, since EBCDIC characters are the norm when using BSC. The receiving end can then check to be sure that it has received an odd number of ones and, if not, may request retransmission. The difficulty with parity checking is that line noise may alter more than one bit of a seven- or eight-bit character, thereby confusing the parity check. To eliminate this problem, BSC also calculates a checksum on the BCC. If either the appropriate redundancy checks or the BCC spots an error, retransmission is requested. Block sequence errors are tested by alternating positive acknowledgments (ACK0 and ACK1, respectively) to even and odd numbered blocks in the message.

Information Coding

Although BSC supports ASCII, EBCDIC, and six-bit Transcode for coding information, most installations use EBCDIC. This may seem a problem to micro users, but it is not—at least not for the end user. If a communications network that requires BSC from micro to mainframe is being used, the microcomputer software should make the code conversion transparent to the user. Conversely, if a network is being used where the micro transmits and receives ASCII, then code conversion will take place in a transparent fashion in a protocol converter, an FEP, or elsewhere. Some characters in both ASCII and EBCDIC have been reserved for control purposes. Only the first 128 characters of an ASCII character set have been defined, although EBCDIC has definitions extending beyond 128 characters. Both systems have a maximum of 256 bit patterns for use as characters.

Information Transparency

To send control characters as data there must be some form of information transparency. With BSC, transparency is initiated by starting the text field with DLE STX. In addition, any Data-Link Control characters transmitted in the transparent mode must be preceded by a DLE character. If the DLE bit pattern is actually a part of the data to be transmitted, a second DLE must be inserted. At the receiving end, one DLE is discarded, and the other is treated as data. Transparent transmission is terminated with a DLE ETB sequence, and a DLE ITB pair signals the end of transparency but continues normal transmission. This use of pairs of characters to control transparency is called *data stuffing*. In data-transmission systems without transparency, it is necessary to use a protocol that can convert control characters to "printable" bit strings and then decode them at the other end.

Line Characteristics

Bisync is a communications protocol based on half-duplex data transmission. With half-duplex systems, data can be sent both ways, but only one way at a time. Distinguished from half-duplex is simplex, which can transmit one way only, and full-duplex, which can handle two-way transmissions simultaneously. Half-duplex transmission introduces some inefficiencies in the process. With 3x74/6 cluster controllers, addressing information is not a part of the definition of the BSC block. This eliminates an additional overlay for addressing on top of the block to be transmitted.

Synchronization

As noted earlier, character synchronization is achieved in BSC by sending at least two SYN (01010101) characters before each block. When a line is idle, SYN characters are sent continuously. Some BSC-based systems can automatically insert and delete SYN characters.

After its introduction in 1968, BSC became a de facto data-communications standard and is one historic root of several contemporary data-communications protocols. Although BSC is efficient compared to asynchronous data transmission, it is inefficient compared to synchronous transmission, partly as a result of operating with half-duplex. Turnaround is demanded twice between each block, and an acknowledgment sequence is used with each block. Because of the manner in which control characters are used, the logically distinct functions of link control, device control, and information representation were mixed.[21] Most of these problems were confronted and cured by SDLC, although it did not stabilize until some years following its introduction.[22]

Synchronous Data Link Control (SDLC)

Originated in 1973, IBM's SDLC was overshadowed by BSC partly because of the slow acceptance of SNA in data processing installations. During the 1980s, however, growth was substantial. Additional causes for slow acceptance included bugs in early releases of SNA software, lack of trained IBM personnel, cost of conversion, and availability of appropriate hardware. The first cluster controller introduced for SNA, the 3271, supported SDLC but few of the SNA protocols. Consequently, uses of the 3271 were limited to its BSC capabilities. Unlike BSC, SDLC is bit oriented and is designed for both half- and full-duplex operation.

Data Transfer and Control

Synchronous Data Link Control is the fundamental data link control for IBM's SNA. It is a subset of ISO's High-level Data Link Control (HDLC)—or maybe HDLC is a superset of SDLC—promulgated in 1974. The SDLC message format is depicted in Figure 7.9. As noted, SDLC is bit, not byte, oriented, although it does use an eight-bit bit pattern for synchronization flags. The eight-bit control field has three formats: One for information transfer, a second for supervisory services, and a third nonsequenced format. A more thorough discussion may be found in Weitzman[23] and in several IBM publications, including *IBM SDLC General Information*.[24] The information-transfer format contains frame-sequence information and a send/receive control signal to simplify data transfers. With the supervisory format, no data transmission takes place, but ready or busy conditions can be designated. The nonsequenced format is for such data-link management functions as the initialization of secondary stations or nodes.

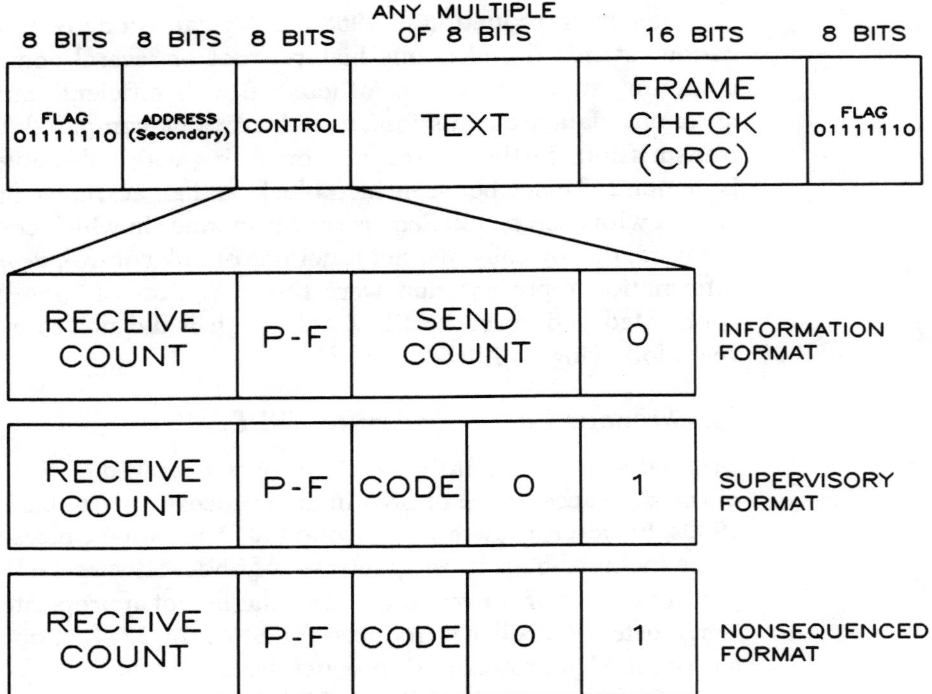

Figure 7.9. SDLC Message Format.

Error Checking and Recovery

Error checking is accomplished in SDLC through CRC, which can detect transmission errors. When an error has been detected, the receiving node sends a message to the sending node indicating that the message containing the error has not been received. The original sender then retransmits after a time-out period.

Information Coding

Since SDLC is bit oriented, the information exchange code used (ASCII or EBCDIC) is irrelevant. Some higher level of SNA (or other network architecture) must define the information exchange code to be used for data transfer.

INFORMATION TRANSPARENCY

For the reasons noted, any "text" data are transparent to SDLC.

LINE CHARACTERISTICS

Both half- and full-duplex can be used with SDLC, although part of the power of SDLC derives from its use of full-duplex lines. Control information is lower for SDLC (48 bits) than for BSC (64 bits in 8 characters), and no separate ACK messages are necessary.

SYNCHRONIZATION

The flag bit strings between messages are used for synchronization. This eliminates the need for the SYN characters of BSC.

A major difference between OSI and SNA is that, although OSI provides only a functional model, SNA defines not only functions but also protocols that are to be used within the single-vendor IBM environment. Compatibility with SNA clearly involves more than consistency with the Data-Link Control Layer. Nor is SNA merely a replacement for BSC networks, since SNA is a network *architecture*. In contrast, BSC is only a method for Data-Link Control.

SNA Overview

This book is not the place for a full-scale discussion of SNA, but some SNA concepts are necessary to have a firm understanding of the context in which LANs exist in an IBM network. Much of IBM's office automation emphasis for the next few years will be based on SNA, as will the methods used to integrate PCs into that environment. Synchronous Network Architecture is also a dynamic and growing concept within IBM itself. The fundamental design objectives and features for SNA were and are similar to other data-communications networks:

- Easy communication between or among end users including network transparency.
- Separation of function based on SNA's layered architecture.
- Ability to use many types of devices, with the network doing any necessary protocol conversion to SNA device-independent protocols.

- Support for distributed functions.
- Support for resource sharing by allowing end users to dynamically allocate or deallocate resources.
- Ability to dynamically reconfigure or modify the network.
- Clear definition of formats for data that flow in the network and the protocols used between layers.

Support for resource sharing is particularly important because, in a modern data-communications network, one primary objective is, or should be, extensive connectivity among end users and devices. Among other things, resource sharing can be thought of as the end user's ability to switch from one application to another from a single terminal—a feature not usually available in a BSC network. "Application" in the sense used here means from one teleprocessing (TP) monitor to another, including the possibility of moving from one IBM host to another through an FEP.

There are some SNA terms and concepts that will prove useful in later discussions:

- A *domain* consists of all the physical and logical components controlled by one common point in the network.
- The *Systems Services Control Point (SSCP)* is the common control point.
- A *node* is a logical grouping of network components that have uniquely defined characteristics.
  - Each node contains a *Physical Unit (PU)* that is the resource controller for the node.
  - Nodes normally contain *Logical Units (LUs)* to interface end users to the network, including a network address.
  - An LU or a PU is addressed through a logical entity assigned a unique network address called the *Network Addressable Unit (NAU)*. Network addressable units defined by SNA include PUs, LUs, SSCPs, and data links. A node summary can be found in Table 7.1.

    Physical Unit-T2.1 was defined in 1983 and is designed for Peer-to-Peer (for PCs, for example) coupling or subarea (see the following) routing. The former is, in principle, nonmediated—that is, it is not necessary for routing through VTAM or NCP,

TABLE 7.1. SNA Node Summary

Node	*PU-Type*	*IBM Hardware*	*Software*
Host	PU-T5	308x, 43xx	VTAM
Com Ctrl	PU-T4	37x5	NCP
Cluster Ctrl	PU-T2.1	PC, Office Automation	—
Cluster Ctrl	PU-T2.0	3174, 3274, 3276, 3790	—

Note: Many manufacturers produce compatible equipment and boards that allow PCs to emulate 3x78 and 3x79 terminals. This summary is not complete and includes only the most commonly used PU types.

although two PCs communicating with one another through different SNA cluster controllers will likely have to pass through the communications FEP.

- An SNA *subarea* is either a host subarea or a communications controller subarea, producing a higher level grouping of nodes.
- A *network address* is 16 bits long and contains both a subarea address and an element (individual NAU).

  In some segments of the network only short, local addresses are desirable and the translation between local and network addressing is through the *boundary function* that resides in either the host or communications controller.

A diagram of a complete SNA network may be seen in Figure 7.10. Microcomputers, as will be seen, can replace the 3174/3274 (or 3x76) and/or the 3x78/9 terminals in an SNA network. Logical Unit 2.2 was designed to provide the basic services necessary to have consistent data transfer among LUs. Remember that an LU exists within a PU.

In 1991, IBM announced APPN architecture as an extension to SNA and Systems Applications Architecture (SAA). According to IBM, these announcements continue "to evolve SNA and preserve SNA investments, while expanding the concepts of Open Communication Architectures and peer-to-peer networking." The shift in IBM's approach to the changing character of modern networking environments is clearly spelled out in this announce-

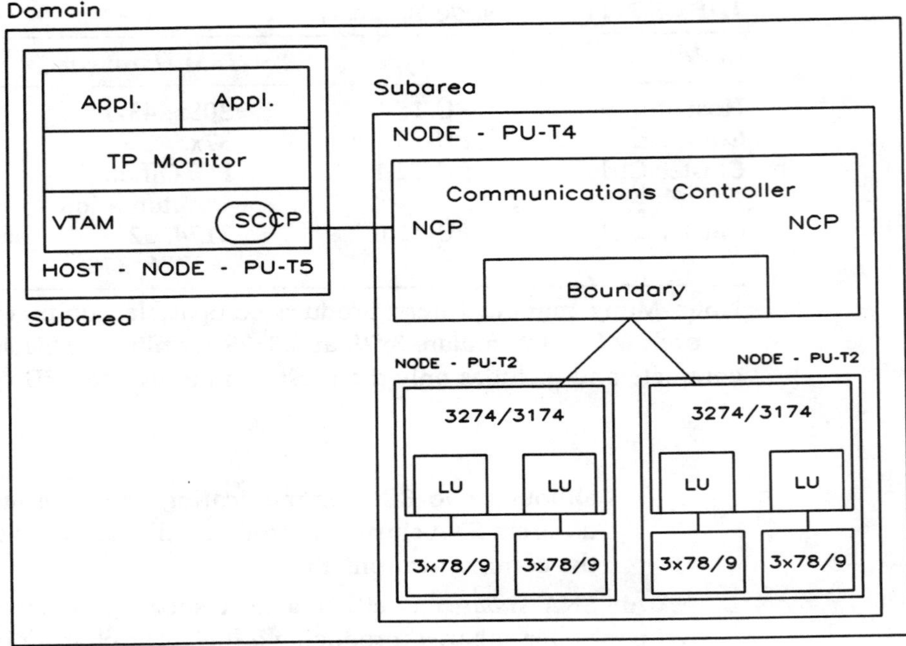

Figure 7.10. Example of an SNA Network.

ment. It professes to provide improved access to distributed customer data, to facilitate multivendor SNA networking, and to protect current SNA investments while providing advanced networking dynamics. The claims for APPN include (among other things) the following:

- Expanded distributed networking that allows both APPN and low-entry nodes to participate peer-to-peer.
- The ability to record network topology changes in a dynamic network topology database.
- A means for automatically registering and locating network resources in a distributed network directory.
- Enhanced control over network installation and change, routing, congestion, and priority.

Unlike mainframe computers, where IBM was able to drive non-IBM architecture vendors out of the market, customers for networking products have proven more flexible. Consequently, there has been significantly more competition for available dollars as well as significant evidence that other approaches are at least as good as IBM's, and often better. This view is also buttressed by an increasing number of announcements from IBM providing OSI links and services. The latter, of course, arises in large part from the European Economic Community's (EEC's) demands that have given much of the impetus to the standards movement in recent years. IBM simply cannot give up the European market after 1992 (when many of the economic integration plans for Europe become a reality).

Software Connectivity Products

The IBM software products that affect the connectivity among micros and the relationship of micros in a wider SNA network are as follows:

- NetBios on the micro specifically designed to be used in conjunction with IBM's LAN hardware.
- Enhanced Connectivity Facilities (ECF), which provide virtual disk and file services for a microcomputer connected either through a Token Ring LAN gatewayed to an SNA network or through a 3270 Display Station emulation card connected through a 3174 cluster controller.
- Advanced Program-to-Program Communication and LU 6.2 for the micro, mini, and mainframe for application-to-application communication at the highest layers of network architecture.
- Systems Application Architecture (SAA), which provides a framework for the development of "consistent applications across the future offerings of the major IBM computing environments—System 370, System/3x and Personal Computer." (Announcement 287-088, March 17, 1987.)

APPC and LU 6.2

Of particular importance to the micro-to-mainframe connection is IBM's development of APPC and LU 6.2, which were designed to provide enhanced SNA support for distributed processing.[25] The express purpose of APPC is to provide a single strategic LU type for all IBM products that support distributed processing. Although SNA supports several different types of sessions, LU-to-LU sessions are among the most important, but they can be established only between or among LUs of the same type. Logical Unit Type 6.2 is the architectural base for APPC. A *distributed transaction* within SNA consists of user application processing executed cooperatively on multiple systems. Advanced Program-to-Program Communication and LU 6.2 provide the structure for making that cooperative execution possible.

Therefore, LU 6.2 specifies a consistent set of functions, formats, and protocols for conversations (sessions) between programs on separate processors. Those processors may be mainframes, minis, or micros, although appropriate software implementing LU 6.2 must be available. Technically, "processor" means an execution environment supplied by an LU. Facilities are furnished for LU-to-LU and LU-to-SSCP conversations. An LU-to-LU session may not include access to any central processor, a significant departure for IBM, although in an SNA network, it is likely that peer-to-peer communications from a micro to a micro would still route through the FEP.

Logical Unit 6.2 provides protocols primarily for session management at the upper layers of SNA. Error recovery within LU 6.2, for example, is at a much higher layer than is error recovery with SDLC. In an LU 6.2 transaction, errors can occur in program logic where the transaction program is responsible for error recovery, in synchronization processing, or in the session itself. In the latter case, the transaction is informed of the error by a return code indicating conversation failure. Action can then be taken to deallocate the conversation, which releases the dead session. This is somewhat similar to automatic logoff when a line drops, a condition that many applications written for IBM mainframe environments do not handle well. Systems that do not handle this condition properly create both technical and security problems. "Synchronization" in this instance means the synchronization of linked transaction processes rather than anything having to do with a data-link protocol.

In an SNA environment, APPC/LU 6.2 provides support for the transparent interchange of data stored consistently with Document Content Architecture (DCA), data organized and addressed according to Document Interchange Architecture (DIA), and data distributed by System Network Architecture's Distribution Services (SNADS), responding to a request by an application program somewhere on the network. System Network Architecture Distribution Services operates at SNA's "Function Management" layer (see Figure 7.7), higher than APPC/LU 6.2.[26]

There has been considerable confusion evidenced in industry literature concerning the future software environment for IBM networks, resulting at least in part from IBM's integration efforts. One report suggested that IBM confused software developers with an announcement concerning protocols at the Communications Networks '87 show (held in February 1987 in Washington, D.C.). Since late 1985, IBM has encouraged developers to support APPC protocols in their communications software. A senior market support representative from IBM, Robert D. Dill, seemed to suggest that developers should not use NetBios, but should instead use the Enhanced Connectivity Facility (ECF). Dill said that ECF is advantageous both in creating peer-to-peer networks between mainframes and personal computers and in the personal computer environment itself. Dill described the move away from Netbios and toward ECF as "strategic."[27] The widespread use of NetBios, however, has assured its continued support into the 1990s, and APPC is one cornerstone of IBM's integration strategy.

Although NetBios, APPC, and ECF may seem to overlap, they were designed to meet somewhat different needs. Parenthetically, note that IBM has also started dropping "support for" statements concerning IEEE 802.2 (LLC) software interfaces into its literature. NetBios extends the PC's operating environment to allow applications to communicate with the Network Interface Card (NIC), and therefore the network (whether that be the PC Network, the Token Ring, or something else). Advanced Program-to-Program Communication is a subsidiary architecture within the context of SNA that provides the set of rules necessary for interapplication communications. Enhanced Connectivity Facility is designed to allow IBM host operating environments (MVS/TSO and VM/CMS) to operate as servers for PCs communicating in a variety of ways. In a LAN environment, both APPC and ECF would be layered on top of NetBios, not necessarily substituting for it. Furthermore, none of these software structures have anything to do with the LAN protocols (CSMA/CD, Token Ring, et cetera). Enhanced Connectivity Facility is irrelevant if there is no micro-to-mainframe connection, and it is unlikely that APPC would be implemented without that same connection.[28] The use of APPC or ECF also assumes, of course, a central IBM system operating under MVS with TSO or VM/CMS. In other words, it is unlikely that software written to either APPC standards, or ECF, will replace NetBios at any time in the near future for LANs operating independently of IBM mainframe systems.

SAA

The SAA seems to be a recognition by IBM that its computer and connectivity products must now be brought together. The elements of SAA are as follows:

- Common user access.
- Common programming interface.
- Common communications support.

The third element is of greatest importance for the subject of this book, although the common programming interface will have impact on software development. The most important feature of the common programming interface is IBM's reendorsement of COBOL, FORTRAN, and C as the primary programming languages. Common versions of these languages will be supplied for all computer products from micros to mainframes, thus allowing the easy porting of applications from one system to another. The endorsement of C is also of great importance because this will provide a common systems programming language (which heretofore has been the local Assembler languages) across all computer systems regardless of hardware architecture.

Common communications support is designed to interconnect SAA applications, systems, networks, and devices. This connectivity will come about through designated communications architectures for each SAA environment. These are the building blocks for IBM's approach to distributed processing. The SAA is a combination of SNA and international standards, and its announcement "reaffirms" IBM's commitment to openness. Considering the amount of speculation and fear expressed in the trade press concerning the possibility of IBM closing down it's previous openness, this is likely to be an important announcement. The original 1987 announcement included support for several functional elements.

Data Streams. Data stream support includes the 3270 Display System, Document Content Architecture, and Intelligent Printer Data Stream. The 3270 Display System continues to be important in IBM's strategy. Systems Application Architecture support for the 3270 data stream consists of user-provided data and commands, as well as control information that governs the way data are handled. Likewise, the System/3x family will continue to support the 5250 data stream. Document Content Architecture (DCA) defines the rules for specifying the form and meaning of a text document. Within an SNA network, DCA provides uniform textual information interchange and consists of format elements optimized for document revision. Other manufacturers, such as DEC and Wang, are beginning to provide translation systems from DCA into their own document-processing systems. Intelligent Printer Data Streams (IPDS) is a high-function data stream intended for use with all-points-addressable page printers.

Application Services. Application services include support for SNADS, DIA, and the SNA Network Management Architecture. System Network Architecture's Distribution Service provides *asynchronous* distribution capability in an SNA network, thereby avoiding the need for active sessions between end points. As IBM is becoming more open, and is recognizing that national and international standards are important, it is providing greater support for communications techniques that have received short shrift in the past, particularly asynchronous support. Document Interchange Architecture provides a set of protocols that define several common office functions performed cooperatively by IBM products. IBM's approach to managing networks is described by the SNA Network Management Architecture. This architecture provides a set of protocols for monitoring network operations from a central location.

Session Services. The only session service protocol family supported in the initial announcement is LU 6.2. As noted elsewhere, LU 6.2 is a program-to-program communications protocol. Logical Unit 6.2 is a set of interprogram communications services that includes a base subset and optional supplementary services. The objective is to provide communications compatibility across systems. At the microcomputer level, this may suggest some replacement for functions currently supported by NetBios, although this is far from clear.

Network. Two types of network support are encompassed within SAA: An SNA low-entry networking node (Type 2.1 node) and X.25. The former supports peer-to-peer communication through a common set of protocols that allow multiple and parallel SNA sessions to be established between Type 2.1 nodes that are directly attached to one another. X.25 support illustrates IBM's adherence to international standards and defines a packet–mode interface for attaching data terminal equipment (DTE) to packet-switched networks. Data terminal equipment may include host computers, communications controllers, and terminals.

Data-Link Controls. Although SNA has never supported a single Data-Link Control, the emphasis has been on SDLC, and this emphasis is reaffirmed in SAA. Synchronous Data Link Control is a discipline for managing synchronous, code-transparent, serial-by-bit information transfer between nodes that are joined by telecommunications links. The system used by the IBM Token Ring Network is added to SDLC for Data-Link Control. An important omission in SAA is the lack of support for the Ethernet data-link protocol. Even though IBM has been forced to recognize the importance of Ethernet it is still referenced only begrudgingly. This is surprising because 1987 announcements from IBM reaffirmed PC Network support in both its broadband and baseband versions. The data-link protocol used by PC Network is a CSMA/CD system similar to IEEE 802.3, and the baseband version is very like StarLan, which served as the basis for the low-speed, twisted pair 802.3 standard. IBM's literature only claims 802.2 (LLC) conformance for the PC Network. Regardless of explicit products, however, IBM supports the 802.3 Data-Link Control standard.

Microcomputer Hardware/Software Connectivity Products

Perhaps the best way to describe IBM's 1987 announcement of the PS/2 family of microcomputers is to suggest that they seem to be viewed strategically as connectivity products themselves. The PS/2 microcomputers are clearly directed toward large organizations and large networking environments. The IBM LANs were also enhanced to take advantage of the new PS/2 microcomputers. Continued support for NetBios was illustrated with an enhanced version of the PC Network Program, and PS/2 versions of all LAN interface cards were announced, including the Token Ring, PC Network (broadband), and PC Network (baseband). This allows older PCs to be connected in a common network with PS/2 machines. Although most existing PC software should work on the new systems, even under OS/2, applications written specifically for the new machines under OS/2 will probably not work on the older systems. One software enhancement, the LAN Manager, enhances the Token Ring's network management capability and provides network management capability to the broadband IBM PC Network.

Although the IBM LAN Support Program has had many limitations, one of its strengths was cost. Some of the announced enhancements will likely make it a more important NOS contender, although Novell, Banyan, and others will likely follow suit. The important enhancements include support for the new PS/2 boards for Token Ring and PC Network (both broadband and baseband). Most importantly, it extends support not only for NetBios, but also for an IEEE 802.2 interface. In addition, support for APPC/PC is provided for both Token Ring and PC Network. Although the PC Network (LAN) Support Program contains considerable improvements, both the old NICs, as well as newly enhanced NICs, are supported. Applications written for IEEE 802.2/LLC, NetBios, or APPC/PC application interfaces can be run on *all* IBM LANs, thus providing portability across LAN technology. Novell, Banyan, and other manufacturers of generic NOSs, provide support for IEEE and APPC/PC interfaces as well as for their own NOSs and NetBios.

The key elements of IBM's connectivity products for microcomputers are LANs and terminal-emulation capabilities. The terminal emulations are focused on the 3270 Display System for System/370 users, and on 5250 Display Station emulation for the old S/34, S/36, and S/38 minicomputers as well as the AS/400. The Token Ring, while the primary strategic LAN product, does not seem to have obliterated the PC Network in either the broadband or baseband versions. The broadband version, particularly, is being enhanced for what IBM regards as a specialized niche in the market: Those users that must combine their LANs with other services, such as video, voice, security, and/or additional data channels on a common broadband medium. All LANs, of course, can be used to meet the requirements of small businesses and individual work groups.

Trying to follow what IBM is doing is always complicated. Part of the problem is that IBM has been around a long time and has an impact in most parts of the information processing industry. They have, consequently, produced a large number of connectivity products over the years and must now attempt to bring some order out of their own somewhat chaotic product inventory. At the same time, they must avoid alienating large customers that have a major impact on IBM's sales. An IBM networking environment will, therefore, always be a compromise among what is best, what is new, and what is installed. Moreover, even within IBM, these compromises are not entirely driven by technology. Different IBM divisions engineer and manufacture different connectivity products. Consequently, there will be the inevitable jockeying for position and prestige within IBM's organization. The competitive tools for the contending groups are the old and new products they produce. As a result of such conflicts, there must be political as well as technical compromises. The concept of an overarching connectivity architecture such as SAA is one approach to managing these compromises. One clearly evident, if not explicitly stated, IBM strategy in managing outside competition is to coopt popular technology. This is evidenced by a growing number of products supporting Ethernet and connectivity to asynchronous computers (always referencing the Series/1, but often informally acknowledged to support DEC's VAX family and similar systems).

VTAM

Virtual Telecommunications Access Method, as a component of SNA, operates on the IBM mainframe computer system and complements the 37x5 (and compatible) front-end communications processors. By operating with the 37x5, the number of functions performed by the central computer for remote terminals is reduced. Virtual Telecommunications Access Method performs the following functions:[29]

- Establishes, controls, and terminates access between user-application programs and the terminals.
- Moves data between user-application programs and the terminals.
- Allows user-application programs to share communications lines, communications controllers, and telecommunications terminals.
- Permits network monitoring and alteration.
- Provides an environment that allows dynamic network reconfiguration.

Virtual Telecommunications Access Method's primary role is data transmission, although it facilitates building telecommunications systems of any size. Features of VTAM include the following:

- Reducing line costs and improving network efficiency by sharing network resources.
- Reducing processing loads on the host CPU by distributing network control functions.
- Serving on-line inquiries and updates.
- Supports attached devices, including a wide variety of terminals (for example, the 3270 Information Display System) using various line disciplines (start-stop, BSC, and SDLC).

Virtual Telecommunications Access Method is a component of several of IBM's batch operating systems, the most important of which is OS/MVS. Application programs use VTAM to communicate with the terminal network.

FEPs (Communications Controller)

IBM mainframes were originally designed as batch processing machines with card input and card and printed output. When those systems began interfacing with terminals in the late 1960s, it was necessary to attach those terminals in some fashion. High-speed peripherals were attached to 360/370 series and later machines through channels. There are byte-multiplexer, block-multiplexer, and selector channels. Front End Processors were developed to provide a means for linking low-speed terminal devices to the mainframe. The first of these FEPs (called *transmission control units* by IBM) were the 2701, 2702, and 2703 series, of which the 2703 became the standard. The FEP was, in turn, channel attached. During the 1980s, the 2703 was displaced first by the 3704 and then by the 37x5 series of FEPs (the 3745 being the most recent as of this writing). The 37x5 communications controller can be attached to any of the three channels. The 3704 (and the 2703 before it) was attached to the byte-multiplexer channel.

There are several plug compatible FEPs, some of which, like the old Memorex 1270, emulated a 2703. Others, like NCR-COMTEN's series, behave like a 37x5. The 37x5s are programmable controllers that allow several modes of operation. The functions provided by the newer controllers include the following:

- Hardware support for BSC, SDLC, and start-stop Data-Link Control.
- Communications line control.
- Line error detection and recovery.
- Acquisition of line statistics and error reporting to VTAM.
- Line activation and deactivation as well as the ability to close down the network.
- For start-stop and BSC terminals, the translating of character codes from ASCII to EBCDIC and EBCDIC to ASCII and date and time stamping.

Some non-IBM FEPs provide added functions that extend beyond the normal duties of a 37x5. Both the Memorex 1270 and the NCR COMTEN, among others, provided fully flow-controlled, full-duplex, asynchronous start-stop ports running at 9,600 b/s or higher. As noted elsewhere, flow control is of significant importance in some networks. IBM's original start-stop capability was half-duplex, without flow control, although it now may be possible to obtain, through special order, flow-controlled async ports. On machines that provide at least the functions of the 37x5, several control programs are typically available. To be fully compatible with IBM, however, it is necessary to have control programs that are compatible with the network control mode (NCP), or emulation mode (EP), or both (PEP).

Emulation Programming (EP)

A 37x5 or similar machine operating in emulation mode, with EP, behaves like a 2703 transmission control unit. This is the mode of operation if the FEP is to function with only Bisync and/or Async communications. Bisync and Async are available only under EP. Although VTAM can control these lines, the access method is often TeleCommunications Access Method (TCAM) or Basic Telecommunications Access Method (BTAM). Either or both TCAM and BTAM can coexist with VTAM on the same host, although SNA services are not available through those systems.

Network Control Programming (NCP)

Like EP, NCP is stored in an FEP and controls the FEP's operations. Network Control Programming is smarter than EP and can fully interact with VTAM. This interaction provides full control of an SNA network. Successive versions of NCP are generated on the mainframe and downloaded to the 37x5 processor.

Partitioned Emulation Programming (PEP)

The functions of both EP and NCP can be run concurrently on 37x5s or similar machines with PEP. Partitioned Emulation Programming partitions the 37x5 so that both NCP and EP are running. Because many installations have a mixture of SDLC/SNA, BSC, and Async devices, a combination of the old and new technologies is needed.

Terminal Requirements

This book is still about LANs and EWC, but terminal requirements continue to be important. Further discussion will focus on the way in which a terminal device—in this case, a micro—can actually be attached in an IBM network. Networks communicate through either asynchronous terminals or synchronous (SDLC or BSC) terminals. The typical problem in either an SNA or BSC network is to make the micro or other asynchronous ASCII devices behave as if they were synchronous members of IBM's 3270 Information Display System. Many or most applications on an IBM mainframe are written to take advantage of the full-screen capabilities of the 3270 device. Before describing the microcomputer as a 3270 device, it is necessary to discuss the 3270 Information Display System.

To understand the role of micros in an IBM environment, some understanding of the 3270 Display System is necessary. Figure 7.11 is a diagram

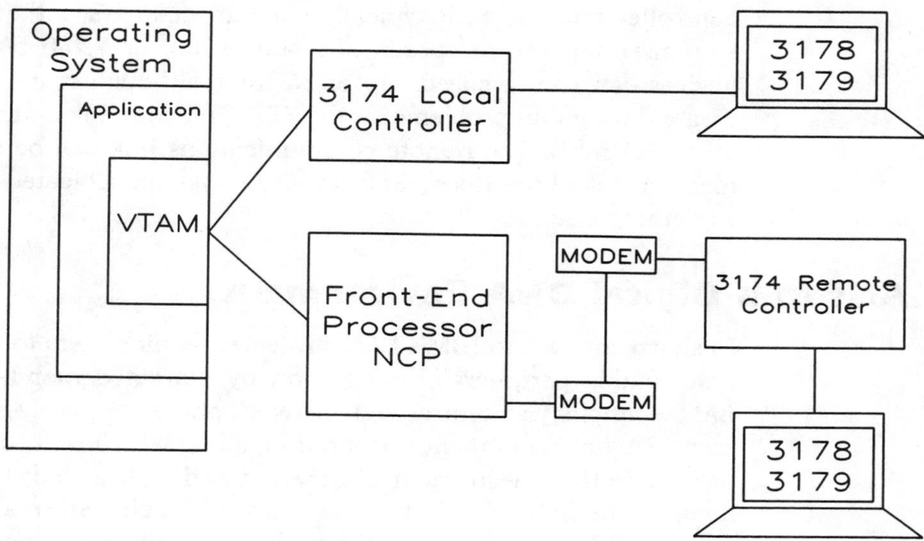

Figure 7.11. 3270 Information Display System Network.

of a simplified network based on the 3270 Display System. Fundamentally, it is composed of 3x78/9 (monochrome or color) transaction terminals connected to a 3x74 locally or remotely attached cluster controller. If the 3x74 is locally attached, it is plugged directly into a channel. If the 3x74 is remotely attached, it communicates via an SDLC (or BSC) communications line, usually through modems, to the FEP. When a display terminal and a cluster controller are combined, the device is a 3x76 and will normally support another seven display terminals. The local controller is directly controlled by VTAM. The remote controller is preprocessed by NCP running in the FEP, then by VTAM. The 3x74 can also support a variety of printers ranging from dot-matrix and daisy-wheel printers, to high-speed, heavy-duty production printers.

The 3x78/9 terminal is buffered and is usually used for full-screen applications. Applications operate on one page at a time, and a synchronous block can be composed of sufficient data to fill a screen. If only part of a screen is to be updated, typically only the part that changes will be transmitted. At least for display purposes, the 3x78/9 is a relatively smart terminal; however, part of the intelligence of the SNA network exists in the 3x74 controllers. The link between the 3x78/9 and the controller is via coaxial cable running at 56 Kb/s. The communications line between the remote controller and the FEP typically runs at 9,600 b/s, although older BSC systems often ran at speeds of 2,400, 4,800, or 7,200 b/s. Some newer devices can run at speeds up to 56 Kb/s, although many such lines will create throughput problems for the FEP. The local link is at channel speeds, up to 1.5 Mb/s. The remote communications link can be any convenient medium: telephone lines, cable television system, dedicated twisted pair, or something else.

LANs in a Digital DNA Environment

In sharp contrast to IBM's LAN strategies—which seem to regard LANs as unavoidable peripherals brought on by market demand—DEC adopted LAN technology as central to its network philosophy early in LAN development. Digital Equipment Corporation, along with Xerox, became an early partner in the development of Ethernet and later a leader in the development of the IEEE 802.3 standard. Today it is almost impossible to buy a large DEC VAX computer without also buying at least one small Ethernet system. Digital Equipment Corporation has developed DNA as a response to the need for an integrated approach to networking that includes both WANs and LANs. Digital Network Architecture is the framework for all DEC's communications products.

Whereas the broad outline of IBM's SNA has remained relatively constant for many years, DEC's DNA has undergone several major changes, starting with Phase I in 1978 through Phase V, announced in 1987. The current installed base is an amalgam of Phase IV and Phase V protocols. Phase V is a major move to a largely OSI-compliant network architecture. At the three upper layers (Application, Presentation, and Session), Phase V retains older Phase IV elements to support existing products. OSI-compliant software products are added to the older products. At the lower four layers, Phase V moves almost enirely to OSI-compliant protocols, although it does retain DDCMP (Digital Data Communications Message Protocol) at the Data-Link Layer. For an overview of this evolution, see Figure 7.12.

Within the framework of DNA, network managers can configure either WANs or LANs. Of particular importance to the discussions in this book are the Network Application Layer and the Data-Link Layer. The Network Application Layer may contain both user- and DEC-supplied modules. It defines network functions used by the User and Network Management layers. Access to other networks, including X.25 and IBM's SNA, is included as a function of the Network Application Layer. So ubiquitous is IBM's

OSI	DNA Phase IV	DNA Phase V	
Application	User	User	FTAM, X.400 Others
	Network Mangement	Network Management	
Presentation	Network Application	Network Application	OSI Presentation
Session	DECnet Session Control	DECnet Session Control	OSI Session
Transport	End-to-End Communication DECnet Transport (NSP)	Common Transport Interface	
		DECnet Transport (NSP)	OSI Transport
Network	DECnet Routing (Adaptive Routing)	ISO Connectionless Service ISO Connection-Oriented Service ISO ES-IS Routing Protocol IS-IS Routing Protocol	
Data Link	Ethernet DDCMP X.25	X.25 DDCMP Ethernet/802.2 LLC/802.3 MAC HDLC	
Physical	Physical	802.3 Physical Others as Necessary	

Figure 7.12. Scope of OSI and DNA Models.

influence in the information processing industry that virtually all other manufacturers must supply links into IBM systems. The Data-Link Layer is important because it supports DEC's DDCMP, X.25 protocol, and Ethernet protocol. Within DNA, software and hardware modules within layers are linked by protocols, and modules between layers are linked by interfaces. The result of a DNA-structured network is DECnet.[30]

As was implied with IBM's synchronous Data-Link Control within SNA, DDCMP, X.25, and Ethernet are, among other things, protocols for organizing the data-bit stream on the appropriate medium. Data are, therefore, organized in packets (or blocks) that are rigidly defined. This is also true for Token Ring and PC Network. Standards typically allow each manufacturer some protocol flexibility so that even when MAC and Physical Layer conditions are identical, two Ethernets on the same physical cable may not be able to communicate with one another. Further, an additional file transfer protocol may be overlayed on the Data-Link Control structure. Digital

Equipment Corporation's implementation of Ethernet is sufficiently important to its view of networking to mention some highlights at this point.

In recognition of the growing need for organizations to rely on more than one or two vendors, and on the growing demand for EWC, DEC now supports a unified network-management architecture. The new Enterprise Management Architecture (EMA) is a foundation for developing network-management products for managing resources in a multivendor environment. Such an environment can be either a local or a dispersed network. Components that can be managed under the architecture include data and voice networks, communications systems, applications, and computer-based data.[31] The arrival of DEC's multivendor network-management scheme in 1990 followed IBM's NetView, AT&T's Unified Network Management Architecture (UNMA), and Hewlett-Packard Co.'s OpenView. Digital Equipment Corporation's EMA is more open and more comprehensive than some of its predecessors, according to Jack Freeman, senior data-communications analyst at the Boston-based consulting firm, Yankee Group. "NetView is superbly designed to manage an SNA network; it doesn't manage a hybrid environment at all. AT&T's UNMA is a very good product for managing telephone lines, but it has no real capability to manage anything else," he pointed out.[32] Enterprise Management Architecture is designed to support both central and distributed control of network management in an enterprise-wide network. It uses a peer-to-peer architecture based on OSI network-management standards, including Common Management Information Protocols. Enterprise Management Architecture addresses OSI's five functional network-management areas for standards development, including configuration, fault identification, performance, security, and accounting.

DEC Ethernet Messages

Ethernet (IEEE 802.3) is a standard that lies at OSI layers 1 (Physical) and 2 (Data-Link). The part of the standard that falls in the Data-Link Layer consists only of the MAC sublayer, rather than encompassing a full data-transmission protocol. The MAC services for Ethernet include CSMA/CD and the basic frame format. There is flexibility within the frame format, particularly with respect to source and destination addresses, which may be either 16 or 48 bits long. Manufacturers are free to use either the 16- or 48-bit format, or to support both (although this is not required by the standard). Developers are also free to link the frame to higher level protocols, which is what DEC does. This results in many manufacturers using the same equipment, possibly over the same cable, without the ability for network devices defined by protocol to communicate with one another.

The Ethernet Data Link has one type of message or frame. The construction and processing of frames is the result of the data-encapsulation function of the Data-Link Layer. The subfunctions of framing include addressing and error detection. No explicit framing information is required with Ethernet because the access method (CSMA/CD) provides the necessary framing cues. Two addresses—for source and destination stations—are provided. Error detection is accomplished with a Frame Check Sequence (FCS)—a 32-bit CRC. In a DNA (Phase IV) network environment composed of DDCMP media, Ethernets, and X.25 systems, every node has a unique address. This requires the use of the 48-bit address field. The Ethernet Data-Link Frame format, as used by DEC, may be seen in Figure 7.13.

The implementation flexibility provided within the 802.3 standard is clearest in the definition of the source and destination addresses. As previously noted, the address fields may be either 16 bits or 48 bits. The 48-bit field allows a specific Ethernet node to have a unique address across all interconnected Ethernets or other networks. In DNA (Phase IV), each

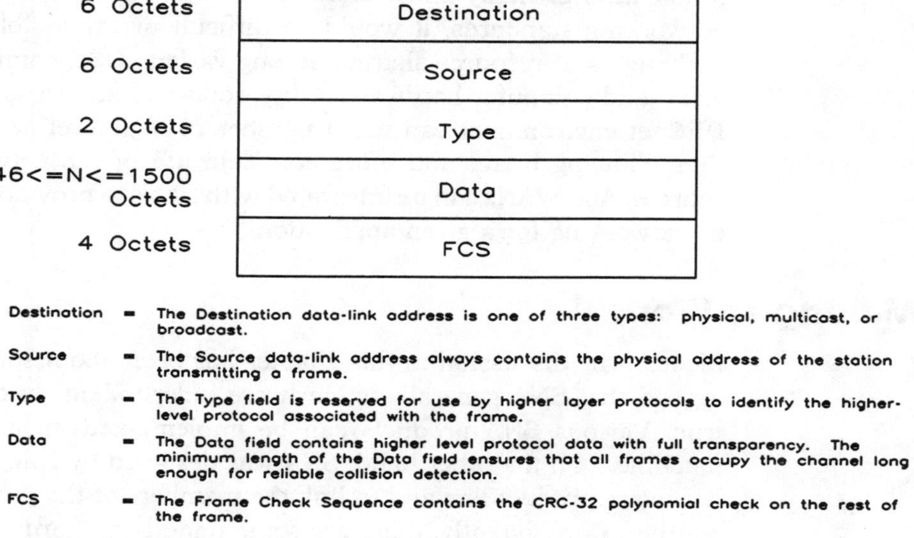

Figure 7.13. DEC Ethernet Data-Link Frame Format.

Ethernet node has a 16-bit node address. If that node is also a DNA node, the 16-bit address is prefixed by a 32-bit address assigned to DNA nodes. Digital Network Architecture addresses are, therefore, unique over a single DNA network, which may include multiple Ethernets, DDCMP links, and X.25 links. The Type field, which identifies any higher level protocols associated with the frame, is associated with this capability. Type values are assigned to the DNA routing protocol and to the DNA Maintenance Operation protocols. In the 802.3 standard, the field DEC labels "TYPE" is actually defined as a length field that stipulates the length of the data field. Note also that, for DEC, the error-control functions necessary for reliable communications are provided by the Network Services Protocol (NSP) in a DNA environment.

DECnet Summary

Both SNA and DNA are network architectures designed to absorb new and increasingly efficient communications technologies. Communications technology is among the fastest changing within the information processing industry. Consequently, a network architecture must be capable of change and adaptation. Moreover, a network architecture can also specify common communications mechanisms and user interfaces that allow the intercommunication of many kinds of computer systems. In the absence of such networking standards, it would be difficult or impossible to effect data exchange and resource sharing among various OSs, communications devices, and computer hardware. A by-product of all this is that a user in a DECnet environment can use a number of high-level network functions, thus allowing better and more complete use of the network and its resources. And WANs can be integrated with LANs to provide the correct level of networking for a given application.

Making It Work

Most of the discussion in this chapter has been about software. It can be argued that SNA generally is hardware independent. In one sense this is true: Various SNA products can be implemented on a wide variety of machines. On the other hand, SNA was designed by IBM to support their hardware product line and to link the members of the product line to one another. Consequently, there are some underlying hardware assumptions implicit in all elements of IBM's approach to networking. To ignore those assumptions would be to build a nonfunctional network when dealing with IBM's products or ones that look and act like IBM's.

In a distributed-processing environment, connectivity is clearly a major objective. Through resource sharing, SNA allowed applications to be shared across communications lines and terminals. The communications lines can also be shared across different terminals. All this was achieved through the development of a single teleprocessing access method (VTAM), supported by uniform multiplexing facilities (NCP in the FEP), and a single Data-Link Control (SDLC). Any combination of devices having SDLC support can be mixed on a multidropped line.

There is a tendency for the uninitiated to believe that data communications is easy to accomplish. From the perspective of a micro user establishing communications via telephone to some mainframe network, that may be the case. A few terminals linked via a hard-wired cable is also simple and straightforward. In a large network with hundreds or thousands of terminals, and with many design objectives, the problem is much more complex. Some sense of that complexity has been conveyed in the discussion of SNA and elsewhere in this book. In an IBM mainframe environment, complexity is the name of the game. Selected communications software is needed to fill the various layers of SNA, but even in a simpler bisync environment the problems multiply. Many people, familiar only with Data-Link Control methods such as bisync or asynchronous start-stop technologies, tend to think these are the beginning and end of data communications. Alas, this is not the case. For SNA, the other two communications elements (in addition to SDLC)—a telecommunications access method and a front-end communications processor with a uniform multiplexing system—are useful regardless of the Data-Link Control system.

Conclusions

This chapter only introduces some of the elements of IBM mainframe networking. Many elements were omitted, and other topics were considered only in a cursory manner. Clearly IBM is on track to engineer a flexible, yet complex network environment. Although SNA represents IBM's strategic planning, many BSC networks still exist. What is new with IBM's approach, however, is its recognition of intelligent end user devices such as the personal computer. This, more than anything, has led to the development of APPC and LU 6.2 as a software technology for dealing with data exchange in a distributed, connective network. Most large system managers will have to deal with the demand for significant micro-to-mainframe connections that go beyond the use of micros as dumb terminals.

Notes

1. James Martin, *Design and Strategy of Distributed Data Processing* (Englewood Cliffs, NJ: Prentice-Hall, 1981), pp. 10, 11.
2. Paul R. Strauss, "The Standards Deluge: A Sound Foundation or a Tower of Babel?" *Data Communications*, Vol. 17, No. 10, Sept. 1988, p. 160.
3. J. L. Hullett and P. Evans, "New Proposal Extends the Reach of Metro Area Networks (Dual Bus Scheme)," *Data Communications* (USA), Vol. 17, No. 2, Feb. 1988, pp. 139–140, 143–144, 147. Much of the information regarding QPSX is taken from this article. See also, R. M. Newman, Z. L. Budrikis, and J. L. Hulett, "The QPSX MAN," *IEEE Commun. Mag.* (USA), Vol. 26, No. 4, Apr. 1988, pp. 20–28.
4. Ibid., p. 139.
5. J. F. Mollenauer, "Networking for Greater Metropolitan Areas," *Data Communications*, Vol. 17, No.2, Feb. 1988, p. 119.
6. Alan Reinhold, "TCP/IP," *Communications Systems Bulletin* (Raleigh, NC: IBM Telecommunications Marketing Center, Feb. 1988), p. 7. Other authors have named these layers somewhat differently, for example, William Stallings, et al., *Handbook of Computer–Communications Standards*, Vol. 3, "Department of Defense (DoD) Protocol Standards" (New York: Macmillan Publishing Company, 1988), p. 21. The formal definitions for the TCP/IP standards are found in the U.S. Military standards documents, in Requests-For-Comments or RFCs available over the Internet, or from the DDN Network Information Center, SRI International, 333 Ravenswood Avenue, Menlo Park, CA 94025.
7. Stallings, et al., *Handbook*, p. 21, have compared TCP/IP (DoD) and OSI Reference Model layering somewhat differently and have named the four layers as Process, Host-to-Host, Internet, and Network Access. RFC: 793 (1981), which is one of the formal documents detailing TCP, labels the layers as Application, Host, Gateway, and Network. My labeling is a modification of that found in Reinhold, *Communications*, p. 33. For a recent overview of TCP/IP see William Stallings, "Tuning into TCP/IP," *Telecommunications*, Vol. 22, No. 9, Sept. 1988, pp. 23ff. Note also, Michael Hurwicz, "TCP/IP: Temporary Glue or Long-Term Alternative?" *ComputerWorld*, Sept. 26, 1988, pp. 73ff.

8. H. Kim Lew and Cyndi Jung, "Getting There From Here: Mapping From TCP/IP to OSI," *Data Communications*, Vol. 17, No. 8, Aug. 1988, pp. 161ff.

9. Jerry Cashin, "ULANA: New Name in Networking," *Software Magazine*, Vol. 8, No. 12, Oct. 1988, pp. 91–94.

10. See, for a brief description, Bill Hancock, "TCP/IP for Network Services," *DEC Professional*, July 1988, pp. 102ff.

11. Defense Communications Agency, *Military Standard Transmission Control Protocol*, MIL-STD-1780, May 10, 1984. It is also reprinted in Defense Communications Agency, *DDN Protocol Handbook* (Menlo Park, CA: DDN Network Information Center, SRI International, Dec. 1985). See also, RFC: 793 (1981), "Transmission Control Protocol." One introduction to TCP/IP is Charles L. Hedrick, "Introduction to the Internet Protocols," Computer Science Facilities Group, Rutgers, the State University of New Jersey, Center for Computers and Information Services, Laboratory for Computer Science Research, Sept. 22, 1988, unpublished paper.

12. Hedrick, "Introduction for the Internet Protocols," pp. 2–3.

13. "ESCON: New IBM Connection Architecture Sends Data Faster & Farther: Fiber-optic Channels Are 1st Major Advance in Channel Architecture Since System/360," *EDGE, on & about AT&T*, Vol. 5, No. 111, Sept. 10, 1990, p. 16(1).

14. Anon., "Introduction to Systems Network Architecture," a report from the Data Communications Technology Series (Cupertino, CA: Communications Solutions, Inc., 1980).

15. See Ibid., pp. 5–7; F. P. Corr and D. H. Neal, "SNA and Emerging International Standards," *IBM Systems Journal*, Vol. 18, No. 2, 1979; and Art Krumrey, "SNA Strategies," *PC Tech Journal*, Vol. 3, No. 7, July 1985, pp. 40ff.

16. For a more detailed treatment of these themes see Anura Gurug, "IBM Radically Reformulates SNA," *Data Communications*, Vol. 20, No. 5, Apr. 1991, pp. 72, 74–82; and Robin Layland, "The End for IBM's FEP?" *Data Communications*, Vol. 20, No. 5, Apr. 1991, pp. 73, 84–92.

17. IBM, "IBM Advanced Peer-to-Peer Networking Architecture and Product Family Overview (291-079)" *Customer Announcement Letters*, Mar. 5, 1991.

18. James Martin, *Introduction to Teleprocessing* (Englewood Cliffs, NJ: Prentice-Hall, Inc., 1972). This paragraph is based on Martin's discussion, pp. 89–90.

19. This organization was suggested by Cay Weitzman, *Distributed Micro/Minicomputer Systems* (Englewood Cliffs, NJ: Prentice-Hall, Inc., 1980), pp. 364ff.
20. Note ibid. and *General Information—Binary Synchronous Communications* (Research Triangle Park, NC: International Business Machines, 1970), document No. GA27-3004-2, for information on binary synchronous communications.
21. Lawrence J. Bolick, "Telecommunications Standards Arrive," *Datamation*, Oct. 15, 1985, pp. 88–89.
22. Anon., "Introduction to Systems Network Architecture," a report from the Data Communications Technology Series (Cupertino, CA: Communications Solutions, Inc., 1980), p. 13.
23. Weitzman, *Distributed Micro/Minicomputer Systems,* pp. 375ff.
24. IBM, *IBM SDLC General Information*, International Business Machines, Inc., document No. GA27-3093.
25. This discussion of ACCP and LU 6.2 is based on Gerard Joseph, *An Introduction to Advanced Program-to-Program Communication (APPC)* (Research Triangle Park, NC: International Business Machines, 1983), document No. GG24-1584-0.
26. For further information, see Krumrey "SNA Strategies"; Robert J. Sundstrom, "Program-to-Program Communications—A Growing Trend," *Data Communications*, Feb. 1984, pp. 87–92; L. David Passmore, "Coming: A New SNA," *Datamation,* Vol. 31, No. 22, Nov. 15, 1985, pp. 102–112; and John W. Verity, "The Shifting Shape of SNA," *Datamation,* Vol. 31, No. 22, Nov. 15, 1985, pp. 93–98.
27. Laurie Flynn, "IBM Changes Its Strategy on Protocols," *InfoWorld,* Vol. 9, No. 7, Feb. 16, 1987, p. 1(2).
28. ECF is described in IBM's program announcement of Mar. 17, 1987 (287-084), and related documents. Some of the misunderstanding about the relationships of the various products, protocols, and architectures continues to be found in the trade literature. See, for example, two articles by Mike Hurwicz: "Not a Standard: When NETBIOS Means Network Bias," *LAN: The Local Area Network Magazine*, Jan. 1987, pp. 60–61; and "APPC Is Coming: LAN Standard of the Future?" *LAN: The Local Area Network Magazine*, Mar. 1987, pp. 50–54. A somewhat better description of NetBios is given by Jamie Lewis, "NETBIOS: Going Beyond Interrupt 5C," *LAN: The Local Area Network Magazine*, Dec. 1986, pp. 23–24.

29. The discussion of VTAM is based on *VTAM: General Information* (Triangle Park, NC: International Business Machines, Inc., 1985), document No. GC27-0608-2.

30. For more detailed discussions of both SNA and DECnet, see Thomas W. Madron, *Micro–Mainframe Connection* (Indianapolis, IN: Howard W. Sams, 1987), Chapters 6 and 8. For a good and reasonably detailed discussion of DNA, see Anon., *Digital's Networks: An Architecture With A Future* (Maynard, MA: Digital Equipment Corporation, 1984).

31. Paula Musich, "Vendors Are Lining Up Behind DEC's New EMA (Enterprise Management Architecture)," *PC Week,* Vol. 5, No. 38, Sept. 19, 1988, p. C1(2).

32. Ibid.

CHAPTER 8

LANs and WANs: The Role of Asynchronous Devices

For a number of years, the death of asynchronous communications has been forecast. They continue to play an important role, however, especially in a situation requiring dial-access over telephone lines. In this chapter we will explore related issues, particularly protocol conversion.

What Is Protocol Conversion?

To be a full-fledged member of an SNA (System Network Architecture) network, an asynchronous, ASCII device like a microcomputer must be made to look like a 3x78/9 display terminal. Existing software and hardware allows micros to look like older equipment, especially the 3275 bisync equivalent of the 3276. This discussion will be confined to the more modern devices, while recognizing that a production network may have a variety of old and new equipment. Even though there are ASCII 3x78 displays, the norm is an EBCDIC-based (Extended Binary Coded Decimal Interchange Code) device. Consequently, complete conversion must be from asynchronous communications to synchronous communications and from ASCII to EBCDIC character codes. This *protocol conversion* can be accomplished at several points in the network, and the options are expanding rapidly.

To do this conversion a computer must be used, along with appropriate software. Figure 8.1 is a simplified flow diagram of the conversion process from one data-link protocol to another. Here asynchronous input is converted in the protocol conversion processor to bisync or SDLC Data-Link Control systems. The conversion process takes place in a computer using appropriate software to take stop-start data flow and place those data into a synchronous block and send it on. On the reverse side, conversion takes place in the other direction when the synchronous device must communicate with the asynchronous machine.

Although the most common form of protocol conversion is from asynchronous devices to IBM synchronous networks, a more general problem exists because of large numbers of incompatible, but useful, devices available in the marketplace. As N. Bapty has pointed out, protocol converters allow for communications among previously incompatible devices on at least one of three levels: communications technique, data code, and terminal-device control.[1] Protocol converters, according to Bapty, evolved from plug-compatible devices supporting asynchronous to synchronous terminals.

Evolution of devices continued with the development of local area networks (LANs). Because of the inherent incompatibility of hardware manufactured by independent companies and the complexity of data communications, the need for protocol converters is expected to increase. V. Altman, another observer of the protocol-conversion scene, has pointed out that protocol converters are used because they are cost-effective or the only solution in some applications for micro–mainframe communication.[2]

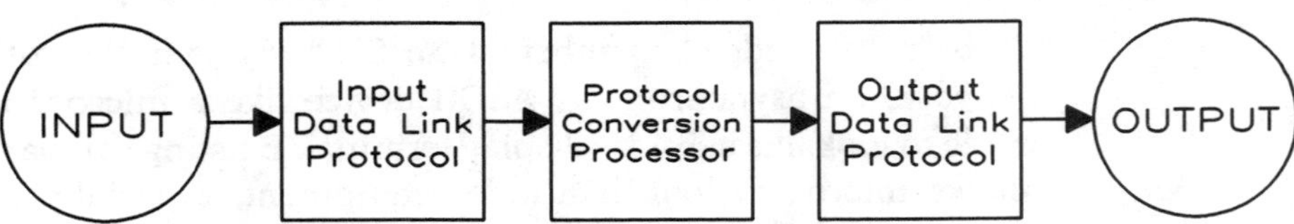

Figure 8.1. The Protocol Conversion Process.

Chapter 7 discussed the characteristics of a 3270 Display System network, and that discussion was summarized in Figure 7.11. To place that discussion in a somewhat different perspective, please note Figure 8.2, which depicts a traditional IBM 3270 star network. Many lines, which may cross many different media, come into the central processor through a Front End Processor (FEP). As previously noted, protocol conversion can take place at several different points in the network. Some of the issues and costs are summarized in Table 8.1.

The actual medium across which the data flow is irrelevant. In a traditional IBM network some lines may be twisted pair, wired via short- or long-haul modems, telephone lines, or even a broadband cable television (CATV) system. To drive home the irrelevance of the medium, some of the figures in this chapter will depict the use of a broadband network, although the actual topology of the synchronous network is star shaped. When using broadband, different frequency ranges take the place of separate wires or telephone circuits. The standard bus diagram for a broadband network, as illustrated in Figure 8.3, will be used from time to time in this chapter. The

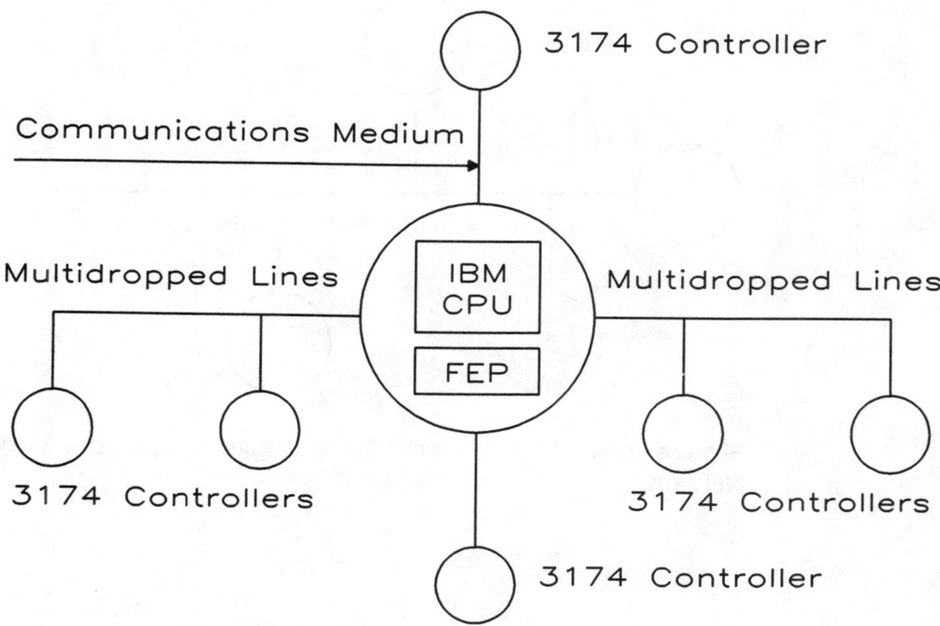

Figure 8.2. Traditional IBM 3270 Star Network.

TABLE 8.1. Summary of Protocol Conversion Points for Micros in an IBM Mainframe Network

Network Link Point	*PC Data-Link Control**	*PC Emulation*†
Internal Coax Board	SDLC	3x78/9
External Converter	Async	ANSI
3x74 Emulation	Bisync	3x78/9
Stand-Alone Converter	Async	ANSI
FEP Conversion	Async	ANSI
LAN Converter	LAN Protocol	3x78/9
Mainframe Converter	Async	ANSI

*Direct link between PC and nearest communications device.
†Type of terminal directly emulated by the PC software. VT100 is a DEC terminal type and is used only for purposes of illustration.

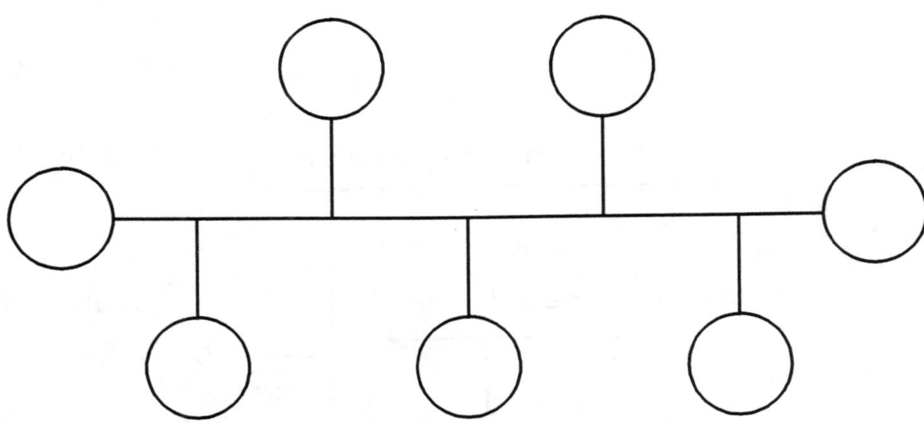

Figure 8.3. Most Network Technologies Can Be the Medium for a 3x70 Network.

result is, of course, a diagram such as that in Figure 8.4, which is a simplified version of the use of broadband in an IBM network.

Protocol Conversion on the Micro

When protocol conversion takes place on the micro, it can be viewed as a specialized form of terminal emulation: Usually the emulation of an IBM 3x78/9 display terminal. In an IBM mainframe network, an important aspect of protocol conversion is to make the target micro appear as a 3x78/9 not only for the end user, but also because considerable IBM mainframe software is written to take advantage of those terminals. Convenience, therefore, is a major issue: Convenience for the end user and convenience for the programmers. On the programmer's side, productivity is improved when only a single-terminal environment can be assumed.

Regardless of where the protocol converter is located on the network, some form of terminal emulation must take place on the micro. Terminal emulation allows for screen addressing, clearing the screen, clearing from the cursor to the end of the screen, clearing from the cursor to the end of the line, and similar services. In an environment that relies heavily on full-

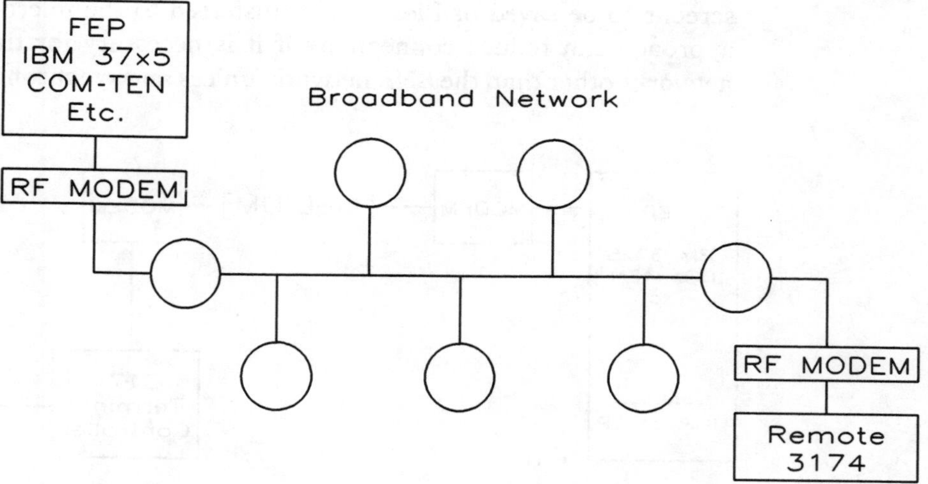

Figure 8.4. Traditional IBM 3x70 Network Using a Broadband Medium.

screen data entry and display, these features are absolute requirements. Table 8.1 is somewhat misleading in its designation of PC emulation as either 3x78/9 or ANSI. Systems designated as ANSI emulation must run a standard asynchronous, ASCII terminal emulator for microcomputer control. Other systems will use other software and hardware for terminal control, but may use ANSI screen control codes to access the screen. They may also, of course, go outside the operating system to directly access video memory for screen control.

3x70 Emulator Cards

One efficient way to make a micro look like a 3x78/9 is to install a 3270 coax board, available from many manufacturers, directly inside the PC. The connector on the back of the PC allows the PC to be connected, via coaxial cable, directly to the 3x74/6 cluster controller. Figure 8.5 illustrates the configuration of an internal coax board. Although the illustration shows a remote 3x74, the cluster controller could just as well be a machine attached directly to a channel.

With a coax board installed, the PC's response time rivals a "real" 3x78/9 terminal and operates in the same fashion as the 3x78/9. Most manufacturers of such boards offer file-transfer software that allows screens to be saved or files to be transferred to the microcomputer. This approach can reduce connectivity if it is necessary for the user to enter networks other than the SNA network, unless an asynchronous adapter and

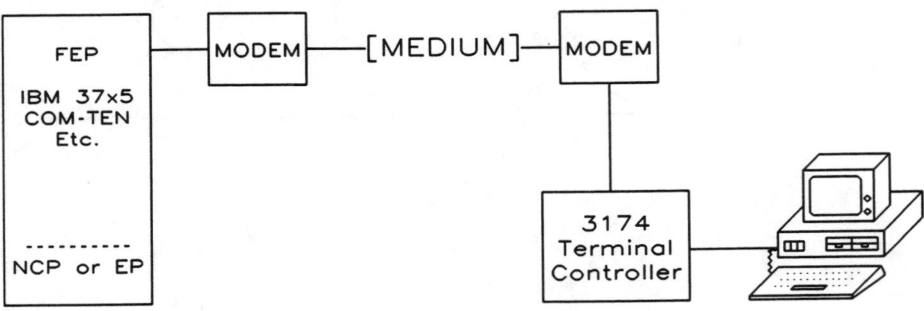

Figure 8.5. Protocol Conversion in the Microcomputer (with a Plug-in Board).

modem are also installed. At this writing the coax boards could add several hundred dollars to the cost of a PC-based workstation, although prices were dropping and volume discounts were commonly available to large organizations. It is also necessary, of course, to have an available port on a conveniently located 3x74/6 cluster controller.

3x78/9 Emulation at the Micro, but Outside It

Similar to an internal coax board, an external protocol converter is attached through a coaxial cable to the 3x74/6, but connected through an asynchronous, RS-232 adapter to the PC. This requires a terminal emulator for the PC, but both the asynchronous adapter and the terminal emulator can be used for other networks as well as the SNA system. Response time is typically degraded through this approach since the protocol converter must furnish complete information to the terminal emulator. Like the internal board, these devices often have a list price around $1,000 and require terminal-emulation software. The method for connecting this device is shown in Figure 8.6.

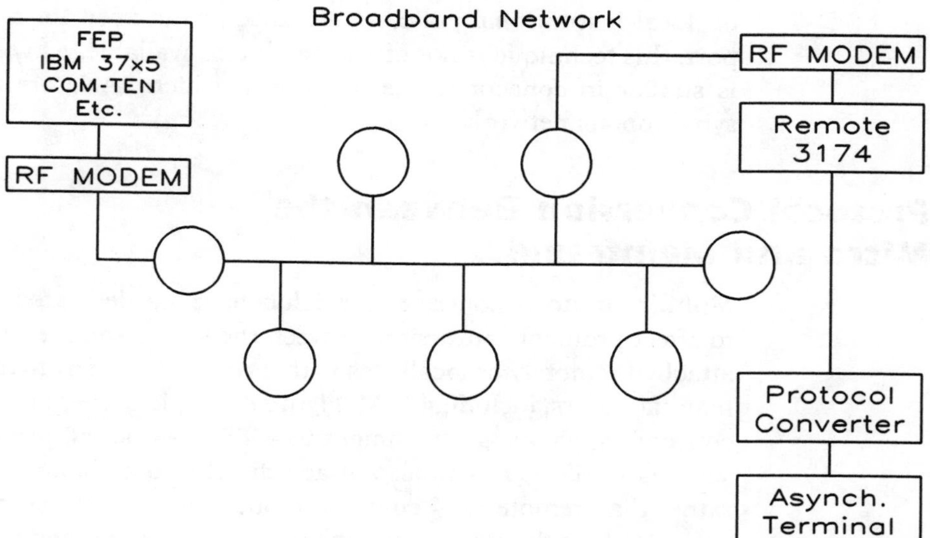

Figure 8.6. A Protocol Converter at the Microcomputer.

A stand-alone, locally attached 3x78/9 protocol converter would not normally be the solution of choice if a LAN or plug-in card is available. If, however, there happened to be a mix of older micros, micros without the availability of a plug-in card, or many standard asynchronous ASCII terminals, then this solution would be an appropriate means for integrating these varied devices within an IBM mainframe network, either SNA or bisync. Reasonably good performance would be achieved on a wide variety of terminal devices, although the cost per workstation can be somewhat high.

3x74/6 Emulation

Protocol conversion can also be achieved by having the PC emulate a 3x74/6 cluster controller. In this mode, the PC is attached, via an RS-232 synchronous interface and cable through the communications link, to the FEP. Sometimes additional PCs can be connected to the base PC, like 3x78/9s can be connected to any cluster controller. A synchronous interface board, like its asynchronous cousin, can cost as little as $200 (for an IBM PC/clone) with similarly priced software. On the other hand, a synchronous modem will likely run $600 to $1000 (and two may be required, depending on local institutional policies). Because of the need for a dedicated FEP port, this technique is not often used but is available. As will be noted, this is similar in concept to the manner in which LANs are connected to a synchronous network.

Protocol Conversion Between the Micro and Mainframe

Multiline protocol converters, which behave like dedicated 3x74 emulators, to effect protocol conversion between the micro and the mainframe either attached remotely or locally, as with a real 3x74, are available from several manufacturers, including IBM. Figure 8.7 depicts this approach to protocol conversion, showing attachment to a FEP. As noted, protocol converters such as IBM's 7171 can also attach directly to a channel, providing local rather than remote 3x74 emulation. Such devices are comparatively cheap per port. Like the single-port external protocol converter, the PC connected to a multiport converter requires an asynchronous adapter, a terminal emulator, and some means of communicating with the converter. An added

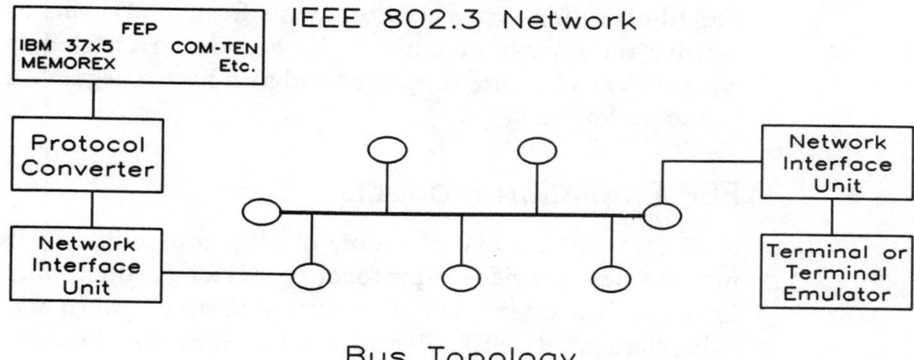

Figure 8.7. Protocol Converter Between the Micro and the Mainframe.

disadvantage for either the single- or multiport protocol converter is that mapping special-purpose 3x78/9 keys to control or escape sequences on the PC can be unhandy.

Clearly, as B. Hendrickson has noted, increasing micro–mainframe communications is putting greater importance on protocol converters.[3] Traditional converters have had a problem with error-free asynchronous data transfer and poor performance with packet-switched networks. Renex, one major manufacturer of stand-alone protocol converters, has developed the Rap message-oriented protocol RLink communications software system solution. Full-screen editing and data entry are done by the software—not the converter. RAP provides for 3270 emulation. The performance of protocol converters can be improved by letting intelligent devices, such as micros, do much of the work rather than passing all control across the communications line.

Protocol Conversion at the Mainframe

There are several ways that protocol conversion can take place at the mainframe. First, the FEP to the IBM/PCM mainframe can do the protocol conversion. This has the advantage of better integration, other control processes take place in the FEP. Second, the conversion can take place on the mainframe as an application running under a host system that supports asynchronous communications, such as VM/SP or MUSIC (both are supported operating system environments from IBM). This approach is inexpensive on a per-port basis. It is, however, restricted in the operating environments that are supported and may have a negative impact on mainframe performance.

FEP Emulation Products

NCR-COMTEN, a manufacturer of plug compatible FEPs for IBM/PCM mainframes, provides a protocol converter product with its "Integrated Protocol Converter," which consists of both software and hardware as a subsystem of its FEP. Figure 8.8 provides an illustration of how this product works. The PC is linked to the FEP through standard asynchronous communications lines; protocol converted to 3270 Bisync; and sent to VTAM, TCAM, or BTAM applications. The conversion takes place in the Integrated Protocol Converter and provides bisync data to the Communications Interface Module. Network Control Programming (NCP), the SNA control program, sees only the bisync information, which it passes to VTAM. The upgrade cost, providing an organization already uses the NCR-COMTEN FEP, is about the same as a stand-alone protocol converter. The

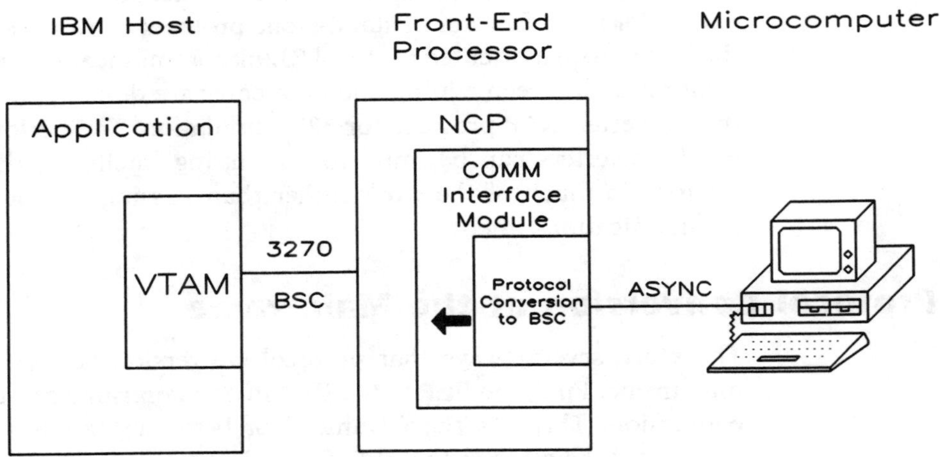

Figure 8.8. Protocol Conversion on the Mainframe.

advantage of protocol conversion integrated with the FEP is that the lines can be controlled and operated through the FEP and maintenance is assured by NCR-COMTEN. The FEP may, however, become overloaded, and the PCs must still communicate with the FEP and use a terminal-emulation program.

3x70 Emulation on the Mainframe

A final point at which conversion can take place is with a VTAM, VM/SP, or some other IBM mainframe operating environment application that does the protocol conversion on the mainframe itself. The PC would communicate through an asynchronous port on the FEP and be sent to VTAM asynchronously through EP (Emulation Programming) (or PEP [Partitioned Emulation Programming]) rather than through NCP. This approach would lose much of SNA's power and could have response-time implications for the mainframe; however, businesses and universities are using these systems. The consulting firm of Towers, Perrin, Forster and Crosby, for example, is using Simware Inc.'s Sim3278/VM software package with PCs and modems to provide a micro-to-mainframe link, according to M. K. Leddy.[4] Sim3278/VM features include compatibility with a variety of personal computers, support for other dumb terminals, and the need for only the software and a modem. Error checking, help screens, and clear documentation are also useful features.

In recent years, Simware's products have grown to include software for MVS as well as VM and support for TCP/IP. Similar growth has taken place with competing products as well. There are several problems with doing protocol conversion on the mainframe. First, a number of products, Simware included, did not always support all of IBM's operating systems. Thus, while such products often started with support of VM it often took several years for support of MVS to follow. Moreover, some products, while they were vended by IBM, were never completely accessible. An example was MUSIC (Multi-User System for Interactive Computing), an interactive operating system written by McGill University but sold as a supported product by IBM for several years. MUSIC was, however, equipped with its own 3278 emulator but it did not work with anything but MUSIC. MUSIC, by the way, was used largely by institutions of higher education with

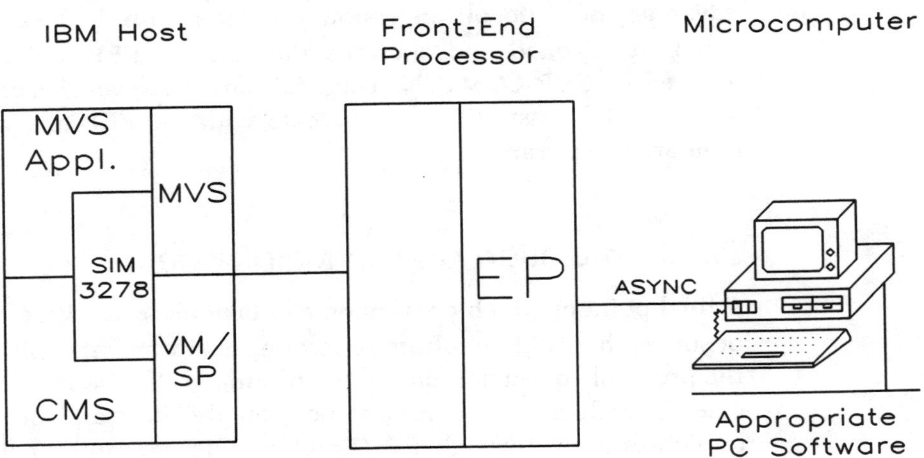

Figure 8.9. Protocol Conversion on the Mainframe.

only a small private-sector clientele. The use of the mainframe as a protocol converter, at least for the two products noted, is illustrated in Figure 8.9.

LANs as Protocol Converters

Local area networks can provide another method of protocol conversion if they are equipped with a 3270 server that acts as a gateway between the LAN and the SNA network. The 3270 server operates as a 3x74 cluster controller (usually an IBM Model C51), and provides terminal emulation to the micros on the LAN. The 3270 server is, in turn, attached through a modem to the FEP. Several LAN manufacturers provide 3270 servers, and they all operate in about the same fashion. If IBM PCs or some reasonable facsimile are on the LAN, the 3270 server will be a PC equipped with both a network adapter for the particular LAN and a synchronous interface card. A program that does the protocol conversion is then run on the server PC, and that program takes the bidirectional data flow and converts it from the LAN protocol to bisync or SDLC and vice versa. Figure 8.10 provides an illustration of a typical setup.

As with other protocol-conversion schemes, opinion varies about the

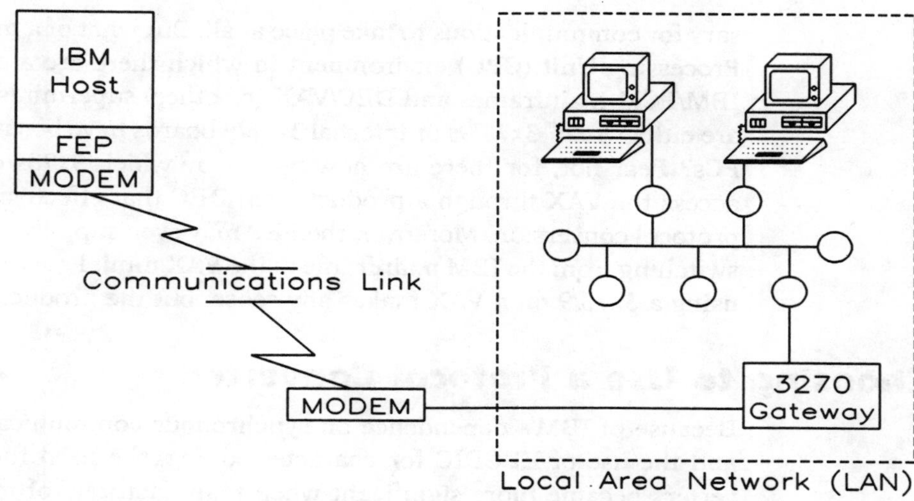

Notes: 1. The communications link is normally SDLC or bisync.
2. The 3270 Gateway is software and hardware running on a micro that emulates a 3x74 terminal controller.

Figure 8.10. A 3x70 Solution Using a PC-Based LAN.

efficiency and effectiveness of using a PC-based LAN for this purpose.[5] Where PCs have connectivity over a LAN, and where use of the 3270 network is light to moderate, this approach can be a cost-effective method for providing users mainframe access. Virtually all the major LAN manufacturers provide an SNA or 3270 gateway. A single server can often accommodate as many as 32 concurrent users. The PC used as a server can be minimally equipped and inexpensive. If the LAN is already in place, then the value-added cost of providing 3270 emulation is low. The use of a LAN to provide 3270 emulation may not solve all problems, but in an SNA environment that approach to emulation should be investigated.

Backward Emulation: 3x70 to Asynchronous

Do not be mislead into thinking that all protocol conversion is designed to let asynchronous devices talk with IBM mainframes: Conversion can go both ways. In a technical sense, of course, all protocol conversion is two ways: async-to-sync and sync-to-async. The two-way conversion is necessary for communications to take place at all. But what of a multiple-Central Processing Unit (CPU) environment in which there are a combination of IBM/PCM mainframes and DEC/VAX (or other) superminis and terminals are either "real" 3x78/9s or internal 3x78/9 boards have been installed in the PCs? Fear not, for there are now means by which 3x78s can be used to access the VAX through a product from DEC that effectively does reverse protocol conversion. Moreover, the FEP may even support systems to allow switching from the IBM mainframe to the VAX mini. I'm not convinced that using a 3x78/9 on a VAX makes any sense, but the products are available.

Choosing to Use a Protocol Converter

Because of IBM's dependence on synchronous communication protocols, and the use of EBCDIC for character coding, the need for protocol converters became more significant when manufacturers of many terminals, mini, and microcomputers adopted a standard asynchronous communication using ASCII character coding.[6] Companies or institutions that do not support anything but the products of a single vendor (IBM, DEC, HP, or others, for example) then may never need to address the specter of protocol conversion. On the other hand, especially in large organizations, mixed-vendor environments are common. This is especially true in universities and engineering-oriented companies. If protocol conversion is desirable, then the specific means for doing it should be based on several criteria:

- Cost can be the overriding consideration.
- Response-time needs, since protocol-conversions systems will not usually be as fast as stand-alone 3x78/9 terminals. Note that where PCs are the primary workstations, internal coax boards can provide service equivalent to the "real" 3x78/9.
- The mainframe or mini operating environment, since some systems cannot be used with some operating conditions.

When protocol converters first came on the market, the argument was made that under some conditions they provided a cheap method for extending 3270 services to users at a low cost. This argument had merit in the early 1980s, before the deployment of PCs became widespread and 3x78/9 devices were still expensive. By the mid-1980s, however, this argument had less merit simply because the price of 3x78/9 devices had dropped, especially among manufacturers of 3270 compatible equipment. Even IBM has dropped its prices on these terminals. Today the primary argument for protocol conversion is convenience and connectivity, although the cost issue can still be argued under some conditions. One such condition is an isolated office with a single user. To buy a 3x74/6 device and a pair of synchronous modems for that use, the total workstation would be expensive. After about four users, however, the cost for the 3x74 plus four synchronous terminals is about the same as providing synchronous equipment. The isolated user, however, may be an appropriate reason for using some protocol conversion. The particular terminal-networking scheme used may also encourage protocol conversion.

The downside of protocol conversion is that asynchronous devices are not structured to make the best use of the features and facilities of a 3x78/9, nor is a 3x78/9 structured to provide optimum use on an asynchronous system. There may also be an ongoing user-education problem so that the protocol-converted devices can be used successfully. On the other hand, since some protocol converters support the use of addressable printers, with the large variety of printers now available, better and more varied printing may result, even when 3x78/9 devices are being used for production work. In any event, protocol converters do provide a useful option for blending any terminal equipment into any host environment.

Finally, in an asynchronous network, the use of protocol converters to connect to an IBM mainframe may be the most cost-effective method for providing asynchronous ports into that mainframe. IBM has never supported asynchronous communications with any degree of enthusiasm, and the 37x5 FEPs are good examples. For many years the only asynchronous ports that one could buy from IBM were slow, half-duplex lines, defeating many of the newer networking schemes. Today, however, with the availability of LANs as well as competing FEP products, such ports are available, and even IBM has acceded to the need. Nevertheless, companies or institutions with enough synchronous ports may find it cost-effective to provide protocol conversion outside the microcomputer.

Notes

1. N. Bapty, "Protocol Conversion—Why and How," *Data Processing* (UK), Vol. 26, No. 9, Nov. 1984, pp. 7–9.
2. V. Altman, "Protocol Converters: A Cost-Efficient Option," *MIS Week Supplement* to *MIS Week*, Vol. 6, No. 14, April 3, 1985, p. 8.

3. B. Hendrickson, "Asynchronous Protocol Boosts Converter Performance: Applications Note," *Telecommunications,* Vol. 19, No. 5, May 1985, pp. 64ff.
4. M. K. Leddy, "Consulting Firm Taps Simware for Link Package," *PC Week,* Vol. 1, No. 44, Nov. 6, 1984, p. 118.
5. G. W. Everhart, "Net Links PCs Directly to IBM Hosts," *Systems & Software,* Vol. 4, No. 2, Feb. 1985, pp. 119–121.
6. G. D. Polk, "The Protocol Converter: Blend Any Equipment into Any Host Network," *DEC Professional,* Vol. 4, No. 5, May 1985, pp. 86–90, 92.

CHAPTER 9

File Transfer Protocols

Discussion thus far has centered on environments in which data communications take place in support of EWC. These discussions have included descriptions of various Data-Link Control methods such as asynchronous, binary synchronous, and synchronous systems and Data-Link Control in LANs (local area networks). The Data-Link Control method organizes the bit- or byte-level information and the manner it is sent over a serial line. I say "serial" line simply because parallel communications is normally applicable only to physically short data-transmission problems, such as the connection of a printer to a computer. The Data-Link Control protocols already discussed are all used in serial data communications. The data encoding method, ASCII or EBCDIC (Extended Binary Coded Decimal Interchange Code), is independent of the Data-Link Control, although most asynchronous communication is accomplished between or among systems using ASCII data encoding. Bisync and SDLC (Synchronous Data-Link Control) are usually used with systems using EBCDIC.

File transfer protocols are at a level higher than Data-Link Control and data-encoding schemes. Within the OSI Reference Model, data transfer protocols are implemented in layers 4 through 7 (Transport, Session Control, Presentation, and Application). Data-Link Control is implemented in Layer 2. Although both Data-Link Control and file transfer protocols may define blocks or packets of data, *only file transfer protocols define end-to-end interactions between user processes*. Data-Link Control has the more fundamental concern with sending blocks of data over a physical link. With synchronous Data-Link Control methods, such as bisync and SDLC, the blocks are large. Asynchronous (start-stop) communication uses blocks of only 10 bits (including start and stop bits). The purpose of a file transfer protocol is to ensure the integrity of data transferred from one machine to another. That transfer may take place between two or more micros, between micros and mainframes, or between mainframes. Many file transfer protocols can be implemented on virtually any physical data communications system, including LANs and more traditional systems.

At the risk of overly belaboring the point, it is important to distinguish clearly between data-link protocols and file transfer protocols. I stress this point because the literature is replete with misunderstandings concerning the relationships between these two sets of protocols by people who should know better. Regardless of how similar the structure of data-link and file transfer protocols may appear, they operate at very different layers of a network architecture. To reiterate, file transfer protocols are implemented in OSI layers 4–7, while data-link protocols are implemented in Layer 2. In fact, there is a third structure that also appears to be very similar to file transfer and Data-Link Controls, and it is often called a datagram or packet. Datagrams are typically formed in the Network Layer (Layer 3). Thus, as an outgoing message is constructed, a unit of data will be encapsulated in a file-transfer block, that block may then be further encapsulated in a datagram, and the datagram encapsulated in the data-link frame with each envelope protected by error-correction codes.

In Figure 9.1 there has been an effort made to make these points explicit. The shaded areas in Figure 9.1 illustrate in which OSI layer each of the blocks/packets/frames are assembled and disassembled. This matter is often made even more irritating in that terms like "block," "packet," "frame," and other related words are used inconsistently throughout the literature. More detailed definitions of these terms are given in the Glossary. Examples of protocols lying at each of these layers would be the OSI FTAM (File Transfer, Access, and Management) and TCP/IP (Transmission Control Protocol/Internet Protocol) FTP (File Transfer Protocol) (Application Layer), the IP datagram of TCP/IP (equating the IP Layer in TCP/IP to the OSI Network Layer), and SDLC, bisync, HDLC (High-Level Data-Link Control), 802.3, 802.4, and 802.5 (Data-Link Layer). One general distinction between file transfer protocols and the others is that file transfer protocols

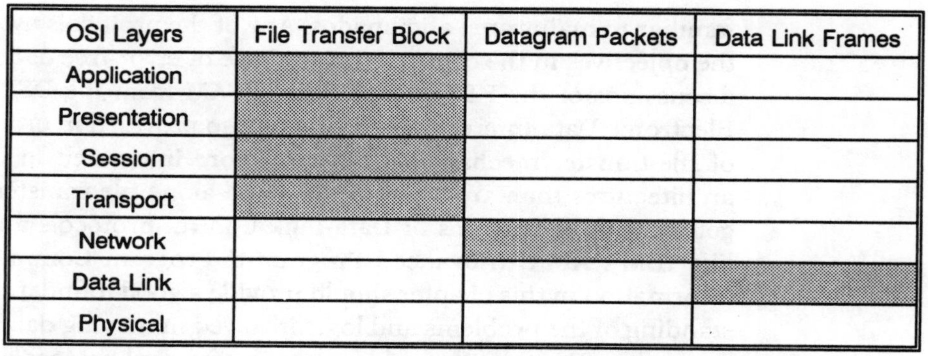

OSI Layers	File Transfer Block	Datagram Packets	Data Link Frames
Application			
Presentation			
Session			
Transport			
Network			
Data Link			
Physical			

Figure 9.1. Protocol Location in the OSI Layered Architecture.

typically do not have address fields defined, assuming that the packet and/or frame structure at other layers will take care of actually routing the information correctly.

The simplest file-transfer mechanism is one where data are spooled out from the device at one end of the connection to a receiving program at the other end. This technique is frequently implemented at the micro end by having the communications program read a line of a file and send each byte out the asynchronous port. Since the receiving end views the incoming data as if it were from a fast typist, a mainframe text editor is often used to capture the incoming data. No control-code conversion takes place, and no checking is done to ensure that all the data sent were properly received. Such an approach, however, is often inadequate in modern data-communications environments.

When speaking of "file transfer protocols" the problem of shipping a file from one computer to another comes immediately to mind. While this is a major objective in the definition of such a protocol, the file-transfer techniques (or similar ones) discussed in this chapter are also used in modern data-communications systems to ensure the integrity of data sent interactively. High-speed dial-access modems are a case in point. Without an extensive error checking and correcting facility there was no way to improve the speed of dial-up lines without using a file transfer protocol even for interactive communications—the telephone lines are too "noisy." The protocol most frequently used by modem manufacturers in the absence of public standards, is MNP from Microcom.

The file transfer protocols selected for inclusion in this chapter will be familiar to large numbers of microcomputer users, although perhaps less familiar to mainframe aficionados. Any of the protocols available illustrate the objectives in the construction and use of error-free data transfer. Short discussions of the FTP from TCP/IP, FTAM from the OSI standards, and Electronic Data Interchange (EDI) are also provided in order to give a view of file-transfer mechanisms that are more integrated in overall network architectures than are some of the stand-alone file transfer protocols. Together with discussions of Data-Link Control protocols and architectures like IBM's APPC (Advanced Program-to-Program Communications), the information in this chapter should provide a good foundation for an understanding of the problems and logic involved in moving data from one point to another. For the sake of completeness, several protocols that are or will become important are briefly discussed at the end of this chapter. The important point to remember, however, is that while each protocol was developed to meet some particular need, they all have similar design objectives: To get a block of data from one end of a connection to the other end with complete integrity in the minimum amount of time.

Issues

The simplest and easiest approach to file transfer requires no error checking or organization of the data being sent. The need for error checking and data organization constitute two of the major reasons why file transfer protocols are necessary. Reliability issues at the Data-Link Control level have already been discussed, but reliability problems also exist at higher layers. In Chapter 7, the discussion about IBM's APPC (LU 6.2) noted the issue of error checking. Advanced Program-to-Program Communications is frequently discussed as a file transfer protocol, but it is more than that. Bear in mind, however, that the list of file transfer protocols discussed in this chapter is not exhaustive, nor is it complete even within the context of this book.

Before a complete file transfer proceeds, several actions must take place on both the sending and receiving end. Figure 9.2 tries to capture the necessary steps. These steps must take place regardless of the Data-Link Control method, and they will take place whether the software handles them in a manner transparent to the user or the user must intervene at one or more steps in the process. Assuming the data to be transferred exists in some format on a disk file and that the sender is a micro and the receiver is an IBM/PCM or other mainframe, then the following steps must take place:

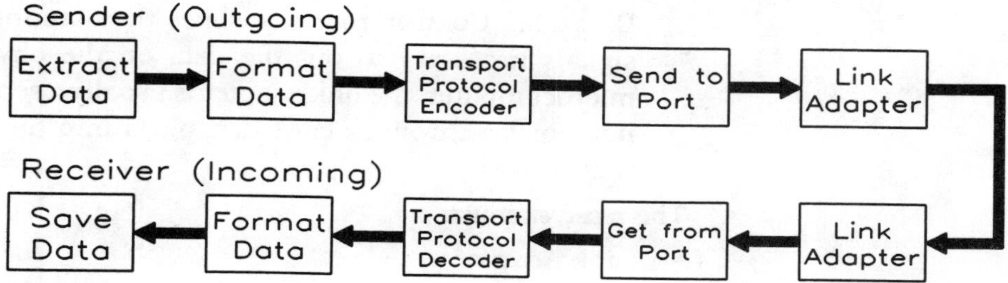

Figure 9.2. The File Transfer Process.

- The *sender* must:
  - Extract Data.

    If the file is a simple record-oriented, ASCII, rectangular file, data extraction is simple—read a record and get on with the transfer. If, however, the data are in a specialized database or spreadsheet file, then the data will have to be extracted with a program or program segment capable of reading (and probably translating) the specialized format.
  - Format Data.

    If the data are in a specialized format, they will undoubtedly have to be reformatted in a form the receiver can handle—frequently a standard record-oriented rectangular data file, although it might be something else.
  - Transport Protocol Encoder.

    Once the data are in the format needed for transmission, they must be placed in the appropriate block or packet format required by the transport protocol, including any error-detection information.
  - Send to Port.

    When the transport packet has been assembled, it must be sent to the port, in whatever format is required by the Data-Link Adapter (usually a byte at a time).
  - Link Adapter.

    The link adapter is a combination of software and hardware that encodes the data for transmission using the appropriate

Data-Link Control, then translates the data into the electrical signals necessary to put the data on the physical line. In a microcomputer, the link adapter is usually a separate asynchronous or synchronous card that plugs into the micro's system unit.

- The *receiver* must:
  - Link Adapter.

    On an IBM mainframe the link adapter will be either at the Front End Processor (FEP) or another channel-attached terminal-control device such as a 3174 cluster controller or a protocol converter emulating a 3174.
  - Get from Port.

    Obtaining a byte of data from a port on a mainframe is rarely the straightforward process it is on a micro. It is a combination of system support software that may include at least the FEP (or cluster controller) and the telecommunications access method program, such as VTAM (Virtual Telecommunications Access Method). By using what is essentially a subroutine call to VTAM, the programmer can extract one or more bytes of data.
  - Transport Protocol Decoder.

    When the full transport packet has been received, the decoder must do all the appropriate error checking. If the data were not correctly received, then a request for retransmission must be sent. If the data are correct, however, they are made available for other processing.
  - Format Data.

    If the data are not already in the appropriate format, then the receiver must format them for the destination program segment. If the data are to be saved as a rectangular file, and if they are coming down the line in the correct format, then no further formatting is necessary. However . . .
  - Save the Data.

    The data must be placed in the specified file. If this is a simple rectangular sequential file, the problem is trivial. If, however, the data must be sent to a database system, a direct (random) access file, or to a VSAM (Virtual Sequential Access Method) file, the problem is more complicated.

The first objective in executing a file transfer is to get the data from one device to another in a correct and useful form. The most primitive approach is to require the user to perform many of the steps of the process individually with separate programs. A second objective *should* be to let the user transfer the file with minimum intervention, except at the inception of the process. A complete file-transfer system, as Figure 9.2 clearly indicates, requires program-to-program interaction between the sending and receiving machines. The process can start on either end, but if the user is required to enter only the filename to be sent, and a receiving filename, then the intervening software must be able to carry on a conversation that provides control over the transfer. The file transfer protocol is only one part of the process, but it guarantees the integrity of the data as it travels through the process.

Reliability in the Transfer of Data

Data can be corrupted at many points in the file-transfer process. One common point is "noise" on the physical medium. On some LANs, data may be corrupted as a result of collisions. On large networks, a session may be established that uses several physical media, with gateways among the different systems. Whatever the source of the corruption, however, error correction may have to take place at various levels of the transfer. Since the file-transfer packet or block is not the same as the Data-Link Control block, then error correction must take place at both levels. All the data in a file transfer protocol packet is perceived by the Data-Link Control as being merely data *qua* data. In an asynchronous system, parity checking is frequently turned off so that a full eight-bit byte can be transferred. Even that simple form of error checking, therefore, may not be available. The typical transport protocol provides, therefore, for a checksum calculation, or something similar, that the receiving end can use to be certain that all the data have been properly received. If the checksum calculated by the receiver is not the same as the checksum sent with the data-transfer packet, then a packet retransmission must be requested. Even this approach to error checking is probably not foolproof, but it does ensure a high degree of reliability.

Interaction of Networks and Data Being Transferred

Unlike simple communications via twisted pair or over telephone lines using modems, communications over a specific network architecture may have pitfalls for data transfer. One problem that confronts a file transfer protocol designer is how to deal with control codes or characters in standard character codes, such as ASCII or EBCDIC. The control codes have been defined for specific functions, usually to control some process. The ASCII codes XON and XOFF, for example, are used for flow control of the data-communications session. In times past, flow control might have been carried on only at the host computer, the terminal, or some combination of the two. Today, the network may be independently flow controlled. If this is the case, then the transmission of XON or XOFF without code conversions may do strange things to the network. A file transfer protocol should be designed to be independent of the network over which it functions. A block or packet of data should not interact in any way with the network over which it is transported.

Asynchronous Modes of Transfer

Trade journals or professional literature dealing with computing make it appear that all communication is accomplished with LANs, IBM's System Network Architecture (SNA), or some other sophisticated system. A look at computers and data-communications equipment on the market, however, will convince anyone that asynchronous serial communications, using ASCII character coding, is not only widespread, but is probably the only Data-Link Control that can provide near universal connectivity. In most organizations with multivendor environments there will almost always be at least some asynchronous communications facilities, or asynchronous links may be dominant. Even in IBM shops using SNA, if dial-access is allowed, there will be some asynchronous ports, even though IBM has historically tried to ignore async access. Recent developments by IBM have suggested that even Big Blue is at last recognizing that async communications is not going away. This section will focus on three file transfer protocols designed to provide error-free file transfers: XMODEM, Kermit, and X.PC.

XMODEM

With the coming of many CP/M microcomputers during the late seventies, it became apparent that some file transfer protocol was needed for transmitting data via phone lines. During 1977, Ward Christensen wrote the first version of XMODEM and produced a major revision in 1979. Christensen made the program and its protocol part of the large store of public domain programs, producing a "definitive" description of the protocol in 1982 in a document called XMODEM.DOC.[1] Various versions of XMODEM are available in the public domain for both CP/M, MS-DOS, and other personal and large-scale computers. They are available, along with XMODEM.DOC, on many of the microcomputer bulletin boards across the United States. With the enormous popularity of micros in the 1980s, the XMODEM transfer protocol has been incorporated into some commercially available communications programs.

The original purpose for writing XMODEM was to provide an error-free method of transferring binary files. XMODEM, using a standard checksum test, reportedly detects 99.6 percent of all data errors.[2] Using a later addition of a CCITT standard Cyclical Redundancy Check (CRC) error detection rises to 99.997–99.998 percent.[3] In the early days of microcomputing it was thought that transferring ASCII files did not merit the same attention as binary files, since printable ASCII files could use parity checking, or even just read the resulting text. For user transparent file transfers, of course, all data must be transferred error free, not just binary files, and the XMODEM protocol will work with ASCII files as well.

Control Characters

There are four control characters used by XMODEM:

```
<SOH>     Start of Header.
<ACK>     Acknowledge.
<NAK>     Negative acknowledge.
<EOT>     End of Transmission.
```

Data-Transfer Control

The format of the XMODEM file-transfer block can be seen in Figure 9.3. The protocol uses the control characters noted for handshaking between the sending and receiving software. The block is a fixed length of 132 characters. The "data" field is a fixed length of 128 bytes, consistent with CP/M's standard record length. When a file transfer is started the receiving machine signals that it is ready by sending a <NAK> to the sending machine. At that point the transmitting computer sends a 132 character block with the 132nd character being a checksum.

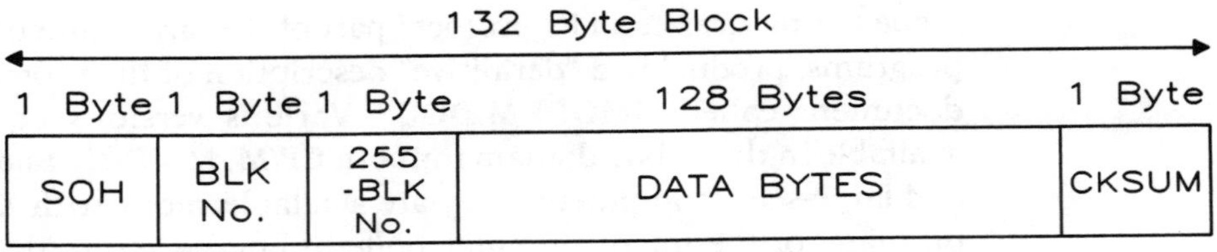

132 Byte Block

1 Byte	1 Byte	1 Byte	128 Bytes	1 Byte
SOH	BLK No.	255 -BLK No.	DATA BYTES	CKSUM

Figure 9.3. Original XMODEM Transfer Block.
Source: From Ward Christensen, "XMODEM.DOC" on Ward's CBBS (Bulletin Board, 312-849-1132, 1986), Messages 4–6.

Error Checking and Recovery

According to Christensen, the checksum is simply the "sum of the [decimal values] of the data bytes only," tossing any carry. A program fragment in BASIC that implements the checksum may be seen in Listing 9.1.

The block number is contained in two different fields. The second block number is the "ones complement" of the first block number. If the data are corrupted (checksums do not match), the receiving station sends a <NAK> to the sending station, requesting a retransmission. Block numbers should always increment by one, or should be the same as the last block if a retransmission was requested. A sample data flow is described in Figure 9.4. Because the simple checksum used in the original XMODEM is subject to duplication even when the data are in error, John Byrnes added the use of a CRC option.

The CRC used in the XMODEM Protocol is an alternate form of block check, which provides more robust error detection than the original

```
5000 CHECKSUM = 0
5010 FOR I = 1 TO 128
5020          CHECKSUM = CHECKSUM + ASC(MID$(XM$,I,1))
5030 NEXT I
5040 CHECKSUM = (CHECKSUM AND 255)
```

XM$ is a string variable of 128 bytes containing the data field of the XMODEM data transfer block.

Listing 9.1. CHECKSUM Calculation on an XMODEM Data Field.

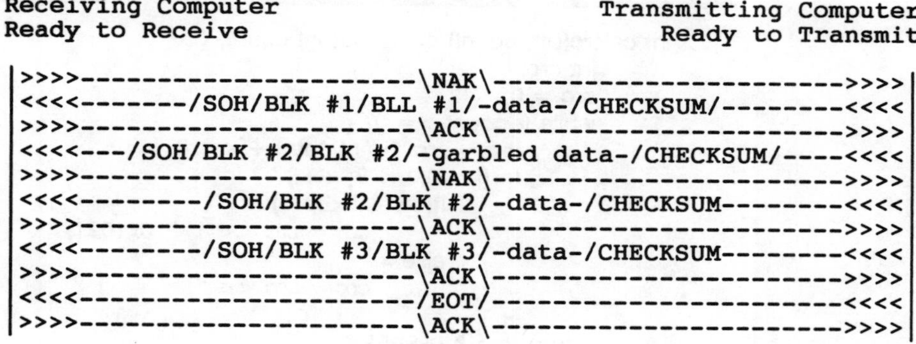

<File Transfer Ends>

Figure 9.4. XMODEM File Transfer Events.
Source: Ward Christensen, "XMODEM.DOC" on Ward's CBBS (Bulletin Board, 312-849-1132, 1986), Messages 4–7.

checksum. The changes to the XMODEM Protocol to replace the checksum with the CRC are straightforward. Byrnes added an initial handshake to solve the problem of incompatibility. The handshake allows a receiving program with CRC capability to determine whether the sending program supports the CRC option, and to switch it to CRC mode if it does. This handshake is designed so that it will work properly with programs that implement only the original protocol.[4] Byrnes has given a C function that implements the CRC, and that function may be seen in Listing 9.2.

This function calculates the CRC now used by XMODEM. The first argument is a pointer to the message block. The second argument is the number of bytes in the message block. The message block used by the XMODEM contains 128 bytes. The function return value is an integer that contains the CRC. The low-order 16 bits of this integer are the coefficients of the CRC. The low-order bit is the low-order coefficient of the CRC. Because the CRC requires 16 rather than 8 bits, the revised transfer block is 133 characters rather than 132. The block format is displayed in Figure 9.5. Unfortunately, C programs are almost unreadable, and Listing 9.2 is no exception. A BASIC (Power/Turbo Basic) translation is, therefore, provided in Listing 9.3 for those readers interested in understanding the details of the method. It should be noted that while Listing 9.3 is a straightforward translation of the logic in Listing 9.2, it is not necessarily the fastest way to

```
int calcrc(ptr, count) char *ptr; int count; {
        int crc, i;
        crc = 0;
        while (--count >= 0) {
                crc = crc ^ (int)*ptr++ << 8;
                for(i = 0; i < 8; ++i)
                        if(crc & 0x8000)
                                crc = crc << 1 ^ 0x1021;
                        else
                                crc = crc << 1;
                }
        return (crc & 0xFFFF);
        }
```

Listing 9.2. C Function to Calculate a CRC.

implement CRC in BASIC.[5] It should be understood that these calculations can reduce overall network performance with the result that improved algorithms for calculating error detecting checksums is of some importance.

The initial handshaking for the CRC option begins by the receiver sending a <C>. If the sender responds within three seconds with an <SOH> then both sides have the CRC option. Otherwise, a time-out occurs and the receiver sends a <NAK> and file transfer takes place using the standard checksum. The sending program always starts in the checksum mode, and all XMODEM programs implement checksum to remain compatible with earlier versions. Sample data flows using the CRC option are given in Figure 9.6 and Figure 9.7.

133 Byte Block

1 Byte	1 Byte	1 Byte	128 Bytes	1 Byte	1 Byte
SOH	BLK No.	255 -BLK No.	DATA BYTES	CRC High	CRC Low

Figure 9.5. XMODEM Transfer Block with CRC.
Source: From John Byrnes, "CRC Option," in Ward Christensen, "XMODEM.DOC" on Ward's CBBS (Bulletin Board, 312-849-1132, 1986), Message 7.

```
    sub CalCRC (v$, crc%, crchi%, crclo%)
'
'   This subroutine is a direct translation from Peter Boswell,
'   "Xmodem, CRC Xmodem, Wxmodem," June 20, 1986, p. 25.  This
'   document may be found on many bulletin boards but is
'   available from CompuServe, in the Borland forum, BPROGA,
'   Library #9, and in the IBM forum, IBMCOM, Library #10.
'
'   The string variable v$ must contain a complete 133 byte
'   XMODEM block.
'
    local a$, carry%, crc$, i2%
    CRC$=CHR$(0)+CHR$(0) 'START AT ZERO
    FOR I2%=4 TO 131
        A$=MID$(V$,I2%,1)
        GOSUB CalculateCRC
    NEXT I2%
    crc% = cvi(crc$)
    exit sub
'
    CalculateCRC:
'
'       CRC bitwise calculation
'
        crchi% = ASC(LEFT$(CRC$,1)) XOR ASC(A$)
        crclo% = ASC(RIGHT$(CRC$,1))
        for i3% = 0 to 7
            carry% = 0
            IF crchi% > 127 THEN carry% = -1  'IS HIGH BIT ON IN CRC?

            crchi% = (crchi% * 2) and 255     'crchi% << 1 and 255
            if crclo%>127 then incr crchi%    'if crclo% carries,
                                              ' then increment crchi%
            crclo% = (crclo% * 2) and 255     'crclo% << 1 and 255
            if carry% then
                crchi% = crchi% xor 16        'if high bit was on,
                crclo% = crclo xor 33         ' xor with &H1021
            end if
        next i3%
        crc$ = chr$(crchi%) + chr$(crclo%)
    return
'
    end sub
```

Listing 9.3. A BASIC Procedure for Calculating a CRC.

```
Receiving Computer                     Transmitting Computer
Ready to Receive                           Ready to Transmit

|>>>>-----------------------\C\-------------------------->>>>|
|3 Second Wait, if no SOH then Shift to CHECKSUM, Send NAK-|
|>>>>----------------------\NAK\------------------------>>>>|
|<<<<-------/SOH/BLK #1/BLL #1/-data-/CHECKSUM/--------<<<<|
|>>>>----------------------\ACK\------------------------>>>>|
|<<<<---/SOH/BLK #2/BLK #2/-garbled data-/CHECKSUM/----<<<<|
|>>>>----------------------\NAK\------------------------>>>>|
|<<<<--------/SOH/BLK #2/BLK #2/-data-/CHECKSUM--------<<<<|
|>>>>----------------------\ACK\------------------------>>>>|
|<<<<--------/SOH/BLK #3/BLK #3/-data-/CHECKSUM--------<<<<|
|>>>>----------------------\ACK\------------------------>>>>|
|<<<<----------------------/EOT/------------------------<<<<|
|>>>>----------------------\ACK\------------------------>>>>|

                  <File Transfer Ends>
```

Figure 9.6. XMODEM with CRC File Transfer Events: Receiver Has CRC Option, Sender Does Not.
Source: John Byrnes, "CRC OPTION ADDENDUM," (1985) in Ward Christensen, "XMODEM.DOC" on Ward's CBBS (Bulletin Board, 312-849-1132, 1986), Message 6.

```
Receiving Computer                     Transmitting Computer
Ready to Receive                           Ready to Transmit

|>>>>-----------------------\C\-------------------------->>>>|
|3 Second Wait, if no SOH then Shift to CHECKSUM, Send NAK-|
|>>>>----------------------\NAK\------------------------>>>>|
|<<<<------/SOH/BLK #1/BLL #1/-data-/CRChi/CRClo/------<<<<|
|>>>>----------------------\ACK\------------------------>>>>|
|<<<<--/SOH/BLK #2/BLK #2/-garbled data-/CRChi/CRClo/--<<<<|
|>>>>----------------------\NAK\------------------------>>>>|
|<<<<------/SOH/BLK #2/BLK #2/-data-/CRChi/CRClo/------<<<<|
|>>>>----------------------\ACK\------------------------>>>>|
|<<<<------/SOH/BLK #3/BLK #3/-data-/CRChi/CRClo/------<<<<|
|>>>>----------------------\ACK\------------------------>>>>|
|<<<<----------------------/EOT/------------------------<<<<|
|>>>>----------------------\ACK\------------------------>>>>|

                  <File Transfer Ends>
```

Figure 9.7. XMODEM with CRC File Transfer Events: Both Sender and Receiver Have CRC Option.
Source: John Byrnes, "CRC OPTION ADDENDUM," (1985) in Ward Christensen, "XMODEM.DOC" on Ward's CBBS (Bulletin Board, 312-849-1132, 1986), Message 6.

Information Coding

XMODEM is designed to work with eight-bit ASCII characters (although only the first 128 are defined with the ASCII standard). It does not have a seven-bit option specifically for transmitting the standard ASCII character set; however, XMODEM will transfer any ASCII data. Because the transfer block is fixed length, it is not possible to confuse any control characters in the data field with control characters used for handshaking. On the other hand, control character coding does not take place in the data field, which means that embedded control characters like XON or XOFF may confuse some networks or devices.

Information Transparency

There is no transparent mode. All data are sent without separate or control character coding.

Synchronization

When a valid block number is received it will be either the expected one (one higher than the last), or a repeat of the previous block number. Any other block number indicates a loss of synchronization, and transmission is aborted by sending a <CAN> (cancel).

Communications Facility Transparency

XMODEM was developed for character-oriented asynchronous transmission over telephone lines. It may not work, or flow control may need to be turned off before use, on some modern communications systems that have flow-control demands outside of the flow control exercised by the communications software at each end of the connection.

Kermit

Unlike XMODEM, which was designed to provide error-free file transfers between microcomputers, Kermit was intended for use in an environment "where there may be a diverse mixture of computers—micros, personal computers, workstations, laboratory computers, timesharing systems—from a variety of manufacturers."[6] The objective of the original design of

Kermit, developed by Bill Catchings under the supervision of Frank Da Cruz at Columbia University in the early 1980s, was to provide error-free file transfers among a DECSYSTEM-20, an IBM 370-series mainframe, and diverse microcomputers. The result was a design that was broad, although the IBM mainframe provided the greatest challenge. The unit of transfer in Kermit is called a "packet," but has a meaning similar to the term "block" used with XMODEM.

Kermit's features address several common file-transfer problems by setting selected minimal transmission standards and by providing mapping from one machine facility to another. Kermit has the following characteristics:[7]

- Communications takes place over standard asynchronous terminal connections.
- Communication is accomplished in half-duplex mode—that is, one way at a time without host echoing.
- Packet length is variable, but relatively short (maximum 96 characters) so that most hosts can accept packets without buffering problems.
- Packets are always sent in alternate directions allowing the participation of half-duplex systems.
- When available, a time-out facility allows the resumption of transmission after a lost packet.
- All transmission is in ASCII.
- Kermit is not written in any particular language: It is a portable protocol, not a portable program.

Control Characters

Kermit is designed to transfer printable ASCII characters from 32 (space or blank) through 126 (tilde), inclusive. The single control character normally used without translation is <SOH> (Start-of-Header, or Control-A, ASCII 1). "ACK" (Acknowledge) and "NAK" (Negative Acknowledge) are used to denote specialized packets instead of the ASCII characters ACK and NAK.

Data Transfer Control

The general structure of a Kermit packet can be seen in Figure 9.8. It is important to note that there are several different types of packets used by Kermit—hence the "TYPE" field. MARK is the Start-of-Packet character, normally an ASCII <SOH>, although this may be changed for machines that swallow that character. Both LEN and SEQ must be transformed into printable ASCII characters by the function char(x). The maximum packet length is 94. Longer packets might be more efficient, but retransmission when an error occurs would take longer. Moreover, most systems can accept short bursts of data without buffer overflow, possibly eliminating the need for a flow controlled network. This makes it feasible to use Kermit with half-duplex systems and in full-duplex environments. The packet TYPE is a single printable ASCII character:

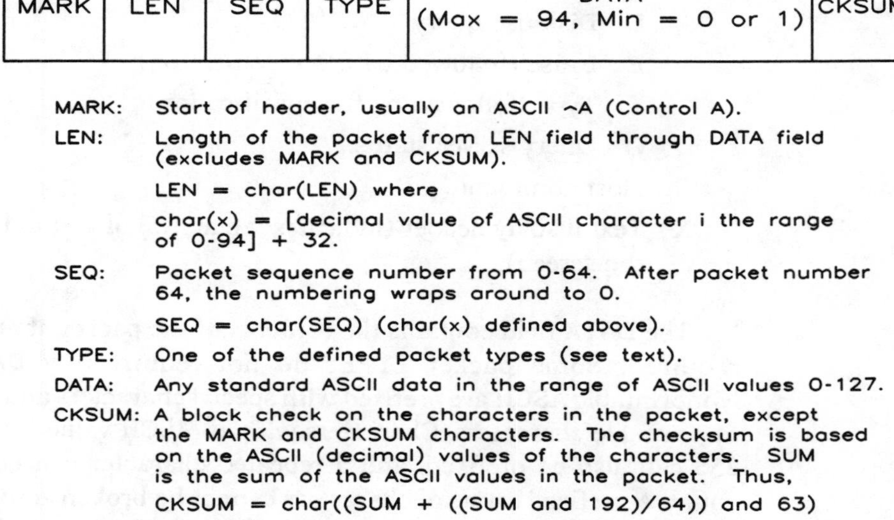
MARK
LEN
SEQ
TYPE
DATA
(Max = 94, Min = 0 or 1)
CKSUM
MARK: Start of header, usually an ASCII ^A (Control A).
LEN: Length of the packet from LEN field through DATA field (excludes MARK and CKSUM).
LEN = char(LEN) where
char(x) = [decimal value of ASCII character i the range of 0-94] + 32.
SEQ: Packet sequence number from 0-64. After packet number 64, the numbering wraps around to 0.
SEQ = char(SEQ) (char(x) defined above).
TYPE: One of the defined packet types (see text).
DATA: Any standard ASCII data in the range of ASCII values 0-127.
CKSUM: A block check on the characters in the packet, except the MARK and CKSUM characters. The checksum is based on the ASCII (decimal) values of the characters. SUM is the sum of the ASCII values in the packet. Thus,
CKSUM = char((SUM + ((SUM and 192)/64)) and 63)
char(x) defined above. Other block checks are allowed, although this is the default, and all Kermits must be capable of performing it.

Figure 9.8. Kermit Packet Format.

D Data.

Y Acknowledge (ACK).

N Negative Acknowledge (NAK).

S Send Initiate.

R Receive Initiate.

B Break Transmission (EOT).

F File Header.

Z End of File (EOF).

E Error.

G Generic command. A single character in the data field, possibly followed by operands, requests host-independent remote execution of the command.

- L Log out, bye.
- F Finish, but don't log out.
- D Directory query (followed by optional file specification).
- U Disk use query.
- E Erase (followed by file specification).
- T Type (followed by file specification).
- Q Query server status.

C Host command.

X Text display header (indicates the arrival of text to be displayed on the screen).

The DATA field contains the contents of the packet, if any contents are required. Some packet TYPEs do not require any DATA contents. Nonprintable ASCII are prefixed with special characters and then converted to printable characters. Characters with an ASCII value from 128 through 255 can also be prefixed, and a repeated character can be prefixed by a count. A prefixed series of characters cannot be broken across packets. The CKSUM is normally a simple checksum similar to that used in XMODEM, although alternative systems, including a CRC, can be used. Although CKSUM is usually only one character, provision has been made for a two- or three-character field as well.

A full-file transfer protocol must be able to take a file from one machine and transport it to some other machine, not necessarily of the same type.

This can sometimes cause problems when the file structures of the two machines are different and when records are delimited in different ways. Kermit handles this problem by delimiting records (regardless of the way in which the local machines delimit them) with a carriage-return and line-feed combination. The specific implementation may have to provide a filtering mechanism if the input delimiters or output delimiters differ from this standard. Within the packet, however, the Carriage Return/Line Feed (CRLF) combination represents the appropriate end-of-record.

Error Checking and Recovery

A block check on the characters in the packet, except the MARK and CKSUM characters, is calculated. The checksum is based on the ASCII (decimal) values of the characters. "SUM" is the sum of the ASCII values in the packet. Thus,

```
cksum = char((SUM + ((SUM AND 192)/64)) AND 63)
```

char(x)=x + 32 and translates control characters into printable characters. Other block checks are allowed, although this is the default, and all Kermits must be capable of performing it. When the checksum calculated by the receiver does not agree with the checksum in the packet, a request for retransmission is generated.

A typical Kermit file-transfer session is illustrated in Figure 9.9. Note that an acknowledgment packet is sent after each packet containing substantive data. Although the packet is short, it still involves more overhead than the single character ACK and NAK acknowledgments of XMODEM. On the other hand, acknowledgment is not dependent on an ASCII control character and should, therefore, work on most systems. Moreover, rather than waiting for a time-out if an ACK is not received, the appropriate Kermit can determine whether an ACK packet has successfully arrived. As with most data-communications software, however, some time-out mechanism is occasionally required.

Information Coding

Kermit was designed to operate with the ASCII character code. It has been implemented, however, on IBM mainframes—systems that use EBCDIC. Any calculations of checksum or CRC values, however, must convert characters' values to the equivalent ASCII (decimal) values before the calculations are made. System software will typically do the ASCII to EBCDIC

```
Receiving Computer                              Transmitting Computer
Ready to Receive                                   Ready to Transmit

                   <File Transfer Begins>

<<<<---/SOH/LEN/SEQ/TYPE(Send-init)/DATA/CHECKSUM/----<<<<
>>>>-----/SOH/LEN/SEQ/TYPE(Y-ACK)/DATA/CHECKSUM/------>>>>
<<<<---/SOH/LEN/SEQ/TYPE(File-Head)/DATA/CHECKSUM/----<<<<
>>>>-----/SOH/LEN/SEQ/TYPE(Y-ACK)/DATA/CHECKSUM/------>>>>
<<<<------/SOH/LEN/SEQ/TYPE(Data)/DATA/CHECKSUM/------<<<<
>>>>-----/SOH/LEN/SEQ/TYPE(Y-ACK)/DATA/CHECKSUM/------>>>>
<<<<------/SOH/LEN/SEQ/TYPE(Data)/DATA/CHECKSUM/------<<<<
>>>>-----/SOH/LEN/SEQ/TYPE(Y-ACK)/DATA/CHECKSUM/------>>>>
<<<<------/SOH/LEN/SEQ/TYPE(Data)/DATA/CHECKSUM/------<<<<
>>>>-----/SOH/LEN/SEQ/TYPE(Y-ACK)/DATA/CHECKSUM/------>>>>
<<<<-----/SOH/LEN/SEQ/TYPE(Z-EOF)/DATA/CHECKSUM/------<<<<
>>>>-----/SOH/LEN/SEQ/TYPE(Y-ACK)/DATA/CHECKSUM/------>>>>
<<<<-----/SOH/LEN/SEQ/TYPE(B-EOT)/DATA/CHECKSUM/------<<<<
>>>>-----/SOH/LEN/SEQ/TYPE(Y-ACK)/DATA/CHECKSUM/------>>>>

                   <File Transfer Ends>
```

Figure 9.9. Kermit File-Transfer Events.
Source: Cruz and Catchings, "Kermit: A File-Transfer Protocol for Universities, Part II: States and Transitions, Heuristic Rules, and Examples," *Byte*, Vol. 9, No. 7, July 1984, p. 400.

character translation automatically, so the implementation of Kermit on the IBM system must take this into account.

Information Transparency

Because all control codes are translated into printable ASCII characters, all information, including binary files, can be passed transparently with Kermit. When a control code (ASCII 0-31 and DEL [127]) is encountered, it is translated to a printable character with the char(x) function, then a special character (usually a pound sign: #) is prepended. This adds about 26.6 percent overhead to a binary file transfer, according to Cruz and Catchings. Other special characters are used to handle data values above the usual printable character range.

The status of the eighth bit of a byte can also be indicated by a prefix character, the ampersand: &. The standard ASCII character set is defined by the first 128 of a possible 256 characters, capable of being represented by seven binary digits. The second set of 128 characters is numerically the same as the first 128, but with the eighth bit set. If the low-order seven bits coincide with a control character, the control-character prefix is added as well. Eighth-bit prefixing can add as much as 50 percent overhead in the number of characters transmitted. When either a # or an & are to be transmitted, they must be prefixed by a #. A third prefix: the tilde (~), followed a single byte representing the number of repeated characters transformed to a printable character, followed by the repeated character, provides a rudimentary form of data compression.

Synchronization

Synchronization is effectively accomplished by use of the <SOH> character and the packet-length parameter. If either of these are corrupted, a time-out will be generated resulting in the sending of a <NAK>packet. Initial synchronization is established by the successful reception of the Receive Initiation packet, which has several setup parameters embedded in the DATA field of the packet.

Communications Facility Transparency

Kermit, like XMODEM, was developed to provide error-free file transfer using asynchronous communications. Because processors or networks may react differently to various ASCII control codes, all control codes are altered to printable ASCII characters, ensuring transparent transmission. The design differences arise largely because Kermit was developed in the context of a large organization with multiple processors and varying networking requirements, not for the simpler communications between micros over a telephone line.

X.PC

Unlike XMODEM and Kermit, X.PC was not designed to be a complete file transfer protocol. As has been noted, a file transfer protocol must deal essentially with a complete program-to-program or application-to-application session. It must include the ability to take files from one system and place them on another, possibly disparate, system. On the other hand, X.PC provides essentially the packet definition, including error correction, for getting data from one machine to another. It was structured in 1983 by Tymnet—a value-added network (VAN)—to complement Tymnet's X.25 VAN. X.PC can, therefore, be incorporated into file transfer protocols for interaction with Tymnet; other VANs; and other mainframe, mini, and microcomputer systems that have software supporting X.PC. Tymnet has placed X.PC in the public domain, hoping for broad acceptance as a de facto standard for error-correcting, asynchronous file transfer systems.

X.PC is similar in concept to X.25,[8] a synchronous protocol based on the European HDLC, of which IBM's SDLC is a subset. X.PC is dissimilar, of course, in that it is an asynchronous protocol. Instead of data being sent to a host system (either a network or another computer) asynchronously with a simple terminal emulation, the data are first grouped into packets protected by the X.PC link frame. At least conceptually this is similar to the block structure in XMODEM and the packets in Kermit. Like the other two protocols, the packets are numbered sequentially so that lost packets can be transmitted in the appropriate order. The packets are then sent over the communications line.

As implemented on a microcomputer, X.PC has two parts. An X.PC program module is loaded as a memory-resident driver (not an MS-DOS-device driver) that provides packet assembler/disassembler (PAD) services. The application (user-provided) software makes proper linkages to the X.PC module to assemble and disassemble data into or from packets. The second part of X.PC is the reverse of this process on the host end. If the "host" is Tymnet, and the target or host is some computer, an X.PC Network Server strips the X.PC packet frame and repacketizes in whatever format is required by the target host and interface.

For the MS-DOS implementation, the concept is depicted in Figure 9.10. The application program, which includes a linkage module to make

<table>
<tr><td colspan="2">Application
Channel</td></tr>
<tr><td colspan="2">Linkage Module</td></tr>
<tr><td colspan="2">Interface: INT 7ah</td></tr>
<tr><td colspan="2">Driver</td></tr>
<tr><td>Device
Packet Assembler/Disassembler
(PAD)</td><td>Device
Packet Assember/Disassembler
(PAD)</td></tr>
<tr><td>COM1 Port</td><td>COM2 Port</td></tr>
</table>

Figure 9.10. MS-DOS X.PC Driver Architecture.
Source: Tymnet, X.PC Driver Interface Specification, San Jose, Calif.: Tymnet, Inc., 1984; 3. The specification is in the public domain.

interrupt calls to the X.PC driver through interrupt vector 7Ah, allows the driver to operate between the application and communications port 1 or 2. The normal terminal emulator usually operates through interrupt vector 21 for COM1 or COM2. The X.PC driver module provides a series of function calls capable of being used by the application program. The result is that the application furnishes to X.PC byte-by-byte data or receives byte-by-byte data for further processing. All packetizing takes place within the X.PC driver. A "channel" is thereby established from the application through the Device PAD. A PAD module could be written for almost any other machine, mainframe, mini, or micro to perform the same services.

The unique feature of X.PC is its ability to establish multiple logical channels, enabling a personal computer to concurrently connect with other PCs, mainframes, or VANs with up to 15 logical circuits multiplexed into one asynchronous interface board. This feature is applicable only when X.PC is being used with Tymnet and resources available through Tymnet. The multiple logical channel feature can be effective only when a local X.PC micro is connected to an X.PC Network Server (XNS) on Tymnet. This is done by dialing a local Tymnet node, then requesting X.PC service. Unfortunately, Tymnet has taken the position that the XNS is proprietary and this may limit the acceptance of X.PC as a de facto standard. An application could be written that allows two directly connected (via hard-wire or modem) PCs to use the existing X.PC code, but use of the protocol on a private network could be limited. The use of multiple logical channels could be implemented on a micro, however, with multitasking software, such as Microsoft's WINDOWS or Quarterdeck's Desqview.

Data-Transfer Control

When it defined the X.PC protocol, Tymnet managed to use some nonstandard terminology. The terminological problems are a function of following the X.25 standard. "Packets" and "frames" are seen as existing at different layers of a protocol. A packet contains user or other data, and a frame contains a packet. Bytes (or eight-bit words) are called "octets." The octet concept makes sense in the context of X.25, since it defines a synchronous protocol in an HDLC Data-Link Control system. The use of octet in the context of an asynchronous protocol glosses over the two-bit overhead for each eight-bit byte sent or received in a stop-start environment, since the stop and start bits must also be included. With X.PC, an "octet" and a "byte" are equivalent.

The basic packet structure of X.PC may be seen in Figure 9.11. The first

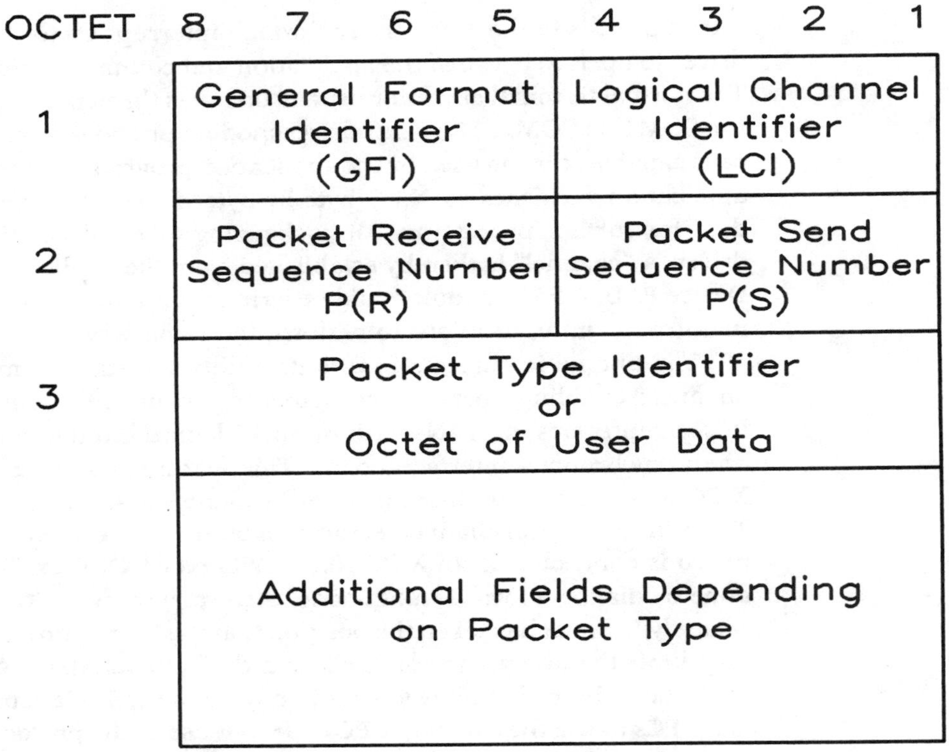

OCTET	8 7 6 5	4 3 2 1
1	General Format Identifier (GFI)	Logical Channel Identifier (LCI)
2	Packet Receive Sequence Number P(R)	Packet Send Sequence Number P(S)
3	Packet Type Identifier or Octet of User Data	
	Additional Fields Depending on Packet Type	

Figure 9.11. X.PC Basic Packet Structure.

two octets are divided into two four-bit fields. The first octet contains the General Format Identifier (GFI) and the Logical Channel Identifier (LCI). The GFI is required since, as with Kermit, there are many packet types. The LCI is necessary since there can be multiple logical channels through which a particular packet might be sent. The second octet contains a packet-receive sequence number and a packet-send sequence number, both necessary for tracking the correct sequencing of packets. The third octet is either a packet-type identifier or the first byte of user data if the packet is a data packet.

To be completely comparable with the block structure of XMODEM or the packets of Kermit, it is necessary to also note the data-link frame structure of X.PC. The format of a frame can be seen in Figure 9.12. X.PC's Data-Link "Layer" provides the full-duplex transfer of Network Layer packets between the local and remote system. This is accomplished in transparent, error-protected frames. Each data-link frame has one packet. The first octet or byte is an STX (Start-of-Text, Control-B) character, which is not included in the CRC1 calculation. There is double error checking within the frame. Framing information, including the first three octets of the data

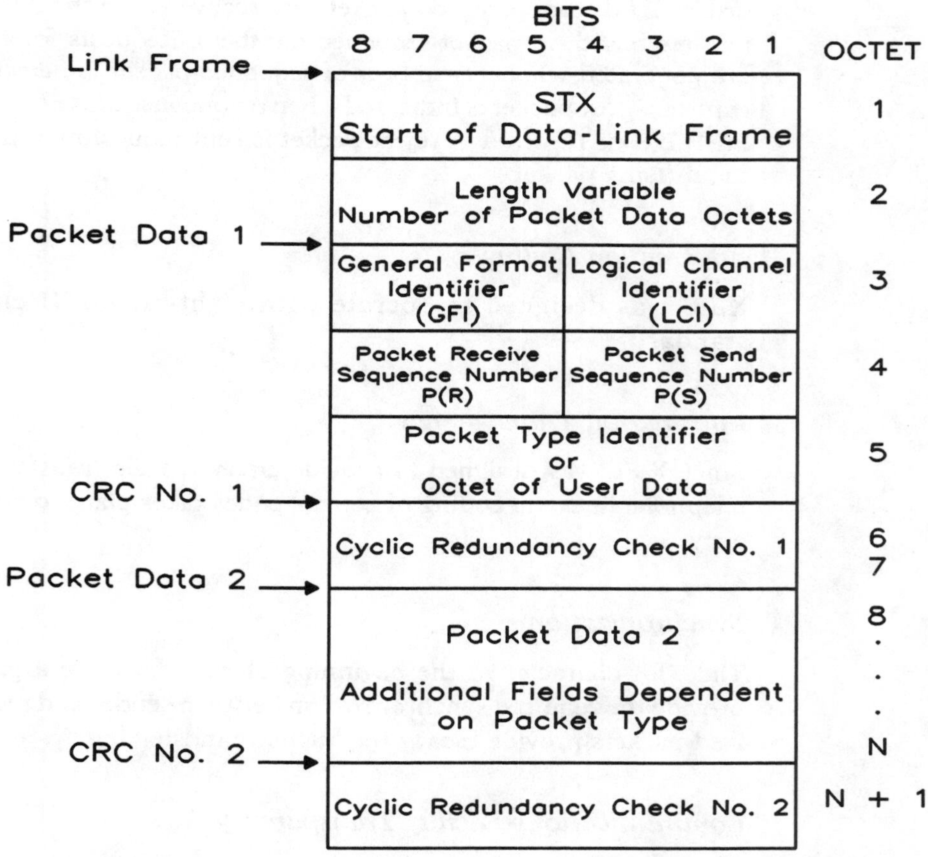

Figure 9.12. X.PC Data-Link Transmission Frame Format.

packet, are checked with CRC1, while CRC2 is calculated for all bytes contained in the length variable (octet 2). If the value of LENGTH is zero, no packet data follows CRC1, and CRC2 is not used.

Error Checking and Recovery

Like XMODEM, X.PC was designed to solve the problem of error-prone telephone lines from a local PC to another node, presumably a local Tymnet access point. It uses the CCITT standard for X.25 error correction: V.41 CRC-16. Each packet is numbered to ensure that packets are sequentially ordered. Lost or corrupted packets are recovered by the retransmission of packets based on packet-sequence numbers. Requests for retransmission are generated whenever an out-of-sequence packet is detected or a timer expires. A lost packet is indicated when a nonconsecutive (with the previous P(S)) P(S) is received. A reject packet is sent requesting retransmission of the missing packet.

Information Coding

X.PC was designed to operate with eight-bit ASCII character code standard.

Information Transparency

Since X.PC was designed to provide error-free file transfer over standard telephone lines, no coding of control codes takes place to ensure transparency.

Synchronization

The STX character at the beginning of each frame and packet numbers provide the required synchronization between sender and receiver. Specialized packets provide means for further handshaking.

Communications Facility Transparency

Because no coding of control characters takes place, a network flow controlled by characters such as XON or XOFF could be flow controlled off by the contents of packets, or other control characters could be swallowed by devices.

Microcom Networking Protocol (MNP)

Since the parent to this book was published in 1987, MNP has been widely adopted by manufacturers of high-speed (2400 bps and greater) dial-up modems as an error-correction system. This is particularly important on voice-grade, dial-access telephone lines, which even with increasing use of fiber-optic cable are still relatively noisy. It also competes with X.PC to provide error-protected asynchronous access to packet-switching networks (PSNs).[9] CCITT recommendation V.42, a proposed standard for error-correcting modems, is based on MNP. The primary competitor with MNP for the modem business is the *Link Access Protocol Balanced (LAPB)*, the most common frame-level protocol used by X.25. Error-correcting modems, when in communication with other, compatible, error-correcting modems, provide communication between the two modems at the Data-Link Layer. Those modems and their associated protocols can organize the bit stream and, in fact, provide synchronous communication between the two modems even though the communicaton between the modem and the data device (micro, terminal, or computer) is taking place asynchronously.

Microcom Networking Protocol was originally designed by Microcom, a modem manufacturer, for use in electronic mail (EMail) systems. The MNP specificiation defines three related protocols: the *link*, the *session*, and the *file transfer*. The link and session protocols implement data-communication activities at the equivalent of the OSI layers of the same name. The link protocol that has turned out to be the most used of the MNP specifications, since it is the link protocol that is used with error-correcting modems. The higher level session and file transfer protocols (the latter providing services at the Presentation and Application layers) are used relatively little. The link protocol can operate either synchronously or asychronously and initiate communication in an asynchronous mode. If both modems are capable of synchronous communication, however, they both switch to it. Much of the total MNP specification has remained proprietary to Microcom. About two-thirds of the link protocol, however, has been put in the public domain and is part of the CCITT V.42 recommendation.

Because the purpose of this chapter is to provide an understanding of file transfer protocols, further discussion of MNP is not necessary. It is, however, important to understand the place of MNP in the marketplace.

Strengths and Weaknesses of Asynchronous File Transfer Protocols

The three asynchronous file transfer protocols described herein are not exhaustive. There are others attempting to make a mark. Most are proprietary to specific terminal-emulation products. An example is the proprietary file-transfer system by Microstuf in its popular Crosstalk XVI program. The difficulty with Microstuf's approach is that it is a file-transfer system designed for micro-to-micro communications, not for micro-to-mainframe loops.

The primary difficulty with protocols like XMODEM or Kermit is that support is dependent on the interest of a few individuals, rather than on the resources of a large organization. The difficulty with XMODEM and X.PC is that they were designed with somewhat limited networking protocols in mind. In particular, the strength of Kermit is its ability to transfer even binary files independent of the network over which the data are passing. The ability to make the data transparent to the network is important in the varied networks of today.

As a final note, look at Table 9.1, which compares the overhead necessary for the three different transfer protocols. My numbers are somewhat different from those reported by others, including some of the documentation for one or another of the systems. The overhead percentages were derived by counting the total number of *bits* per packet or block, including stop-start bits. Overhead is the sum of the bits of bytes required by the protocol other than user data, including stop-start bits and the stop-start bits represented by each byte of user data. The total was then divided into the number of bits of overhead, resulting in the figures in Table 9.1. For a full packet, the overhead is similar for all three systems, but for the transmission of only a single byte, XMODEM is worse because of its fixed block-length structure. The X.PC CRC-16 error checking is probably the best of the three, but both XMODEM and Kermit have had similar, though optional, algorithms implemented. Of the three, Kermit comes closest to providing error-free transmission independent of the network over which the data flow.

TABLE 9.1. Overhead Comparisons for Asynchronous Protocols (Data Packets)

	*Maximum Packet**			*Minimum Packet†*		
	XMODEM	*Kermit*	*X.PC*	*XMODEM*	*Kermit*	*X.PC*
Number Bits Overhead	296	238	592	1312	52	62
Total Bits	1320	990	2640	1320	60	70
Percent††	22.4	24.0	22.4	99.4	86.7	88.6
Data Bytes	128	94	256	128	1	1

*The maximum packet contains the most data bytes that can be sent with the protocol.
†The minimum packet contains the fewest data bytes that can be sent with the protocol.
††The percent overhead is calculated by dividing the number of bits of overhead by the total bits. (Since XMODEM has a fixed block size, even if only one data byte is present, 128 bytes are sent.) This takes into account the standard 20 percent overhead implicit in all start–stop communications. XMODEM and Kermit assume one-byte checksums, X.PC a two-byte CRC-16.

Synchronous File Transfers

In an IBM bisync communications environment, file-transfer systems have been available since the 1960s. This discussion centers on IBM protocols, and the file-transfer systems use either bisync or SDLC, which have already been described in detail. Synchronous Data-Link Control and Bisync, like asynchronous start-stop are Data-Link Control systems operating in Layer 2 of the OSI Reference Model. File transfer protocols generally take advantage of the capabilities of bisync and SDLC block structures rather than defining something else, which would be difficult to overlay in any event. Since asynchronous communications are byte, not block oriented, asynchronous file transfer protocols must define packet or block structures themselves. One well-known file transfer protocol—one for which software and hardware is available for a wide variety of microcomputers, is the 2780/3780 Remote Job Entry (RJE) file transfer protocol.

RJE with 3780

Remote Job Entry stations were originally designed to transfer batches of punched cards to a central mainframe where they were read into software capable of decoding the associated job-control language and, presumably, used to execute a batch job. On the reverse side, RJE stations were also designed to receive data back, primarily to be printed. The 3780 protocol has restricted record-length features—either card image (80 columns) or print image (132 columns), and nothing else. Applications on either end must be written to compose and decompose longer record lengths into 80 or 132 columns.

The HASP Workstation

The 3780, operating as it did and does on a half-duplex bisync line, was not designed to provide concurrent two-way communications. This and other limitations led to the development of what is sometimes called a HASP Workstation, originally developed to run on an IBM 360/Model 20 computer. The HASP Workstation software met many of the shortcomings of the 2780/3780 by using a multileaving system that gave the appearance, if not the reality, of concurrent two-way communications. This made possible the implementation of limited operator-console operations at the remote site, and it ran on more intelligent and powerful machines and provided additional peripheral devices such as tape and disk. The record restrictions, however, remained largely as they were with 3780 devices. IBM has since produced a series of RJE devices such as the 3770 and 3790. The latter operates over an SDLC line with some increases in functionality. Software available on micros generally emulates the 3780.

APPC and Logical Unit (LU) 6.2

The most recent IBM effort to provide transparent file transfer has been the development of APPC and its associated protocols (LU 6.2). Advanced Program-to-Program Communication has been discussed in some detail. One force generating the need for LU 6.2 services is the growth in the use of microcomputers as intelligent workstations. Logical Unit 6.2 provides services to application programs so that they can communicate with one another in an SNA network. Examples of IBM software on mainframes and micros are the programs in DISOSS (an office automation product running on the mainframe) and Displaywriter, which run on dedicated word processors, and IBM PCs that implement IBM's Document Interchange Architecture (DIA). Logical Unit 6.2 is an important building block for DIA systems. The synchronous bisync and SDLC protocols have always allowed transparent data transfer, including binary files.

Remote Spooling Communications System (RSCS)

Unlike the other systems discussed in this chapter, or in this book, for that matter, RSCS is a single-purpose *operating system* that runs under IBM's Virtual Machine Facility (VM/370) on an IBM mainframe host system. It is designed for communication in distributed and networking environments. Remote Spooling Communications System is dedicated to (1) accepting files spooled to it and transmitting these files to the destination specified by the files' submitters, and (2) accepting files transmitted to it and respooling them to appropriate local VM/370 users or transmitting them to other destinations. Data-Link Control is via bisync communications lines or channel-to-channel adapters. Through RSCS, provision is thereby made for establishing a remote store-and-forward system. Telecommunications facilities must be attached to RSCS either permanently or temporarily, but once a remote node is defined to RSCS,it will store the file until a line to the remote system is available.[10]

Although RSCS was designed to operate with mainframe systems or RJE systems tied to IBM mainframes, it is possible to define micros as RSCS nodes if those micros are on an appropriate network. An unsupported module from the University of Waterloo (Canada), probably requiring local modification, that allows addresses on a Sytek LocalNet/20 broadband LAN to be designated as RSCS nodes, is available. A cooperative international network among universities, Bitnet, makes use of RSCS facilities to produce an extensive network, which is used primarily for file transfers. Bitnet is interesting in that a new user institution is responsible only for paying for the communications line to the next nearest Bitnet node. The network topology tends to be somewhat random, but it works effectively at a relatively low cost. Where Bitnet access is through a terminal network, and where the terminals are microcomputers, then the micro-to-mainframe connection is complete.

Other Important Data-Link and File Transfer Protocols

The file transfer protocols discussed thus far are not the only, nor in one or two cases the most important, systems devised or used. Those described thus far are widely used, but an attempt to unravel file transfer needs will generate competing claims from vendors for one protocol over another. Moreover, new protocols are published from time to time. Like IBM, Digital

Equipment Corporation (DEC) realized the need for a stable network architecture and devised DECnet. Because of DEC's prominence in the large computer marketplace it is necessary to cover the file transfer protocol of this important system. Data-Link Control protocols (such as BSC, SDLC, DEC's DDCMP, and others) exist at OSI Layer 2 (Data-Link) while file transfer protocols are defined at the Transport Layer (Layer 4) and above.

Although it must be something of a pain to DEC, TCP/IP is gaining popularity on networks that often revolve around DEC computing equipment. Transmission Control Protocol/Internet Protocol was originally designed by the U.S. Department of Defense (DoD) as a standard protocol that could run on its wide variety of communications subsystems. As automation has hit U.S. manufacturing environments, an application-specific protocol, the Manufacturing Automation Protocol (MAP), was devised by General Motors to enhance the automation process. The Technical and Office Protocol (TOP), originated by Boeing, to encompass the office and technical environments is related to MAP. Both MAP and TOP are conscious implementations of the OSI standards. Manufacturing Automation Protocol and TOP have a common steering committee, although corporate commitments to MAP currently outdistance those to TOP.

There are other protocols that have been mentioned in passing and will be reiterated at this point. The Xerox Network System (XNS) is widely used on various implementations of Ethernet, though not exclusively. Microcom's MNP protocol, designed for reasons similar to Tymnet's X.PC, is still not completely in the public domain, although it is available for "third-party" use. Others exist, of course, but this chapter is not designed to be encyclopedic. Rather, its purpose is to impress the importance of the file transfer protocol system. The important point to remember is that when a network is designed, the data transport protocol must be chosen. That choice can be made by default, or it can be adopted consciously and deliberately.

DEC's Link Protocols

Do organizations really have choices in protocols? The answer is a qualified "yes." Organizations using only IBM (or compatible) mainframes probably should not use something other than IBM's bisync or SNA networks. On the other hand, it is possible to design a network that would be almost all DECnet, but would support IBM SNA devices at all or most nodes. This is because DEC has recognized the impact of IBM in the marketplace and has succumbed to the pressure to provide IBM access for DEC users. The result is an SNA gateway that appears as another DECnet device on a DEC network but allows the connection of IBM SNA devices. In a computing environment with mixed DEC and IBM computers, this may prove to be the most efficient and economical approach to the design of an integrated network, since IBM provides no useful methods for attaching DEC machines to its networks. Alternatively, organizations with largely DEC equipment VAXs of various sizes, running both VMS and Unix, and Unix machines from other manufacturers, may not be able to conveniently use DECnet. An alternative would be to design a network based on TCP/IP, software for which is available for a large variety of DEC computers and for most other Unix machines. Choices can and should be made in order to provide a high degree of integration.

At this writing there were three protocols residing in the DEC Network Architecture (DNA). These are regarded by DEC to be data-link protocols, residing at a lower layer of the OSI hierarchy than do standard file transfer protocols, although these distinctions are often blurred or misinterpreted in the literature. The three protocols supported by DEC areas follows:[11]

- Digital Data Communications Message Protocol (DDCMP), which is a byte-oriented protocol.
- Ethernet protocol, which meets the IEEE 802.3 standard at the Physical and Data-Link layers (CSMA/CD) but uses DEC's own data-link frame format (since the standard does not define a frame format).
- X.25 Levels 2 and 3. These operate over Level 1 of the CCITT X.25 standard, which defines the interface between data-terminal equipment and data-circuit terminating equipment of a packet-switched network.

The discussion in this section will be confined to DDCMP and Ethernet.

DDCMP

As has been noted elsewhere, there are three general types of data-link protocols: byte oriented, character oriented, and bit oriented. Digital Data Communications Message Protocol is a byte-oriented protocol with some resemblance to IBM's BSC, designed in 1974 for DNA. Unlike BSC, however, it is a full duplex protocol that allows concurrent two-way data transmission both synchronously and asynchronously.

Data transfer control. Digital Equipment Corporation prefers to use the term "frame" rather than "block" or "packet." The DDCMP data-message frame format can be seen in Figure 9.13. Like many such protocols there are variations on this basic format for various purposes, such as message acknowledgement. Any node initiating a message transfer must send an inquiry and receive an acknowledgement before message transfer can take place. One or more of the frames depicted in Figure 9.13 are then transmitted as numbered blocks. A single following acknowledgement may acknowledge up to 255 previous message frames.

Error checking and recovery. Block checking is accomplished using 16-bit CRC. Two CRC fields are used, the first to verify the header information, the second for the data. When an error is detected, a NAK message is sent to the transmitting node. The sequence number in the NAK message indicates the last good message received. In a full-duplex environment the NAK message can be sent while an incoming data frame is on the line, unlike the half-duplex turnaround problem with BSC. Messages are always retransmitted if the sender does not receive an acknowledgement before time-out occurs.

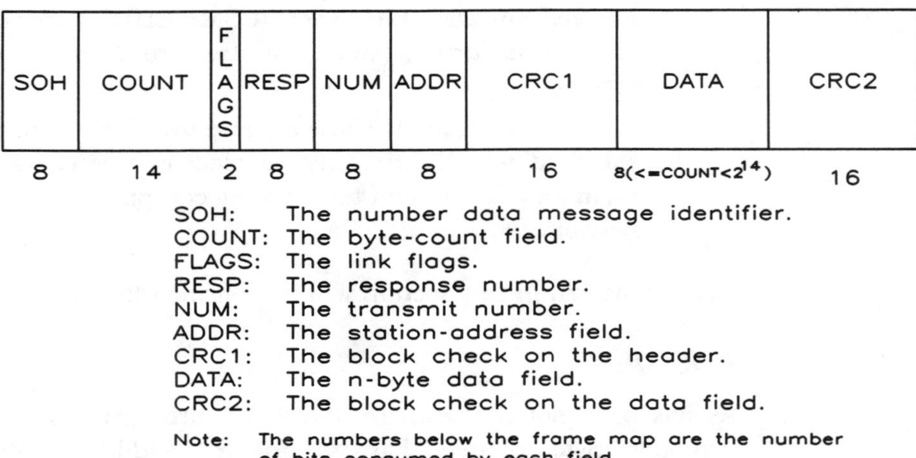
SOH
COUNT
FLAGS
RESP
NUM
ADDR
CRC1
DATA
CRC2
8
14
2
8
8
8
16
8(<=COUNT<2^14)
16
SOH: The number data message identifier.
COUNT: The byte-count field.
FLAGS: The link flags.
RESP: The response number.
NUM: The transmit number.
ADDR: The station-address field.
CRC1: The block check on the header.
DATA: The n-byte data field.
CRC2: The block check on the data field.
Note: The numbers below the frame map are the number of bits consumed by each field.

Figure 9.13. DDCMP Message-Frame Format.

Information coding. All information is coded in ASCII. Three ASCII control characters are used for message identification: SOH for numbered data messages, ENQ (Enquiry) for control messages (such as acknowledgements), and DLE (Data Link Escape) for maintenance messages. The remainder of the message, both text and header, is transparent.

Information transparency. The text or data field may be of any length from zero to two^{14} (16,383) bytes of transparent data. Any ASCII character can be used for header and text. The header CRC is validated before COUNT is used to receive data.

Synchronization. Digital Data Communications Message Protocol provides for synchronized transmission and reception on byte and message levels. When synchronization occurs, two ASCII SYN characters are used preceding the SOH. Syncronization is not needed between messages as long as there are no gaps between them.

Communications facility transparency. Digital Data Communications Message Protocol is totally transparent and handles control character transparency efficiently. This means that DDCMP can be made to run over virtually any communications system regardless of the control facilities required by that system.

Higher Layer File-Transfer Mechanisms

The several protocols described in this section could, just as easily, have been incorporated into the previous section. They are separated because the previous section deals with the essentially proprietary aspects of IBM and DEC networking. This section, by way of contrast, deals with standardized or public-domain file-transfer techniques within broader networking architectures or techniques. These include TCP/IP's FTP, the OSI FTAM, and a brief description of EDI. The latter can, of course, be implemented within DEC or IBM networking architectures as well as within OSI or TCP/IP architectures.

TCP/IP FTP

Internetworking has become a major issue in most large organizations, although it is probably nowhere more complicated than in the DoD. Several years ago DoD's Defense Advanced Research Projects Agency (DARPA), through its Internet research program, developed standards for internetworking through its TCP/IP. Together they form a reliable, virtual-circuit oriented, peer-to-peer communications protocol. Transmission Control Protocol and IP are layered protocols that fit below network-applications protocols and above access and data-link protocols. Internet Protocol resides at about the Network Layer (Layer 3) of OSI and TCP at the Transport Layer (Layer 4). File-transfer systems making use of TCP/IP typically fall at Layer 5 (Session).[12]

Transmission Control Protocol and Internet Protocol is not tied to any single type of network or technology. Rather, it was developed as a means for tying together diverse networks with gateways. The composite network provides the capability for devices on different physical networks to communicate as if they were on the same network. As a result of these objectives, TCP provides reliable, sequenced, byte-stream virtual circuits. It uses checksums, sequence numbering of all data, retransmissions for reliability, reliable connection establishment and clearing, and a flow-control mechanism. The features of TCP make it suitable for a variety of networks, making no assumptions about the reliability of the underlying network services. The TCP virtual circuit remains intact even when components of internetwork fail. Assuming that there are multiple paths between nodes, TCP will switch paths as necessary to guarantee connectivity. Internet Protocol provides TCP with addressing and internetworking capabilities. Addressing is based on a 32-bit address. Three formats for the addresses allow a range of network classes from small to large networks.[13]

The file-transfer process as it is managed by FTP is not intended to handle all the issues or steps of the process previously described. Rather, FTP presumes some basic properties, such as data type, file organization, and file ownership, and provides a means by which one computer can manipulate these properties on another computer system without either computer knowing details about the other. Files on a remote system are manipulated through a series of commands and responses, performing such functions as *get a file from*, or *send a file to* a remote system. File Transfer Protocol itself does not translate files from one computer type to another, nor does it establish any kind of virtual network file. More fundamentally, it provides three dimensions: data types, file types, and transmission modes. These dimensions can then be used by the two computers to establish a common ground. Problems such as data extraction, formatting, and translation (EBCDIC to ASCII, for example) are accomplished prior or subsequent to submission to FTP. A file transfer using FTP can be initiated by either a human or another computer program. The human user will use a program called the *User FTP Program*. User FTP provides access to all FTP services. In some installations, FTP may also be called (like a subroutine) from other application programs. This would be the approach if there were complex data extraction, formatting, and translation issues to be handled.

File Transfer Protocol has been implemented on every size machine from large mainframes to personal computers under a variety of operating systems (OS) and environments. It rests, of course, on TCP/IP to actually get the data from one host to another. In the FTP process the initiating host constitutes a client and the remote host is the server. Files can be transferred in either direction, from client to server or server to client. Prior to file transfer, however, a remote login must be accomplished by the client, often using TELNET facilities. The client user must, of course, be authorized to access files on the server through whatever mechanisms are appropriate to the server. By providing a mechanism for negotiating a file transfer's options in three dimensions (data type, file type, and transfer mode), support has been provided for a variety of hardware and operating environments.

Data Types

Four data types are defined for FTP: ASCII, EBCDIC, Image, and Logical Byte Size. ASCII is the most common representation for FTP text files, although on IBM hosts such files would be EBCDIC. NVT ASCII consists of ASCII codes 0–127. The eighth bit (high-order bit) of the standard eight-bit byte is not used. When two IBM hosts are communicating with one another, it is often more convenient to use EBCDIC rather than translate from EBCDIC to ASCII and back. Both types may be further specified as to whether they will be presented to a line or page printer. Three options for providing printer control characters are offered: nonprint, TELNET formatting, and carriage-control formatting. With the latter, FORTRAN carriage-control conventions are used.

Image or binary data is used to exchange data between machines of the same type. No bits are skipped, preset, or otherwise modified. This data type is used to transfer executable programs or other data in binary form. Type Image could be used to transfer either ASCII or EBCDIC files since Image preserves all the information in the file; however, it would not be useful to use type Image to transfer files between different kinds of machines. Sometimes it is useful to store a binary file from one machine in a library on another, dissimilar, machine. For such purposes, the Logical Byte Size type is provided. Logical Byte Size takes an argument, which is the size of the "byte." Size is somewhat arbitrary and in this instance does not conform to the normal definition of "byte."

File Types

Three file types are defined: File Structure, Record Structure, and Page Structure. For other file types, client and server computers must be programmed to take what is offered and place them in an appropriate format. File Transfer Protocol is designed to provide a very low level of file compatibility among computers and their OSs. Type File Structure is the simplest and most frequently used. It assumes that a file is simply a sequence of bytes (defined by the data type) followed by an End-of-File marker. The destination operating environment must make sense out of this approach. On an MS-DOS machine, for example, lines or records of a file are delimited by a carriage return/linefeed (<CRLF>) combination, and MS-DOS knows that when it sees <CRLF>, as do most applications running under MS-DOS. Some systems, however, prefer a defined Record Structure for files. Record Structure allows the transmission of individual records, separated by the standard End-of-Record marker for the specified data type. In the early days of ARPANET, when TCP/IP was being developed, DEC's TOPS-20 OS was prominent, and it used files composed of pages. The Page Structure of TOPS-20 continues its life in FTP, although TOPS-20 itself is outmoded and obsolete.

Transmission Modes

The Transmission Mode options are provided to optimize the use of the communications network. There are three transmission modes: Stream, Block, and Compressed. Stream Transmission is the default transmission mode for all transfers. In this mode the unmodified raw data are sent to TCP. This mode requires the lowest overhead since it imposes the lowest computational burden on the receiving machine. For Record Structure files a two-byte control code is used to mark the End-of-Record (EOR) and the End-of-File (EOF). The first byte is all ones, while the second byte has a value of one, two, or three to indicate EOR, EOF, or both. If a byte of all ones is to be sent, it is appended to a second byte of all ones. The second byte is stripped off by the receiving FTP. Block Mode is used to allow for restarting failed transfers and may be needed with very large files. In this mode, the source host breaks the data into well-defined blocks—the destination machine reassembles the blocks into an appropriate file. The client and server FTPs cooperate to determine when blocks are successfully transferred and will request retransmission when this does not occur. The block mode is most like many of the other commonly used file-transfer mechanisms. Some files contain series of the same byte replicated many times. Since large files can sometimes take many hours to transfer, it is useful to compress files as much as possible before transmission. In compressed mode, the sending FTP removes excess bytes, while the receiving FTP expands the compressed data.

OSI FTAM

File Transfer Access and Management provides a set of services for transferring information between application processes and filestores. The specification is contained in ISO 8571, Parts 1–4 and requires, at least in the MAP implementation, ISO 8822 (Presentation Service Definition) and ISO 8823 (Presentation Protocol Specification). File Transfer Access and Management guarantees the ability to do the following:

- Work with binary or text files.
- Create files.
- Delete files.
- Transfer entire files
- Read file attributes.
- Change file attributes.
- Erase file contents.
- Locate specific records.
- Read and write records of a file.

The optionally supported file types include sequential files, random-access files, and single-key indexed sequential files.

A virtual filestore is defined by the FTAM standard, to describe the service provided by the FTAM service element. The function of the virtual filestore is to map FTAM services onto the local (real) filestore, thus making FTAM independent of any particular brand of computer. The FTAM standard does not provide an interface to the FTAM services, assuming that the implementor will define such an interface. The MAP specification, however, does define an FTAM application-interface specification, and those implementing MAP are strongly encouraged to include the FTAM interface services as specified in the MAP "Application Interface Model and Specifications Requirements."

Manufacturing Automation Protocol's FTAM Application Interface Specification is designed to provide a programming interface for the use of FTAM fto provide easy access to the FTAM service. It provides the user with the capability to access various FTAM functions as detailed in the ISO FTAM Protocol and Services standards. Within FTAM there are both REQUESTER (local) and RESPONDER (remote) services and filestores. Manufacturing Automation Protocol defines the application-interface specification largely from the perspective of the REQUESTER, assuming that the RESPONDER behaves consistently with the FTAM standard. There are two forms of request: "context free" and "context sensitive." A context-free service requires no special user knowledge of FTAM protocols, providing a complete and autonomous action on the specified filestores. An example might be a File Copy request. By way of contrast, context-sensitive procedures require knowledge of the FTAM protocol. Typically the context-sensitive services would be used by programmers implementing an application requiring FTAM services.

EDI

A massively growing need has given rise to EDI—the intercompany, computer-to-computer exchange of business documents in standard formats. Electronic Data Interchange allows common business forms such as invoices, bills of lading, and purchase orders to be transformed into a standard data format and electronically transferred between or among trading partners. Although similar systems may operate internally in an organization, EDI is designed to work between or among companies without human intervention and without paper documents. The advantages of an EDI system are monetary savings, accurate transmission, and fast transmission. Thus, it is possible for some companies to send bills or invoices electronically and to have funds transferred electronically to pay the bills.[14]

The American National Standards Institute (ANSI) has published the X.12 standards, which support EDI implementation efforts. The X.12 standards consist of:

- Transaction-set standards.
- Data-element dictionary.

- Data-segment directory.
- Transmission-control standards.

Each of the four points listed cover a part of the data-interchange process, which when integrated as a system, ensure that the documents received are identical to those sent. Why does this seem somewhat more complex than the simple file transfer protocols described earlier? The reason is because EDI is designed to operate between or among machines on a network with minimal human intervention, with the high degree of security necessary when financial instruments or documents that have financial or other security implications are being exchanged. Moreover, at each end of the transaction, it is desirable that a document not only be sent, but also that the document's contents be automatically posted to an appropriate application at the receiving end. Since different organizations have their preferred formats for invoices or other documents, it is necessary to translate such documents into a standard format prior to transmission and then to reconstruct the document on the other end in whatever manner the receiver requires.

The format and context of data used within specified business documents, such as invoices, are defined by the *transaction-set standards*. A number of transaction sets have been defined. The invoice transaction set (810) is designed to provide the funcationality of the paper invoice, although it does not contain all the information of its paper counterpart since it is not intended for direct human consumption. A standard *data dictionary* contains codes for types of information used in business documents, thus reducing large amounts of information to two-digit data elements. This eliminates the need for large amounts of descriptive information in the electronic document itself. Data segments are the electronic equivalent of "line items" in business documents, and their definitions are contained in the *data segment dictionary*. The document is enclosed in an interchange envelope, which provides control information for the data interchange. The format of the envelope, data element delimiters, and transaction-set separators are all defined by the *transmission-control standards*.

Electronic Data Interchange, as defined by X.12, is essentially an Application Layer mechanism that interacts with lower layer entities, to use OSI Reference Model concepts. The interchange envelope is then presented to lower level network layers for actual transmission. At the time the EDI envelope is generated, the nature of the network becomes irrelevant. It might be a MAN, a WAN, a point-to-point telephone link, or whatever. The key is that on the receiving end the software mechanisms are available to do something with the interchange envelope when it arrives.

Reflections on the File Transfer Process

There are clearly some useful synchronous and asynchronous file transfer protocols available today. Unfortunately, they all have some limitations, and few are designed to be network independent. Moreover, even fewer are designed to be user transparent. An ideal approach to file transfer would be to provide a user interface that was simply an extension of the micro's OS so that file transfers could simply use DOS commands, like COPY, to move a file from the micro to the mainframe. Admittedly that approach leaves something to be desired when line speeds are low, but increasingly, at least within the campuses of corporations and universities, lines run at 9,600 or 19,200 bps. Increasingly, people are attached through LANs, and even dial-up modem speeds of 9,600 bps are becoming common. At least the user interface should be easy and straightforward. In the context of the entire end-to-end file-transfer system, data-format conversions, including character formats and file formats, should be accomplished without pain to the user. Significant strides toward appropriate file transfer protocols are clearly being made, but the technology is not yet perfected.

Notes

1. Ward Christensen, "XMODEM.DOC" on Ward's CBBS (Bulletin Board, Telephone 312-849-1132, 1986), Messages 4–6.
2. The format is based on Jim Rector, "Xmodem Protocol," *TI Professional Computing*, March 1985, p. 32.
3. John Byrnes, "CRC Option" in Ward Christensen, "XMODEM.DOC" on Ward's CBBS (Bulletin Board, Telephone: 312-849-1132, 1986), Message 7.
4. Ibid.
5. This subroutine is a direct translation from Peter Boswell, "Xmodem, CRC Xmodem, Wxmodem," June 20, 1986, p. 25. This document may be found on many bulletin boards but is available from CompuServe, in the Borland forum, BPROGA, Library Number 9; and in the IBM forum, IBMCOM, Library Number 10. The documents by Ward and Byrne, along with the commentary by Boswell, probably represent the defini-

tive statements concerning what constitutes XMODEM, notwithstanding the fact that they are all now several years old.

6. Frank da Cruz and Bill Catchings, *Kermit Protocol Manual* (New York: Trustees of Columbia University in the City of New York, 1983), p. 3. For further information see also, Cruz and Catchings, "Kermit: A File-Transfer Protocol for Universities, Part I: Design Considerations and Specifications," *Byte*, Vol. 9, No. 6, June 1984, pp. 255–278; and Cruz and Catchings, "Kermit: A File-Transfer Protocol for Universities, Part II: States and Transitions, Heuristic Rules, and Examples," *Byte*, Vol. 9, No. 7, July 1984, pp. 143–145, 400–403. See also, Augie Hansen, "Kermit," *PC Tech Journal*, Vol. 3, No. 1, Jan. 1985, pp. 110–123. More recently, Cruz has published *KERMIT: A File Transfer Protocol* (Bedford, MA: Digital Press, 1987).
7. Cruz and Catchings, "Kermit: A File-Transfer Protocol for Universities, Part I," p. 264.
8. For an explanation of X.25, see R. J. Deasington, *X.25 EXPLAINED: Protocols for Packet Switching Networks* (Chichester, UK: Ellis Horwood Limited, 1985).
9. David A. Honig and Kenton A. Hoover, *Desktop Communications* (New York: John Wiley & Sons, Inc., 1990), p. 197. This section rests heavily on the work of Honig and Hoover.
10. See *Remote Spooling Communications Subsystem Networking General Information* (Endicott, NY: International Business Machines Corporation, 1983), document Number GH24-5004-4, for an introduction to RSCS.
11. See *Digital's Networks: An Architecture with a Future* (Maynard, MA: Digital Equipment Corporation, n.d.), p. 27. While this is a good overview of DEC networking, most of the technical information in this section is taken from *DECnet: DIGITAL Network Architecture, General Description*, Document No. AA-N149A-TC (Maynard, MA: Digital Equipment Corporation, 1982), pp. 2.2ff.
12. See, for example, Defense Communications Agency, *Military Standard File Transfer Protocol*, MIL-STD-1780, May 10, 1984. The preceding is also reprinted in Defense Communications Agency, *DDN Protocol Handbook* (Menlo Park, CA: DDN Network Information Center, SRI International, Dec. 1985). Note also, RFC: 765 (1985). An easily found analysis of the protocol is Tony Micel, "File Transfer Protocol," in William Stalling, et al., *Handbook of Computer Communications Standards: Department of Defense (DoD) Protocol Standards*, Vol. 3 (New

York: Macmillan, 1988), pp. 92–119. Before other LAN standards were available, suggestions were made that all or part of the Internet be adopted for that use. See, "Options for Implementing LAN Protocols Before Standards Gel," *Digital Design*, Jan. 1985.

13. Jack Haverty and Robert Gurwitz, "Protocols and Their Implementation: A Matter of Choice," *Data Communications*, March 1983, pp. 153ff.

14. This discussion of EDI is based largely on Kathleen Conlon Hinge, *Electronic Data Interchange* (New York: American Mangement Association, 1988).

CHAPTER 10

Data Extraction, Data Format, and Application-Specific File Transfers

Were it but possible to have a universal means for doing file transfers among users, life would be much more pleasant in an enterprise-wide computing (EWC) environment. Unfortunately, even in the early 1990s, that ideal is more wish than reality. Some of the reasons why universal solutions are hard to come by include the following:

- Continued use of proprietary schemes by some major manufacturers.
- The corollary to the foregoing, insufficient distribution in the use of international standards for file transfer.
- Multivendor environments for EWC.

- Lack of adequate strategic and tactical network planning *and* implementation control to assure interoperability of all potential network components.

Standing at the foundation of EWC "file transfer" represents the larger issue of effective and efficient distributed computing. Writing in *Scientific American* about supercomputer centers, Elizabeth Corcoran observed that in the not too distant future "scientists working at personal computers in their offices [will have] the flexibility to solve parts of problems on specialized architectures (including workstations, special-purpose processors and supercomputers), regardless of where the machines are located."[1] The developments in network standards, technology, and software that took place in the 1980s are making distributed computing available not only to scientific establishments, but also to business and governmental organizations. While the reality of distributed architectures extends considerably beyond file-transfer issues, these issues must be confronted and solved by any networking system.

Data are kept in various ways by different software and hardware, which inhibits transparent file transfers among different machines. When data are organized in a flat, rectangular file, with a record length not exceeding 80 columns, and providing that not more than one record at a time will be sent down the line, file transfers can be handled in a straightforward manner. Unfortunately, much of the data that people must use is not so conveniently maintained on all systems. Data organized by database systems or spreadsheets or other specialized software are certain to be in formats peculiar to the system. Moreover, records, even in flat files, are terminated differently by various systems. IBM mainframes, for example, have system software organized to operate on records, making it sometimes difficult to work with data on a character-by-character basis.

The result is that even if the physical file transfer from one machine to another is accomplished, it still may not be useful. As previously emphasized, the more comprehensive objective is to pass a file from one application to another in a usable form. This process often requires the user to do each task using a separate program on each computer system involved in the file transfer. Some manufacturers provide end-to-end processes for specific applications, but laudable as that may be, it may create the need for a user to interact with several communications programs and systems. From a systems perspective, it may also create the need for multiple methods for physical communication between or among computers. Working from either the server or the client, the actual steps required at each end, up to entering the communications process, are illustrated in Figure 10.1.

In the not too distant past the micro-to-mainframe file-transfer process was the significant issue in distributed computing. It is clear today, however, that the micro-to-mainframe concept is much too narrow. Rather, the concept is one of client and server. The client–server model of interaction in a distributed system is one in which a program at one site sends a request to a program at another site and awaits a response. The requesting program is called a client; the program satisfying the request is called the server. It is usually easier to build client software than server software.

This chapter is not concerned with communication between the client and server, it is concerned with what must happen before and after that transfer takes place. The problem with the simple file-transfer techniques implemented by terminal emulators is that they only take an existing file in an appropriate format and send it to the receiver, saving it as another file

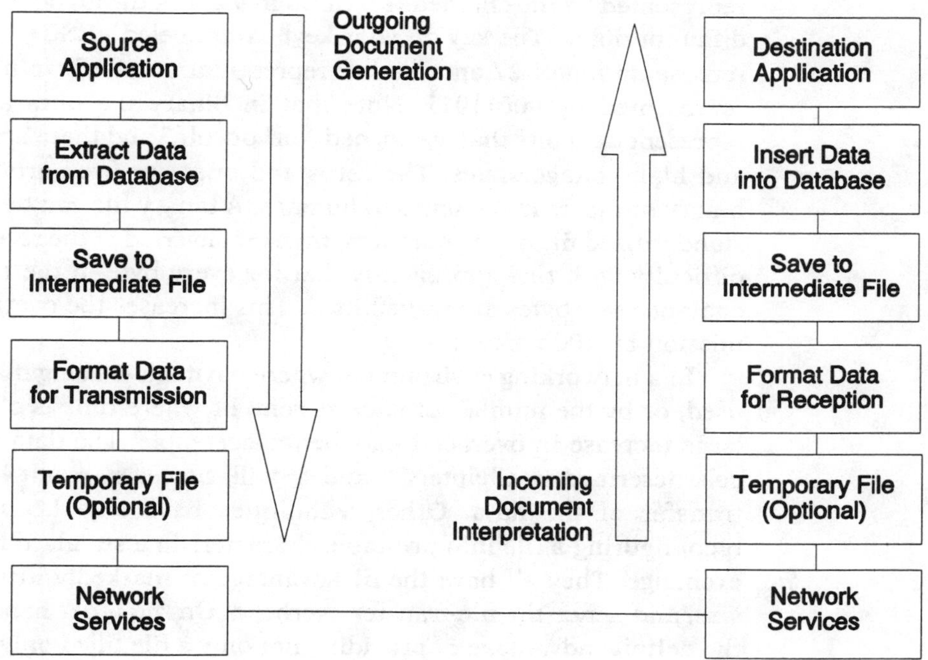

Figure 10.1. The Data Interchange Process.

that may not have any relationship to the intended application. The nature of the file used for transmission between the two computers can help determine what is required of the file transmission protocol (see Chapter 8). If, for example, any file transmitted will already use only printable characters, then a transparent mode for the file transfer protocol is redundant. One way to produce a file that contains only printable characters is to convert the data before transmission.

One example of file conversion is to convert the file to a hexadecimal (hex) representation before file transmission. This has been used for executable program and other binary files. Recall from Chapter 8 that one major problem encountered for a network-transparent file transfer protocol is how to transfer a binary file without interaction with the network or other elements (software and hardware) between applications. Both hex and decimal representations are used by humans and are, therefore, printable. Hex numbers can often be used in computer applications more directly than can decimal numbers. Moreover, every byte is represented by exactly two hex digits, rather than by one to three decimal digits. A hex digit is represented by the characters 0 through 9 and A through F, for a total of 16 different digits. The key on your keyboard labeled <ESC> has the decimal representation of 27 and the hex representation of 1B. In binary it can be represented by 00011011. Note that in binary the ones and zeros only represent data bits that are turned "on" or "off," and these are normally low and high voltage states. The zeros and ones are used arbitrarily to have binary numbers make sense to humans. A binary file can be converted to a standardized file of hex numbers, then reconverted at the receiving end. The difficulty with this approach is that for every byte in the binary file, two characters or bytes are transmitted. This increases the overhead for transmission by 100 percent.

In a networking environment where payment is being made by the time used, or by the number of packets sent, or where time is of the essence, a large increase in overhead may be unacceptable. The data transfer protocols described in Chapters 7 and 8, will, however, result in the accurate transfer of the data. Other techniques have also been designed for reconfiguring a file into printable characters in a standard format for data exchange. They all have the disadvantage of markedly increasing the file size, and hence the file-transfer overhead. On the other hand, they all have the definite advantage of providing not only a file filled only with printable characters, but they also have a well-defined and known file structure that can be reconverted on reception.

Accessing Common Databases

Today, most corporate information is kept by a database management system on the corporate mainframe, a large minicomputer, or for smaller organizations, a file server on a LAN. Whether that mainframe is blue (IBM) or an IBM Plug Compatible Machine (PCM), or supermini such as a large DEC (Digital Equipment Corporation) VAX, the data in the database are arranged according to current theories of the "best" in database management. The database may exist as a relational system, a hierarchical system, or something else. It is accessed through a program that makes use of what are essentially structured subroutine calls that allow easy (for a programmer) access to the database information. In a microcomputer database package, a specialized "language" is often used to access the data. An alternate approach would be a subroutine package that could be used within a FORTRAN, COBOL, or BASIC program, similar to the traditional methods used in large-scale systems (although some programming is now being done with 4GL).

Because of the cost and time involved in having a programmer extract data from a corporate database, both institutions and end users have demanded simplified access, especially for doing ad hoc reporting. This problem has been attacked in several ways. First, producers of database systems have provided simplified (though not necessarily simple) languages or command systems for data extraction. IBM has Data Language 1 (DL1) for IMS and Software AG has Natural for ADABAS. Natural, for example, is an interpreted language not unlike BASIC, but like any interpreted language, applications written in it are slow. Moreover, it is not "simple" enough for many end users. Data Language 1 is designed to improve programmer productivity rather than end users.

The problem of extracting corporate data for additional use either on the mainframe or to be downloaded to a micro has been attacked in at least two ways. First, database manufacturers have attempted to provide micro-to-mainframe links that allow access to the database through "simplified" languages. An example of this approach is a product from Software AG called the Natural Connection. The difficulty with this approach is that support for various communications and network facilities may be limited. A vendor is dictating auxiliary equipment and software to the user organization. Moreover, such manufacturers can be unresponsive to either specialized user needs or to a recognition that their design decisions are not necessarily the only or best ones.

An alternative approach has been provided by "third-party" manufacturers, usually with products that also need access to the corporate database. An example of this is Focus and its associated micro-to-mainframe link, FocTalk, from Information Builders, Inc. Particularly if Focus is running on each computer on the network, requests for corporate information can be set up, transmitted, the data extracted, and downloaded back to the local Focus system in a simple fashion. Focus has interfaces to a wide variety of micro, mini, and mainframe database products and can communicate with a variety of networks, making it a flexible tool.

Focus and SAS (from SAS, Inc.) are two of the most frequently used products in corporate information centers across the country. SAS, Inc. has some interface facilities similar to those found in Focus but in a less integrated and less expansive fashion. The SAS interface to ADABAS, for example, has been written by yet another software manufacturer and must be purchased independently of SAS itself. SAS, Inc., like Software AG, has had a limited perspective on communications and networks, but with its micro-to-mainframe link, and with SAS at both the micro and mainframe ends, some transparency can be achieved.

A last caveat about the data-extraction issue is needed. All the products mentioned, as well as many others on the market, can be expensive. Moreover, most of the manufacturers of these products attempt to remake the buyer in the manufacturers' own image of what is appropriate. This has caused many large organizations to put their resources into writing their own data extraction and downloading software. Producing one's own software is sometimes the best approach, but not all the time, and maybe not even most of the time. Moreover, it may be necessary for an organization to have multiple products to do the same job, simply because there may be no communication among the products. Hence, it may be necessary to have Focus, SAS, and Natural Connection rather than identifying one basic package that could be used as a general-purpose interface for multiple applications. This results in added cost and can result in a training and learning nightmare, since end users might be forced to use multiple systems and even several terminal emulators, depending on the applications involved.

The strategy with the products just described is to extract data from the database and save it to an intermediate file. In each instance the microcomputer usually acts as the client and the mainframe as the server. At that point processing can continue either on the mainframe end or on the micro side. As networks come to link more diverse processors, the data extraction/

translation issue becomes more important. Any ad hoc reporting requirement will likely require extraction software, whether that ad hoc reporting will be done on the mainframe or micro end of the connection. The next section addresses what must happen to the data either before transfer, or after transfer, so that those data will be in a format useful at the other end. Regardless of where the data originate, there remains the need to translate those data from the server's application to the client's application, and to transfer the data from the server to the clients.

Client–Host Data Format Issues

The extraction program may, of course, include a module that places the data from the server in a format ready for transfer to the client, but many times that will not be the case. Although the current objectives in providing EWC include such seamless data transfers, that step may have to be accomplished by a separate program. There are at least two strategies that might be pursued at this point. The data might be formatted only for transmission to the client. It might be placed in a specialized format for file transfer in preference to a form required by the target application. Alternatively, the data might be placed in a format that can be directly read by the target application when the transfer is complete, if the needs for transmission and use are the same or similar. There are a number of formatting issues that arise, including data compression, encryption, character coding, and file structures.

Data Compression

As the files to be transferred grow in size and number, the issue of how fast they can be sent also grows in importance. The limiting factor on how many files of a given size can be sent is a function of bandwidth. Bandwidth is the range of frequencies assigned to a channel or system. The difference, expressed in Hertz, between the highest and lowest frequencies of a band is the measure of bandwidth. Sometimes bandwidth is also referred to in terms of the number of bits per second that can be processed over a given frequency range. Thus, the greater the bandwidth, the higher the number of bits per second (b/s) that can be transmitted. Because bandwidth is always finite, no matter how large the channel, data are often compressed prior to sending and decompressed on reception. While this is not the medium to discuss compression/decompression algorithms, suffice it to say that in a network environment the algorithms used must be fast and capable of being used "on-the-fly." Both client and server must be capable of doing the compression/decompression. While data compression can assist in using bandwidth parsimoniously, it will also have an adverse effect on throughput, since all the data must be compressed and decompressed. Like most networking issues, there are advantages and disadvantages in the use of many techniques, and data compression is a case in point.

Encryption/Decryption

In Chapter 5 the problem of network security was discussed in some detail. One of the primary points made in that chapter was that data encryption was the primary method for securing information being transmitted across a network. Note, therefore, that the encryption (and decryption) of information is also a format problem in that once encrypted, the material must also be decrypted for it to be used. Like data-compression techniques, encryption/decryption can also have an adverse impact on throughput, since it takes time to encrypt and decrypt the information. Note also that these various techniques tend to be cumulative. That is, if a file is encrypted then compressed, the time for encryption must be added to the time for compression. At the other end, the reverse flow must take place. The point to be made here is that all of these issues interact with one another to affect throughput.

Character Coding: EBCDIC Versus ASCII

Whatever the nature of the file that resulted from the extraction program, it is likely to be a file in standard EBCDIC (Extended Binary Coded Decimal Interchange Code) or ASCII character format. It was once necessary for an application program to make the character conversions between two such systems of character representation, and that may still be true under some circumstances. Today, however, system software often takes care of that problem. It is important to remember, however, that some calculations, like checksum and CRC (Cyclical Redundancy Check) values, will be different if done on an EBCDIC file on one end and an ASCII file at the other. Some character conversion may be required, if only temporarily, at both ends of the connection. Transfer between ASCII systems or between EBCDIC systems will not have that problem, of course. Just as this issue is important for file transfer protocols, it is also important for compression and encryption techniques, as well.

File Structure Format Issues

Although many intermediate files will be rectangular sequential files, this will not always be the case. In a rectangular file it is not only assumed that each record will have the same length, but it is also assumed that each record will have the same number of fields. Moreover, some data transmission techniques limit physical record lengths to 80 or 132 characters. A file with larger records may also have to be cut up to conform to the data-transfer system and then reassembled on the other end. The structure of the dataset may also have to be preserved. Few data elements extracted from a database will have been part of a neat rectangular file, although the data may be capable of being put into such a format. On the other hand, some data, even in their "natural" state, have other structures. Census data, for example, is often structured in hierarchical files, since data are collected at both the household (family) level and for individuals. One data unit has one or more records of household data along with one or more records on each individual within the household. When analyzed, this hierarchical structure must be taken into account and when transferred to another system, must be preserved.

"Standard" Data File Formats

One possible solution to some of these problems is to adopt a standard data-interchange format for any file to be transferred. Software manufacturers could implement that format as an output choice for users of their software. This approach has been attempted, albeit informally, at the micro level. There are several widely used data formats. The Intel Hex Format, for example, is used primarily for binary files. The Data Interchange Format (DIF), as another example, is for data that have been converted to printable form. There are other approaches that could be (and are) used, but these examples will suggest the strengths and weaknesses of these approaches. Consider first, the small rectangular dataset found in Table 10.1.

The data in Table 10.1 consist of four records, each with ten fields. The first field is the record identifier and is two columns long. The remaining nine fields are each three columns in length (a space followed by two digits).

TABLE 10.1. Sample Data

01	11	22	33	44	55	66	77	88	99
02	10	11	12	13	14	15	16	17	18
03	19	20	21	22	23	24	25	26	27
04	28	29	30	31	32	33	34	35	36

The file can be converted into an Intel Hex Format file. The converted file is found in Table 10.2. The Intel Hex Format is designed primarily for binary program files, but any file can be converted to the format and reconverted later.

The first subtable in Table 10.2 is the sample dataset, the second is the same data converted to Hex, and the third is the Hex file reconverted to the original. The process is straightforward and it works. The primary difficulty with this approach is that the Hex file is much larger than the original. The conversion does nothing except take every byte in an input file and convert it to Hex, assuming ASCII to be the base character-code definition. On reconversion everything will be put back as it was in the original. The "gotcha" in this is that the precise format (end-of-record and end-of-file characters, for example) may not be identical for the source and destination machines or operating systems (OS). Although a technique such as Hex conversion will work, additional information may have to be added at the sending or receiving station to ensure identity of the files.

A somewhat different approach is exemplified by the DIF format, devised by Robert M. Frankston of Software Arts, Inc. (the creators of VisiCalc), which was designed to ease exchanges of data between different computer programs.[2] In DIF files, records are called "TUPLES" and columns (fields) are called "VECTORS." Many programs like Lotus 123 can import or export data as DIF files.[3] A DIF file resulting from the conversion of the sample data is shown in Table 10.3. Each field of the original data is broken out into a single, short record, associated with information describing the size and type of data. The data may be either numeric or alpha. Other control information is sent as other record types at the beginning of the file.

Data Interchange Format files are limited to converting flat, rectangular files with equal numbers of fields per record. Moreover, the size of the file increases enormously. The DIF version is 5.12 times (640 characters) the size of the original and 1.71 times the size of the Hex file. The significance

TABLE 10.2. Sample Data Converted to Intel Hex Format

Original Data

01	11	22	33	44	55	66	77	88	99
02	10	11	12	13	14	15	16	17	18
03	19	20	21	22	23	24	25	26	27
04	28	29	30	31	32	33	34	35	36

Converted to Intel Hex Format

```
:10010000303120313120323220333320343420352 5
```

Converted Back to Original Form

01	11	22	33	44	55	66	77	88	99
02	10	11	12	13	14	15	16	17	18
03	19	20	21	22	23	24	25	26	27
04	28	29	30	31	32	33	34	35	36

of these file-size differences is that, if transferring asynchronously at 9,600 b/s, 1,000 records each of 100 characters would take about two minutes (1.7) to transmit in the original format. After conversion to DIF format, the same file would take nearly nine minutes (8.9). Differences of this magnitude could have a significant impact on the capacity of a network if many file transfers were taking place.

The concept of a "standard" file format for data interchange is a useful idea, but its limitations place strictures on its use. An interchange format that gained general acceptance, or was endorsed by a standards organization, would go a long way toward simplifying data transfers. Many microcomputer products support the DIF file and one or two other widely used

TABLE 10.3. Sample Data Converted to DIF File

```
TABLE
0,1
"SAMPLE DATA"
VECTORS
0,10
""
TUPLES
0,4
""
DATA
0,0
""
-1,0
BOT
0,1
""
0,11
""
0,22
""
0,33
""
0,44
""
0,55
""
0,66
""
0,77
""
0,88
""
0,99
""
-1,0
BOT
0,2
""
0,10
""
0,11
""
0,12
""
0,13
""
0,14
""
0,15
""
0,16
""
0,17
""
0,18
""
-1,0
BOT
0,3
""
0,19
""
0,20
""
0,21
""
0,22
""
0,23
""
0,24
""
0,25
""
0,26
""
0,27
""
-1,0
BOT
0,4
""
0,28
""
0,29
""
0,30
""
0,31
""
0,32
""
0,33
""
0,34
""
0,35
""
0,36
""
-1,0
EOD
```

file formats, one of which is a simple print image. Unfortunately these approaches have severe limitations and are inappropriate for many database files.

EDI

Chapter 9 introduced EDI as a file-transfer system. In this chapter it may be useful to note EDI again and to highlight further some of the issues relating to data extraction and format. As previously noted, there is a need to translate files into some standard format for transmission to a remote system. Electronic Data Interchange is an example of a service that actually defines such an intermediate file standard. The standard file is actually transferred rather than the original form of the document because the receiving end must know precisely the format of the document in order to handle it automatically. It cannot assume some large number of randomly designed documents, as is the case with the more informal file transfers characteristic of less-formal systems, such as PC-based bulletin board systems. With the latter a human being typically initiates the file transfer, and when it is complete does something manually to make use of the incoming data. With EDI all of this is automated so that no human intervention is necessary.[4] Software is available for EDI applications for micros, minis, and mainframes. Moreover, value-added networks (VANS) will also provide EDI services. In the latter case the electronic document is furnished to the VAN, and the VAN takes if from there.

In order for application-to-application EDI transfers to take place, there must be an appropriate *application*, *application-translator link*, and *document translator*. It goes without saying that each system must also be connected to a network or have at least primitive data communications capabilities. The application is the busines function in which information is either generated or needed. Examples are order entry and accounts payable systems. Information flow between the application and the document translator is handled by the application-translator link. This link may be a flat file with a defined format or some similar mechanism. The document translator reformats the data into some EDI standard for outgoing documents. For incoming data it reformats the EDI data into the format required by the internal application. For outgoing documents the process is called "document generation," while for incoming documents it is called "document interpretation."

Application-Specific Micro-to-Mainframe Systems

Selected types of applications are particularly well suited to both mainframe and micro implementations. Data management and reporting systems such as Focus are prime candidates, as are decision support systems (DSS). Decision support systems vendors, according to one writer in *MIS Week*, seem to have adopted one of three strategies to capture the micro-to-mainframe DSS market: Allow the user to download data from the host to the micro and then manipulate the data with standard micro software packages such as Lotus 1-2-3;[5] develop a downsized version of the mainframe DSS package for the micro; or transport the complete mainframe DSS package to a micro environment.[6] Although microcomputer-based stand-alone software has become increasingly sophisticated, many users will continue to rely on micro-based software with links to a host package. Consequently the third alternative is likely to appeal to an end user. Within such systems users can sometimes do transparent client–server transfers. This makes the link to the corporate database easy and straightforward. At least within a limited environment, the data extraction and formatting issues are solved by "built-in" file transfer protocols. It is easier, of course, to successfully implement a client–server link if both ends of the link are tightly controlled by versions of the same program. In that controlled framework, data extraction and formatting problems are well known and understood by the developers, and when an end user is conversant with the system being used, the file transfer is seen simply as another option within the system. If there are special file formats, they can be handled with a special-purpose approach rather than a general-purpose file-transfer system.

Applications and Products

More than anywhere else in this book there is the need in this chapter to mention specific products, since the strategies described here are specific to such products. The products mentioned are neither the only ones on the market, nor necessarily the best. They are, however, widely used and may provide particularly useful links. New products are also frequently entering the market, so use all available reference sources to determine the current crop of products.

Database and Transfer (The Information Center)

As was implied by earlier sections of this chapter, many users demand access to the corporate database so that ad hoc reporting can be accomplished quickly and easily. Several products have been implemented or reimplemented to attack this need. Many of the products mentioned in this section have the capacity to create their own file structures, others can be used to directly access the organization's database, reformat the data, and transmit those data to a micro.

Focus

As has already been mentioned, one example of the trend toward equivalent systems on both the micro and mainframe has been Focus from Information Builders, Inc. Information Builders, Inc., has introduced a micro-to-mainframe communications software package for floppy- and hard-disk-based systems. FocTalk provides access and bidirectional file transfer from a personal computer to and from those systems its "Focus Report Writer" supports.[7] An interesting example of one use of Focus was during the Los Angeles Olympics in 1984. Coca Cola's Olympic Systems Group used PC/Focus to reserve Olympic event tickets for Coca Cola's guests. They developed five primary databases, which were linked using PC/Focus's join facility to help allocate 41,000 tickets to visitors.[8]

SPSS/PC and SAS

Two products that have been available on mainframe systems for many years is the Statistical Analysis System (SAS) from SAS, Inc., and the Statistical Package for the Social Sciences (SPSS) from SPSS, Inc.[9] They have also been direct competitors for years. Well-known in universities, strong marketing efforts have increased the use of these systems in the private sector. SAS, Inc,. has been more successful than SPSS, Inc,. in this endeavor. SAS has been particularly successful in selling to technical support units responsible for performance monitoring and capacity planning. Both companies are marketing for "Information Centers," and since the term "4th Generation Language" (4GL) has become popular seem to have discovered that their products are, indeed, 4GLs.

The file-transfer problem has been attacked somewhat differently by SAS and SPSS. Both have implemented large subsets of their mainframe products on micros with the attendant need to transfer their system files (binary) back and forth from system to system. SAS has implemented a system similar in concept to the dedicated approach used by Focus. SPSS, possibly as a stopgap measure, is distributing Kermit (see Chapter 8) with its SPSS/PC product, which uses an intermediate file format. Because of the varied consumers using both SAS and SPSS, they will ultimately have to implement both synchronous and asynchronous file-transfer systems.

Natural Connection (Software AG)

A somewhat different strategy has been followed by Software AG with its Natural Connection product. With its Natural language for easier data extraction, a user (not a naive user) can take data from the corporate database, and through Natural Connection tied to a micro over a synchronous line with the micro using a 3x78/9 emulation board, download/upload data to/from the micro. Unlike Focus, SAS, or SPSS, which have impressive micro versions of their software, Software AG is making arrangements with vendors of micro-based database products to directly interact with the micro software. Ashton-Tate and Software AG, for example, in a cooperative agreement, announced in 1985 an interface for Ashton-Tate's products and AG's microcomputer to mainframe link.[10] A similar agreement was developed between AG and Lotus Development Corp. The purpose of the Ashton-Tate agreement was to provide software packages to IBM mainframe accounts. While the success of these efforts was mixed, at best, they represented early recognition of the importance of EWC. Software AG's products are closely tied to IBM mainframe environments, although network users on many different systems may need access to similar centralized database systems.

Computer Based Instruction (CBI) as a Micro-to-Mainframe Link

A somewhat specialized market for micro-to-mainframe links has developed around computer based instruction (CBI). For many years CBI was a mainframe province, although during the early 1980s, in a separate development, micros also became important for training purposes. Several manufacturers of computer-based training authoring systems now include PC/mainframe links in their system.[11] Connecting PCs with mainframe computers offers many advantages for certain training applications. Some manufacturers recognize that the mainframe can be a useful development system. Micros, however, offer many presentation advantages, not the least of which is the ability to provide CBI without taxing the mainframe.

Alternatively, providing presentation services on the mainframe may also offer some advantages, particularly in an environment where "dumb" terminals are more common than micros. Moreover, a CBI training package can be easily distributed through downloading from the mainframe system.

Authoring systems such as Scholar/Teach, from Boeing Computer Services; ADROIT, from ADR; and PHOENIX/Micro, from Goal Systems offer different approaches to the use of PC/mainframe links in developing and using computer-based training systems.

Bibliographic Access and Capture

An emerging class of micro-to-mainframe software involves the access to and capture of bibliographic data. Especially in schools, universities, and private research establishments this can be an important issue. Many private (school, university, corporate) and public libraries are now automated, and given the availability of services like Lockheed's Dialogue and other online bibliographic reference services, the possibility of developing an extensive local bibliographic file, at a reasonable cost, now exists. The typical method of downloading such information is to use a standard terminal emulator with the capability of downloading ASCII files. The problem is what to do with the information. Several products are now on the market that will take such data, in several different, but known, formats, and automatically place them in a local, microcomputer-based database that can be searched at will. This has the advantage of minimizing communications costs when the communications network is the telephone system. In a university or corporation with a private network, this can also be useful in allowing researchers to develop specialized bibliographic files that can be quickly and easily searched.

Other Dedicated Systems

A myriad of other dedicated micro-to-mainframe links built around specialized software are coming to market. Accountants Microsystems Inc. (AMI) is marketing Datawrite Corporate General Ledger, a banking package that transmits data automatically to a mainframe computer. Report formats can be altered using 60 command keys. The bank must have the data link. Another example is the Rating, Auditing and Payment Authorization System (RAPAS) from Distribution Science, which uses micro-to-mainframe communication. A microcomputer user enters the bill of lading data; it is transferred to the mainframe for prices; it is routed to accounting to check the freight bill for a price check; and data goes to accounts payable or original entry point to check freight discrepancy.

Multimedia Systems

So far discussion has centered on the client-server connection in the context of an individual user wishing to send or receive a particular file. By 1990, a growing market was developing for multimedia applications in a networking environment. Multimedia concepts have been around for many years, but the technology was just becoming available for devising multimedia reports and presentations with a desktop workstation. Voice and video cards are available for insertion into a relatively fast PC (80386 class) so that application programs can now use such media for input or output, along with the more traditional printed reports on screen or paper. One problem facing many organizations is report distribution, but the nature of those reports may change to multimedia presentations. Depending on the kind network available, broadcast downloading of information may be an appropriate method for distributing such reports. Devices are now available that allow one-way file transfer over FM radio or cable television (CATV) systems. At this writing these systems were slow and subject to problems that require appropriate processing on the receiving end to ensure correct reception. Since these systems are one-way, file transfer protocols such as those discussed earlier, cannot be used. Many of the experiments taking place at this writing revolved around the distribution of software to home computers, but the technology opens up many avenues for mainframe-to-micro file transfers. In an organization that must distribute memos, newsletters, and similar communications to all employees, if data communications are via CATV, inexpensive receivers equipped with a tape recorder could capture broadcast information for later review on a microcomputer-based workstation. On a more public scale, such technology might make possible a long-held dream of some for the electronic distribution of newspapers and other similar documents.

Other Extraction and Format Problems

There are two approaches to the problem of data extraction and formatting for the client-server relationship: general-purpose, network-independent systems or application-specific systems. At this writing no true general-purpose system existed, although strides were being taken in this direction. There were, however, several application-specific approaches that could be used. The problem with application-specific systems is that the end user might have to learn several different methods for file transfer, and it might even be necessary for the managers of EWC systems to provide more than one technology for communications among systems. The latter problem is the most severe from a cost-efficient perspective, while the former might lead to resistance from end users.

Several problems that stand in the way of a generalized solution to the successful implementation of a user-friendly method for file transfer can be identified:

- Lack of appropriate standards.
- The use of multiple operating environments on a single mainframe (VMS or UNIX on DEC machines; the concurrent use of VM/CMS, MVS, MUSIC, TSO, CICS, IMS, COMPLETE/ADABAS, on IBM machines).
- A multivendor "mainframe" computing environment (a combination of IBM, DEC, and Hewlett-Packard, for example).
- A multivendor microcomputer environment.
- Use of multiple networks.
- And sundry other problems.

One way to overcome these problems is by establishing national or international standards for extracting and formatting data for file transfer. Such standards would encourage manufacturers of software to include standard approaches to data extraction and file formats as well as providing vendor-specific solutions. The obvious alternative for an organization consuming computer hardware and software is to surrender to a single vendor and accept that vendor's solution to all these problems. Many shops are all IBM, or all DEC, or all something else. Such an approach limits consuming organizations to vendor specific solutions instead of acquiring what is best for a particular environment. Regardless of what a particular manufacturer claims, no one, including IBM, yet has a perfect solution to the enterprise-wide data extraction and formatting problem.

The lack of adequate standards for software has led many large organizations to spend the time and money on producing highly specialized solutions by writing their own systems revolving around the hardware at their disposal. Although this may be an appropriate solution for a large organization, it is clearly inappropriate for a small company. If the cost itself is not prohibitive, it may not be possible to find the appropriate technical personnel. In the meantime, as software manufacturers continue to deal with the problem, the market may drive those vendors to broader, more general solutions. Hints of such developments have been discussed in this chapter. Certainly with the increasing use of multisystem computing and networking environments, there is an increasing need for general solutions.

Notes

1. Elizabeth Corcoran, "Calculating Reality," *Scientific American*, Vol. 264, No. 1, Jan. 1991, p. 108.
2. A detailed treatment of the DIF file may be found in Donald H. Beil, *The DIF File* (Reston, VA: Reston Publishing Co., 1983).
3. The inventors of VisiCalc, the "granddaddy" of the contemporary spreadsheet programs, also were resposible for devising the DIF file format. With respect to new developments, especially those concerning enterprise spreadsheet computing, see "Lotus Development's Frank Moss Heralds the Era of Enterprise Spreadsheet Computing," *Computergram International*, No. 1405, April 12, 1990.
4. This discussion is based on Kathleen Conlon Hinge, *Electronic Data Interchange* (New York: American Management Association, 1988), pp. 25–31.
5. Although note that at this writing Lotus was looking at directly providing connectivity. See, for example, "Connectivity Now: 1-2-3/M and T-A-C," *Lotus*, Vol. 6, No. 3, March 1990, p. 84(1).
6. E. Nee, "Reaching Decisions with Micro-to-Mainframe DSS," *Mis Week*, Vol. 5, No. 46, Nov. 14, 1984, pp. 5, 8, 14.
7. "'FocTalk' Ties PC-CPU," *Mis Week*, Vol. 5, No. 31, Aug. 1, 1984, p. 36. See also, "PC/Focus 5.5 Sets Stage for Cooperative Processing," *PC Week*, Vol. 7, No. 16, April 23, 1990, p. 1(2). See also, "Focus Ready to Shift Back to Large Systems," *Computing Canada*, Vol. 16, No. 4, Feb. 15, 1990, p. 16(1).
8. B. Freedman, "PC/FOCUS Helped Coke Sponsor Olympic Games," *PC Week*, Vol. 2, No. 4, Jan. 29, 1984, p. 95.
9. For relatively up-to-date information see "SPSS Packs 'Mainframe Functionality' in Mac Version of Statistics Package," *MacWEEK*, Vol. 4, No. 10, March 13, 1990, p. 18(1), and "Testes Laud OS/2 SAS for Mainframe Data Links," *PC Week*, Vol. 7, No. 7, Feb. 19, 1990, p. 27(2).
10. W. P. Artorelli, "Software AG Makes a Natural Connection," *Information Week*, Vol. 16, May 27, 1985, p. 16.
11. K. Barnes, "Tapping Mainframe for PC Training—Without Taxing It," *PC Week*, Vol. 2, No. 13, April 12, 1985, p. 39.

CHAPTER 11

Successful Networks for EWC

"There is a revolution in the making for the management of centralized, mainframe computer systems. Over the next few years the emphasis will move from the management of computers to the management of networks."[1] When I wrote those two sentences in 1986, the idea that the emphasis in computing would move from processors to networks was still controversial. Few would debate that issue today. Yet the concept of enterprise-wide computing (EWC) is still not widely understood, even though there have been many attempts to provide integrated networks for corporations, universities, governmental agencies, and other organizations. A major part of the reason why organizations do not have true EWC is due more to failures in management than to a lack of technology.

Management's failure to use information technology well is not a recent phenomenon but rather stems from the fact that information systems are not often part of an institution's strategic planning. The lack of strategic thinking about information systems has meant that in many organizations mainframe systems are controlled and planned by one group, networks by another, minis by a third, and micros by a fourth. When local area networks (LANs) became popular, yet a fifth group might have been formed. Moreover, most organizations were slow to adopt organization-wide standards for hardware and software, which has led to the inability to communicate adequately. Sometimes, when organizations have been willing to plan strategically for information systems, the technology has not been quite ready, although this has been the case less often than the lack of strategic planning. These historical factors have provided impediments that stand in the way of developing true EWC.

Has this book provided a comprehensive definition of EWC? Perhaps not, but it has attempted to identify those issues that contribute to such a definition. We have, therefore, discovered that enterprise-wide computing means at least the following:

- A strategic concern for the total computing needs of the organization.
- The ability to do distributed computing using distributed databases.
- The capacity for each computing entity on the network to communicate with any other entity as required by the organization.
- Provisions to protect the integrity of information throughout the organization (security).
- Adoption of internal and national/international standards.
- An integrated network management system capable of managing components from multiple vendors.
- Enhancements that improve the capacity to use the system by the people in the organization, possibly including:
    - A common user interface (CUI)
    - Sufficient bandwidth to move multimedia information (including not only voice, video, and images, but also text) in a timely fashion.
    - "Seamless" and "transparent" interactions among users of diverse computing hardware.
    - Access to information internal to the organization and acquisition of relevant information available on networks external to the organization.

This book has not tried to define enterprise computing in terms of the specific approaches to enterprise networking suggested by mainframe/mini vendors like IBM and DEC (Digital Equipment Corporation) or LAN vendors such as Novell and Banyan. Moreover, much of the essence of enterprise networking is tied up in network management, and the availability of management resources was still sparse in the early 1990s. According to James Herman the "industry has set its sights on open, multivendor networks and distributed computing, but missing in action so far are the enterprise management architectures that can integrate diverse and farflung network devices into a cohesive, controllable whole."[2] IBM's catchall for enterprise computing is the new Enterprise Systems Connection (ESCON) architecture, while DEC's contribution is called Enterprise Management Architecture. Both Novell and Banyan are explicitly aimed at the enterprise networking market, as well.[3]

Yet these developments do not mean that large mainframe systems, or smaller multiuser computers, will go away. In fact, IBM's enterprise strategy is built on its newest series of mainframe computers. Such systems are necessary for problems that cannot be handled by a desktop computer, or that archive data necessary for running an organization. Even with a distributed database, however, central supervision of data integrity, security, and backup will continue to be important for the well-being of organizations large and small. The key to either distributed processing or distributed database systems, however, is data communications and the ability for system users to pass information back and forth in a friendly and transparent manner. As advances in data communications occur, information transfer will become more efficient. Most LANs demonstrate this trend, as does the introduction of higher speed (9.6 Kpbs and higher) dial-up modems. The way in which a data-communications network is presented to those who use the system will determine the character of computing into the twenty-first century. Fundamental to the changes taking place in the computing environment is what is called "enterprise-wide computing."

Networks and EWC

For EWC to take place, a highly connective network or set of networks must be in place. Like computers themselves, networks come in small, medium, and large, and all sizes will probably be used by even the most technologically casual person in the years to come. Small networks are designed to serve a small organization or a single department in a larger organization. Medium-sized networks connect the components of a single organization to one another. Large networks are designed to connect otherwise unrelated individuals and organizations to one another. Small networks will almost always be LANs. Medium size networks may be LANs, Metropolitan Area Networks (MANs), or Wide Area Networks (WANs). Metropolitan Area

Networks and WANs may or may not be wholly owned by a single organization, but the likelihood is that the physical media for such networks would include lines provided by public utilities of one form or another (telephone sysems, CATV systems, and so forth). A large company may operate a private network that uses various private and public technologies. Finally, a large network will normally be a WAN, using public communications carriers and serving a variety of needs on regional, national, or international levels. Note that I have defined network size not in numbers of nodes, but by the potential size and complexity of the organization or group the network serves. Another way of thinking about networks is the way in which they serve the goals of people: Small networks serve departmental goals, medium networks serve larger institutional goals, and large networks serve public or "global" goals. Each of these networks gives rise to a variety of problems in making the micro-to-mainframe connection.

Although technical issues have been discussed in some detail, I have also tried to give some sense of the importance of organizational problems in seeking an appropriate micro-to-mainframe connection. Implicit and explicit organizational goals determine the extent to which the demand for a micro-to-mainframe connection is taken seriously. This may include proper funding for networks and the associated software, the political strength to establish organizational standards, and the level of concern for appropriate security and backup.

What Is the Client-Server Connection?

With the development of technology in the 1980s, the micro/mini/mainframe distinction, couched in the language of the power of the computers, has become of limited value, if not outright obsolete. One more useful distinction was described in Chapter 10: The client–server model. Another more useful distinction is between single-user and multiuser systems. A third distinction might be one of function: The need of one user to use data amassed by someone else. The classic and traditional need has been for interactive or transactional access of a single user to the resources and services found on a "central" system.[4] This use might include the use of data found on the central system, or it might be using a powerful resource for computating and calculating.

Today, however, the computing "climate" is changing rapidly. Traditional micro-to-mainframe applications will continue to be important, but the micro will be used as a terminal in a terminal-emulation mode, no matter how many "bells-and-whistles" the terminal emulator contains. Increasingly, however, it is important to move quantities of data from one location to another for highly specialized local processing. This phenomenon is taking place for a variety of reasons. First, large central machines are still expensive, no matter how "expense" is measured. The unbridled expansion of applications on a central system that can be handled as well or better on some other node in a distributed network is economically inappropriate. Second, microcomputers, like the reinvention of movable type in the fifteenth century, is in large part a technology for the distribution of information. Emphasis is placed on the "distribution" of information rather than interactive and transactional processing. Third, the quantity of information now available either publicly or in organizations requires tools that can reduce the information to usable dimensions.

The Economy of Scale

Large central computers and their associated networks were originally used because it was cheaper for several people to share the costs of expensive technology. Today, sales people market LANs with many of the same economy-of-scale arguments. The economy-of-scale argument as applied to hardware, or even software, is becoming less persuasive with every passing day. What is less well-recognized, however, is that there is also an economy-of-scale argument to be made about acquiring and archiving information. This argument may keep central systems around for years to come, or perhaps forever. Large computer systems will also remain for the foreseeable future because of the development time required for new computer applications. An illustration of this is the Japanese Fifth Generation project, designed to bring the support of artificial intelligence to the public. Many artificial intelligence problems (though by no means all) are computer-intensive, requiring expensive machines that can process information at high rates of speed using large amounts of memory. Other development projects in many areas of science are also computer bound in a similar manner.

Every organized human activity requires acquiring and archiving information. For thousands of years people have put large amounts of time, energy, and money into these activities. One thing that distinguishes humans from other animals is our ability to use information as a tool. For any human society, information is as important as any physical tool. At first, information was acquired and archived by the human mind. Pictures were then used to ensure that others would be able to have common knowledge. Then writing was developed to retain and transmit information. Once the technology of writing developed, it was then necessary to retain, archive, and retrieve the resulting documents in libraries. The development of computers in the twentieth century simply allow us to retain and archive more information and retrieve it faster.

Because information is generated at many different points in society, for many different purposes, current technology dictates that the information so acquired be accessible by many different people within organizations or within society as a whole. Although most information in today's technological society is acquired through machine-readable methods, or immediately placed in machine-readable form, it requires large data storage facilities. If the cost-per-character of storage is calculated—and this is difficult—machine-readable storage is already competitive with paper storage. But the vast quantity of storage still implies large expenditures to acquire sufficient computing power to access that storage quickly and efficiently. Advances in technology are bringing down the cost-per-character of storage, and what is expensive for organizations today will be available to individuals tomorrow. There will be even more information with which to contend, and the character of that information is being enhanced. In the not-too-distant future most people will have to deal with files composed not only of characters to be printed to screen or paper, but also digital voice and video information as well as other image data.

The Distribution of Information

This book is an information-distribution method that has been around for thousands of years—the use of a written or printed document. Unfortunately, the moment this book was first placed in a bookstore the information in it was a minimum of 12 months old. It takes from 6 to 12 months to write such a book. It then takes from 6 to 9 months for a publisher to produce the book. There are some other time delays, as well. An author will require anywhere from one to six months to find a publisher and negotiate the contract, for example. The time the process takes has been reduced over the past 20 years, but a significant part of the reduction has been in the improved productivity of writers with the widespread use of word processing on microcomputers. Both my first book in the 1960s and my last book took about the same time to produce once the publishers had the manuscript, though I now provide the copy in both printed and machine-readable form. Although there are some processes in publishing that simply take time—editing copy, for example—similar problems occur with all paper-production methods. And many (perhaps most) documents no longer need be committed to paper.

Yet the publishing business is one where the micro-to-mainframe link is becoming increasingly important. Newspapers and magazines have been using computerized systems since the 1970s to help write and produce those publications. Several publishers with which I deal encourage uploading the original text to their editing computers, rather than sending a traditional paper manuscript. This saves everyone time and effort. In many publishing environments, the publisher subcontracts the printing of the documents. This happens, at least logically, inside large organizations, as well.

Many colleges and universities publish a daily newspaper, as did one for which I was a computing center manager. The newspaper staff uses its own editing computer to generate the copy for the paper. The paper is printed by the university's print shop, on the other side of the campus. Not many years ago paper copy was simply taken to the print shop, where it was typeset. Then paper copy was generated by the newspaper's computer and it was reentered by the print shop. Later it became possible to transport copy via diskette from the newspaper to the print shop. Today, text is transmitted directly over the network from the newspaper's computing facility to the print shop's computer for automatic composition. The computing center's only role in this process is to furnish the network through which the information flows, and it does not flow through any central computer system. This is one of my favorite examples of the way in which the role of enterprise computing management is changing.

A traditional problem in any organization is report distribution. The way this has traditionally taken place is for someone to run a program on the corporate machine, print the results in a report, then have someone else deliver or pickup the report. Most such reports are for reference purposes only, and are important only when the information is needed. Many such reports are generated on a daily, weekly, or monthly basis. Sometimes these reports are very long, running to hundreds of pages of printed output. It is frequently necessary for the user of such reports to analyze part of the data for further reporting, and by the time the "bottomline" gets to a vice-president or president, it has been reduced to a one sentence summary. Two approaches to this classical organizational problem are available in most large organizations (and many smaller ones as well). First, software, which allows easy access to the information through a terminal on a central system, can be placed on the central system. Second, the report itself can be distributed electronically to the end user's microcomputer for massaging and local inquiry. It is, of course, easier to say these things than do them.

The advantage of the first approach—do everything on the central system—is that data does not move very far and it will be available to all who need the information. The systematic methods for backing up and securing information on the mainframe will limit the possibility of loss. There are, however, several disadvantages. Higher use rates of the central system are ensured, thereby creating a demand for spending more money on large machines. Methods for subsetting and manipulating parts of the data may require that many different copies of the information are being kept on the central system's disks. The software available on the mainframe may not be as convenient or easy to use as would a microcomputer-based software system.

There are also advantages and disadvantages in transporting the reports to local microcomputers. Although many copies of the data may exist, once downloaded to a micro, those copies can be retained or released at the discretion of the end user. It may be easier to incorporate segments of the data into higher level reports through local word processors than if the data were retained on the central system. Further data processing may also be easier with spreadsheets and similar microcomputer-based software products. On the downside, however, the information will almost certainly not be protected the same way on the micro as it was or would be on the mainframe. The institution can no longer guarantee the integrity of the data. And decisions may be made based on out-of-date data. If the data are retained too long by an end user, excessive demands for ever larger amounts of storage on the micro may be generated.

A final illustration of saving significant amounts of paper in an organization is with electronic mail (EMail). It is clearly more costly to distribute paper memoranda than it is to use EMail. Like the report-distribution issue, EMail systems can be either centralized or distributed. Since many organizations still use many dumb terminals as well as microcomputer-based workstations, some combination of both might be necessary. Nevertheless, retaining memoranda on a micro, rather than in paper form, has many distinct advantages for the recipient. With software currently on the market it is possible to store and retrieve such documents easily, although as with any filing system it takes some discipline.

In this section I have tried to give a sense of the current state of the art in information distribution. I have not even mentioned public distribution of documents such as newspapers, magazines, or even books. The technology for this is also coming into place and may become cost-effective. Nor have I mentioned the need for various groups of people to move documents. Lawyers, physicians, and researchers of all kinds have frequent need to transfer manuscripts, data, and other documents across the street, across the nation, or across the world. Be that as it may, the thing that binds all these applications is that none is only, or even primarily, transaction or interactively oriented. Instead, they all involve file transfer, sometimes large-scale file transfers. Clearly the issue of error-free file transfer, and the protocols that make this possible, constitute a major area of concern for networking in the 1990s.

Understanding the Information

Just getting a file transferred does not solve the problems, of course. The data must be manipulated once received. It is desirable, therefore, to think about application-to-application transfers instead of machine-to-machine methods. Machine-to-machine document distribution has been around for a long time, but it is hardly transparent to the user. The ideal system would be one sufficiently universal so that any information transferred would be placed in a format most appropriate for the retrieval, inspection, and manipulation of those data, whether they were text or numbers, memos, books, or bibliographic materials. Such universality may not be possible, and it is not available today. With appropriate integration of micro and mainframe products, however, a high degree of transparency is possible.

Open Issues

A major problem confronting enterprise computing is software. The software problem revolves around both a better understanding of user needs and demands and the cost of producing adequate solutions. An IBM solution and a DEC solution and an HP (Hewlett-Packard) solution, or some other set of solutions, is not needed. Solutions should be driven by the real needs of the organizations that pay for the commodities and services. Unfortunately it is easier to make these assertions than to do anything about them. Part of the problem is that different organizations have different needs. Another part of the problem is that with enough money organizations can produce their own solutions, but rarely is that much money available. Especially when funding for networking solutions is competing with funding for more explicit software projects. Other unresolved issues include the user interface and management issues.

The User Interface

The typical user interface for the micro-to-mainframe connection was, through the 1980s, not very friendly. It frequently took several steps, started by the user, to move a file from one computer to another. Using the micro as a terminal emulator was only slightly more friendly. One approach is to standardize on the micro's DOS (disk operating system) as the standard environment, or on the mainframe system as the standard. From that point it will be necessary to provide access to the full facilities of the other system. Any effort to provide a standard environment will require software development at both the mainframe and micro, or it will require a more comprehensive perspective on the problem than that evidenced by most commercial software developers.

Several manufacturers of microcomputer LANs or LAN software have chosen to have the remote file server appear as simply another disk drive to the user. Thus, drives A: and B: may be local floppy disks; C: a local hard disk; and G: and Z: remote virtual disks. Once the software is installed, therefore, except for having to know how to access a resource on some disk drive, the user need not be concerned with much else. Some micro-to-mainframe link software is taking a similar approach. It may not be possible to build an appropriate shell around a mainframe operating environment, but to the extent it is possible, this would seem to be a promising approach. With the advent of the 1990s, industry thinking has turned to the graphical user interface (GUI) as the appropriate way of allowing end users to access computer resources. There is, indeed, something elegant in thinking that the appropriate way to transfer a file from one network node to another is to drag an icon from one dialog box to another. While not all the components are available for a seamless GUI in a complex network environment, the time is not far off when such an interface will be in place.

An alternative to dealing with an OS-level micro-to-mainframe interface is the direction taken by several software developers: An application-to-application link. Some things are simplified for the user in an application-to-application link, but once into the application, getting to the link may be something else. In any event, forging a user-friendly micro-to-mainframe connection is one current challenge for software developers.

Management Systems for EWC

The idea of distributed computing is fundamental to the building of enterprise-wide systems. Distributed computing is to be distinguished from decentralized computing, for they are not the same thing. The terms are confused because of the movement in the 1980s to place more computing responsibility on the end user rather than a central computing center trying to do everything. If computing is decentralized, it is just that, and nothing more. A company with several plants, each having its own computer facility, has decentralized computing. Even if these computers are linked together for convenience, but without a systematic approach to distributing computing, it is still a decentralized system.

In contrast to the decentralized system, distributed or cooperative computing implies that computing will take place at appropriate points among a set of coordinated computers. Systematic program-to-program links, or archiving data on a mainframe with reporting on a micro, is truly distributed computing. Distribution may be loose or it may be tight, but it requires a different perspective on networking and software development for the micro-to-mainframe link than is true of a decentralized approach. It does, indeed, imply a system. Systems that support an organization might be distributed, but probably should not be decentralized.

With enterprise computing/networking, the multivendor environment is not the enemy but an opportunity. Unfortunately, even though vendors such as IBM and DEC imply that they can handle different vendors, they tend to support only their own devices adequately. IBM, for example, continues to use its established proprietary management interfaces to monitor and control its own products. "Meanwhile," according to Herman, "there are a number of standards being developed for different kinds of network and system environments, including IEEE LANs, TCP/IP internets, OSI backbones, and Unix operating systems."[5]

One perplexing problem to overcome is the way to confront a multivendor computing environment. This is probably more of a problem than a multivendor network, since there are some standards for at least components of networks. But, for organizations with PCs and mainframes from several different vendors, the problem of integration is difficult. Similarly, if software systems are used for which there is no independent "third-party" support, an organization may be at the mercy of its primary software vendor. This is all well and good if the system has been constructed to add facilities, but may be problematic if growth is unavailable or difficult to manage. The moral of all this is that when major system software and hardware is being selected, the long-term implications of those selections must be weighed, if any long-term trends are apparent.

Inadequate or Nonexistent Standards

The development of file transfer protocol standards would help software manufacturers pursue many of the developments described or alluded to throughout this book. Such standards should include not only an approach to packetizing data, but should also include an approach to the interface between the computer system and the application software. Although the X.PC file transfer protocol is too specialized to be even a de facto standard, the approach used in its development is good. The concept of a standard, memory-resident module that contains the channel between the application and the hardware communications adapter, as well as the packet assembler/disassembler, seems like one ideal solution.

The construction of the packet should provide for transparent data transfer completely independent of the physical network over which the data are passed. Similar concepts could be put to work on mainframes as well as micros. The result would be a uniform set of system calls that any software developer might write. On the PC end, the module could also include the software necessary to guide the PC's DOS to the communications interface through a virtual disk. Unfortunately, standards do not guarantee consistent use by different manufacturers. Nowhere is this more apparent than with implementations of the RS232C standard. But standards can help, and a standard data-transfer packet definition, along with a standard access method at both the PC and mainframe end, could go a long way toward encouraging the software development necessary for good micro-to-mainframe connections.

Finding the "Right" Solution for the Enterprise

Considering the multitude of micro and mainframe application and communications products, not to mention the number of hardware manufacturers, there is no "right" micro-to-mainframe solution. But there are solutions. To find the appropriate solution it is necessary to look at the issue systematically in a specific local context. Some of the questions that must be answered include broad ones: "What do we want to accomplish?" "What do we want the user interface to look like?" "Are we willing to commit the resources to get it done?" Then determine what products are available for accomplishing the goals.

On the mainframe end, analysis must include an evaluation of existing teleprocessing monitors or access methods. On the micro end, organizations will need to evaluate what products they need for their standard PC, if there is a standard. And they must come to some understanding of the role of the physical network at their disposal. Once that analysis has been accomplished organizations may find that they can use available software or that they must write their own. Either way, it will probably not be an inexpensive solution.

Facing the Organizational Problem

Because the loud demand for a good micro-to-mainframe connection is of relatively recent origin, many organizations have not yet recognized either the importance of the demand or the need to budget for the project. The budgetary problem will, of course, probably be resolved if the importance of the issue is recognized. Part of the problem in many organizations is that although lip service is paid to making cost savings, there is no real commitment if it requires changes in the way things are done. In every organization there is the tendency to respond to the "squeaky wheel" rather than to larger, general problems that may have few or no lobbyists for the service. Another part of the problem is simply convincing management that the micro-to-mainframe link has no simple solution. This attitude is the downside of the wide deployment of micros. Many people who have used micros for some period of time have used terminal emulators to download sequential datasets and saved them locally. If that was all there was to the problem, there would be no problem. That simpleminded approach does not begin to touch the needs of many people.

There are other organizational problems, as well. Software and hardware decisions made before the demand for a micro-to-mainframe connection became important may limit the range of solutions. Those decisions may preclude some solutions or require a single-vendor solution when something else may be technologically better. Prior decisions may be a hindrance because those decisions are likely to have resulted in enough investments of time and money to make a change in direction impossible.

On the other hand, large organizations, unlike smaller ones, may have the resources and talent to build solutions unique to that organization.

EWC and You

Is it possible to build an effective, user-friendly micro-to-mainframe connection? Maybe. Is it necessary to build a connection useful to end users? Without question. It is necessary, however, to approach the problem systematically by considering the purposes for the connection. In that sense it is desirable to look at the connection as a part of a growing network for distributed processing. Instead of thinking about the connection as a simple problem of uploading or downloading data, recognize that the micro-to-mainframe connection requires an application-to-application or program-to-program system. Recognize also that such a system will have to work as well for naive computer users as it does for computer professionals. Achieving that objective will move computing a step closer to realizing the value of both micros and mainframes in the contemporary computing environment.

Notes

1. Thomas W. Madron, *Micro–Mainframe Connection* (Indianapolis, IN: Howard W. Sams & Co., 1987), p. 213.
2. James Herman, "Enterprise Management Vendors Shoot It Out," *Data Communications,* Vol. 19, No. 14, Nov. 1990, p. 92.
3. See, for example, Cheryl Snapp, "Cerberus on the Enterprise," *LAN Times,* Vol. 6, No. 8, Aug. 1989, p. 85(2).
4. Note that even in the 1990s this aspect of computing is still important. See, for example, Charles C. Thomas, Jr., "Hosts and PCs Profit by Sharing," *Data Communications,* Vol. 19, No. 7, June 1990, pp. 121ff.
5. Herman, "Enterprise Management Vendors Shoot It Out," p. 94.

Glossary

Because many of the terms used in this book may be unfamiliar to the more casual reader, a short glossary is provided. The glossary generally follows definitions given in the text and follows common industry sources.

acceptable risk—in *risk analysis:* An assessment that an activity or system meets minimum requirements of security directives.

access control—in a network or its components: The tasks performed by hardware, software, and administrative controls to monitor a system operation, ensure data integrity, perform user identification, record system access and changes, and grant access to users.

active threats—unauthorized use of a device attached to a communications facility to alter transmitting data or control signals or to generate spurious data or control signals.

amplifier—in a broadband system, a device for strengthening the radio frequency signal to a level needed by other devices on the system.

answer modem—see modem.

ASCII—American (National) Standard Code for Information Interchange, X3.4-1968. A seven-bit-plus parity code established by the American National Standards Institute to achieve compatibility among data services and consisting of 96 displayed upper- and lowercase characters and 32 nondisplayed control codes.

asynchronous transmission—a mode of data-communications transmission in which time intervals between transmitted characters may be of unequal length. The transmission is controlled by start and stop elements at the beginning and end of each character; hence it is also called start-stop transmission.

attachment unit interface (AUI)—the cable, connectors, and transmission circuitry used to interconnect the physical signaling (PLS) sublayer and MAU (medium attachment unit).

authentication—(1) ensuring that a message is genuine, has arrived exactly as it was sent, and came from the stated source; (2) verifying the identity of an individual, such as a person at a remote terminal or the sender of a message. *Data origin authentication* is the corroboration that the source of data received is as claimed. *Peer-entity authentication* is the corroboration that a peer entity in an association is the one claimed.

bandwidth—the range of frequencies assigned to a channel or system. The difference expressed in Hertz between the highest and lowest frequencies of a band.

baseband (signaling)—transmission of a signal at its original frequencies, that is, unmodulated.

batch—a group of records or programs that is considered a single unit for processing on a computer.

batch processing—a technique in which a number of data transactions are collected over a period of time and aggregated for sequential processing.

baud—a unit of transmission speed equal to the number of discrete conditions or signal events per second. Baud is the same as "bits per second" only if each signal event represents exactly one bit, although the two terms are often incorrectly used interchangeably.

bisynchronous transmission—binary synchronous (bisync) transmission. Data transmission in which synchronization of characters is controlled by timing signals generated at the sending and receiving stations, in contrast to asynchronous transmission.

bit-mapped graphics—a method of representing data in a computer for display in which each dot on the screen is mapped to a unit of data in memory.

block—a group of digits, characters, or words that are held in one section of an input/output medium and handled as a unit, such as the data recorded between interblock gaps on a magnetic tape or a data unit being transmitted over a data-communications system; a block may or may not contain control information. A group of N-ary digits, transmitted as a unit. An encoding procedure is generally applied to the group of bits or N-ary digits for error-control purposes.

b/s (bits per second)—see baud.

BNC-connector—a 50-Ohm BNC-series coaxial cable connector of the kind commonly found on RF equipment.

BR—the bit-rate of data throughput on the trunk coaxial medium expressed in hertz.

branch cable—the AUI cable interconnecting the data terminal equipment (DTE) and MAU (medium attachment unit) system components.

bridge—the hardware and software necessary for two networks using the same or similar technology to communicate; more specifically, the hardware and software necessary to link segments of the same or similar networks at the Data-Link Layer of the OSI Reference Model, (that is, a MAC Level bridge; a router that connects two or more networks and forwards packets among them). Usually, bridges operate at the physical network level. Bridges differ from repeaters because bridges store and forward complete packets, while repeaters forward electrical signals.

broadband—a communications channel having a bandwidth characterized by high data-transmission speeds (10,000 to 500,000 bits per second). Often used when describing communications systems based on cable television technology. In the 802 standards, a system whereby information is encoded, modulated onto a carrier, and band-pass filtered or otherwise constrained to occupy only a limited frequency spectrum on the coaxial transmission medium. Many information signals can be present on the medium at the same time without disruption, provided that they all occupy nonoverlapping frequency regions within the cable system's range of frequency transport.

bus—the organization of electrical paths within a circuit. A specific bus, such as the S-100, provides a standard definition for specific paths.

carrier sense—the signal provided by the Physical Layer to the access sublayer to indicate that one or more stations are currently transmitting on the trunk cable.

CATV—Community Antenna Television. See broadband.

CCITT—Consultative Committee International Telegraph and Telephone. An organization established by the United Nations to develop worldwide standards for communications technology, as for example *protocols* to be used by devices exchanging data.

central processing unit—see CPU.

centralized network—a computer network with a central processing node through which all data and communications flow.

Centronics—a manufacturer of computer printers. Centronics pioneered the use of a parallel interface between printers and computers, and that interface, using Centronic standards, is sometimes referred to as a Centronics parallel interface.

character user interface (CUI)—classical character-based system for computer/human communications.

checksum—a fixed-length block produced as a function of every bit in an encrypted message; a summation of a set of data items for error detection; a sum of digits or bits used to verify the integrity of data.

cipher—an algorithm for disguising information according to a logical principle by working within the elements of whatever alphabet is in use, such as by shift substitution of the letters of the alphabet with other letters a certain number of places toward the beginning or end of the alphabet. Not to be confused with a *code*.

ciphertext—encrypted text that cannot be read without decryption; data in its encrypted form that is cryptologically protected; the opposite of *plaintext* or *cleartext*.

client–server—the model of interaction in a distributed system in which a program at one site sends a request to a program at another site and awaits a response. The requesting program is called a client; the program satisfying the request is called the server. It is usually easier to build client software than server software.

code—a technique by which the basic elements of language, such as syllables, words, phrases, sentences, and paragraphs, are disguised through being replaced by other, usually shorter, arbitrarily selected language elements, requiring a codebook (table) for translation. A term not generally used in relation to encryption. Not to be confused with cipher.

collision—multiple concurrent transmission on the cable resulting in garbled data.

command languages—software in which commands are typed in, rather than selected from, a set displayed on the screen.

communications—see data communications. Transmission of intelligence between points of origin and reception without altering the sequence or structure of the information content.

communications network—the total network of devices and transmission media (radio, cables, et cetera) necessary to transmit and receive intelligence.

communications security (COMSEC)—the protection resulting from the application of cryptosecurity, transmission security, and emission security measures to telecommunications and from the application of physical security measures to communications security information. These measures are taken to deny unauthorized persons information of value that might be derived from the possession and study of such telecommunications. COMSEC includes: 1. Cryptosecurity: The component of COMSEC that results from the provision of technically sound cryptosystems and their proper use. 2. Transmission security: The component of COMSEC that results from all measures designed to protect transmissions from interception and exploitation by means other than cryptanalysis. 3. Emission security: The component of COMSEC that results from all measures taken to deny unauthorized persons information of value that might be derived from intercept and analysis of compromising emanations from cryptoequipment and telecommunications systems. 4. Physical security: The component of COMSEC that results from all physical measures necessary to safeguard classified equipment, material, and documents from access thereto or observation thereof by unauthorized persons.

communications security equipment—equipment designed to provide security to telecommunications by converting information to a form unintelligible to an unauthorized interceptor and by reconverting such information to its original form for authorized recipients; also, equipment designed specifically to aid in, or as an essential element of, the conversion process. COMSEC equipment is cryptoequipment, cryptoancillary equipment, cryptoproduction equipment, and authentication equipment.

computer conferencing—a process for holding group discussions through the use of a computer network.

computer network—one or more computers linked with users or each other via a communications network.

confidentiality—the property that information is not made available or disclosed to unauthorized individuals, entities, or processes.

connectionless applications—those applications that require routing services but do not require connection-oriented services.

connectionless service—a class of service that does not establish a virtual or logical connection and does not guarantee that data-units will be delivered or be delivered in the proper order. Connectionless services are flexible, robust, and provide connectionless application support.

connection-oriented services—services that establish a virtual connection that appears to the user as an actual end-to-end circuit. Sometimes called a virtual circuit or virtual connection. See also *virtual circuit*.

connectivity—in a local area network, the ability of any device attached to the distribution system to establish a session with any other device.

CP/M—Control Program for Microcomputers. Manufactured and marketed by Digital Research, Inc.

CPU—Central Processing Unit. The "brain" of the general-purpose computer that controls the interpretation and execution of instructions. The CPU does not include interfaces, main memory, or peripherals.

cryptochannel—a complete system of cryptocommunications between two or more holders. The basic unit for naval cryptographic communication. It includes: (a) The cryptographic aids prescribed; (b) The holders thereof; (c) The indicators or other means of identification; (d) The area or areas in which effective; (e) The special purpose, if any, for which provided; and (f) Pertinent notes as to distribution, usage, et cetera. A cryptochannel is analogous to a radio circuit.

cryptogram—the ciphertext.

crypto-information—information that would make a significant contribution to the cryptanalytic solution of encrypted text or a cryptosystem.

cryptology—the science that investigates hidden, disguised, or encrypted communications. It embraces communications security and communications intelligence.

cryptomaterial—all material, including documents, devices, or equipment, that contains crypto-information and is essential to the encryption, decryption, or authentication of telecommunications.

CSMA/CD—Carrier Sense Multiple Access with Collision Detection. A network access method for managing collisions of data packets.

CUI—see character user interface.

cursor—a position indicator frequently employed in video (CRT or VDT) output devices or terminals to indicate a character to be corrected or a position in which data is to be entered.

cyclic redundancy check (CRC)—an algorithm designed to generate a check field used to guard against errors in data transmission; the check field is often generated by taking the remainder after dividing all the serialized bits in a block of data by a predetermined binary number.

database—a nonredundant collection of inter-related data items processable by one or more applications.

data communications—the transmission and reception of data, often including operations such as coding, decoding, and validation.

data encryption standard (DES)—an algorithm to be implemented in electronic hardware devices and used for the cryptographic protection of digital, binary-coded information. For the relevant publications see "Data Encryption Standard," *Federal Information Processing Standard (FIPS) Publication 46*, 1977 January 15, also published as *American National Standard Data Encryption Algorithm*, American National Standards Institute, Inc., December 30, 1980, and supplemented with "DES Modes of Operation," *Federal Information Processing Standard (FIPS) Publication 81*, 1980 December 2; "Telecommunications: Interoperability and Security Requirements for Use of the Data Encryption Standard in the Physical Layer of Data Communications," *Federal Standard of the General Services Administration*, August 3, 1983, FED-STD-1026; "Telecommunications: General Security Requirements for Equipment Using the Data Encryption Standard," *Federal Standard of the General Services Administration*, April 14, 1982, FED-STD-1027; and "Telecommunications: Interoperability and Security Requirements for Use of the Data Encryption Standard with CCITT Group 3 Facsimile Equipment," *Federal Standard of the General Services Administration*, April 4, 1985, FED-STD-1028.

data file—a collection of related data records organized in a specific manner. In large systems, data files are gradually being replaced by databases in order to limit redundancy and improve reliability and timeliness.

datagram—a finite-length packet with sufficient information to be independently routed from source to destination without reliance on previous transmissions; typically does not involve end-to-end session establishment and may or may not entail delivery confirmation acknowledgement.

datagram service—a service that establishes a datagram-based connection between peer entities. In OSI parlance this type of service is called a *connectionless service*.

data link—an assembly of two or more terminal installations and the interconnecting communications channel operating according to a particular method that permits information to be exchanged.

data-link layer—the conceptual layer of control or processing logic existing in the hierarchical structure of a station that is responsible for maintaining control of the data link.

data-management system—a system that provides the necessary procedures and programs to collect, organize, and maintain data files or databases.

data security—procedures and actions designed to prevent the unauthorized disclosure, transfer, modification, or destruction, whether accidental or intentional, of data.

DB-25—a 25-pin connector commonly used in the United States as the connector of choice for the RS-232-C serial interface standard.

dialog box—a rectangle that appears onscreen, prompting the user to enter data or mutually exclusive selection.

digital signature—a number depending on all the bits of a message and also on a secret key. Its correctness can be verified by using a public key (unlike an authenticator, which needs a secret key for its verification).

disk storage (disc storage)—information recording on continuously rotating magnetic platters. Storage may be either sequential or random access.

distributed data processing (DDP)—an organization of information processing such that both processing and data may be distributed over a number of different machines in one or more locations.

distributed network—a network configuration in which all node pairs are connected either directly, or through redundant paths through intermediate nodes.

DOS (Disk Operating System)—a general term for the operating system used on computers using disk drives. See also, operating system.

download—the ability of a communications device (usually a microcomputer acting as an intelligent terminal) to load data from another device or computer to itself, saving the data on a local disk or tape.

EDI—see electronic data interchange.

electronic data interchange (EDI)—the intercompany, computer-to-computer exchange of business documents in standard formats.

electronic mail (EMail)—a system to send messages between or among users of a computer network and the programs necessary to support such message transfers.

emulator, terminal—see terminal emulator.

encryption—the translation of one character string into another by means of a cypher, translation table, or algorithm in order to render the information contained therein meaningless to anyone who does not possess the decoding mechanism. It is the reverse of *de*cryption.

encryption algorithm—a group of mathematically expressed rules that render information unintelligible by producing a series of changes through the use of variable elements controlled by the application of a key to the normal representation of the information.

end-to-end encryption—the encryption of data in a communications network at the point of origin with decryption occurring at the final destination point.

envelope—a group of binary digits formed by a byte augmented by a number of additional bits that are required for the operation of the data network; the boundary of a family of curves obtained by varying a parameter of a wave.

Ethernet—a local area network and its associated protocol developed by (but not limited to) Xerox. Ethernet is a baseband system.

FAX (facsimile)—devices that consist of three basic components: an image scanner, a FAX modem, and a printer. Often integrated in a single unit with each FAX file treated as a cohesive image (rather than character data).

F-connector—a 75-Ohm F-series coaxial cable connector of the kind commonly found on consumer television and video equipment.

fiber optics—a technology for transmitting information via light waves through a fine filament. Signals are encoded by varying some characteristic of the light waves generated by a low-powered laser. Output is sent through a light-conducting fiber to a receiving device that decodes the signal.

floppy disks—magnetic, low cost, flexible data disks (or diskettes) usually either 5.25 inches or 8 inches in diameter.

flow control—a speed matching technique used in data communications to prevent receiving devices from overflow, thus losing data.

FEP (Front End Processor)—a communications device used for entry into a computer system. The FEP typically provides either or both asynchronous or synchronous ports for the system.

frame—in data transmission, the sequence of contiguous bits bracketed by and including beginning and ending flag sequences. A typical frame might consist of a specified number of bits between flags and contain an address field, a control field, and a frame-check sequence. A frame may or may not include an information field. A transmission unit that carries a protocol data unit (PDU).

gateway—the hardware and software necessary to make two technologically different networks communicate with one another; a gateway provides protocol conversion from one network architecture to another and may, therefore, use all seven layers of the OSI Reference Model; a special purpose, dedicated computer that attaches to two or more networks and routes packets from one to the other. The term is loosely applied to any machine that transfers information from one network to another, as in *mail gateway*.

graphical user interface (GUI)—a means for computer/human communications characterized by ease of use, interaction, and intuitive feel providing visual, direct, immediate feedback in a WYSIWYG environment.

GUI—see graphical user interface.

HDLC—Hierarchical Data Link Control: A highly structured set of standards governing the means by which unlike devices can communicate with each other on large data-communications networks.

headend—in a broadband local area network or CATV system, the point at which a signal processor upconverts a signal from a low inbound channel to a high outbound channel.

Hertz—a unit of frequency equal to one cycle per second. Cycles are referred to as Hertz in honor of the experimenter Heinrich Hertz. Abbreviated as Hz.

high-split—in a broadband system the organization of the spectrum that places the guard band at about 190 MHz. The midsplit system offers the greatest amount of spectrum for return path channels (14 channels).

IBM—International Business Machines: One of the primary manufacturers of computer equipment (usually though not exclusively large-scale equipment).

IEEE—Institute of Electrical and Electronic Engineers.

icon—a small graphic image on a computer screen that represents a function or program.

impedance—in a circuit, the opposition that circuit elements present to the flow of alternating current. The impedance includes both resistance and reactance.

integrity (of data)—the property that data have not been altered or destroyed in an unauthorized manner.

interactive processing—processing in which transactions are processed one at a time, often eliciting a response from a user before proceeding. An interactive system may be conversational, implying continuous dialogue between the user and the system. Contrast with batch processing.

interface—a shared boundary between system elements defined by common physical interconnections, signals, and meanings of interchanged signals.

ISO/OSI—International Standards Organization Open Systems Interface: A seven-tiered network model.

key—a piece of digital information that interacts with cryption algorithms to control cryption of information and, thus, must be protected from disclosure.

key distribution center (KDC)—the element in a system that generates and distributes cryptographic key variables.

key generator—an object for encrypting-key generation.

key hashing—the method in which a long key is converted to a native key for use in the encryption/decryption process. Each number or letter of the long key helps to create each digital bit of the native key.

key management—control of key selection and key distribution in a cryptographic system.

key notarization—a method for encrypting information at a terminal site before transmission to a host computer over communications media that might not be secure. It is necessary for the host and the terminal to maintain the same encryption key and algorithm. This is frequently accomplished by "downloading" (sending information) from the host to the terminal on key changes. The downloaded information must also be encrypted.

kilohertz—1,000 Hertz. See Hertz.

line extender—in a broadband system, an amplifier used to boost signal strength, usually within a building.

link encryption—application of on-line crypto-operations to a communications-system link so that all information passing over the link is encrypted completely. The term also refers to end-to-end encryption within each link in a communications network.

LLC—see logical link control.

local area network (LAN)—a computer and communications network that covers a limited geographical area, allows every node to communicate with every other node, and does not require a central node or processor.

logical link control (LLC)—that part of a data station that supports the logical link control functions of one or more logical links.

logical record—a collection of items independent of their physical environment. Portions of the same logical record may be located in different physical records.

MAC—see medium access control or message authentication code.

mainframe computer—a large-scale computing system.

manager's workstation—a microcomputer containing an integrated package of software designed to improve the productivity of managers. A workstation will usually, though not exclusively, include a word processor, a spread sheet program, a communications program, and a data manager.

Manchester encoding—a means by which separate data and clock signals can be combined into a single, self-synchronizable data stream, suitable for transmission on a serial channel.

manipulation detection code—see MDC.

masquerading—the attempt to gain access to a system by posing as an authorized client or host.

master–slave computer system—a computer system consisting of a master computer connected to one or more slave computers; the master computer provides the scheduling function and jobs to the slave computer(s).

MDC—manipulation (modification) detection code: A redundancy check field included in the plaintext of a chain before encipherment, so that changes to the ciphertext (an active attack) will be detected.

medium access control (MAC)—the portion of the IEEE 802 data station that controls and mediates the access to the medium.

medium attachment unit (MAU)—the portion of the physical layer between the MDI and AUI that interconnects the trunk cable to the branch cable and contains the electronics that send, receive, and manage the encoded signals impressed on, and recovered from, the trunk cable.

medium dependent interface (MDI)—the mechanical and electrical interface between the trunk cable medium and the MAU.

menu—a multiple choice list of procedures or programs to be executed; a list of command options currently available to the computer user and displayed onscreen.

menu trees—successions of menu displays that become more detailed.

message authentication code (MAC)—a method by which cryptographic check digits are appended to the message. They pertain to the transaction type, transaction account number, destination, and point of origin in computer security. Specifically, by using MAC, messages without the additional check digits are rejected by the computer system, and valid transactions cannot be modified without detection.

microcomputer—a computer system of limited physical size and in former times limited in speed and address capacity. Usually, though not exclusively, a single-user computer.

microprocessor—the central processing unit of a microcomputer. The microprocessor contains the logical elements for manipulating data and performing arithmetic or logical operations on the microcomputer.

midsplit—in a broadband system the organization of the spectrum that places the guard band at about 140 MHz. The midsplit system offers a substantial amount of spectrum for return path channels (14 channels).

minicomputer—a computer system, usually a timesharing system, sometimes faster than microcomputers but not as fast as large main-frame computers.

modem—MODulator/DEModulator. A device that modulates and demodulates signals transmitted over communications facilities. A modem is sometimes called a data set.

modification detection code—see MDC.

multimedia—software that permits a mix of text, speech, and static and dynamic visual images.

multitasking—the ability of a computer to perform two or more functions (tasks) concurrently.

multiuser system—a system where two or more people, using different access systems (terminals), can access one computer concurrently or simultaneously. Such a system must have multitasking capabilities.

National Institute of Standards and Technology—see NIST.

native key—the internal key (string of bits) that is required by the cryption algorithm.

network—see also communications network and/or computer network. (1) A system of interconnected computer systems and terminals; (2) a series of points connected by communications channels; (3) the structure of relationships among a project's activities, tasks, and events.

NIST—National Institute of Standards and Technology: Formerly (prior to 1988) the National Bureau of Standards (NBS) of the U.S. government.

node—any station, terminal, computer or other device in a computer network.

notarization—the verification (authentication) of a message by a trusted third party similar in logic to classic notarization procedures; normally an automated procedure.

octet—a bit-oriented element that consists of eight contiguous binary bits.

office automation—refers to efforts to provide automation for common office tasks, including word processing, filing, record keeping, and other office chores.

off-the-shelf—production items that are available from current stock and need not be either newly purchased or immediately manufactured. Also relates to computer software or equipment that can be used by customers with little or no adaptation, thereby saving the time and expense of developing their own.

on-line processing—a general data processing term concerning access to computers, in which the input data enters the computer directly from the point of origin or in which output data is transmitted directly to where it is used.

operating system (OS)—a program that manages the hardware and software environment of a computing system.

originate-only-modem—a modem that can originate data communications, but which cannot answer a call from another device.

outlet—access point, with an appropriate connector, to a communications medium.

packet—a block of data for data transmission. Each packet contains control information, such as routing, address, error control, and data; a group of data and control characters in a specified format, transferred as a whole; a group of binary digits, including data and call control signals, which is switched as a composite whole; the data, all control signals, and possibly error-control information are arranged in a specific format.

packet switching—a discipline for controlling and moving messages in a large data-communications network. Each message is handled as a complete unit containing the addresses of the recipient and the originator.

passive threats—monitoring and/or recording data while data are being transferred over a communications facility; with *release of message contents* an attacker can read user data in messages; with *traffic analysis* the attacker can read user packet headers to identify source and destination information as well as the length and frequency of messages. See also, threats, active threats.

passphrase—a phrase used instead of a password to control user access.

password—a unique word or string of characters used to authenticate an identity. A program, computer operator, or user may be required to submit a password to meet security requirements before gaining access to data. The password is confidential, as opposed to the user identification.

PBX/PABX—private branch exchange or private automated branch exchange. A switching network for voice or data.

peer protocol—the sequence of message exchanges between two entities in the same layer that use the services of the underlying layers to effect the successful transfer of data and/or control information from one location to another location.

peer systems—computer/communication systems capable of performing equal or comparable tasks within defined limits or parameters.

peripheral—computer equipment external to the CPU performing a wide variety of input and output functions.

personal computer (PC)—an alternative name for a microcomputer, suggesting that the computer is to be used for personal and individual work production or entertainment.

personal identification number (PIN)—a sequence of decimal digits (usually four, five, or six) used to verify the identity of the holder of a bank card; a kind of password.

physical record—a basic unit of data that is read or written by a single input/output command to the computer.

plaintext—text that has not been encrypted (or has been decrypted) and can be easily read or acted upon.

program—a set of instructions in a programming language used to define an operation, or set of operations, to a computer.

protocol—a formal set of conventions governing the format and relative timing of message exchange in a communications network.

protocol data unit (PDU)—the sequence of contiguous octets delivered as a unit from or to the MAC sublayer. A valid LLC PDU is at least three octets long, and contains two address fields and a control field. A PDU may or may not include an additional information field.

public key—a cryptographic key used for encipherment but not usable for decipherment. It is therefore possible to make this key public.

public key cryptosystem—an encryption methodology that depends on two keys: A public key—made available to anyone who wants to encrypt information—is used for the encryption process, and a private key—known only to the owner—is used for the decryption process.

pull-down menu—a menu that appears on-screen when accessed by a cursor placed on a box or bar at the top of the display.

questionnaire—a method of identity verification that makes use of information known to the authorized user but unlikely to be known to others.

RAM—Random Access Memory: Semiconductor memory devices used in the construction of computers. The time required to obtain data is independent of the location.

reliability—in data communications or computer equipment, the extent to which hardware or software operates in a repeatable manner, often characterized (for hardware) as a low mean-time-between-failures.

remote access—pertaining to communication with a computer by a terminal distant from the computer.

remote batch terminal (RBT)—a terminal used for entering jobs and data into a computer from a remote site for later batch processing.

remote job entry (RJE)—input of a batch job from a remote site and receipt of output via a line printer or other device at a remote site.

repeater—a device used to extend the length, topology, or interconnectivity of the physical medium beyond that imposed by a single segment, up to the maximum allowable end-to-end trunk transmission line length by copying electrical signals from one network segment to another. Because repeaters transfer electrical impulses rather than data packets they may also transfer noise.

risk analysis—a process of studying system assets and vulnerabilities to determine an expected loss from harmful events, based upon probabilities of occurrence of those harmful events. The object of risk analysis is to determine the degree of acceptability of each risk to system operation.

ROM—Read Only Memory: A memory device used in computers that cannot be altered during normal computer use. Normally a semiconductor device.

router—the hardware and software necessary to link two subnetworks of the same network together; the hardware and software necessary to link two subnetworks at the Network Layer of the OSI Reference Model; any machine responsible for making decisions about which of several paths network traffic will follow. At the lowest level, a physical network bridge is a router because it chooses whether to pass packets from one physical wire to another. Within a long-haul network, each individual packet switch is a router because it chooses routes for individual packets. In the Internet, each IP gateway is a router because it uses IP destination addresses to choose routes.

security—see also, data security, communications security. The state of certainty that computerized data and program files cannot be accessed, obtained, or modified by unauthorized personnel or the computer or its programs. Security is implemented by restricting the physical area around the computer system to authorized personnel, using special software, and the security built into the operating procedure of the computer.

security mechanisms—operating procedures, hardware and software features, management procedures, and any combinations of these that are designed to detect and prevent either passive or active threats on any component of an information system.

security service—activity or provision of an activity that enhances the security of information systems and an organization's information transfer. In the OSI Reference Model the defined services consist of five groups: confidentiality, authentication, integrity, nonrepudiation, and access control.

security threat—any action that compromises the security of information owned by an organization. See also, active threat, passive threat.

session—active connection of one device to another over a communications system, during which interactions do or can occur.

socket—the abstraction provided by Berkeley 4.3 BSD UNIX that allows a process to access the Internet. A process opens a socket, specifies the service desired (for example, reliable stream delivery), binds the socket to a specific destination, and then sends or receives data. While the functional characteristics remain as defined, the concept has been generalized to include processes that access networks other than Internet.

software—a term used to contrast computer programs with the "iron," or hardware, of a computer system.

spectrum—a range of wave lengths usually applied to radio frequencies.

spreadsheet programs—computer programs that allow data to be entered as elements of a table or matrix with rows and columns and to manipulate the data. Programs widely available on microcomputers are Lotus 1-2-3 and SUPERCALC.

start-stop transmission—see asynchronous transmission.

station—a physical device that may be attached to a shared medium local area network for transmitting and receiving information on that shared medium.

subsplit—in a broadband system the organization of the spectrum that places the guard band at about 40 MHz. The subsplit system offers the least amount of spectrum for return path channels (four channels).

tap—a device that allows an exit from a main line of a communications system.

teletex—one-way transmission of data via a television system.

terminal—a device that allows input and output of data to a computer. The term is most frequently used in conjunction with a device that has a keyboard for data entry and either a printer or a video tube for displaying data.

terminal emulator—a software or software/hardware system for microcomputers that allows the micro to behave like some specified terminal, such as a DEC VT100 or an IBM 3278/79.

text editor—a program that provides flexible editing facilities on a computer for the purpose of allowing data entry from a keyboard terminal without regard for the eventual format or medium for publication. With a text editor, data (text, copy, or what have you) can be edited easily and quickly.

text formatter—a program for reading a data file created with a text editor for transforming the raw file into a neatly formatted listing.

threats—threats to an information system or its networks may be either *active* or *passive*. See also, active threats, passive threats.

token—the symbol of authority that is passed between stations using a token access method to indicate which station is currently in control of the medium.

token passing—a collision avoidance technique in which each station is polled and must pass the poll along.

transaction processing—a style of data processing in which files are updated and results generated immediately as a result of data entry.

trunk cable—the trunk (usually coaxial) cable system.

turn-key system—a system in which the manufacturer or distributor takes full responsibility for complete system design and installation, and supplies all necessary hardware, software, and documentation.

twisted pair—the two wires of a signaling circuit, twisted around each other to minimize the effects of inductance.

Unix—a multitasking, multiuser operating system developed by Ken Thompson, Dennis Ritchie, and coworkers at Bell Laboratories (AT&T); a powerful operating system implemented on a wide variety of computers from mainframes to microcomputers.

upload—refers to the ability to send data from an originating terminal (usually a microcomputer) to another computer or terminal.

videotex—a two-way method of communications, integrating video and a related communications system.

virtual circuit—a communication arrangement in which data from a source user may be passed to a destination user over various real-circuit configurations during a single period of communication (during a single session). Also called a logical circuit. See also, connection-oriented service.

Winchester disks—hard magnetic disk storage media in sealed containers. Not all sealed disks are Winchester drives.

window—a rectangular onscreen image within which the user accesses particular features of a system. With operating environment software, windowing is often combined with multitasking capabilities.

word processing—the transformation of ideas and information into a human readable form of communication through the management of procedures, equipment, and personnel. Generally refers to text editing and formatting on a computer.

WYSIWYG—What You See Is What You Get.

Trademarks

The products and company names listed below, which are referenced in this work, may be protected by federal, state, or common law trademark laws.

3COM/Bridge Communications.

3270, 5250 Display Station, AS/400, BTAM, CICS, ESCON, IBM, Logical Unit (LU) 6.2, MVS, MVS/XA, NetBIOS, NetView, OS/2, PC/AT, PC/XT, PCWS, PS/2, RSCS, SNA, SPF, System/36, System/38, System/370, TCAM, Token Ring, TSO, TSO, VM, VM/PC, VM/SP, VSAM, VTAM, and XEDIT are registered trademarks of International Business Machines Corporation.

ADABAS, COM-PLETE, CTAM, and Natural Connection are registered trademarks of Software AG.

ADM3A is a registered trademark of Lear-Siegler.

ADROIT is a registered trademark of ADR.

ARCnet is a registered trademark of Datapoint, Inc.

ASCOM is a registered trademark of Dynamic Microprocessor Associates, Inc.

Ashton-Tate, Inc.

Bitnet is a registered trademark of EDUCOM.

Burroughs is a registered trademark of Unisys.

Cinemax.

CompuServe Information Manager and CIM are registered trademarks of CompuServe.

Concurrent PC-DOS and CP/M are registered trademarks of Digital Research, Inc.

Corning Glassworks.

CrossTalk is a registered trademark of Microstuff, Inc.

Datawrite Corporate General Ledger is a registered trademark of Accountants Microsystems, Inc.

DEC, DECNet, DNA, Enterprise Management Architecture, MicroVAX, System/10, System/20, VAX, VT100, and VT240 are registered trademarks of Digital Equipment Corporation.

DesqView is a registered trademark of Quarterdeck.

Ethernet, Ventura Publisher, Xerox Network System, XNS, and Xerox Star are registered trademarks of Xerox Corporation.

FOCUS is a registered trademark of Information Builders, Inc.

GE Information Services.

HBO is a registered trademark of Home Box Office, Inc.

HP3000 and OpenView are registered trademarks of Hewlett-Packard.

Intel.

Kermit is a registered trademark of Henson Associates, Inc.

Linkware: Information Server is a registered trademark of Linkware Corporation.

LocalNet/20 is a registered trademark of Sytek, Inc.

Lotus 1-2-3 is a registered trademark of Lotus Development Corporation.

Macintosh is a registered trademark of Apple Computer, Inc.

Manufacturing Automation Protocol, MAP are registered trademarks of General Motors Corporation.

MCI.

MicroCICS is a registered trademark of Unicorn Systems.

Microcom Networking Protocol.

Mobius is a registered trademark of FEL Computing.

Model 204 is a registered trademark of Computer Corporation of America.

Motorola, Inc.

MUSIC and PCWS are registered trademarks of McGill University/IBM.

National Semiconductor.

NCR-COMTEN.

NetWare is a registered trademark of Novell.

PHOENIX/Micro is a registered trademark of Goal Systems.

PROCOMM Plus is a registered trademark of DataStorm Technologies, Inc.

Rating and Auditory and Payment Authorization System is a registered trademark of Distribution Science.

RDISK is a registered trademark of Tangram Systems, Inc.

Remote Access Facility and RAF are a registered trademarks of Datability Software Systems.

RLink is a registered trademark of Renex.

Sammons Cable.

Scholar/Teach, Technical and Office Protocol, and TOP are registered trademarks of Boeing Computer Services.

Showtime.

SPC/PC is a registered trademark of Command Technology Corporation.

StarLAN, Unified Network Management Architecture, and UNIX are registered trademarks of AT&T.

Statistical Analysis System and SAS are registered trademarks of SAS, Inc.

Statistical Package for the Social Sciences, SPSS, SPSS/PC, SPSS/x are registered trademarks of SPSS, Inc.

Tektronix 4010 is a registered trademark of Tektronix.

Telecom Australia.

Telenet.

TELETERM is a registered trademark of Telexpres, Inc.

Tempus-Link and Tempus-Data are registered trademarks of Micro Tempus, Inc.

The Business Library, Inc.

Token/Net is a registered trademark of Concord Data Systems.

Truax and Associates, Inc.

U.S. Sprint.

Ungermann-Bass.

V-Drive is a registered trademark of Virtual Microsystems.

VINES is a registered trademark of Banyan.

VisiCalc is a registered trademark of Software Arts, Inc.

VTERM is a registered trademark of Coefficient Systems.

WangNet is a registered trademark of Wang.

Warner Communications.

Windows is a registered trademark of Microsoft Corporation.

WordStar is a registered trademark of Micropro International Corporation.

X-Windows is a registered trademark of Massachusetts Institute of Technology.

X.PC is a registered trademark of Tymnet.

Index